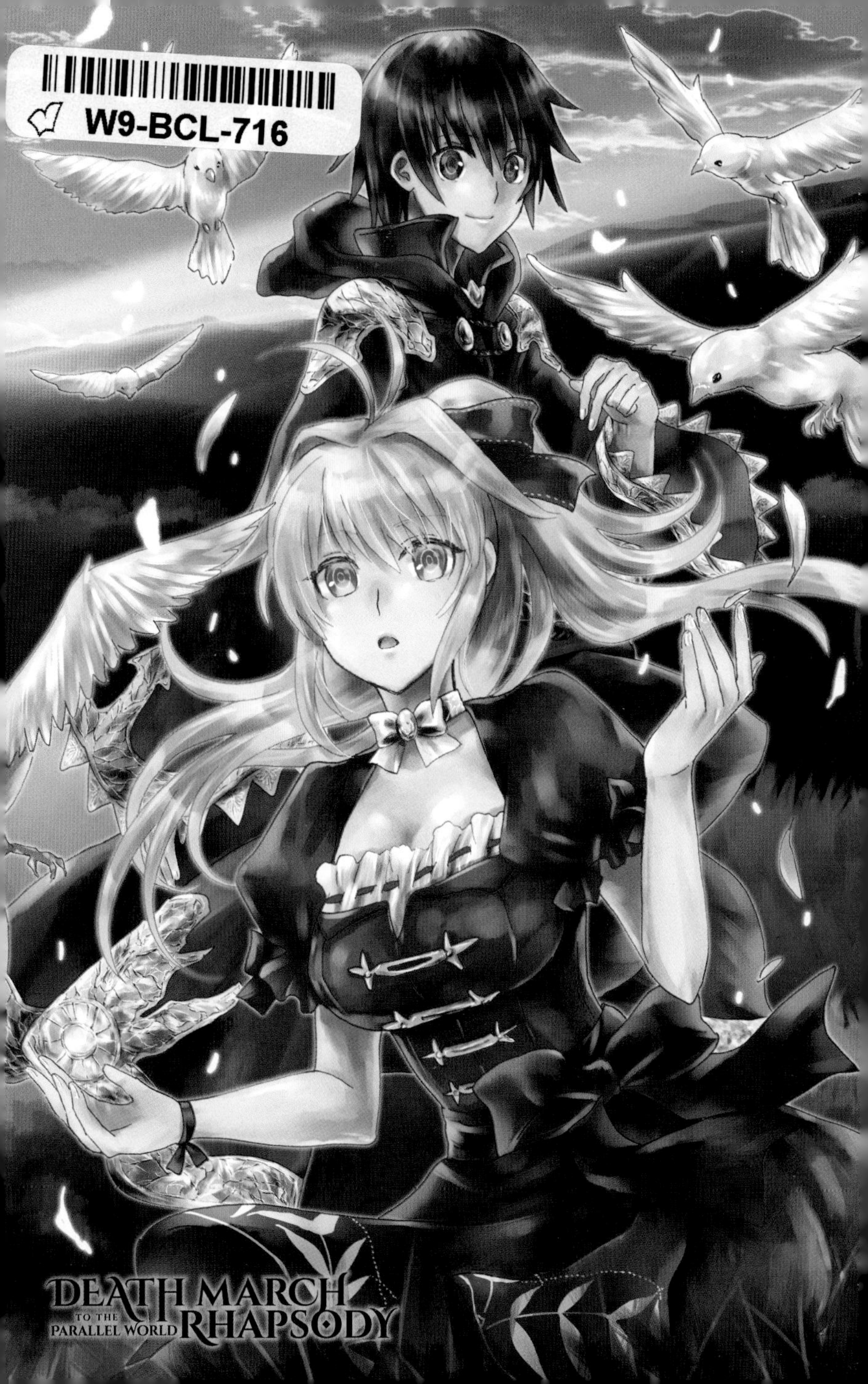
DEATH MARCH
TO THE PARALLEL WORLD
RHAPSODY

C O N T E N T S

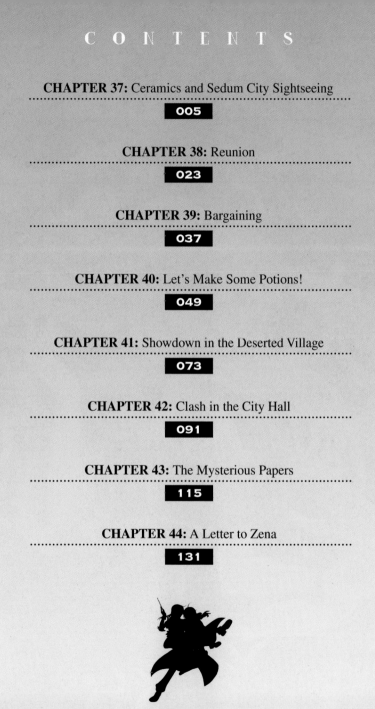

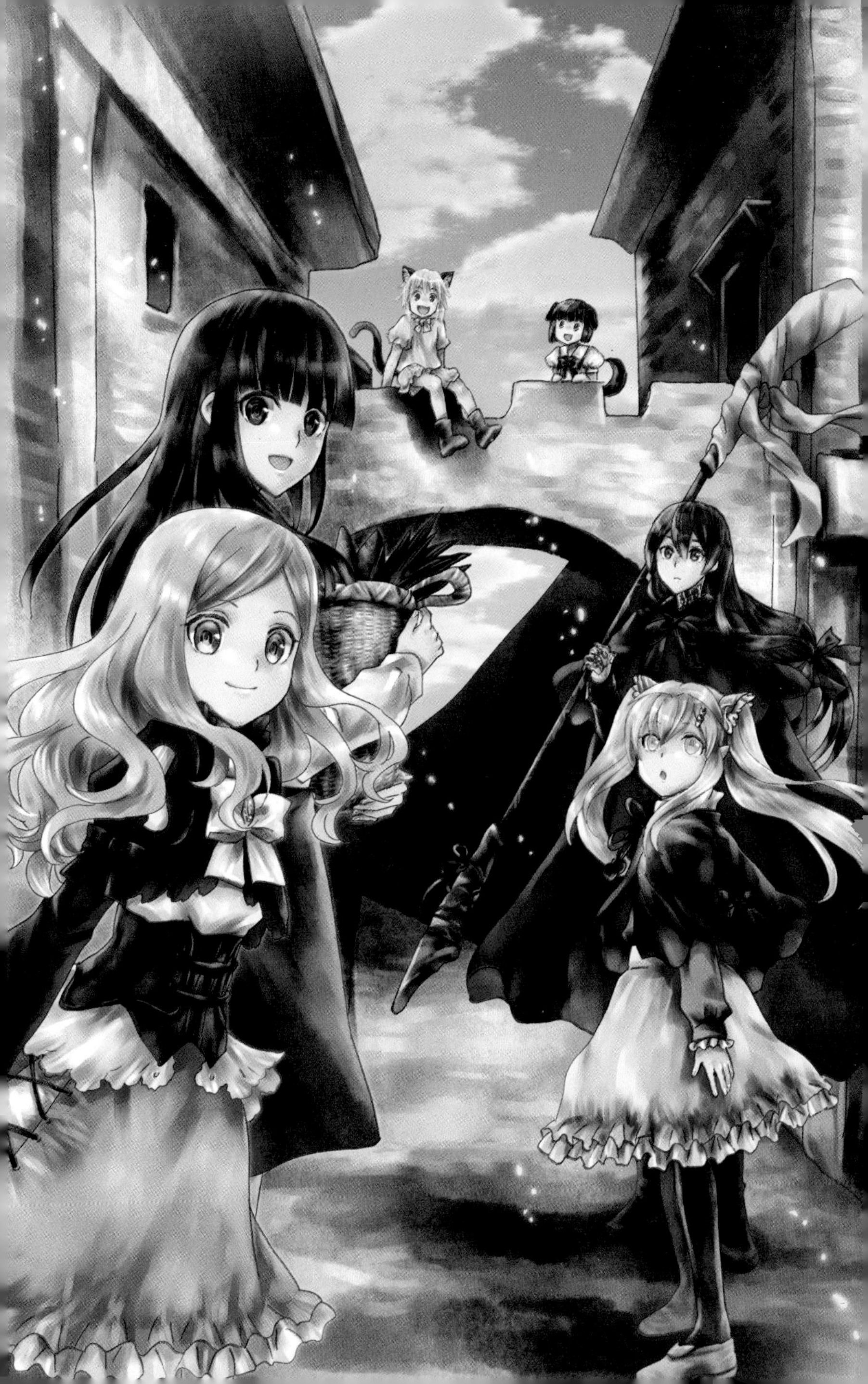

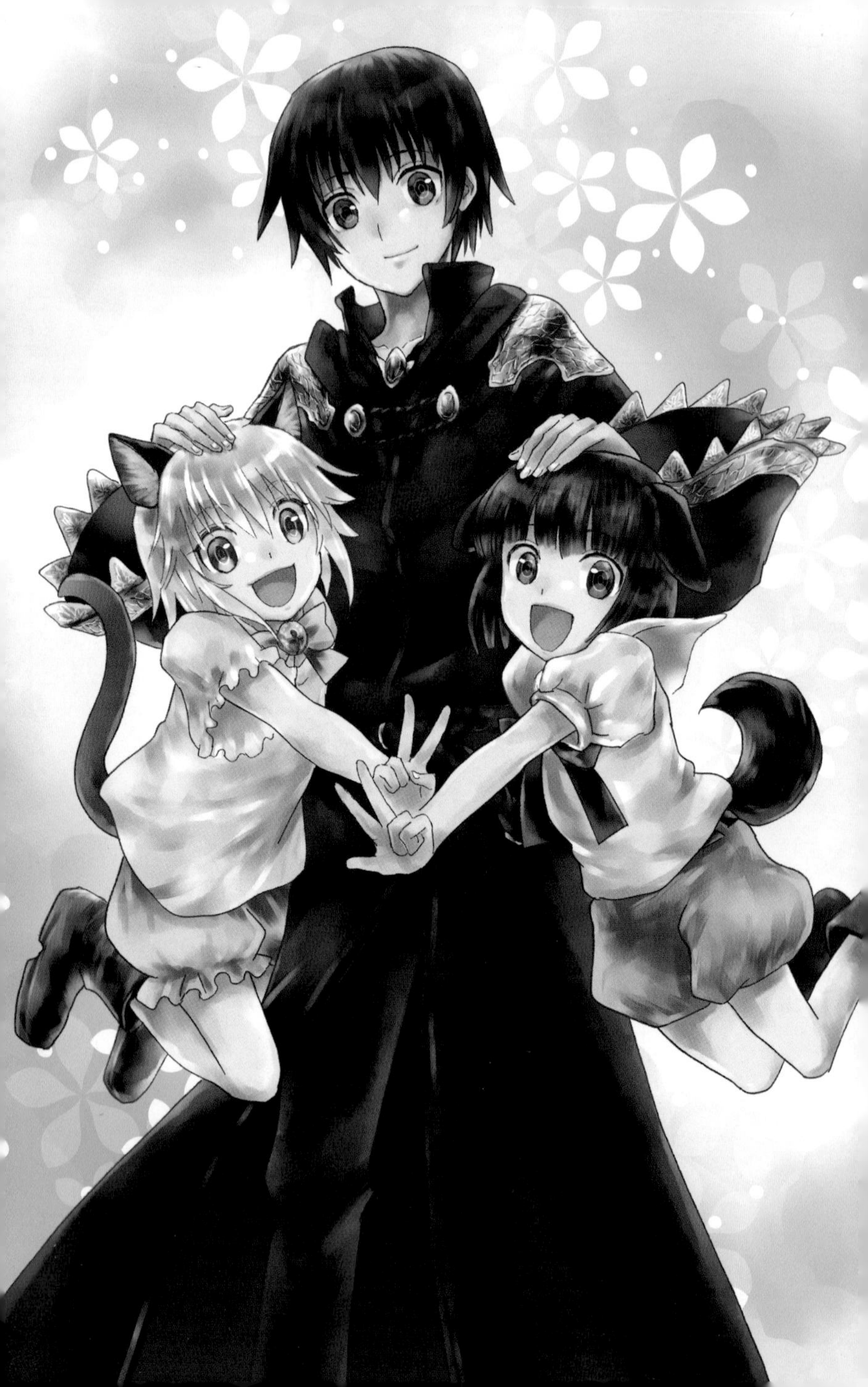

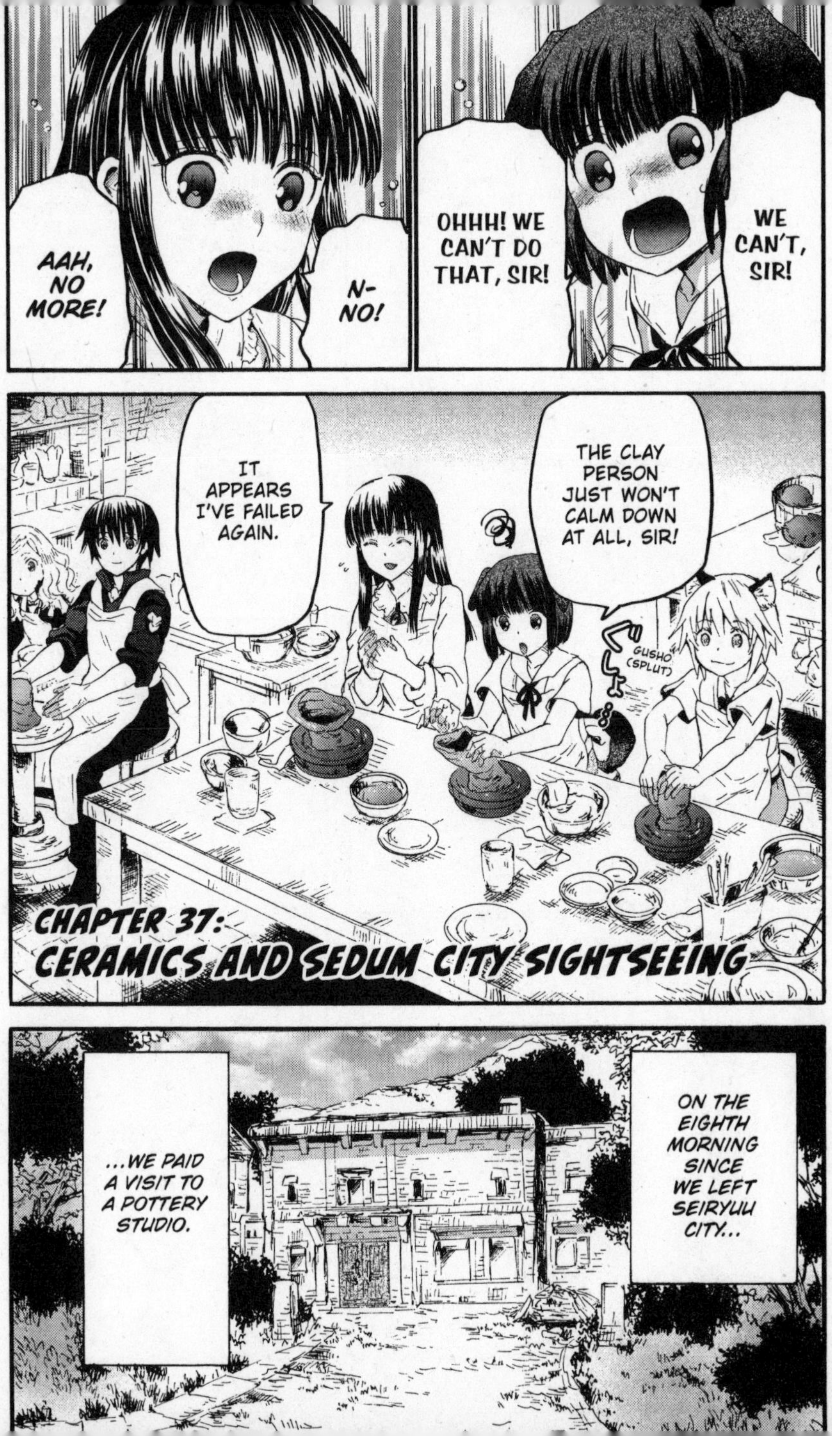
WE CAN'T, SIR!
OHHH! WE CAN'T DO THAT, SIR!
N-NO!
AAH, NO MORE!
THE CLAY PERSON JUST WON'T CALM DOWN AT ALL, SIR!
GUSHO (SPLUT)
IT APPEARS I'VE FAILED AGAIN.
CHAPTER 37:
CERAMICS AND SEDUM CITY SIGHTSEEING
ON THE EIGHTH MORNING SINCE WE LEFT SEIRYUU CITY...
...WE PAID A VISIT TO A POTTERY STUDIO.

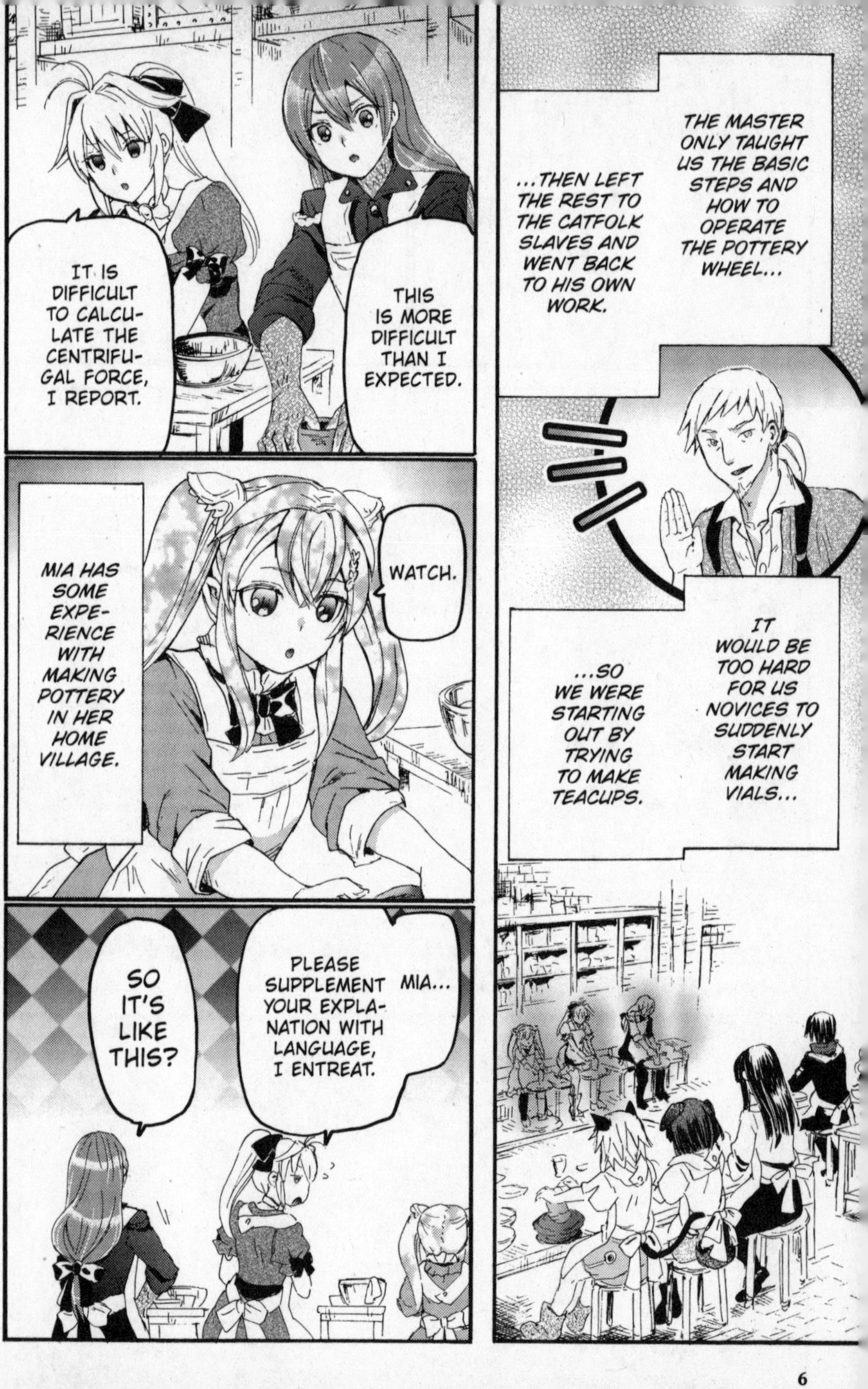
THE MASTER ONLY TAUGHT US THE BASIC STEPS AND HOW TO OPERATE THE POTTERY WHEEL...
...THEN LEFT THE REST TO THE CATFOLK SLAVES AND WENT BACK TO HIS OWN WORK.
IT WOULD BE TOO HARD FOR US NOVICES TO SUDDENLY START MAKING VIALS...
...SO WE WERE STARTING OUT BY TRYING TO MAKE TEACUPS.
THIS IS MORE DIFFICULT THAN I EXPECTED.
IT IS DIFFICULT TO CALCULATE THE CENTRIFUGAL FORCE, I REPORT.
WATCH.
MIA HAS SOME EXPERIENCE WITH MAKING POTTERY IN HER HOME VILLAGE.
MIA... PLEASE SUPPLEMENT YOUR EXPLANATION WITH LANGUAGE, I ENTREAT.
SO IT'S LIKE THIS?

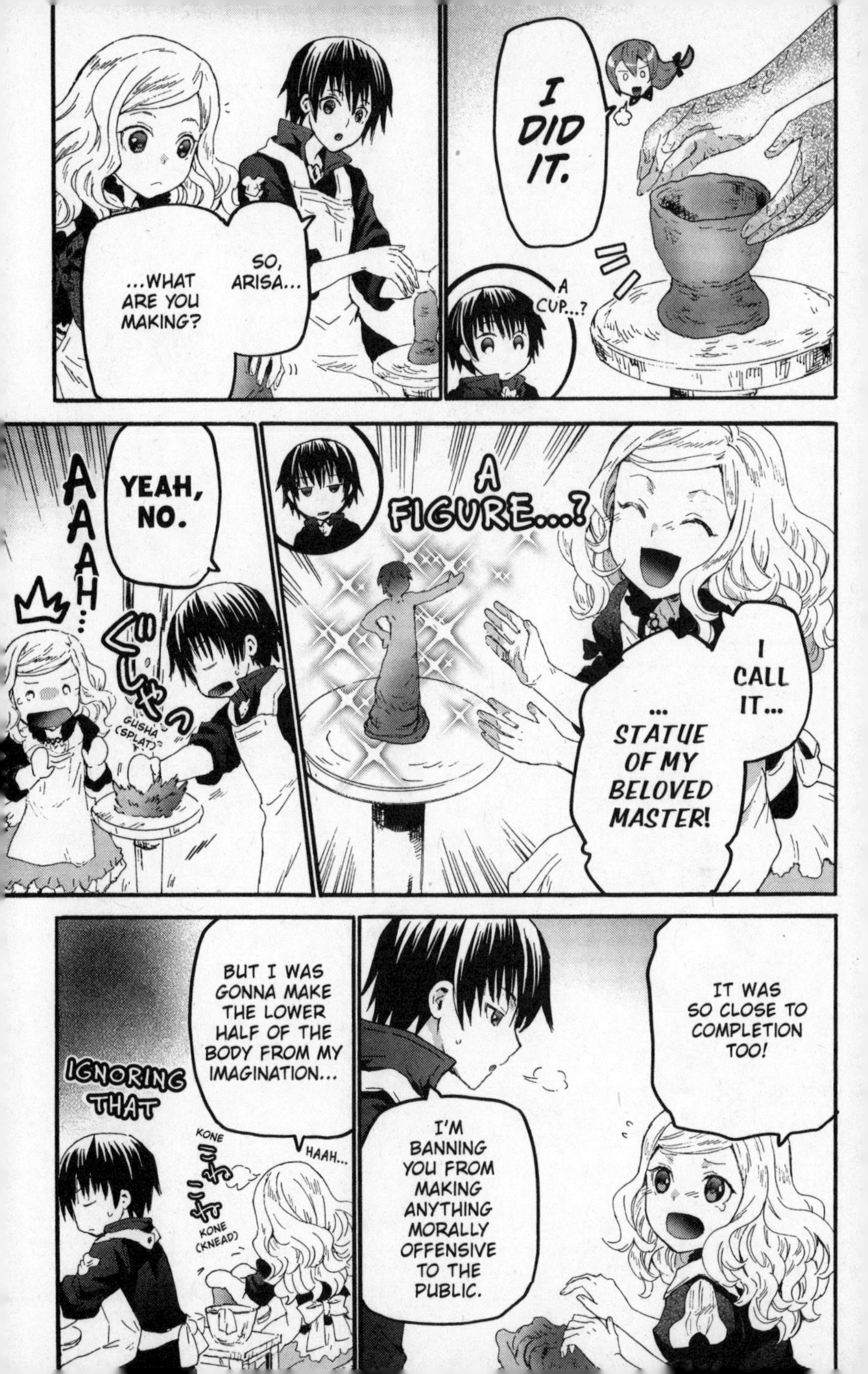
I DID IT.
A CUP...?
SO, ARISA...
...WHAT ARE YOU MAKING?
A FIGURE...?
I CALL IT...
...STATUE OF MY BELOVED MASTER!
YEAH, NO.
AAAAH...
ぐしゃっ
GUSHA (SPLAT)
IT WAS SO CLOSE TO COMPLETION TOO!
I'M BANNING YOU FROM MAKING ANYTHING MORALLY OFFENSIVE TO THE PUBLIC.
BUT I WAS GONNA MAKE THE LOWER HALF OF THE BODY FROM MY IMAGINATION...
IGNORING THAT
HAAH...
KONE こね
こね KONE (KNEAD)

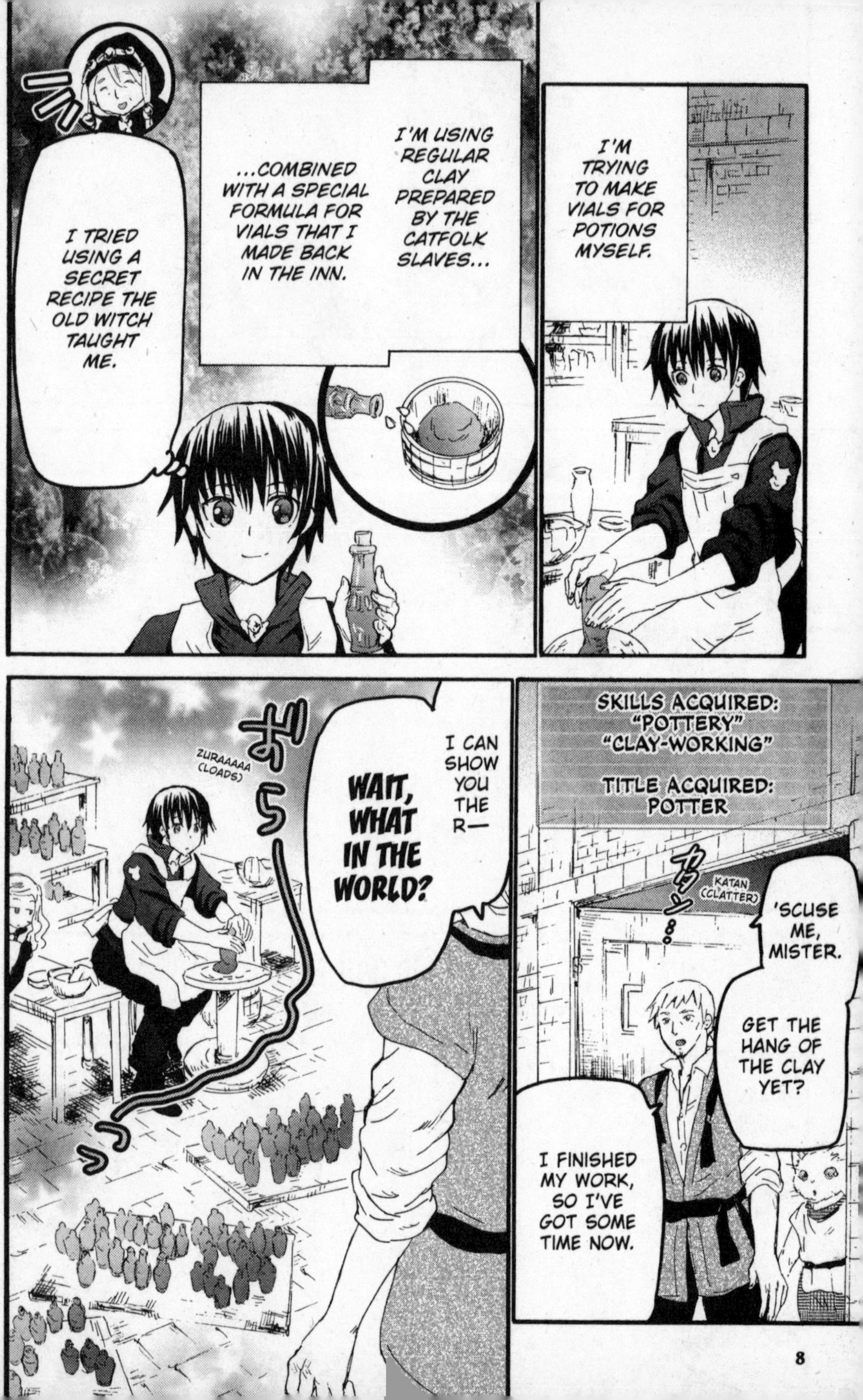
I'M TRYING TO MAKE VIALS FOR POTIONS MYSELF.
I'M USING REGULAR CLAY PREPARED BY THE CATFOLK SLAVES...
...COMBINED WITH A SPECIAL FORMULA FOR VIALS THAT I MADE BACK IN THE INN.
I TRIED USING A SECRET RECIPE THE OLD WITCH TAUGHT ME.
SKILLS ACQUIRED: "POTTERY" "CLAY-WORKING"
TITLE ACQUIRED: POTTER
KATAN (CLATTER)
'SCUSE ME, MISTER.
GET THE HANG OF THE CLAY YET?
I FINISHED MY WORK, SO I'VE GOT SOME TIME NOW.
I CAN SHOW YOU THE R—
WAIT, WHAT IN THE WORLD?
ZURAAAAA (LOADS)

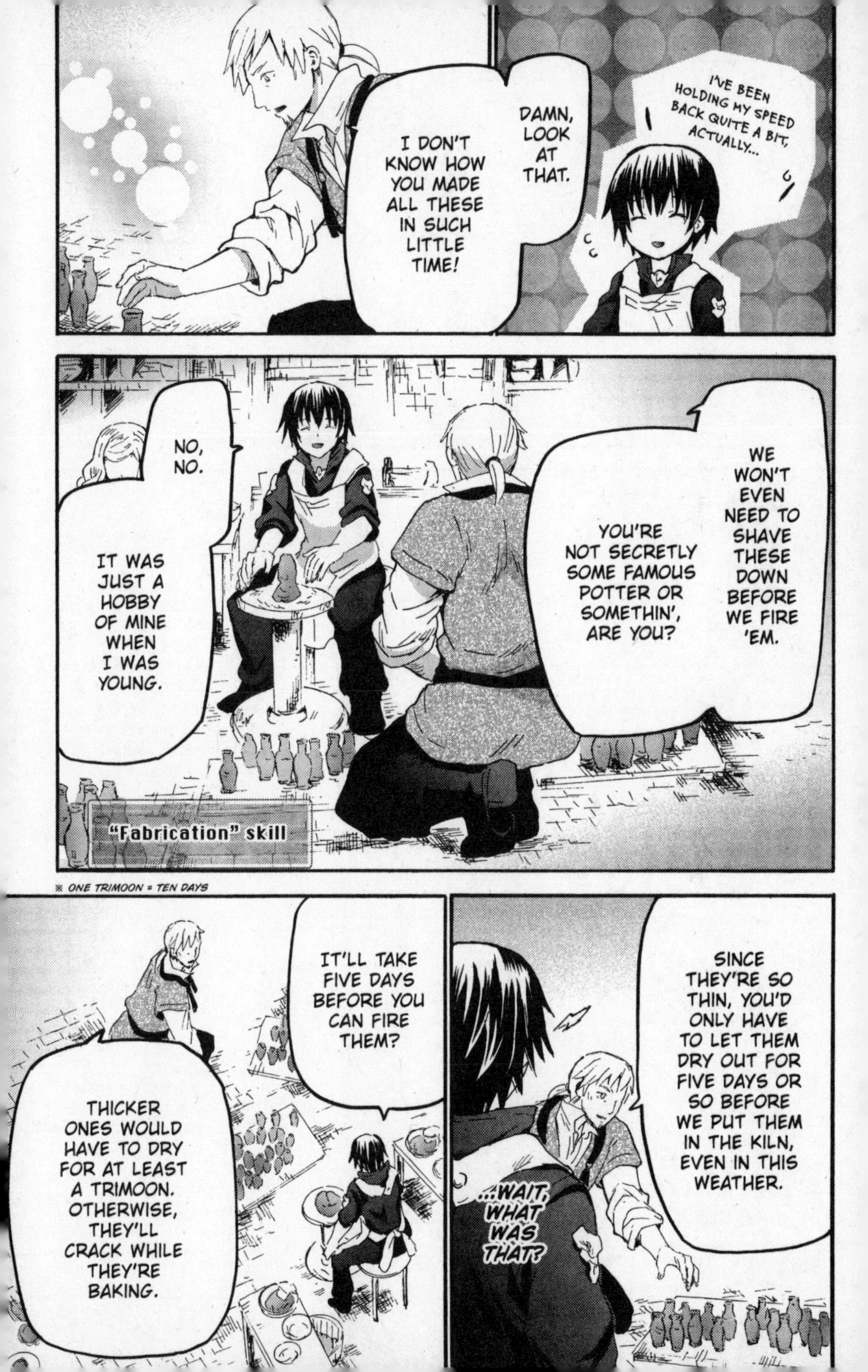
I'VE BEEN HOLDING MY SPEED BACK QUITE A BIT, ACTUALLY...
DAMN, LOOK AT THAT.
I DON'T KNOW HOW YOU MADE ALL THESE IN SUCH LITTLE TIME!
WE WON'T EVEN NEED TO SHAVE THESE DOWN BEFORE WE FIRE 'EM.
YOU'RE NOT SECRETLY SOME FAMOUS POTTER OR SOMETHIN', ARE YOU?
NO, NO.
IT WAS JUST A HOBBY OF MINE WHEN I WAS YOUNG.
"Fabrication" skill
※ ONE TRIMOON = TEN DAYS
SINCE THEY'RE SO THIN, YOU'D ONLY HAVE TO LET THEM DRY OUT FOR FIVE DAYS OR SO BEFORE WE PUT THEM IN THE KILN, EVEN IN THIS WEATHER.
...WAIT, WHAT WAS THAT?
IT'LL TAKE FIVE DAYS BEFORE YOU CAN FIRE THEM?
THICKER ONES WOULD HAVE TO DRY FOR AT LEAST A TRIMOON. OTHERWISE, THEY'LL CRACK WHILE THEY'RE BAKING.

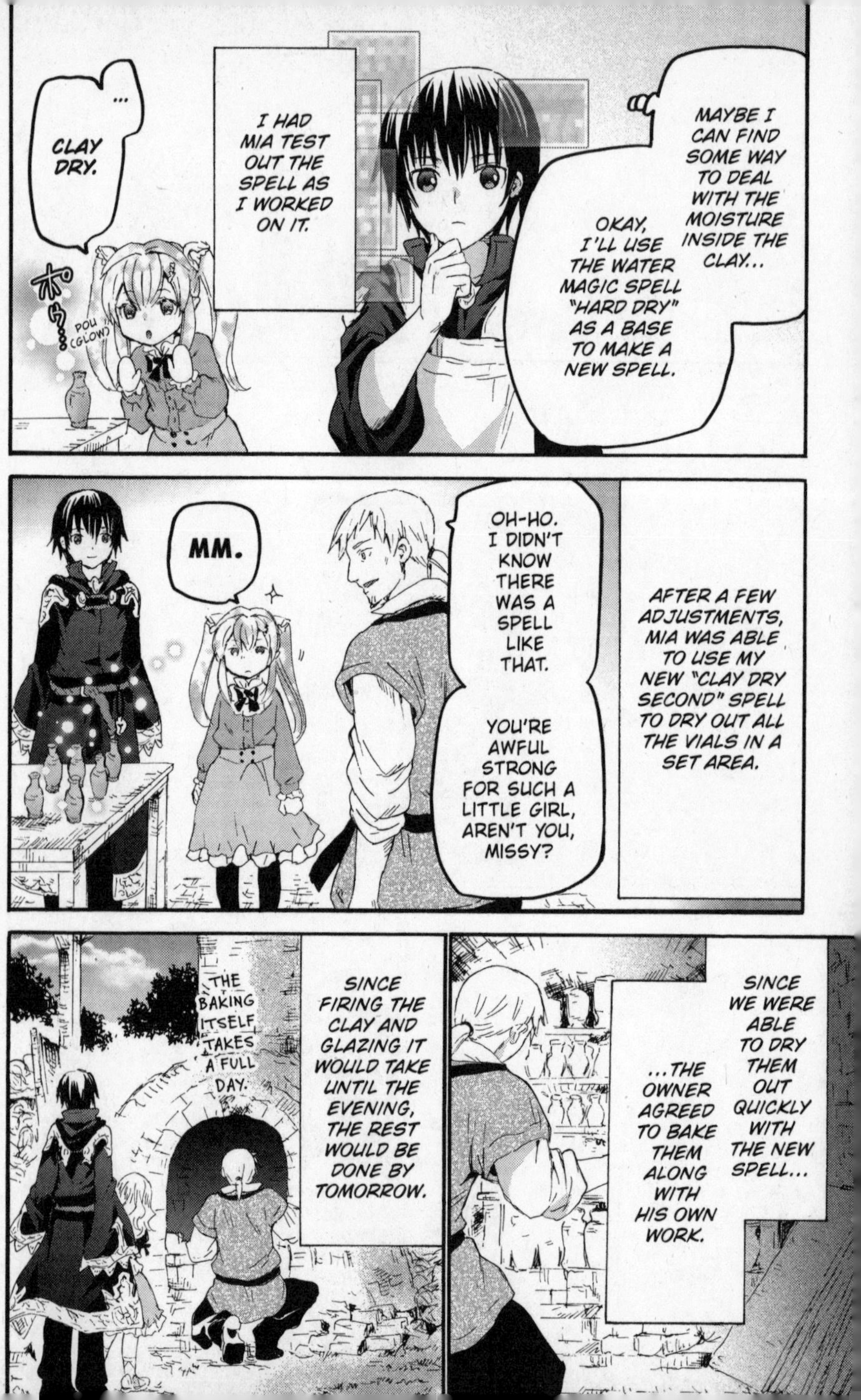
MAYBE I CAN FIND SOME WAY TO DEAL WITH THE MOISTURE INSIDE THE CLAY...
OKAY, I'LL USE THE WATER MAGIC SPELL "HARD DRY" AS A BASE TO MAKE A NEW SPELL.
I HAD MIA TEST OUT THE SPELL AS I WORKED ON IT.
... CLAY DRY.
POU (GLOW)
AFTER A FEW ADJUSTMENTS, MIA WAS ABLE TO USE MY NEW "CLAY DRY SECOND" SPELL TO DRY OUT ALL THE VIALS IN A SET AREA.
OH-HO. I DIDN'T KNOW THERE WAS A SPELL LIKE THAT.
YOU'RE AWFUL STRONG FOR SUCH A LITTLE GIRL, AREN'T YOU, MISSY?
MM.
SINCE WE WERE ABLE TO DRY THEM OUT QUICKLY WITH THE NEW SPELL...
...THE OWNER AGREED TO BAKE THEM ALONG WITH HIS OWN WORK.
SINCE FIRING THE CLAY AND GLAZING IT WOULD TAKE UNTIL THE EVENING, THE REST WOULD BE DONE BY TOMORROW.
THE BAKING ITSELF TAKES A FULL DAY.

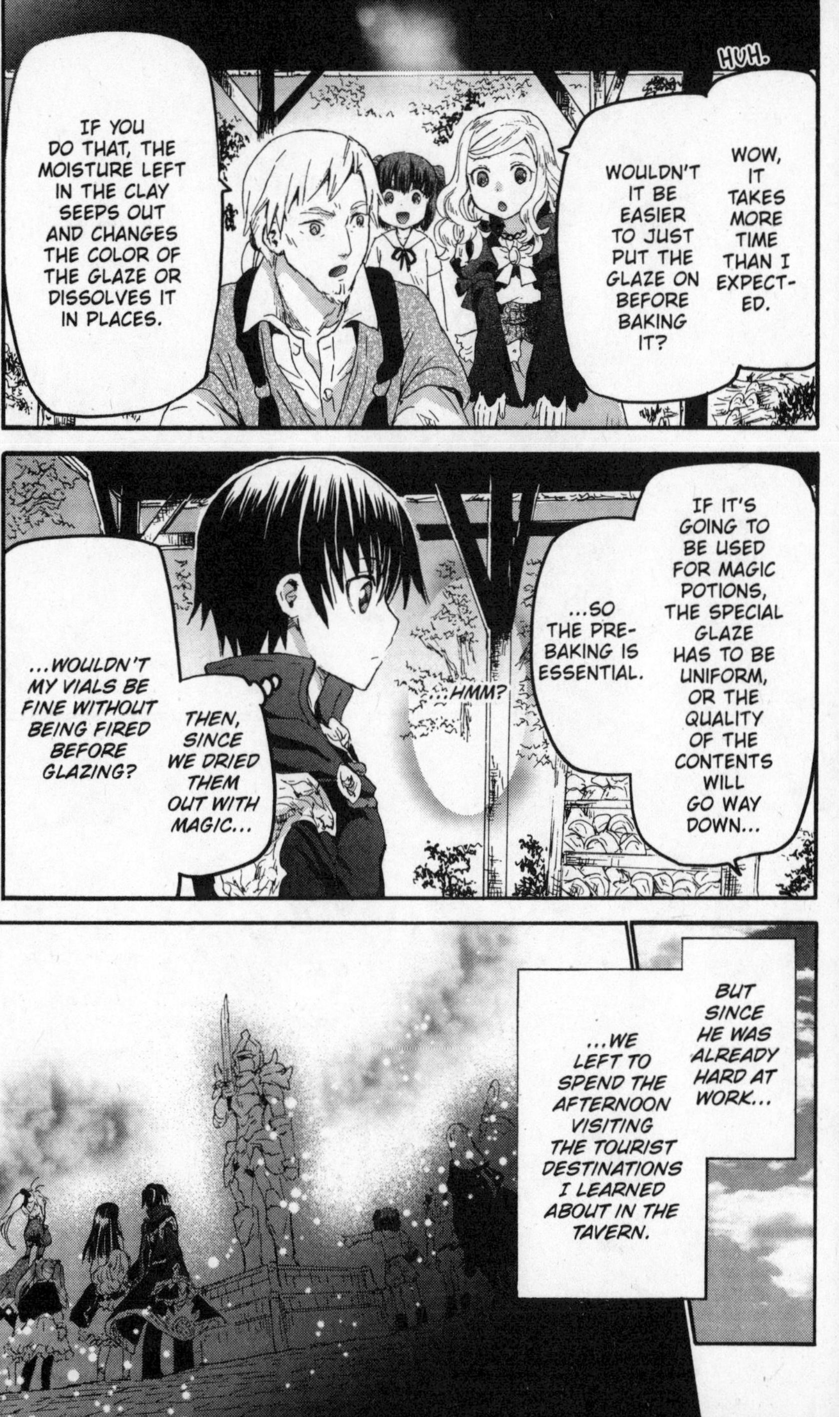
HUH.
WOW, IT TAKES MORE TIME THAN I EXPECTED.
WOULDN'T IT BE EASIER TO JUST PUT THE GLAZE ON BEFORE BAKING IT?
IF YOU DO THAT, THE MOISTURE LEFT IN THE CLAY SEEPS OUT AND CHANGES THE COLOR OF THE GLAZE OR DISSOLVES IT IN PLACES.
IF IT'S GOING TO BE USED FOR MAGIC POTIONS, THE SPECIAL GLAZE HAS TO BE UNIFORM, OR THE QUALITY OF THE CONTENTS WILL GO WAY DOWN...
...SO THE PRE-BAKING IS ESSENTIAL.
...HMM?
THEN, SINCE WE DRIED THEM OUT WITH MAGIC...
...WOULDN'T MY VIALS BE FINE WITHOUT BEING FIRED BEFORE GLAZING?
BUT SINCE HE WAS ALREADY HARD AT WORK...
...WE LEFT TO SPEND THE AFTERNOON VISITING THE TOURIST DESTINATIONS I LEARNED ABOUT IN THE TAVERN.

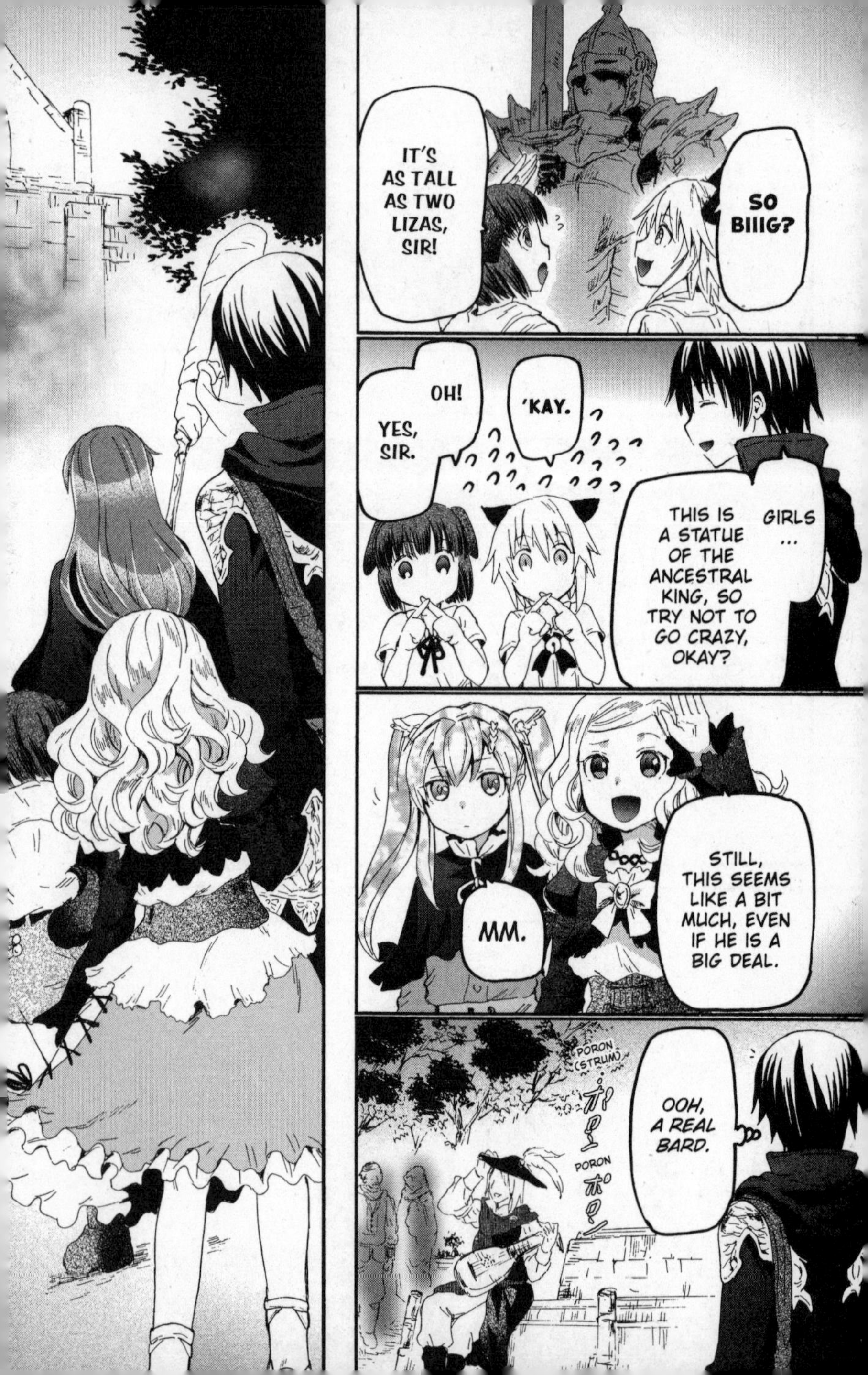
SO BIIIG?
IT'S AS TALL AS TWO LIZAS, SIR!
GIRLS ...
THIS IS A STATUE OF THE ANCESTRAL KING, SO TRY NOT TO GO CRAZY, OKAY?
'KAY.
OH! YES, SIR.
STILL, THIS SEEMS LIKE A BIT MUCH, EVEN IF HE IS A BIG DEAL.
MM.
OOH, A REAL BARD.
PORON (STRUM)
ポロン
PORON
ポロン

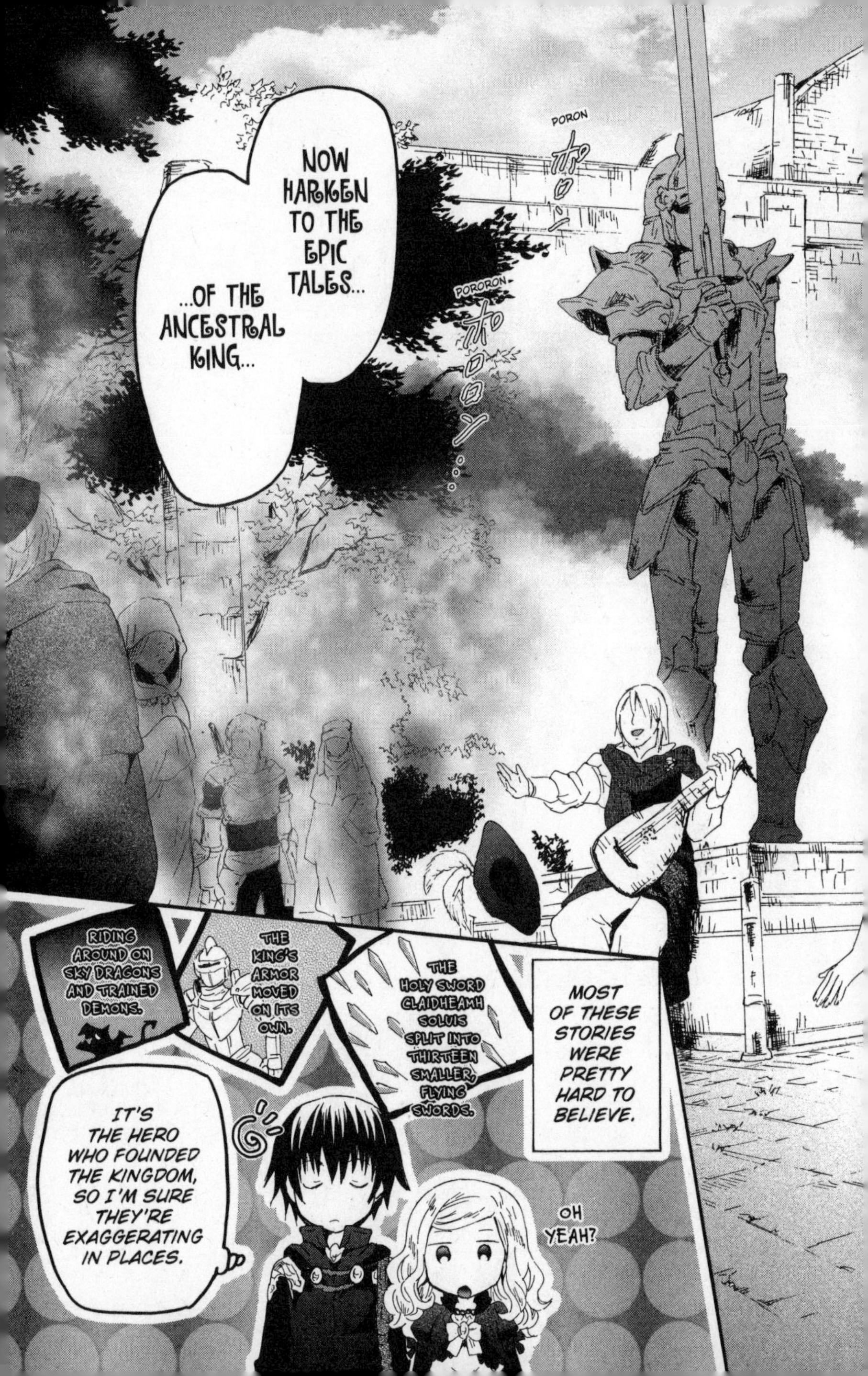
PORON
NOW HARKEN TO THE EPIC TALES...
PORORON
...OF THE ANCESTRAL KING...
MOST OF THESE STORIES WERE PRETTY HARD TO BELIEVE.
THE HOLY SWORD CLAIDHEAMH SOLUIS SPLIT INTO THIRTEEN SMALLER, FLYING SWORDS.
THE KING'S ARMOR MOVED ON ITS OWN.
RIDING AROUND ON SKY DRAGONS AND TRAINED DEMONS.
IT'S THE HERO WHO FOUNDED THE KINGDOM, SO I'M SURE THEY'RE EXAGGERATING IN PLACES.
OH YEAH?

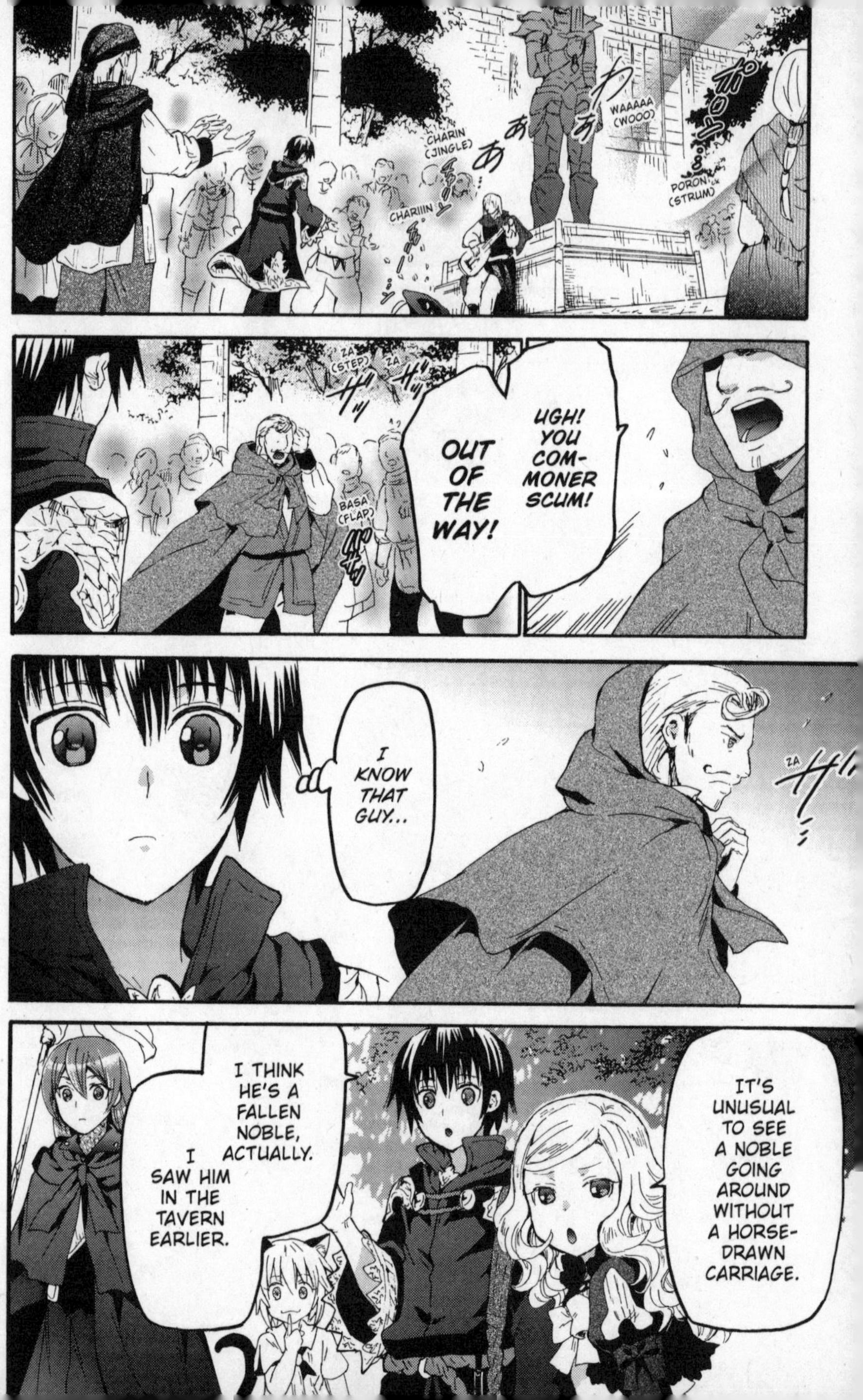
PORON (STRUM)
WAAAAA (WOOO)
CHARIN (JINGLE)
CHARIIIN
UGH! YOU COMMONER SCUM!
OUT OF THE WAY!
ZA (STEP) ZA
BASA (FLAP)
ZA
I KNOW THAT GUY...
IT'S UNUSUAL TO SEE A NOBLE GOING AROUND WITHOUT A HORSE-DRAWN CARRIAGE.
I THINK HE'S A FALLEN NOBLE, ACTUALLY.
I SAW HIM IN THE TAVERN EARLIER.

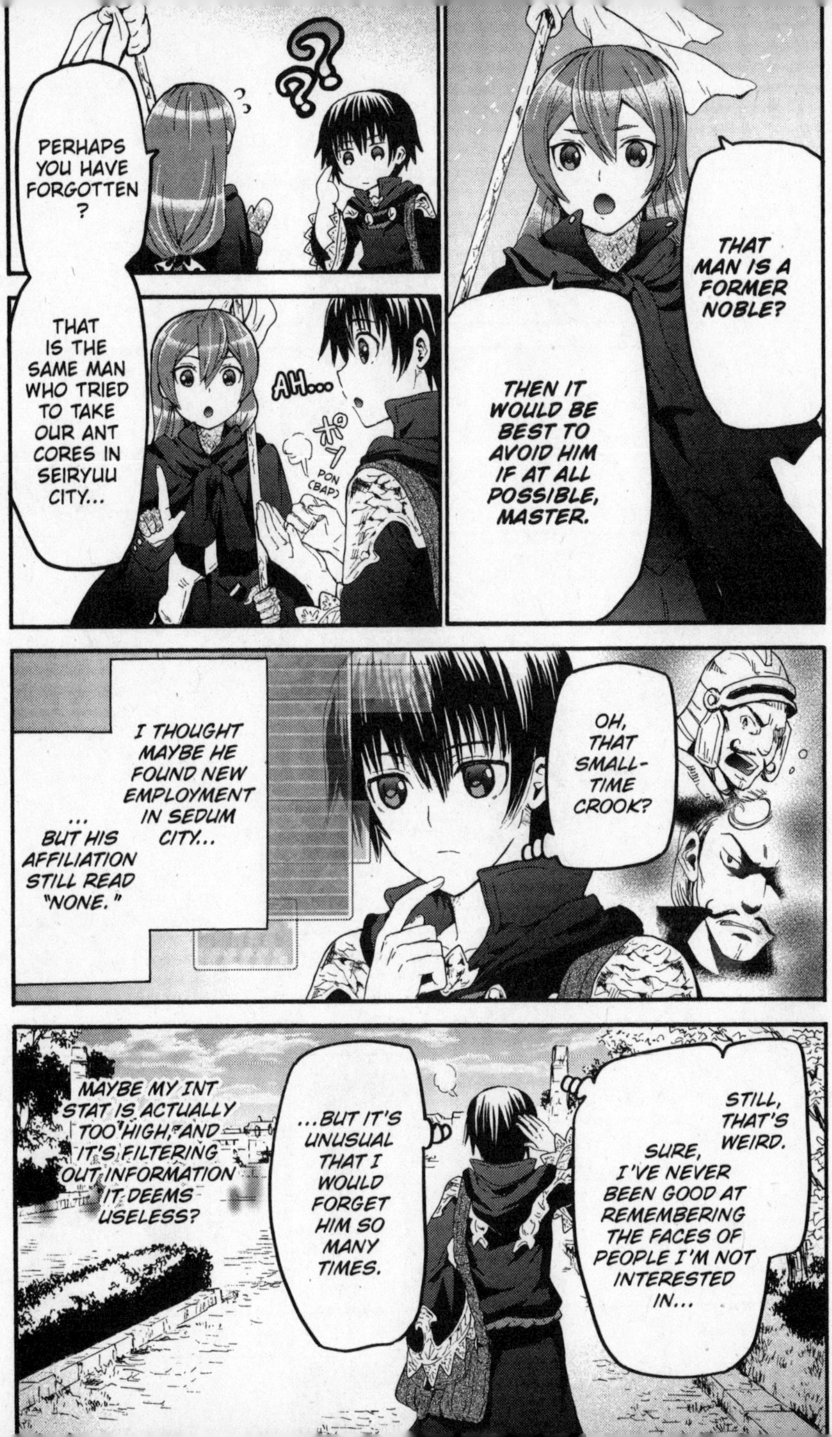
THAT MAN IS A FORMER NOBLE?
THEN IT WOULD BE BEST TO AVOID HIM IF AT ALL POSSIBLE, MASTER.
??
PERHAPS YOU HAVE FORGOTTEN ?
THAT IS THE SAME MAN WHO TRIED TO TAKE OUR ANT CORES IN SEIRYUU CITY...
AH...
ポン
PON (BAP)
OH, THAT SMALL-TIME CROOK?
I THOUGHT MAYBE HE FOUND NEW EMPLOYMENT IN SEDUM CITY...
... BUT HIS AFFILIATION STILL READ "NONE."
STILL, THAT'S WEIRD.
SURE, I'VE NEVER BEEN GOOD AT REMEMBERING THE FACES OF PEOPLE I'M NOT INTERESTED IN...
...BUT IT'S UNUSUAL THAT I WOULD FORGET HIM SO MANY TIMES.
MAYBE MY INT STAT IS ACTUALLY TOO HIGH, AND IT'S FILTERING OUT INFORMATION IT DEEMS USELESS?

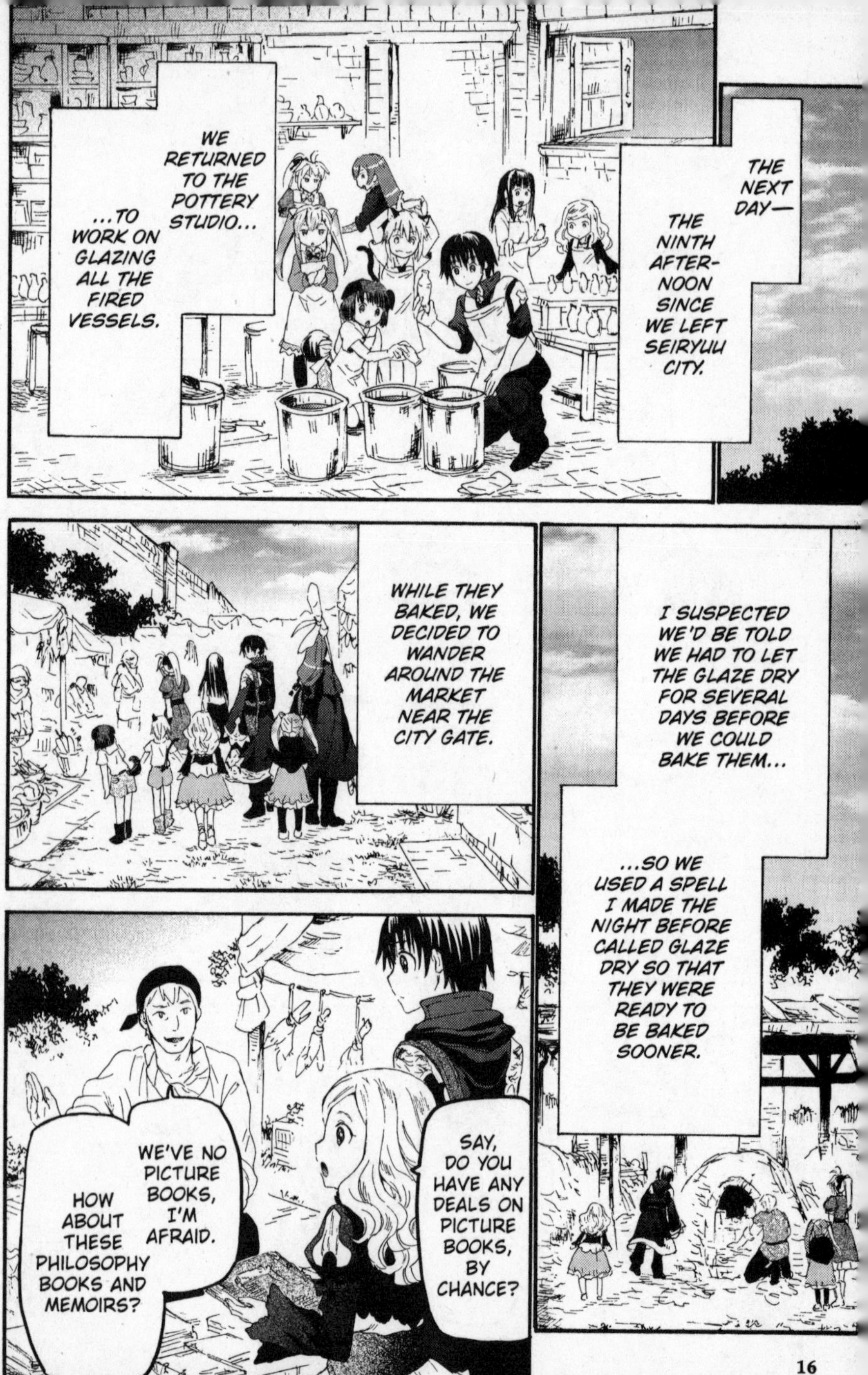
THE NEXT DAY—
THE NINTH AFTERNOON SINCE WE LEFT SEIRYUU CITY.
WE RETURNED TO THE POTTERY STUDIO...
...TO WORK ON GLAZING ALL THE FIRED VESSELS.
I SUSPECTED WE'D BE TOLD WE HAD TO LET THE GLAZE DRY FOR SEVERAL DAYS BEFORE WE COULD BAKE THEM...
...SO WE USED A SPELL I MADE THE NIGHT BEFORE CALLED GLAZE DRY SO THAT THEY WERE READY TO BE BAKED SOONER.
WHILE THEY BAKED, WE DECIDED TO WANDER AROUND THE MARKET NEAR THE CITY GATE.
SAY, DO YOU HAVE ANY DEALS ON PICTURE BOOKS, BY CHANCE?
WE'VE NO PICTURE BOOKS, I'M AFRAID.
HOW ABOUT THESE PHILOSOPHY BOOKS AND MEMOIRS?

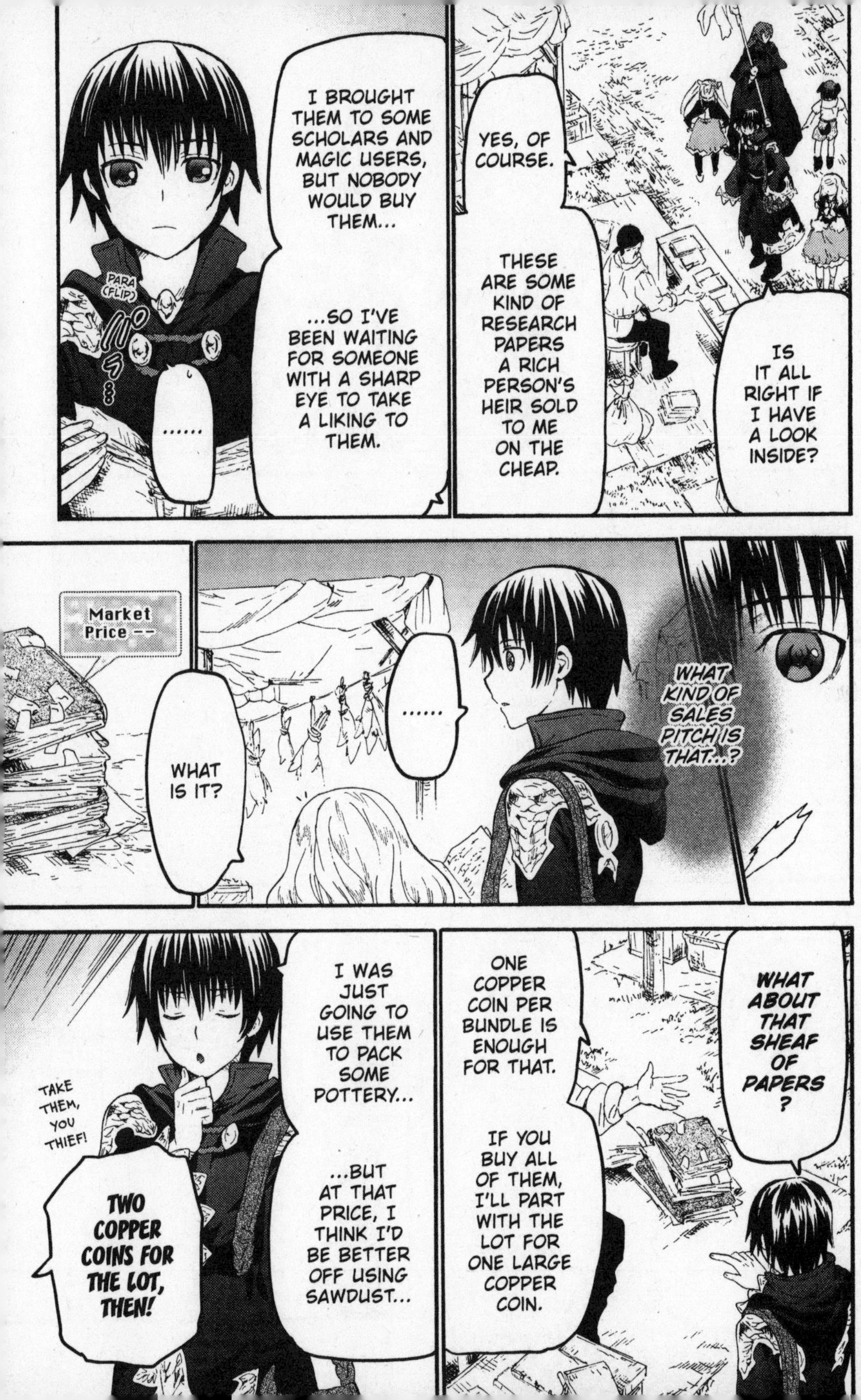
IS IT ALL RIGHT IF I HAVE A LOOK INSIDE?
YES, OF COURSE.
THESE ARE SOME KIND OF RESEARCH PAPERS A RICH PERSON'S HEIR SOLD TO ME ON THE CHEAP.
I BROUGHT THEM TO SOME SCHOLARS AND MAGIC USERS, BUT NOBODY WOULD BUY THEM...
...SO I'VE BEEN WAITING FOR SOMEONE WITH A SHARP EYE TO TAKE A LIKING TO THEM.
PARA (FLIP)
......
WHAT KIND OF SALES PITCH IS THAT...?
......
WHAT IS IT?
Market Price --
WHAT ABOUT THAT SHEAF OF PAPERS?
ONE COPPER COIN PER BUNDLE IS ENOUGH FOR THAT.
IF YOU BUY ALL OF THEM, I'LL PART WITH THE LOT FOR ONE LARGE COPPER COIN.
I WAS JUST GOING TO USE THEM TO PACK SOME POTTERY...
...BUT AT THAT PRICE, I THINK I'D BE BETTER OFF USING SAWDUST...
TWO COPPER COINS FOR THE LOT, THEN!
TAKE THEM, YOU THIEF!

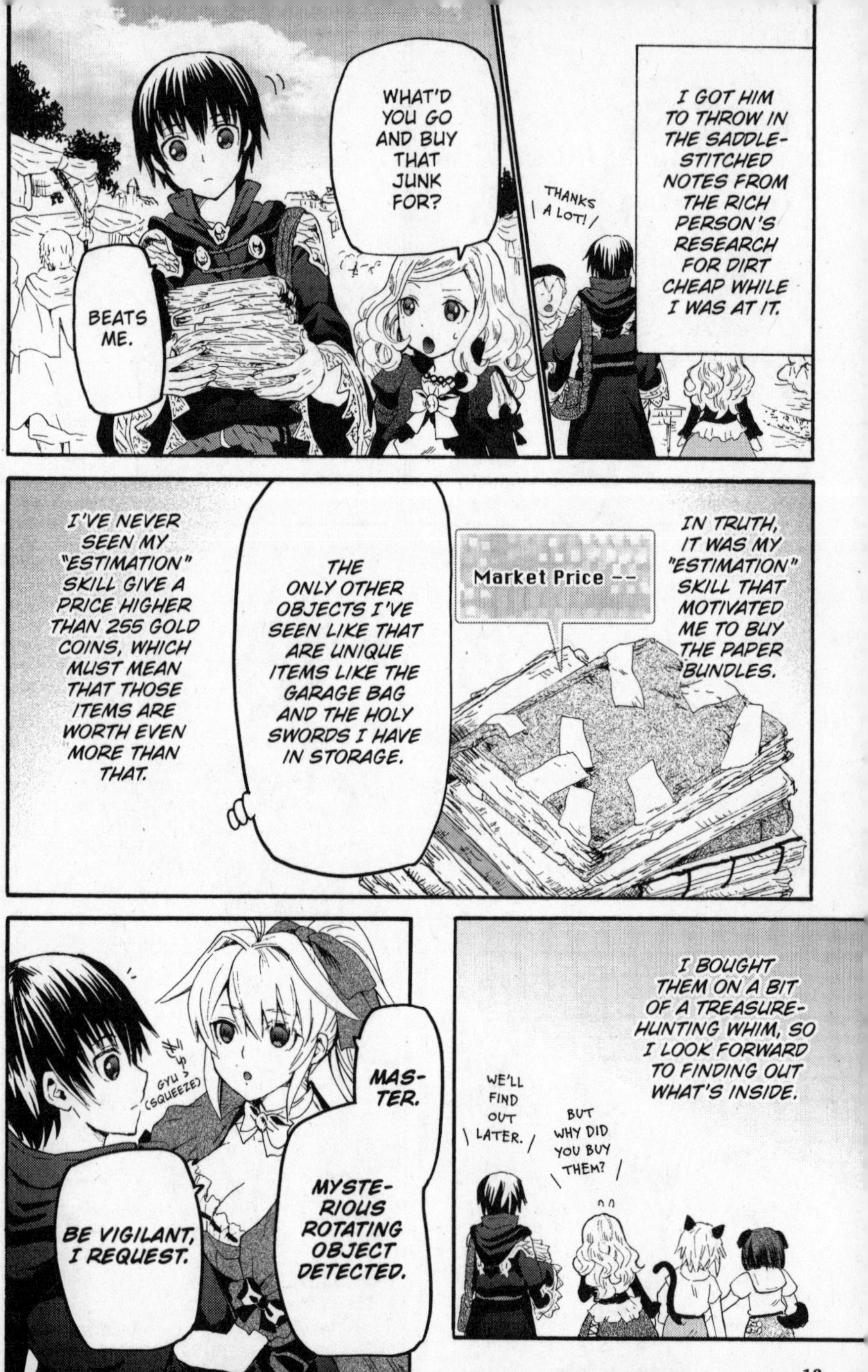
I GOT HIM TO THROW IN THE SADDLE-STITCHED NOTES FROM THE RICH PERSON'S RESEARCH FOR DIRT CHEAP WHILE I WAS AT IT.
THANKS A LOT!
WHAT'D YOU GO AND BUY THAT JUNK FOR?
BEATS ME.
IN TRUTH, IT WAS MY "ESTIMATION" SKILL THAT MOTIVATED ME TO BUY THE PAPER BUNDLES.
Market Price --
THE ONLY OTHER OBJECTS I'VE SEEN LIKE THAT ARE UNIQUE ITEMS LIKE THE GARAGE BAG AND THE HOLY SWORDS I HAVE IN STORAGE.
I'VE NEVER SEEN MY "ESTIMATION" SKILL GIVE A PRICE HIGHER THAN 255 GOLD COINS, WHICH MUST MEAN THAT THOSE ITEMS ARE WORTH EVEN MORE THAN THAT.
I BOUGHT THEM ON A BIT OF A TREASURE-HUNTING WHIM, SO I LOOK FORWARD TO FINDING OUT WHAT'S INSIDE.
BUT WHY DID YOU BUY THEM?
WE'LL FIND OUT LATER.
MAS-TER.
GYU (SQUEEZE)
MYSTE-RIOUS ROTATING OBJECT DETECTED.
BE VIGILANT, I REQUEST.

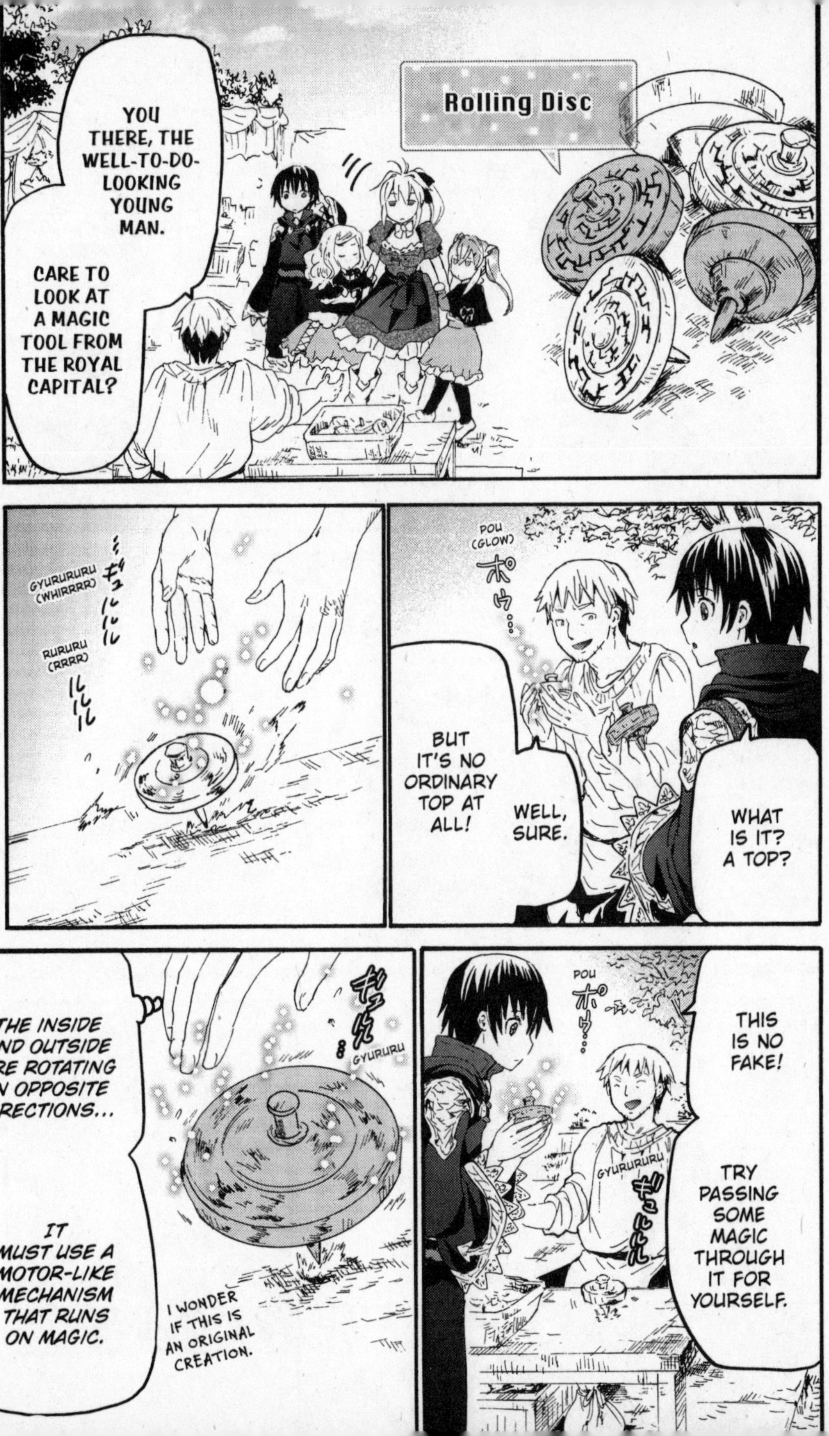
Rolling Disc
YOU THERE, THE WELL-TO-DO-LOOKING YOUNG MAN.
CARE TO LOOK AT A MAGIC TOOL FROM THE ROYAL CAPITAL?
WHAT IS IT? A TOP?
WELL, SURE.
BUT IT'S NO ORDINARY TOP AT ALL!
POU (GLOW)
GYURURURU (WHIRRRR)
RURURU (RRRR)
THIS IS NO FAKE!
POU
TRY PASSING SOME MAGIC THROUGH IT FOR YOURSELF.
GYURURURU
THE INSIDE AND OUTSIDE ARE ROTATING IN OPPOSITE DIRECTIONS...
GYURURU
IT MUST USE A MOTOR-LIKE MECHANISM THAT RUNS ON MAGIC.
I WONDER IF THIS IS AN ORIGINAL CREATION.

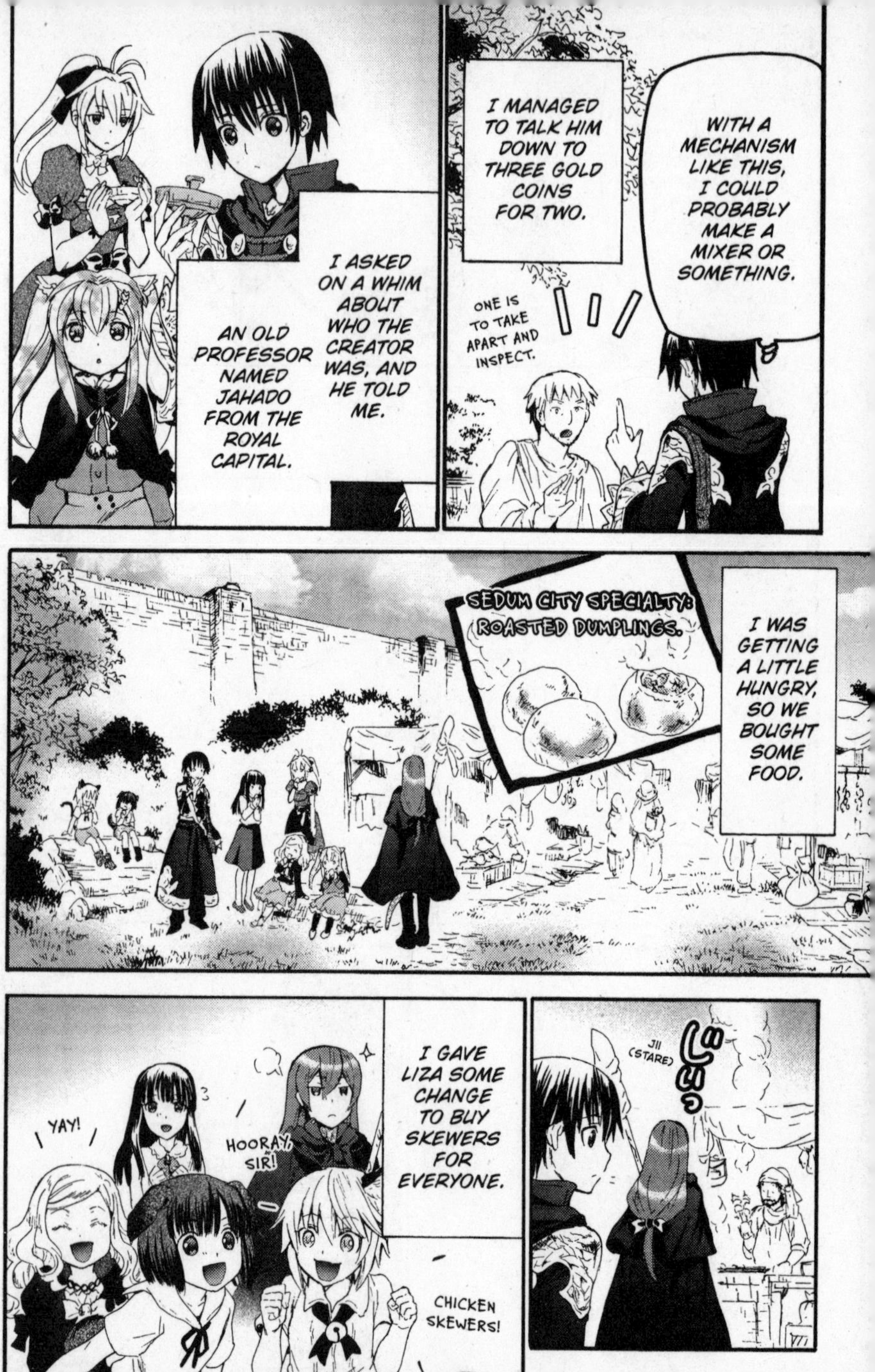
WITH A MECHANISM LIKE THIS, I COULD PROBABLY MAKE A MIXER OR SOMETHING.
I MANAGED TO TALK HIM DOWN TO THREE GOLD COINS FOR TWO.
ONE IS TO TAKE APART AND INSPECT.
I ASKED ON A WHIM ABOUT WHO THE CREATOR WAS, AND HE TOLD ME.
AN OLD PROFESSOR NAMED JAHADO FROM THE ROYAL CAPITAL.
I WAS GETTING A LITTLE HUNGRY, SO WE BOUGHT SOME FOOD.
SEDUM CITY SPECIALTY: ROASTED DUMPLINGS.
JII (STARE)
I GAVE LIZA SOME CHANGE TO BUY SKEWERS FOR EVERYONE.
HOORAY, SIR!
YAY!
CHICKEN SKEWERS!

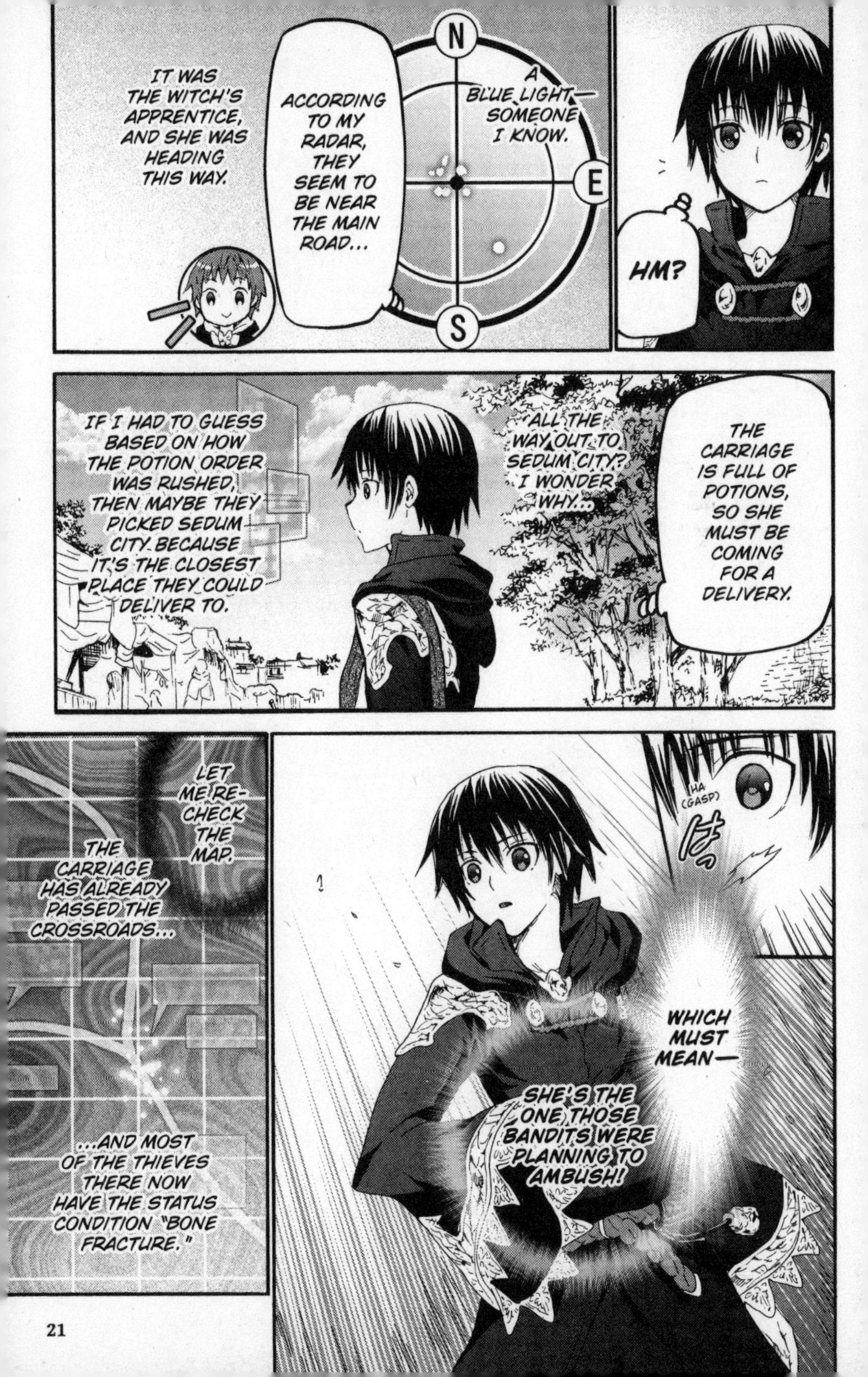
HM?
N
E
S
A BLUE LIGHT— SOMEONE I KNOW.
ACCORDING TO MY RADAR, THEY SEEM TO BE NEAR THE MAIN ROAD...
IT WAS THE WITCH'S APPRENTICE, AND SHE WAS HEADING THIS WAY.
THE CARRIAGE IS FULL OF POTIONS, SO SHE MUST BE COMING FOR A DELIVERY.
ALL THE WAY OUT TO SEDUM CITY? I WONDER WHY...
IF I HAD TO GUESS BASED ON HOW THE POTION ORDER WAS RUSHED, THEN MAYBE THEY PICKED SEDUM CITY BECAUSE IT'S THE CLOSEST PLACE THEY COULD DELIVER TO.
HA (GASP)
はっ
WHICH MUST MEAN—
SHE'S THE ONE THOSE BANDITS WERE PLANNING TO AMBUSH!
LET ME RE-CHECK THE MAP.
THE CARRIAGE HAS ALREADY PASSED THE CROSSROADS...
...AND MOST OF THE THIEVES THERE NOW HAVE THE STATUS CONDITION "BONE FRACTURE."

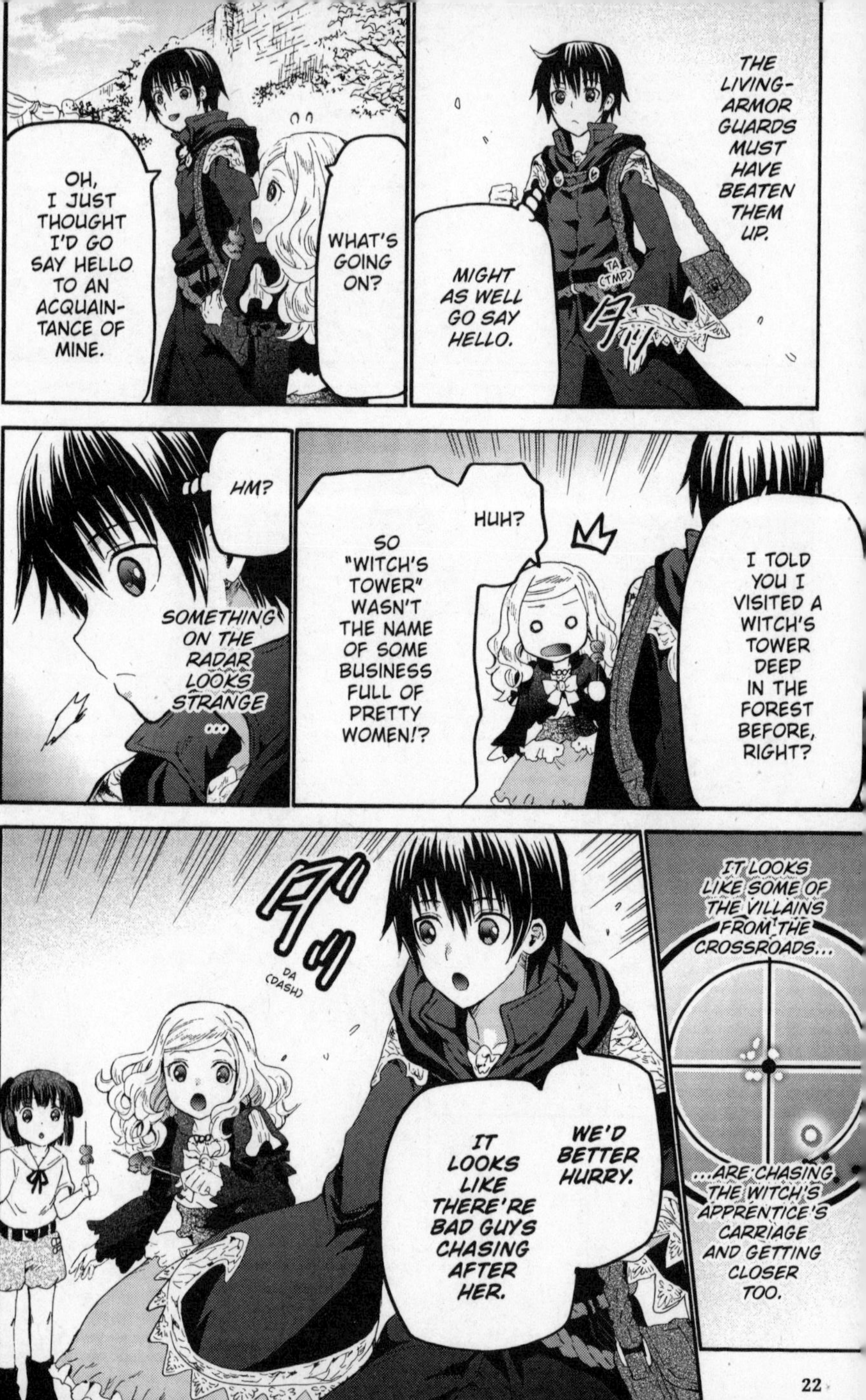
THE LIVING-ARMOR GUARDS MUST HAVE BEATEN THEM UP.
MIGHT AS WELL GO SAY HELLO.
TA (TMP)
WHAT'S GOING ON?
OH, I JUST THOUGHT I'D GO SAY HELLO TO AN ACQUAINTANCE OF MINE.
I TOLD YOU I VISITED A WITCH'S TOWER DEEP IN THE FOREST BEFORE, RIGHT?
HUH?
SO "WITCH'S TOWER" WASN'T THE NAME OF SOME BUSINESS FULL OF PRETTY WOMEN!?
HM?
SOMETHING ON THE RADAR LOOKS STRANGE...
IT LOOKS LIKE SOME OF THE VILLAINS FROM THE CROSSROADS...
...ARE CHASING THE WITCH'S APPRENTICE'S CARRIAGE AND GETTING CLOSER TOO.
WE'D BETTER HURRY.
IT LOOKS LIKE THERE'RE BAD GUYS CHASING AFTER HER.
DA (DASH)

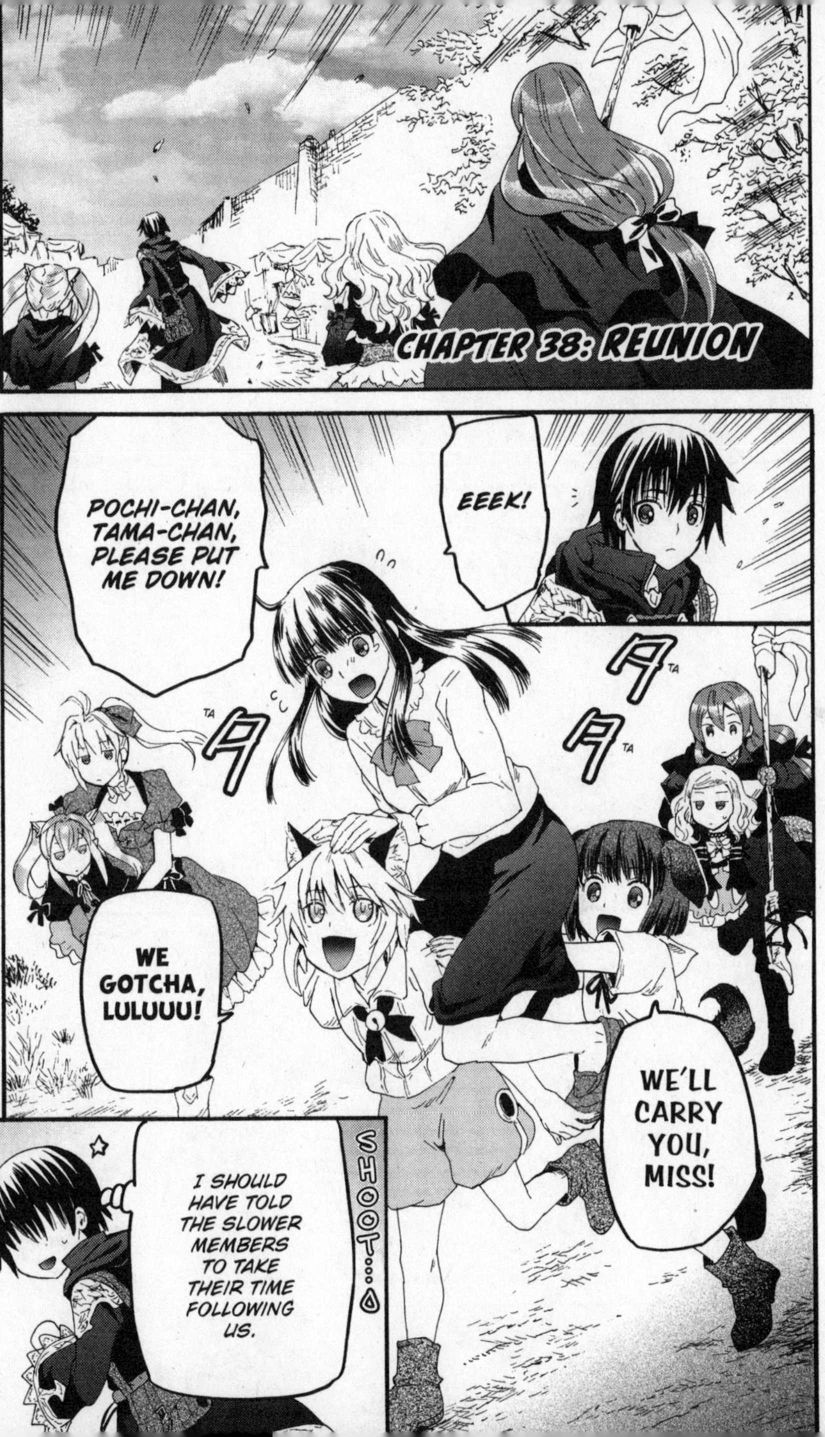
CHAPTER 38: REUNION
EEEK!
POCHI-CHAN, TAMA-CHAN, PLEASE PUT ME DOWN!
TA
TA
TA
WE GOTCHA, LULUUU!
WE'LL CARRY YOU, MISS!
SHOOT...
I SHOULD HAVE TOLD THE SLOWER MEMBERS TO TAKE THEIR TIME FOLLOWING US.

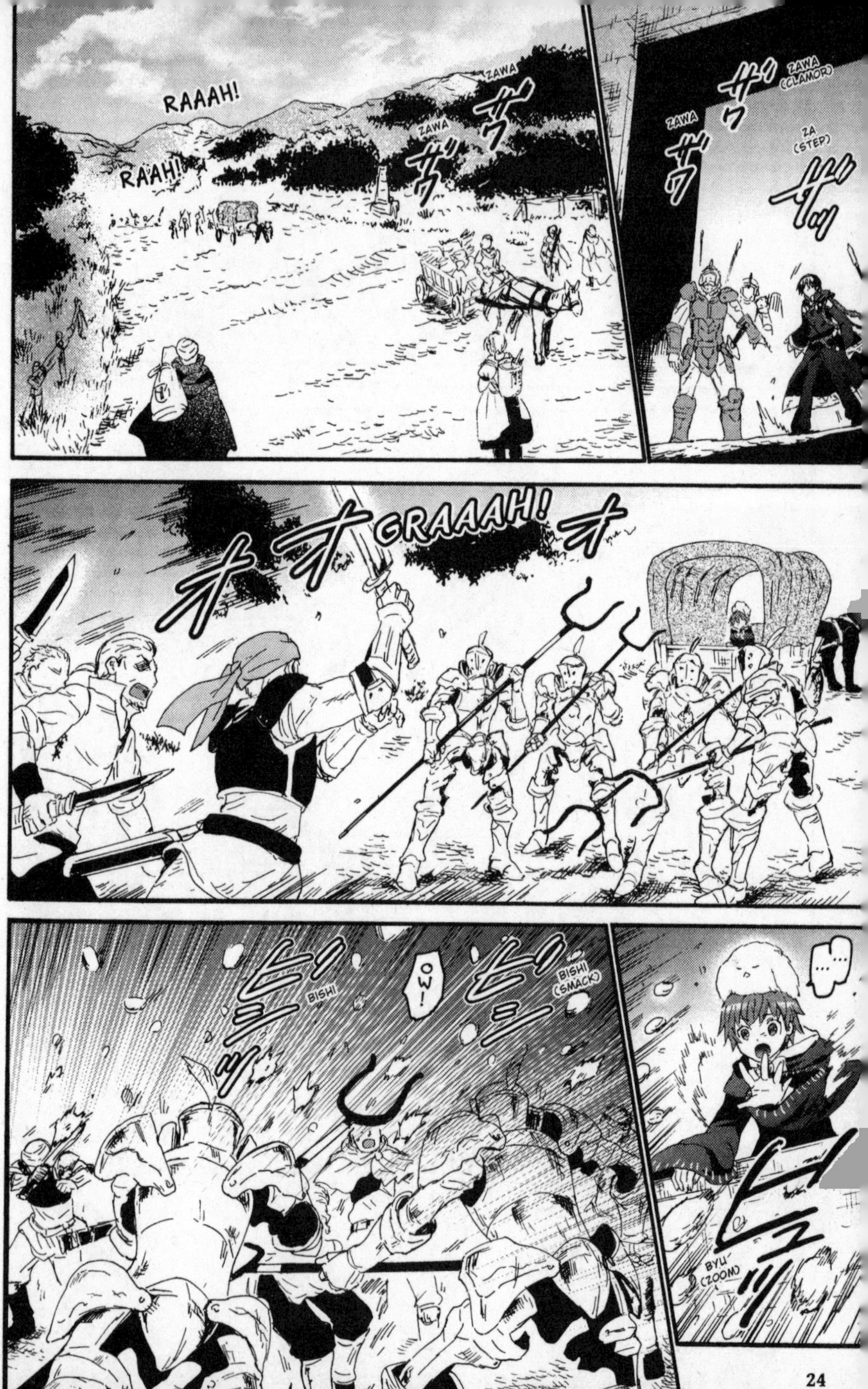
ZAWA (CLAMOR)
ZAWA
ZA (STEP)
RAAAH!
RAAH!
ZAWA
ZAWA
GRAAAH!
......
......
BYU (ZOOM)
BISHI (SMACK)
OW!
BISHI

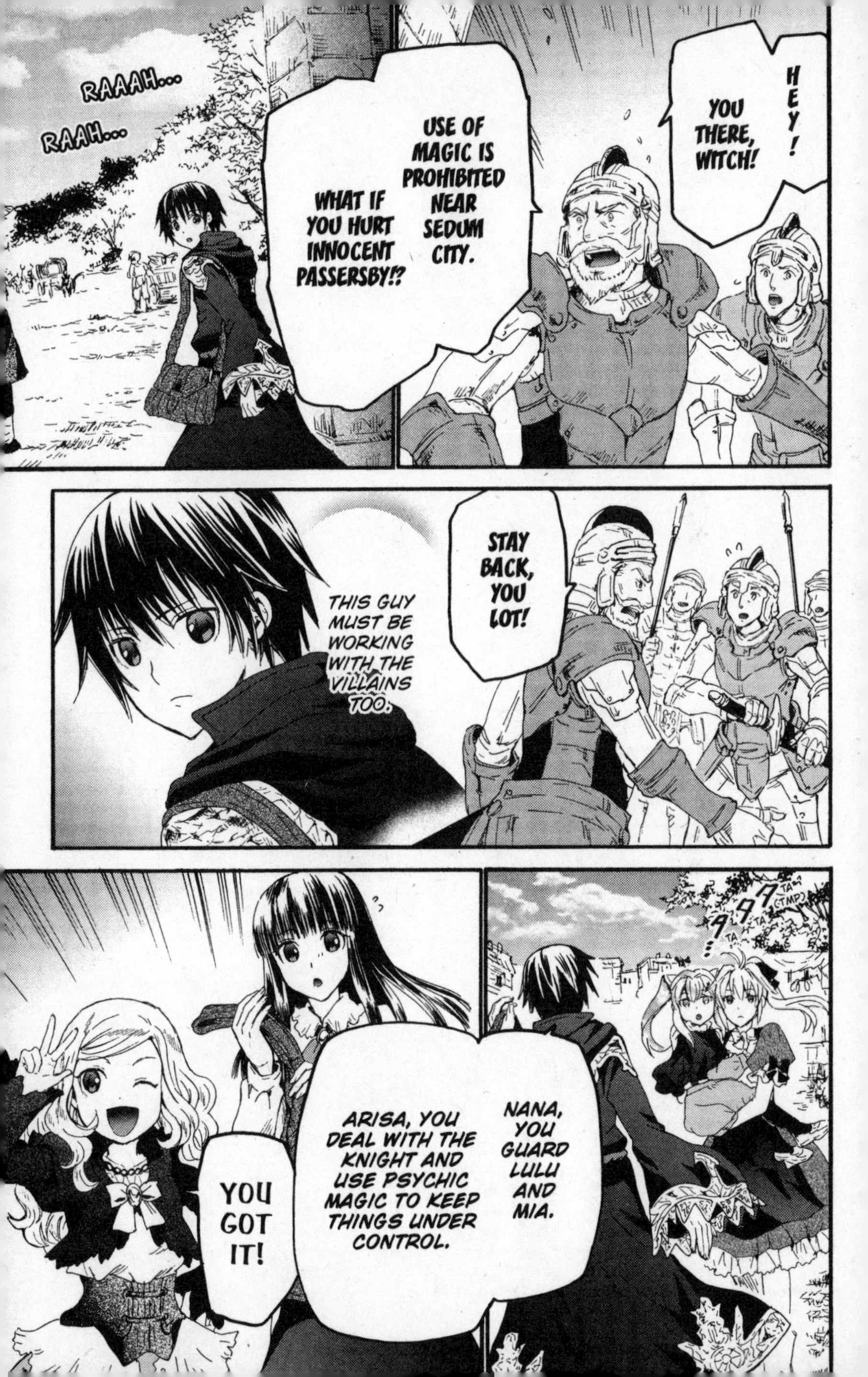
HEY!
YOU THERE, WITCH!
USE OF MAGIC IS PROHIBITED NEAR SEDUM CITY.
WHAT IF YOU HURT INNOCENT PASSERSBY!?
RAAAH...
RAAH...
STAY BACK, YOU LOT!
THIS GUY MUST BE WORKING WITH THE VILLAINS TOO.
TA TA TA (STMP)
NANA, YOU GUARD LULU AND MIA.
ARISA, YOU DEAL WITH THE KNIGHT AND USE PSYCHIC MAGIC TO KEEP THINGS UNDER CONTROL.
YOU GOT IT!

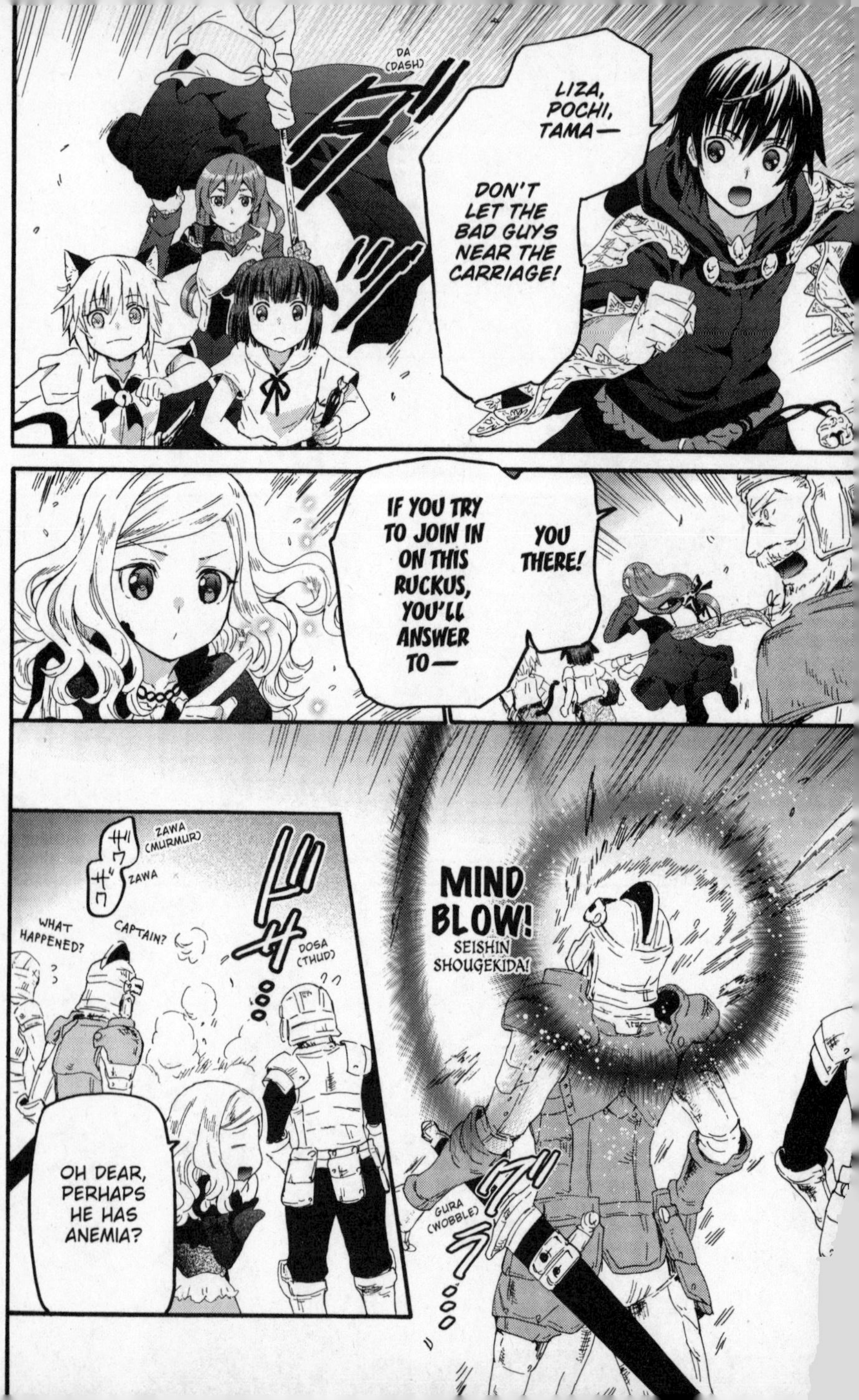
LIZA, POCHI, TAMA—
DON'T LET THE BAD GUYS NEAR THE CARRIAGE!
DA (DASH)
YOU THERE!
IF YOU TRY TO JOIN IN ON THIS RUCKUS, YOU'LL ANSWER TO—
MIND BLOW!
SEISHIN SHOUGEKIDA!
GURA (WOBBLE)
ZAWA (MURMUR)
ZAWA
DOSA (THUD)
CAPTAIN?
WHAT HAPPENED?
OH DEAR, PERHAPS HE HAS ANEMIA?

TA (TMP) TA TA
WAAH!
WAAH!
TA
POU KWEE!
...AH!
IT'S YOU!
THE PERSON WITH THE ELFIN BELL!
TA TA
THE NAME'S SATOU.
YOU'RE INE-SOMETHING-OR-OTHER-CHAN, RIGHT?
GASHA
GASHA (CLANK)
GO ON INTO THE CITY. LEAVE THIS TO US.
SORRY, OUR CAPTAIN WAS STOPPING US...
R-RIGHT!
WAAH!
WAAH!

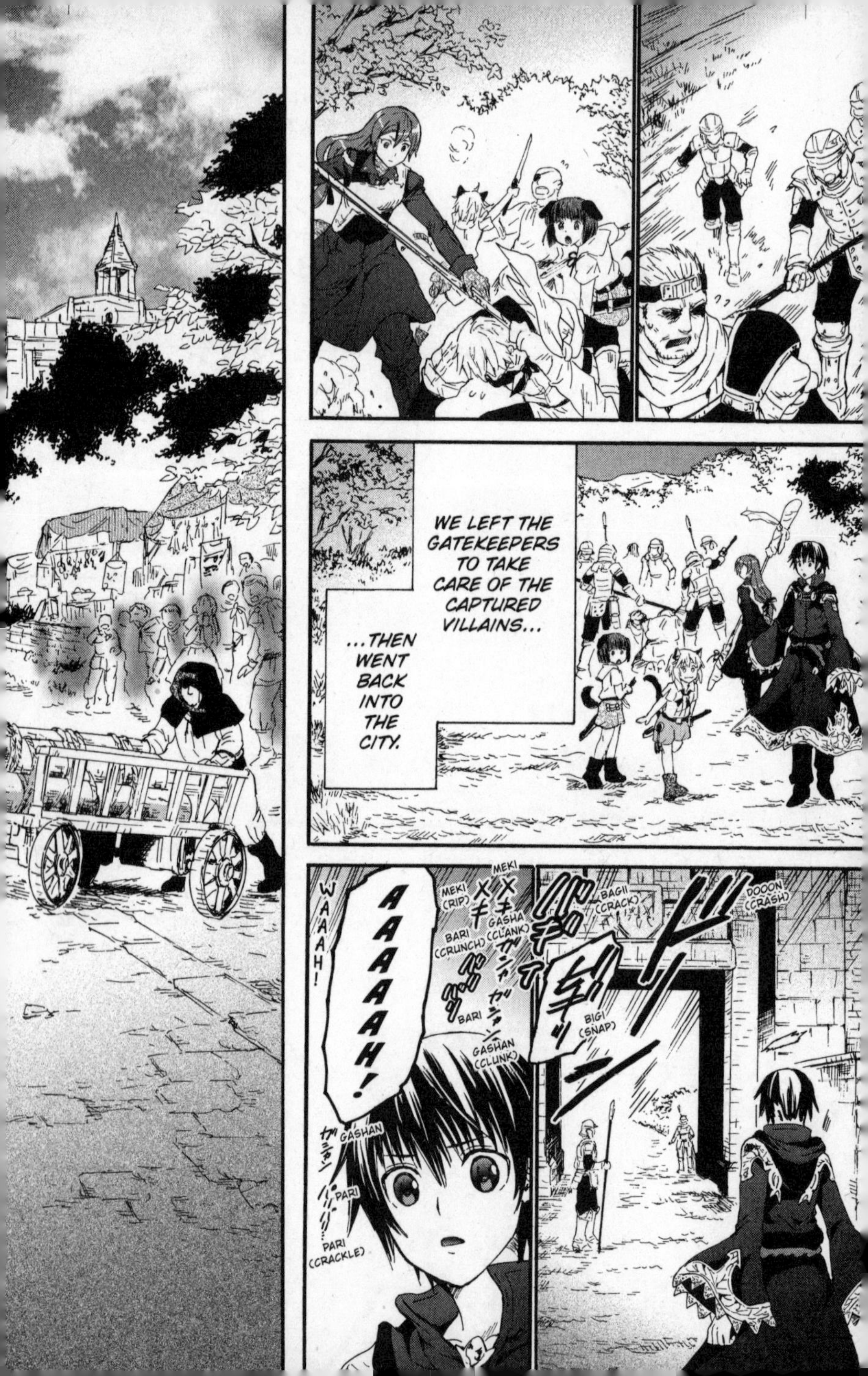
WE LEFT THE GATEKEEPERS TO TAKE CARE OF THE CAPTURED VILLAINS...
...THEN WENT BACK INTO THE CITY.
DOOON (CRASH)
BAGII (CRACK)
BIGI (SNAP)
MEKI MEKI (RIP)
GASHA (CLANK)
BARI (CRUNCH)
BARI
GASHAN (CLUNK)
AAAAAAH!
WAAAAH!
GASHAN
PARI
PARI (CRACKLE)

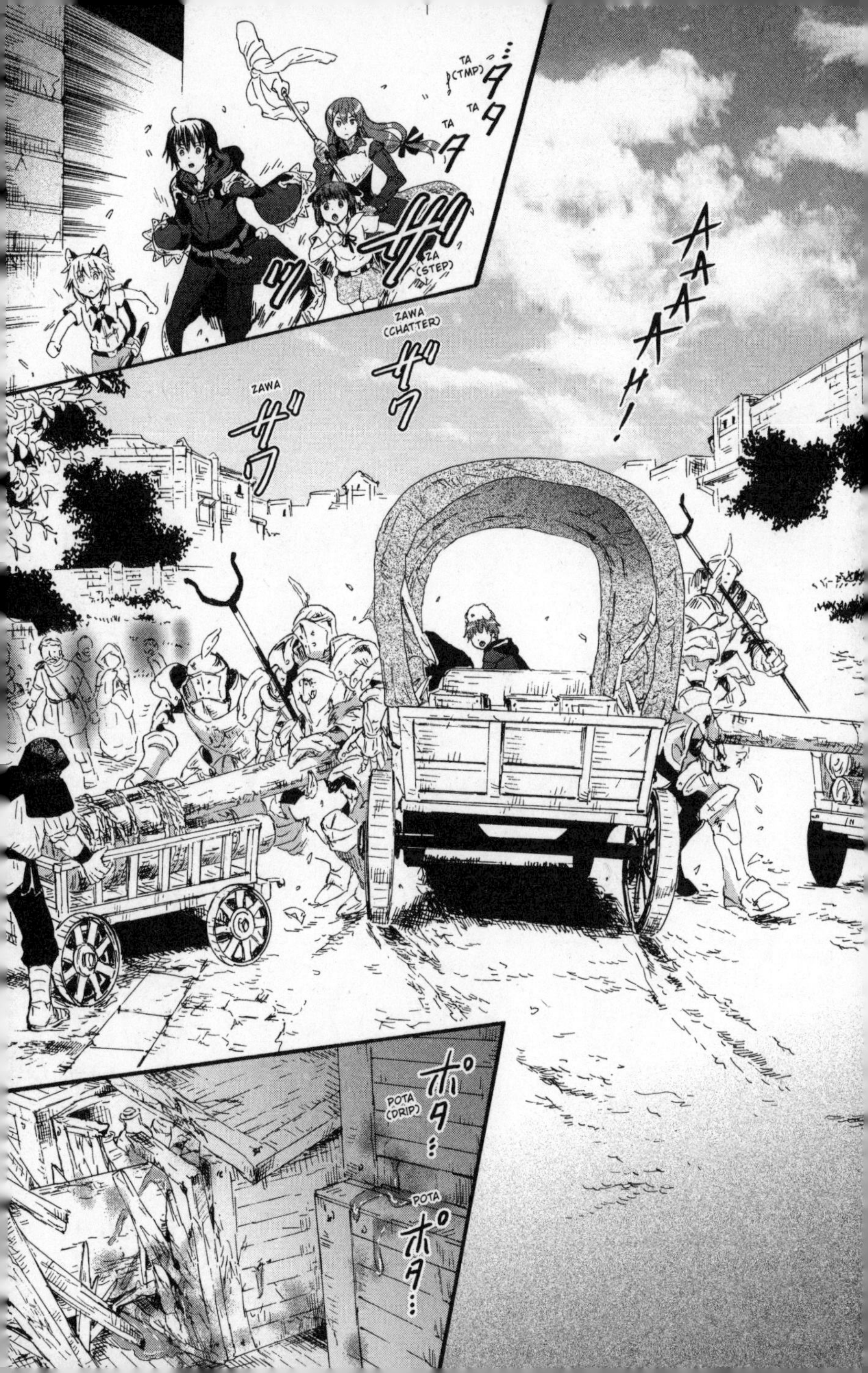

TA (TMP)
タ…
TA
タ
TA
タ
ZA (STEP)
ザッ
AAAAAH!
ZAWA (CHATTER)
ザワ
ZAWA
ザワ
POTA (DRIP)
ポタ…
POTA
ポタ…

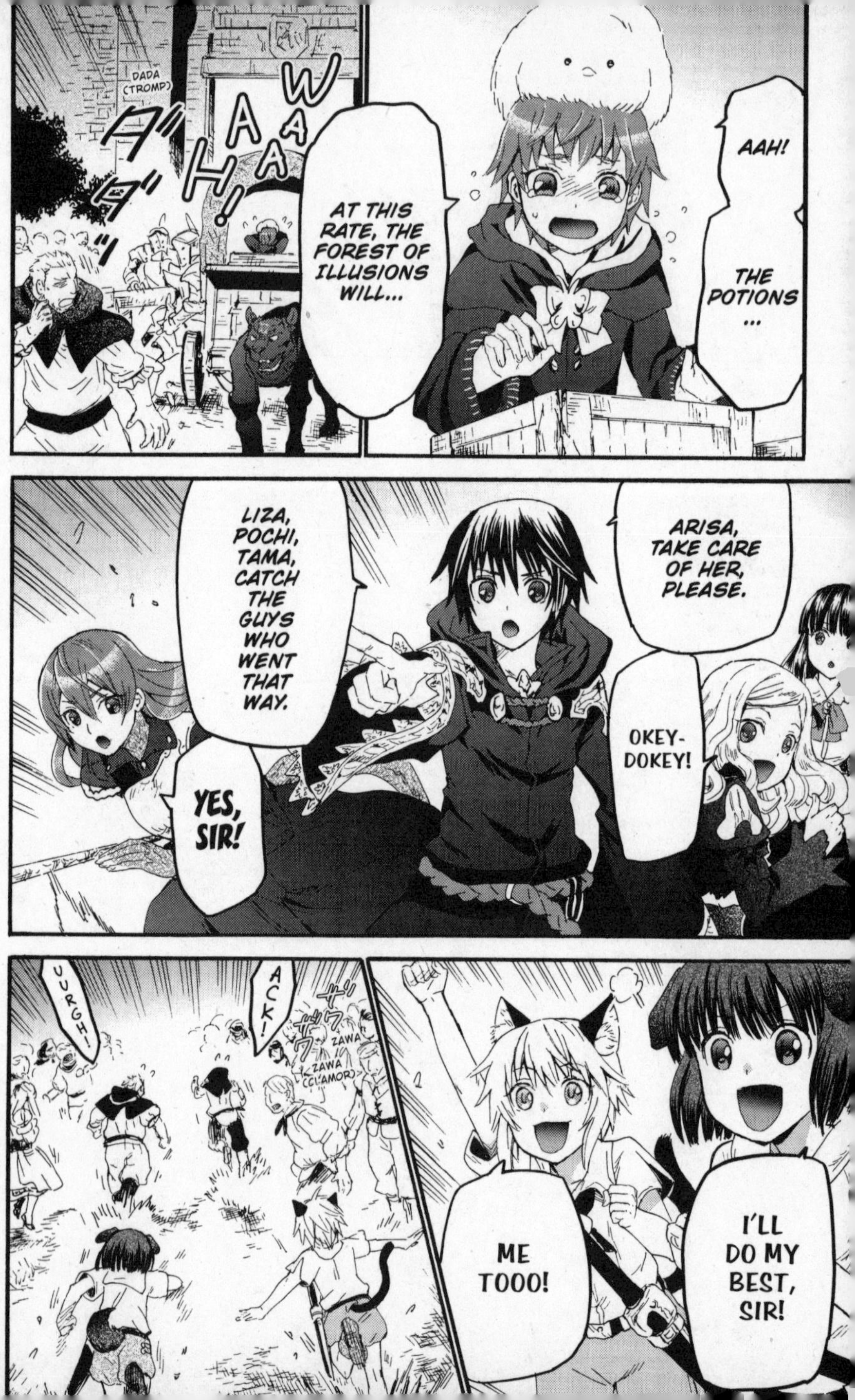
AAH!
THE POTIONS...
AT THIS RATE, THE FOREST OF ILLUSIONS WILL...
WAAAAH!
DADA (TROMP)
ARISA, TAKE CARE OF HER, PLEASE.
LIZA, POCHI, TAMA, CATCH THE GUYS WHO WENT THAT WAY.
OKEY-DOKEY!
YES, SIR!
I'LL DO MY BEST, SIR!
ME TOOO!
ACK!
ZAWA ZAWA (CLAMOR)
UURGH!

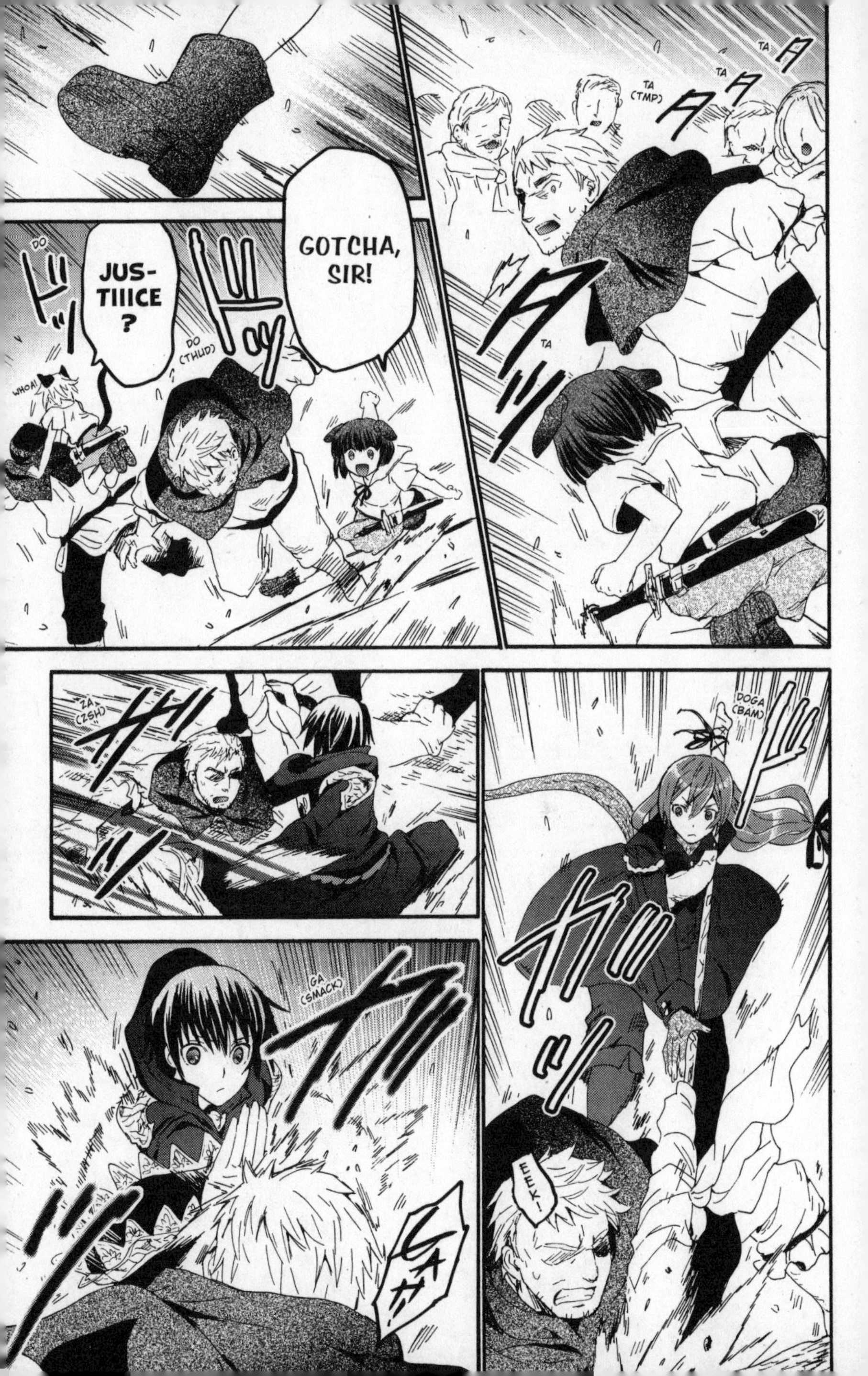
TA
TA
TA (TMP)
TA
GOTCHA, SIR!
DO (THUD)
JUS-TIIICE?
DO
WHOA!
DOGA (BAM)
EEK!
ZA (ZSH)
GA (SMACK)
GAH!

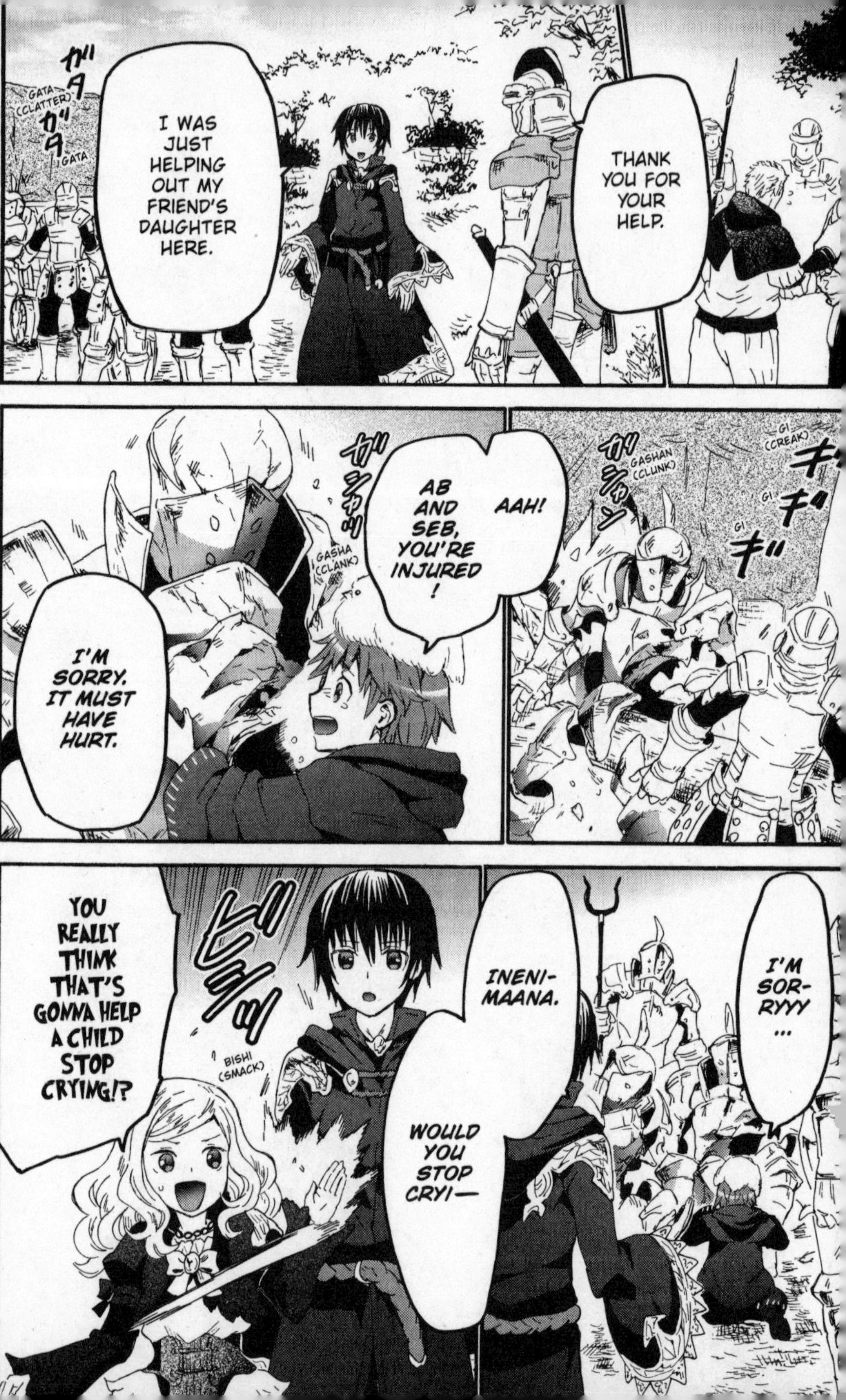
THANK YOU FOR YOUR HELP.
I WAS JUST HELPING OUT MY FRIEND'S DAUGHTER HERE.
GATA (CLATTER)
GATA
GI (CREAK)
GI
GI
GASHAN (CLUNK)
AAH!
AB AND SEB, YOU'RE INJURED!
GASHA (CLANK)
I'M SORRY. IT MUST HAVE HURT.
I'M SOR-RYYY...
INENI-MAANA.
WOULD YOU STOP CRYI—
BISHI (SMACK)
YOU REALLY THINK THAT'S GONNA HELP A CHILD STOP CRYING!?

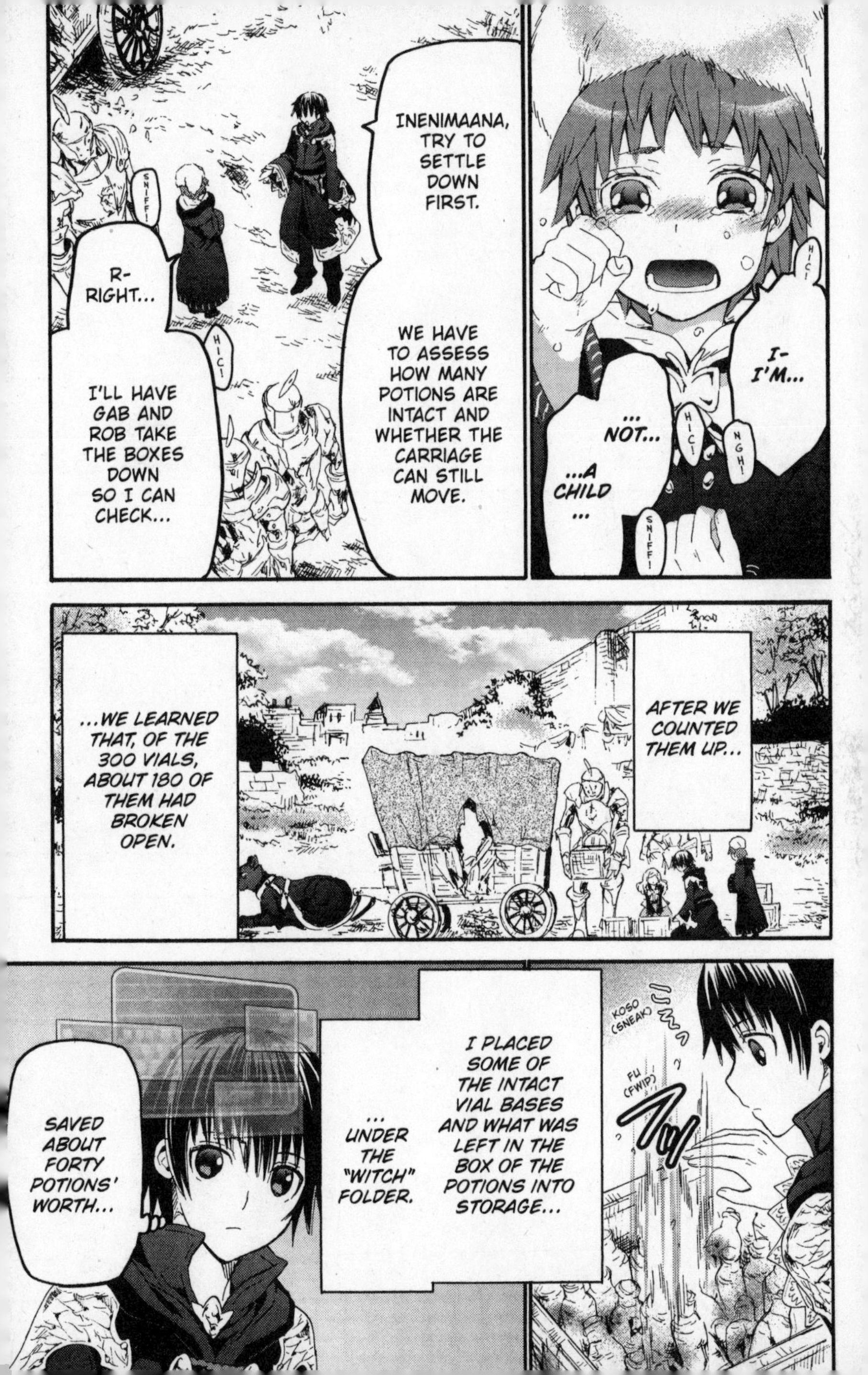
HIC!
I- I'M...
... NOT...
...A CHILD ...
HIC!
NGH!
SNIFF!
INENIMAANA, TRY TO SETTLE DOWN FIRST.
WE HAVE TO ASSESS HOW MANY POTIONS ARE INTACT AND WHETHER THE CARRIAGE CAN STILL MOVE.
SNIFF!
R- RIGHT...
HIC!
I'LL HAVE GAB AND ROB TAKE THE BOXES DOWN SO I CAN CHECK...
AFTER WE COUNTED THEM UP...
...WE LEARNED THAT, OF THE 300 VIALS, ABOUT 180 OF THEM HAD BROKEN OPEN.
KOSO (SNEAK)
FU (FWIP)
I PLACED SOME OF THE INTACT VIAL BASES AND WHAT WAS LEFT IN THE BOX OF THE POTIONS INTO STORAGE...
... UNDER THE "WITCH" FOLDER.
SAVED ABOUT FORTY POTIONS' WORTH...

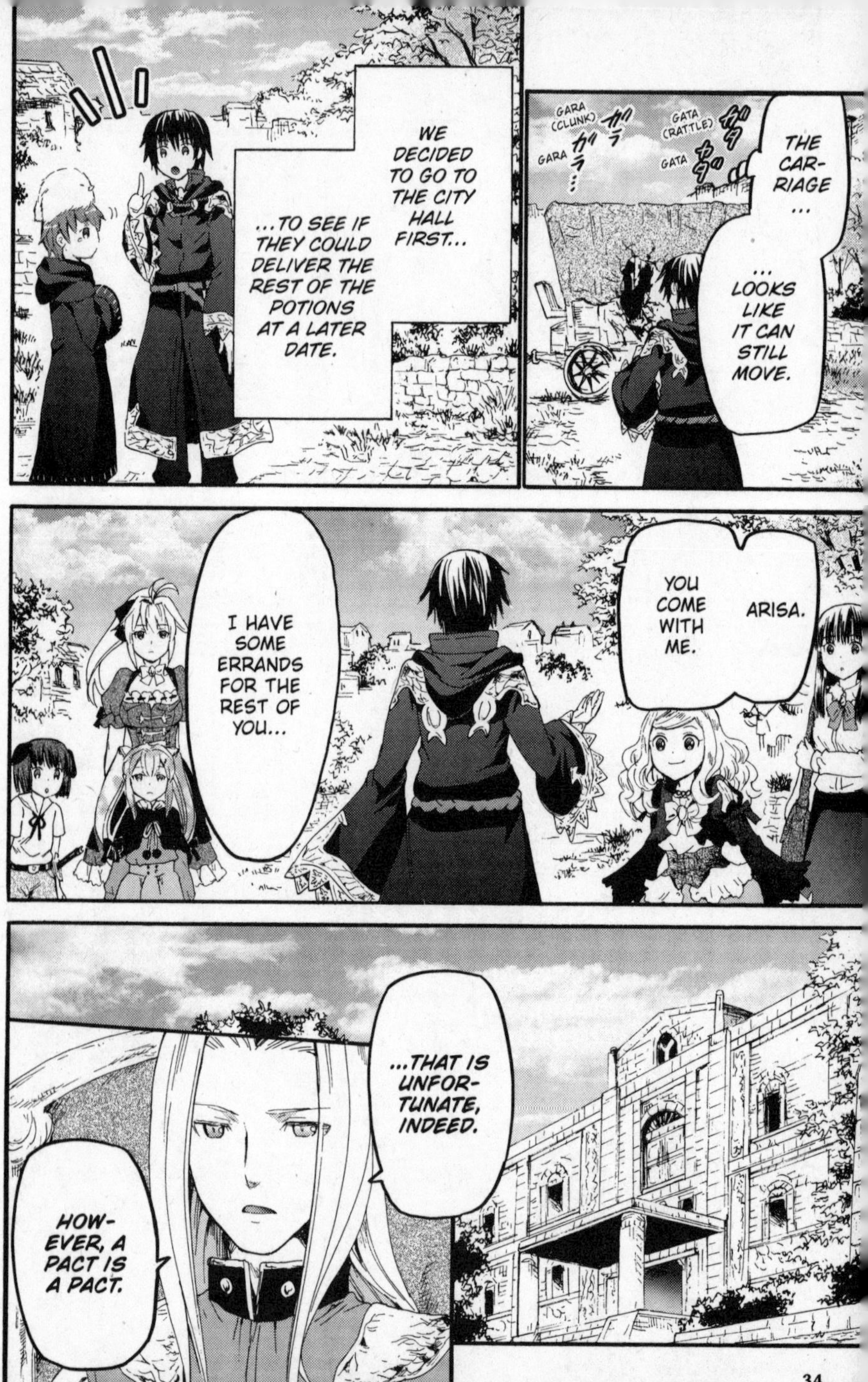
GARA (CLUNK)
GARA
GATA (RATTLE)
GATA
THE CAR-RIAGE...
...LOOKS LIKE IT CAN STILL MOVE.
WE DECIDED TO GO TO THE CITY HALL FIRST...
...TO SEE IF THEY COULD DELIVER THE REST OF THE POTIONS AT A LATER DATE.
ARISA.
YOU COME WITH ME.
I HAVE SOME ERRANDS FOR THE REST OF YOU...
...THAT IS UNFOR-TUNATE, INDEED.
HOW-EVER, A PACT IS A PACT.

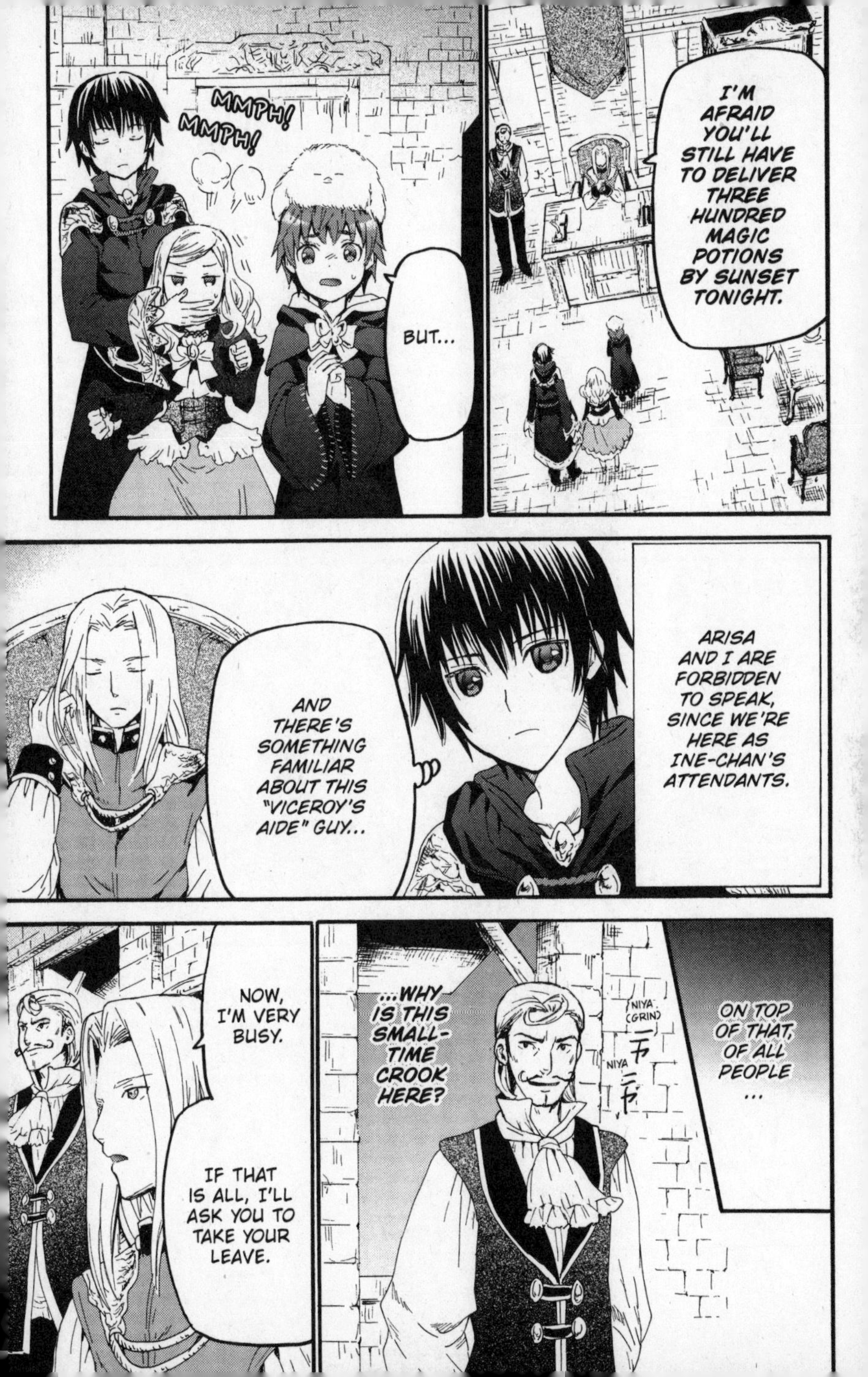
I'M AFRAID YOU'LL STILL HAVE TO DELIVER THREE HUNDRED MAGIC POTIONS BY SUNSET TONIGHT.
BUT...
MMPH! MMPH!
ARISA AND I ARE FORBIDDEN TO SPEAK, SINCE WE'RE HERE AS INE-CHAN'S ATTENDANTS.
AND THERE'S SOMETHING FAMILIAR ABOUT THIS "VICEROY'S AIDE" GUY...
ON TOP OF THAT, OF ALL PEOPLE ...
NIYA (GRIN)
NIYA
...WHY IS THIS SMALL-TIME CROOK HERE?
NOW, I'M VERY BUSY.
IF THAT IS ALL, I'LL ASK YOU TO TAKE YOUR LEAVE.

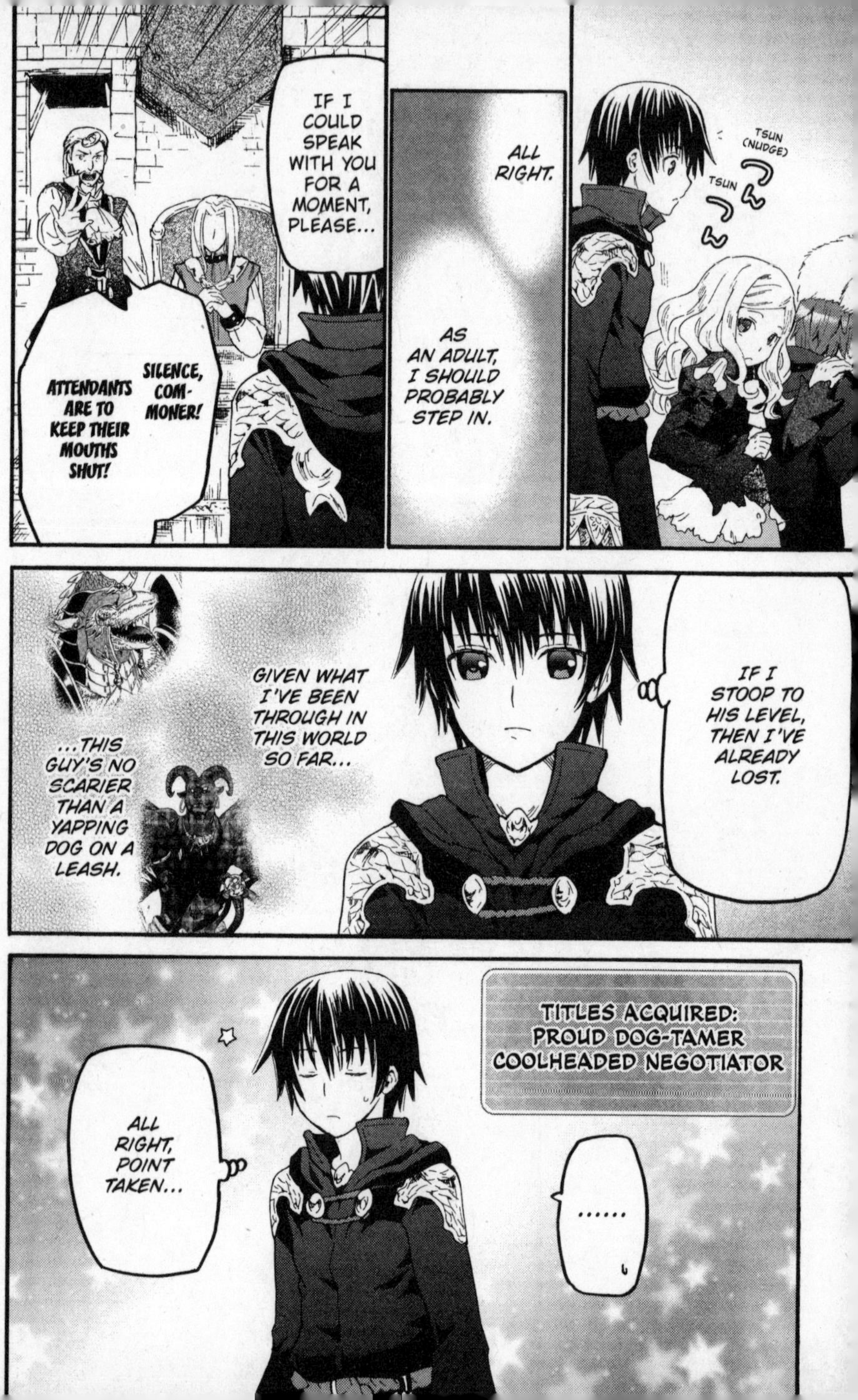
TSUN (NUDGE)
TSUN
ALL RIGHT.
AS AN ADULT, I SHOULD PROBABLY STEP IN.
IF I COULD SPEAK WITH YOU FOR A MOMENT, PLEASE...
SILENCE, COM-MONER!
ATTENDANTS ARE TO KEEP THEIR MOUTHS SHUT!
IF I STOOP TO HIS LEVEL, THEN I'VE ALREADY LOST.
GIVEN WHAT I'VE BEEN THROUGH IN THIS WORLD SO FAR...
...THIS GUY'S NO SCARIER THAN A YAPPING DOG ON A LEASH.
TITLES ACQUIRED: PROUD DOG-TAMER COOLHEADED NEGOTIATOR
......
ALL RIGHT, POINT TAKEN...

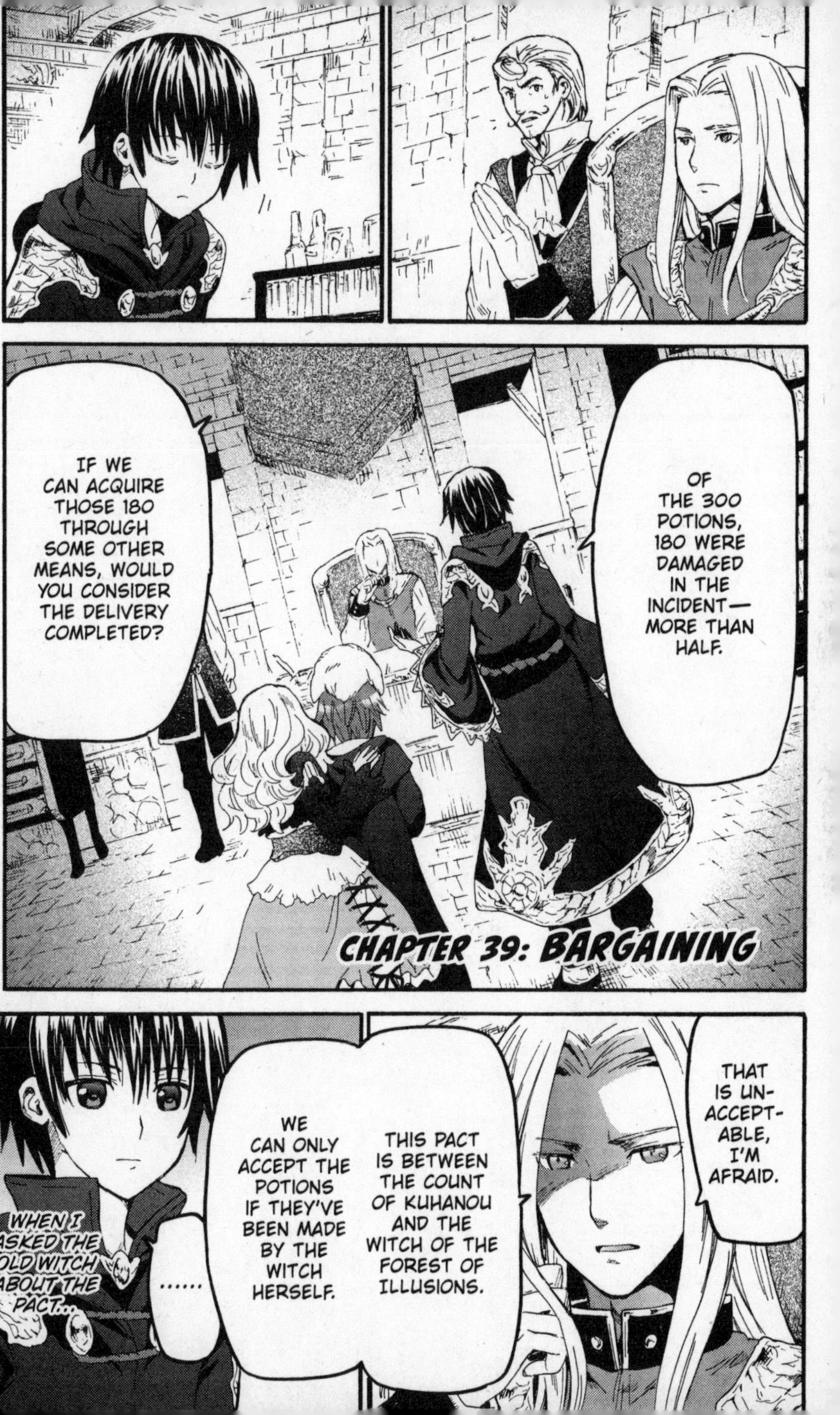
OF THE 300 POTIONS, 180 WERE DAMAGED IN THE INCIDENT—MORE THAN HALF.
IF WE CAN ACQUIRE THOSE 180 THROUGH SOME OTHER MEANS, WOULD YOU CONSIDER THE DELIVERY COMPLETED?
CHAPTER 39: BARGAINING
THAT IS UN-ACCEPT-ABLE, I'M AFRAID.
THIS PACT IS BETWEEN THE COUNT OF KUHANOU AND THE WITCH OF THE FOREST OF ILLUSIONS.
WE CAN ONLY ACCEPT THE POTIONS IF THEY'VE BEEN MADE BY THE WITCH HERSELF.
......
WHEN I ASKED THE OLD WITCH ABOUT THE PACT...

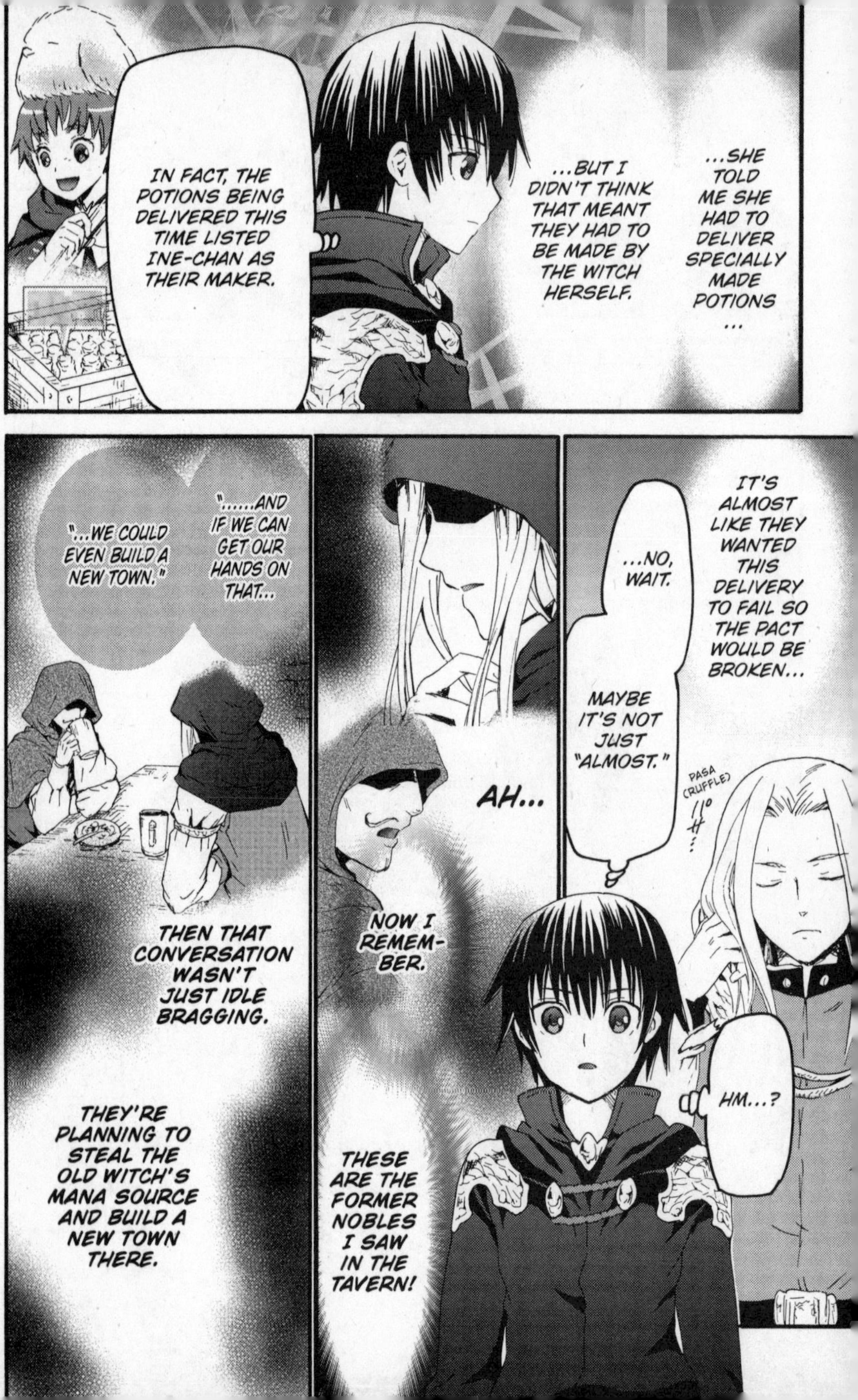
...SHE TOLD ME SHE HAD TO DELIVER SPECIALLY MADE POTIONS...
...BUT I DIDN'T THINK THAT MEANT THEY HAD TO BE MADE BY THE WITCH HERSELF.
IN FACT, THE POTIONS BEING DELIVERED THIS TIME LISTED INE-CHAN AS THEIR MAKER.
IT'S ALMOST LIKE THEY WANTED THIS DELIVERY TO FAIL SO THE PACT WOULD BE BROKEN...
...NO, WAIT.
MAYBE IT'S NOT JUST "ALMOST."
PASA (RUFFLE)
HM...?
AH...
NOW I REMEMBER.
THESE ARE THE FORMER NOBLES I SAW IN THE TAVERN!
"......AND IF WE CAN GET OUR HANDS ON THAT...
"...WE COULD EVEN BUILD A NEW TOWN."
THEN THAT CONVERSATION WASN'T JUST IDLE BRAGGING.
THEY'RE PLANNING TO STEAL THE OLD WITCH'S MANA SOURCE AND BUILD A NEW TOWN THERE.

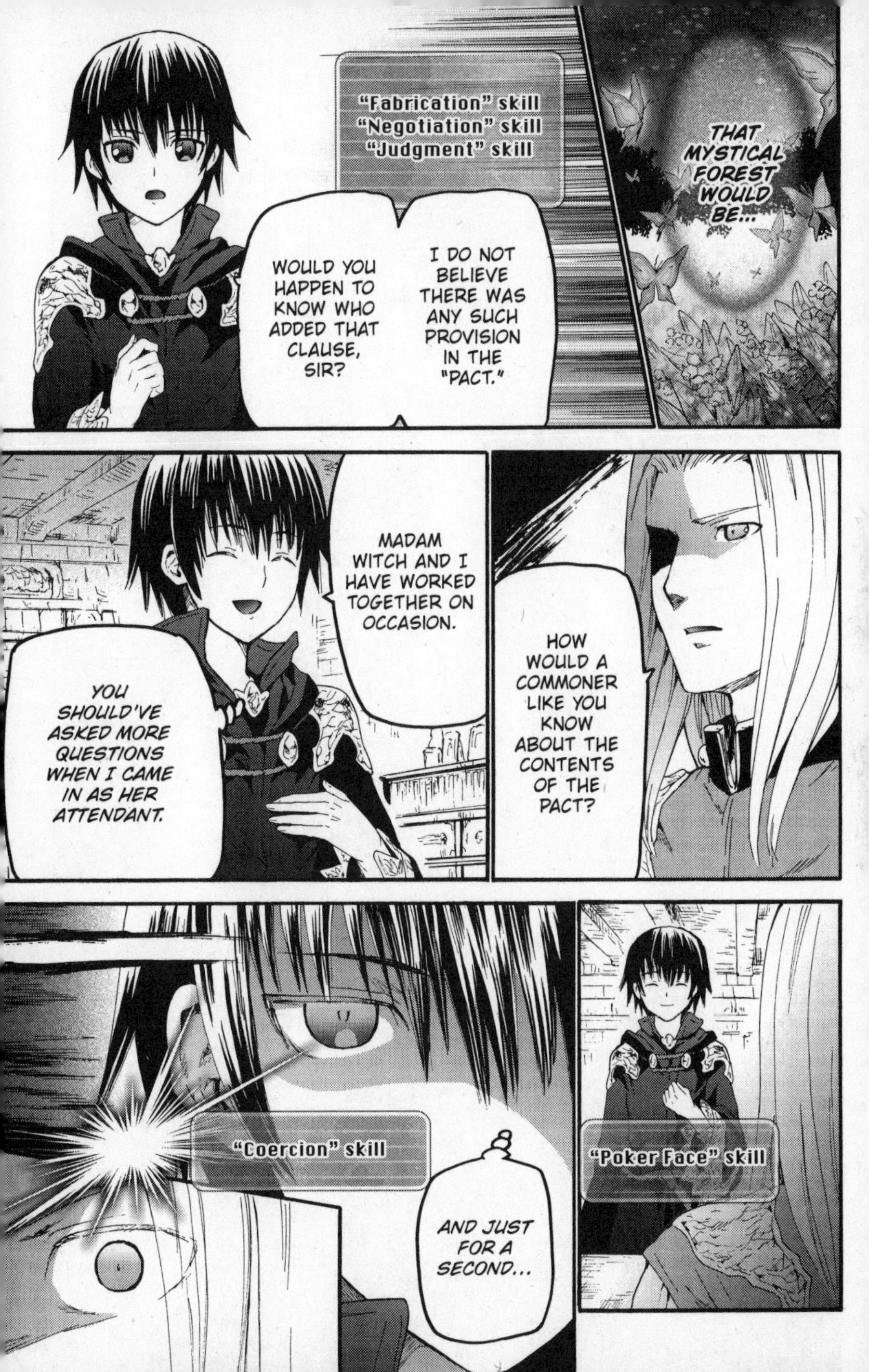
THAT MYSTICAL FOREST WOULD BE...
"Fabrication" skill
"Negotiation" skill
"Judgment" skill
I DO NOT BELIEVE THERE WAS ANY SUCH PROVISION IN THE "PACT."
WOULD YOU HAPPEN TO KNOW WHO ADDED THAT CLAUSE, SIR?
HOW WOULD A COMMONER LIKE YOU KNOW ABOUT THE CONTENTS OF THE PACT?
MADAM WITCH AND I HAVE WORKED TOGETHER ON OCCASION.
YOU SHOULD'VE ASKED MORE QUESTIONS WHEN I CAME IN AS HER ATTENDANT.
"Poker Face" skill
"Coercion" skill
AND JUST FOR A SECOND...

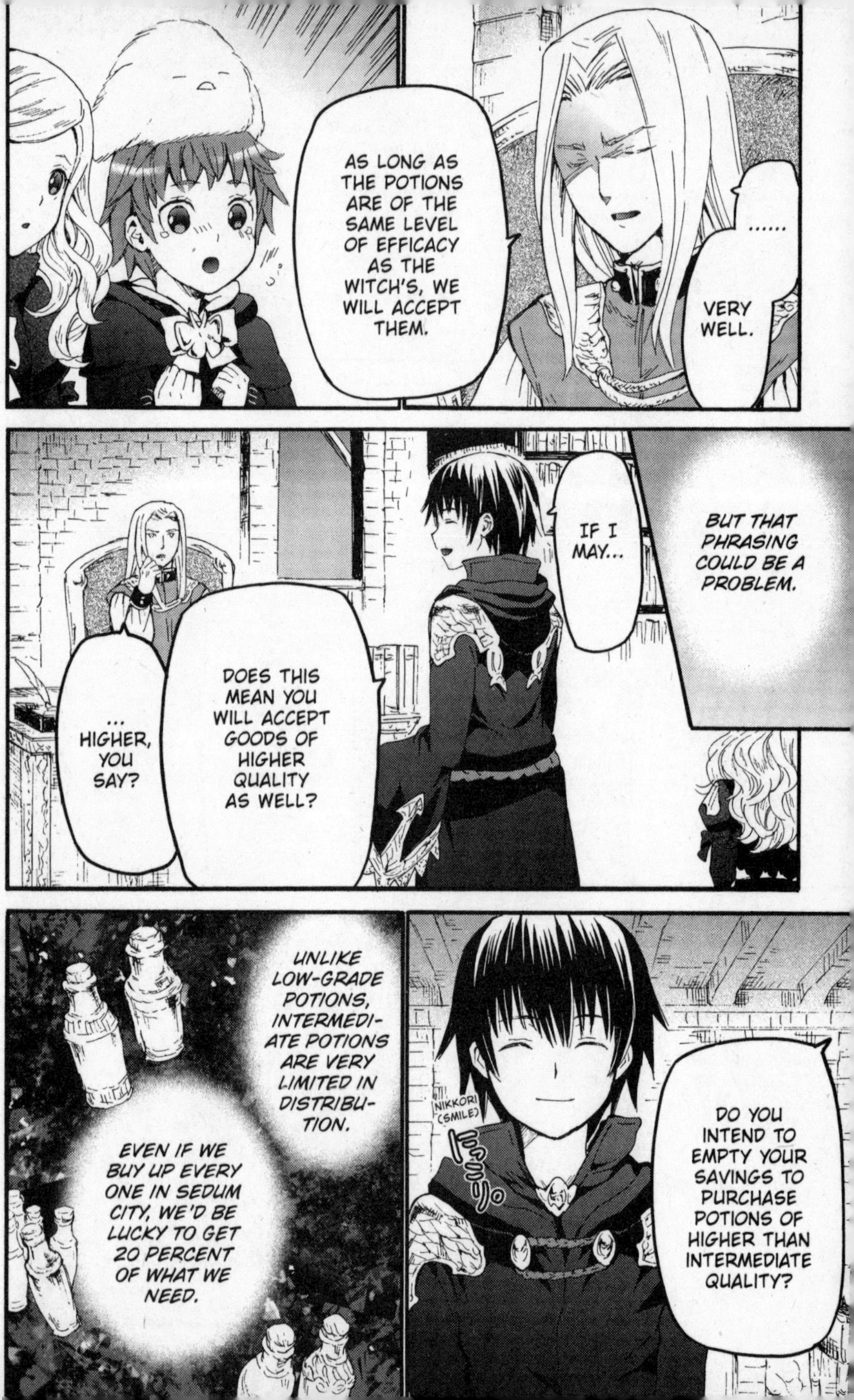
......
VERY WELL.
AS LONG AS THE POTIONS ARE OF THE SAME LEVEL OF EFFICACY AS THE WITCH'S, WE WILL ACCEPT THEM.
BUT THAT PHRASING COULD BE A PROBLEM.
IF I MAY...
DOES THIS MEAN YOU WILL ACCEPT GOODS OF HIGHER QUALITY AS WELL?
... HIGHER, YOU SAY?
NIKKORI (SMILE)
DO YOU INTEND TO EMPTY YOUR SAVINGS TO PURCHASE POTIONS OF HIGHER THAN INTERMEDIATE QUALITY?
UNLIKE LOW-GRADE POTIONS, INTERMEDIATE POTIONS ARE VERY LIMITED IN DISTRIBUTION.
EVEN IF WE BUY UP EVERY ONE IN SEDUM CITY, WE'D BE LUCKY TO GET 20 PERCENT OF WHAT WE NEED.

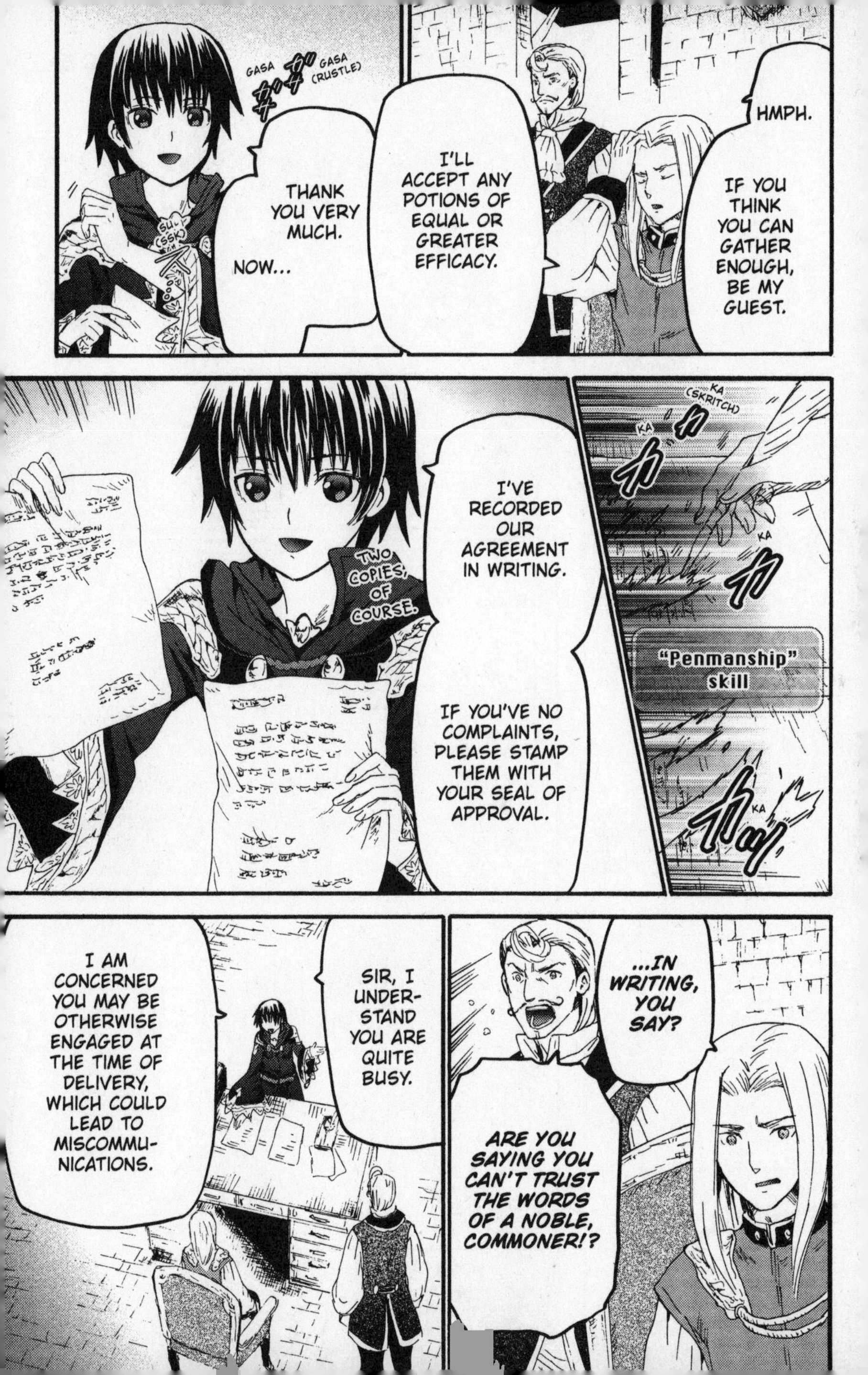
HMPH.
IF YOU THINK YOU CAN GATHER ENOUGH, BE MY GUEST.
I'LL ACCEPT ANY POTIONS OF EQUAL OR GREATER EFFICACY.
GASA GASA (RUSTLE)
THANK YOU VERY MUCH.
NOW...
SU (SSK)
KA (SKRITCH) KA
KA
"Penmanship" skill
KA
I'VE RECORDED OUR AGREEMENT IN WRITING.
IF YOU'VE NO COMPLAINTS, PLEASE STAMP THEM WITH YOUR SEAL OF APPROVAL.
TWO COPIES, OF COURSE.
...IN WRITING, YOU SAY?
ARE YOU SAYING YOU CAN'T TRUST THE WORDS OF A NOBLE, COMMONER!?
SIR, I UNDER-STAND YOU ARE QUITE BUSY.
I AM CONCERNED YOU MAY BE OTHERWISE ENGAGED AT THE TIME OF DELIVERY, WHICH COULD LEAD TO MISCOMMU-NICATIONS.

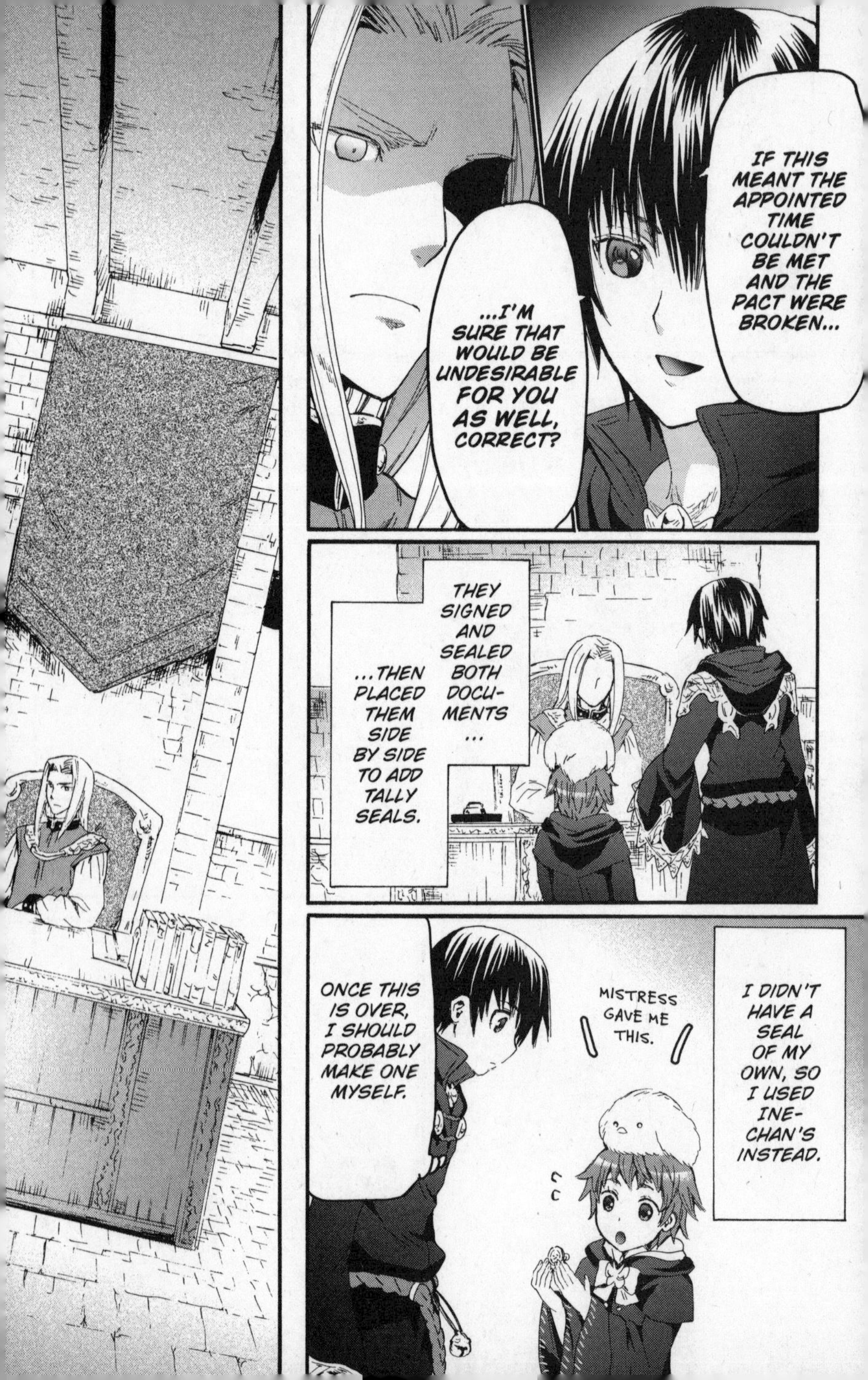
IF THIS MEANT THE APPOINTED TIME COULDN'T BE MET AND THE PACT WERE BROKEN...
...I'M SURE THAT WOULD BE UNDESIRABLE FOR YOU AS WELL, CORRECT?
THEY SIGNED AND SEALED BOTH DOCUMENTS...
...THEN PLACED THEM SIDE BY SIDE TO ADD TALLY SEALS.
I DIDN'T HAVE A SEAL OF MY OWN, SO I USED INE-CHAN'S INSTEAD.
MISTRESS GAVE ME THIS.
ONCE THIS IS OVER, I SHOULD PROBABLY MAKE ONE MYSELF.

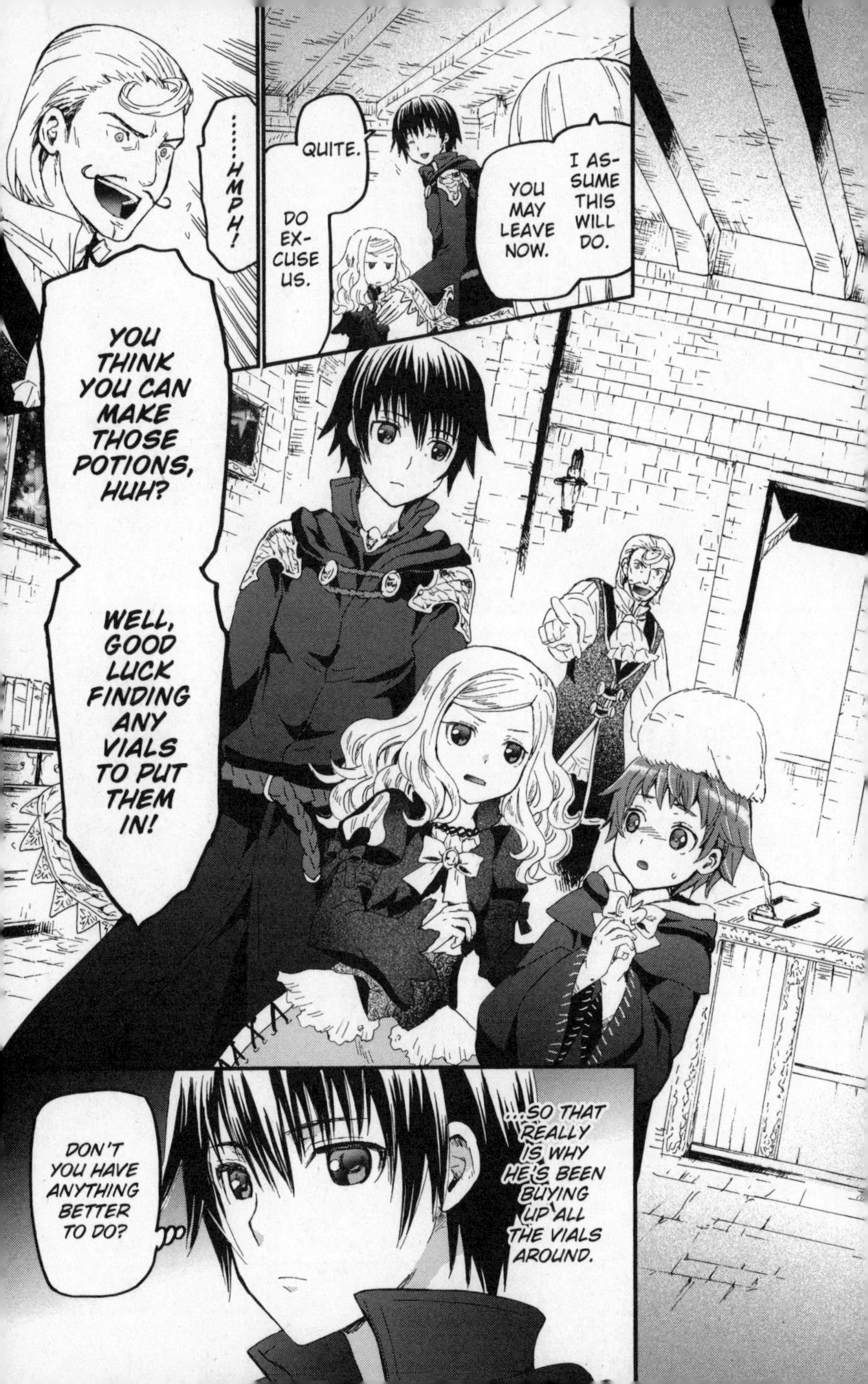

I ASSUME THIS WILL DO.
YOU MAY LEAVE NOW.
QUITE.
DO EXCUSE US.
......HMPH!
YOU THINK YOU CAN MAKE THOSE POTIONS, HUH?
WELL, GOOD LUCK FINDING ANY VIALS TO PUT THEM IN!
...SO THAT REALLY IS WHY HE'S BEEN BUYING UP ALL THE VIALS AROUND.
DON'T YOU HAVE ANYTHING BETTER TO DO?

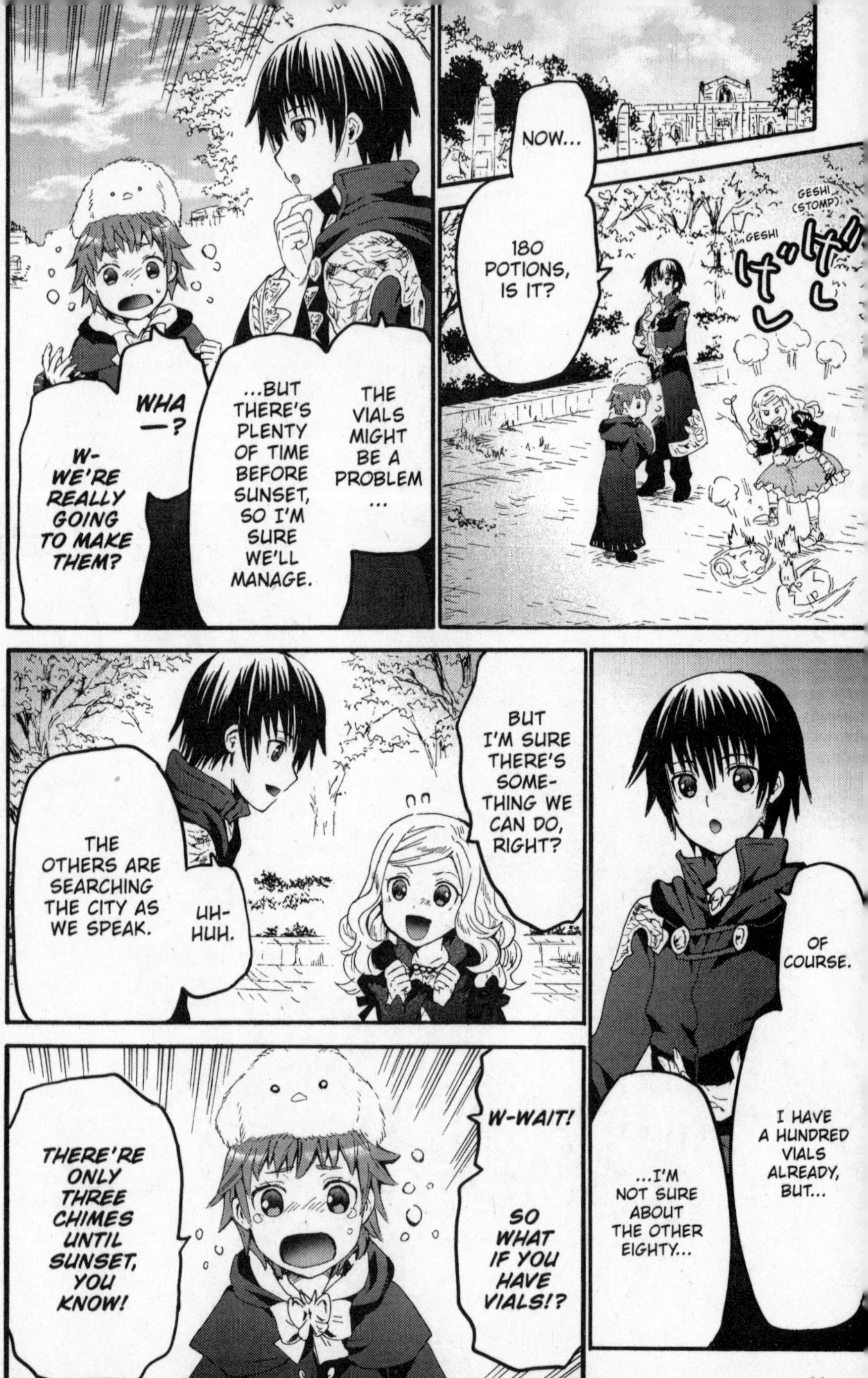
NOW...
180 POTIONS, IS IT?
GESHI (STOMP)
GESHI
THE VIALS MIGHT BE A PROBLEM...
...BUT THERE'S PLENTY OF TIME BEFORE SUNSET, SO I'M SURE WE'LL MANAGE.
WHA—?
W-WE'RE REALLY GOING TO MAKE THEM?
OF COURSE.
I HAVE A HUNDRED VIALS ALREADY, BUT...
...I'M NOT SURE ABOUT THE OTHER EIGHTY...
BUT I'M SURE THERE'S SOMETHING WE CAN DO, RIGHT?
UH-HUH.
THE OTHERS ARE SEARCHING THE CITY AS WE SPEAK.
W-WAIT!
SO WHAT IF YOU HAVE VIALS!?
THERE'RE ONLY THREE CHIMES UNTIL SUNSET, YOU KNOW!

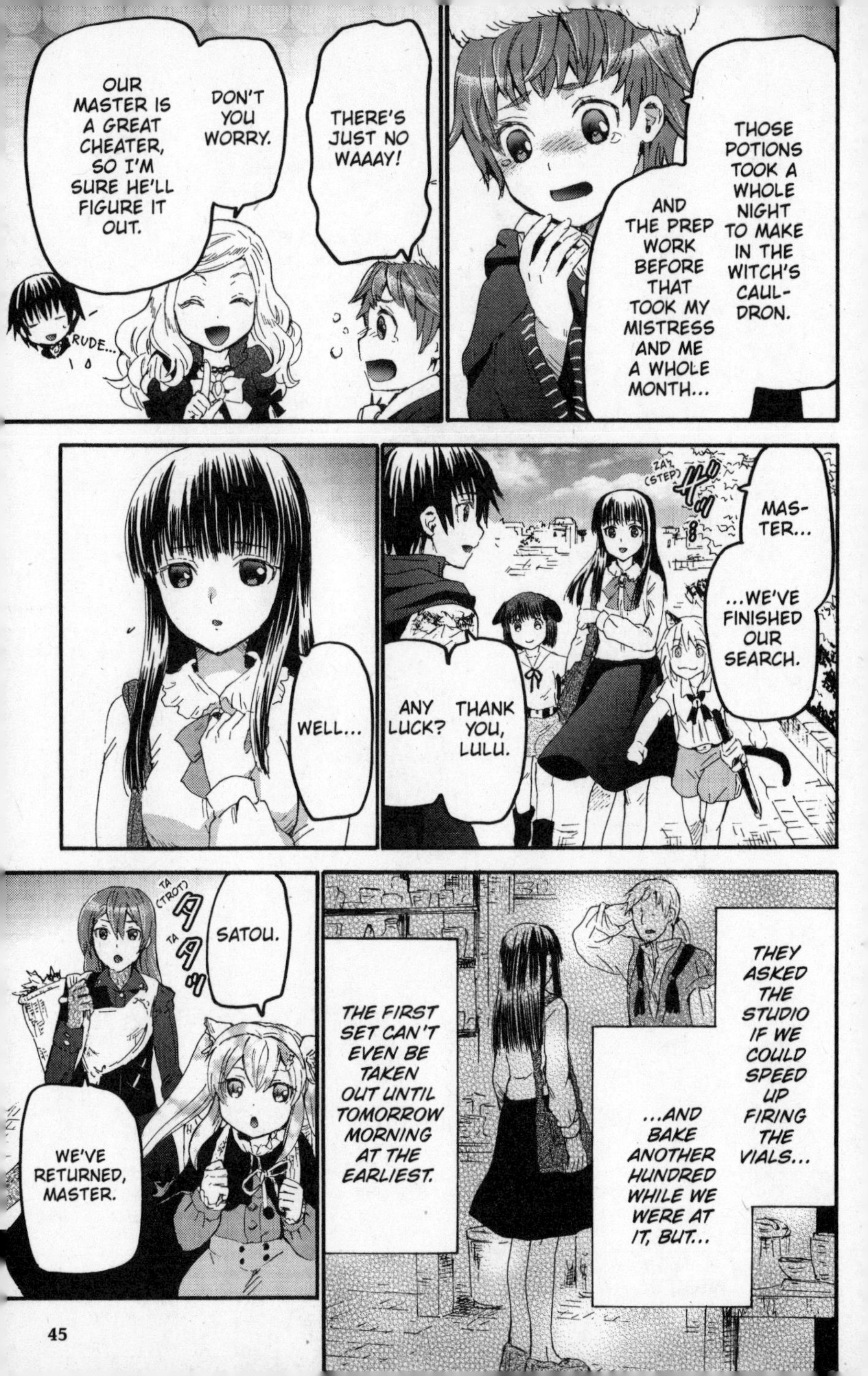
THOSE POTIONS TOOK A WHOLE NIGHT TO MAKE IN THE WITCH'S CAULDRON.
AND THE PREP WORK BEFORE THAT TOOK MY MISTRESS AND ME A WHOLE MONTH...
THERE'S JUST NO WAAAY!
DON'T YOU WORRY.
OUR MASTER IS A GREAT CHEATER, SO I'M SURE HE'LL FIGURE IT OUT.
RUDE...
ZA (STEP)
MASTER...
...WE'VE FINISHED OUR SEARCH.
THANK YOU, LULU.
ANY LUCK?
WELL...
THEY ASKED THE STUDIO IF WE COULD SPEED UP FIRING THE VIALS...
...AND BAKE ANOTHER HUNDRED WHILE WE WERE AT IT, BUT...
THE FIRST SET CAN'T EVEN BE TAKEN OUT UNTIL TOMORROW MORNING AT THE EARLIEST.
TA (TROT) TA
SATOU.
WE'VE RETURNED, MASTER.

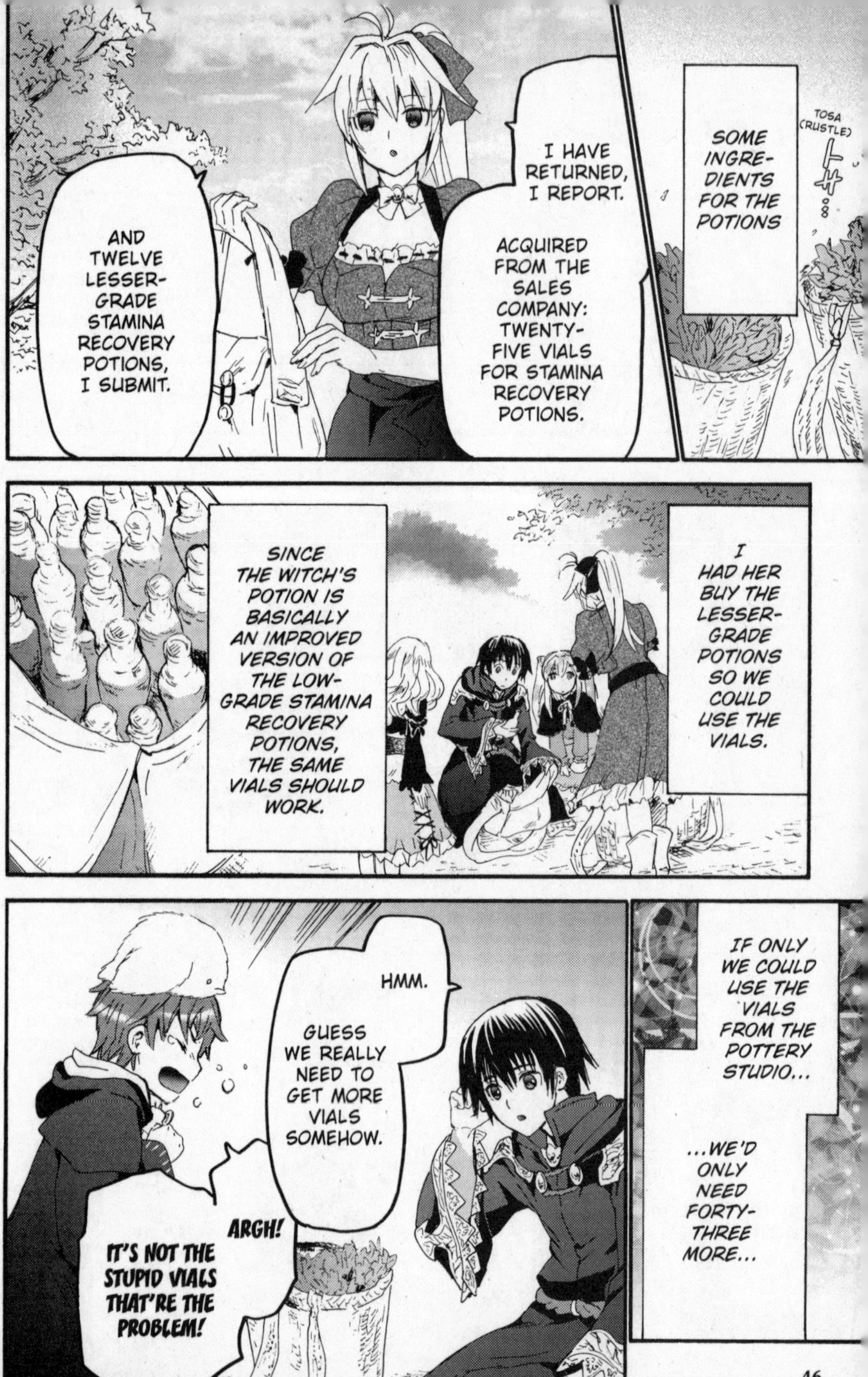
SOME INGREDIENTS FOR THE POTIONS
TOSA (RUSTLE)
I HAVE RETURNED, I REPORT.
ACQUIRED FROM THE SALES COMPANY: TWENTY-FIVE VIALS FOR STAMINA RECOVERY POTIONS.
AND TWELVE LESSER-GRADE STAMINA RECOVERY POTIONS, I SUBMIT.
I HAD HER BUY THE LESSER-GRADE POTIONS SO WE COULD USE THE VIALS.
SINCE THE WITCH'S POTION IS BASICALLY AN IMPROVED VERSION OF THE LOW-GRADE STAMINA RECOVERY POTIONS, THE SAME VIALS SHOULD WORK.
IF ONLY WE COULD USE THE VIALS FROM THE POTTERY STUDIO...
...WE'D ONLY NEED FORTY-THREE MORE...
HMM.
GUESS WE REALLY NEED TO GET MORE VIALS SOMEHOW.
ARGH!
IT'S NOT THE STUPID VIALS THAT'RE THE PROBLEM!

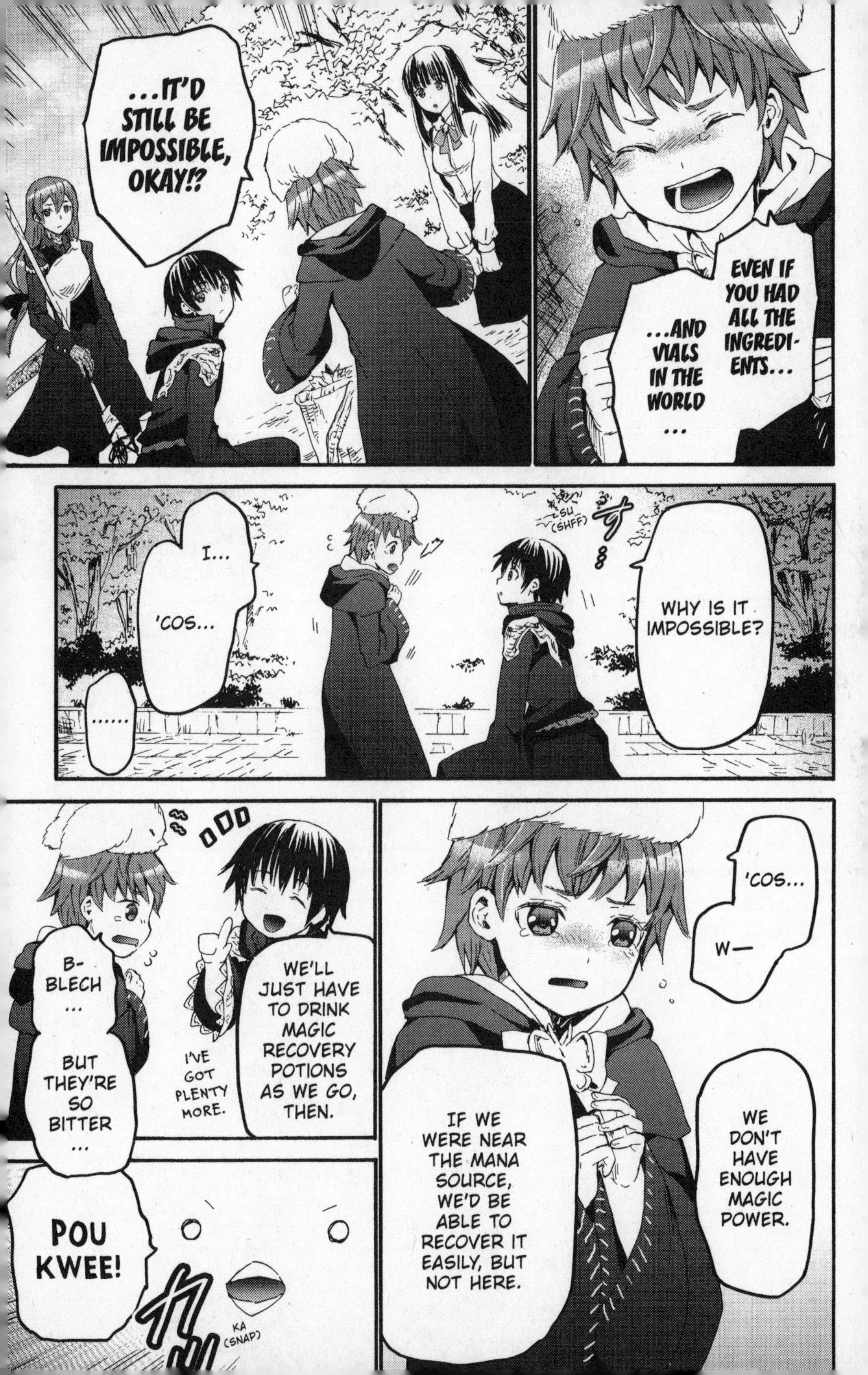
EVEN IF YOU HAD ALL THE INGREDI-ENTS...
...AND VIALS IN THE WORLD ...
...IT'D STILL BE IMPOSSIBLE, OKAY!?
WHY IS IT IMPOSSIBLE?
SU (SHFF)
I...
'COS...
......
'COS...
W—
WE DON'T HAVE ENOUGH MAGIC POWER.
IF WE WERE NEAR THE MANA SOURCE, WE'D BE ABLE TO RECOVER IT EASILY, BUT NOT HERE.
WE'LL JUST HAVE TO DRINK MAGIC RECOVERY POTIONS AS WE GO, THEN.
I'VE GOT PLENTY MORE.
B-BLECH ...
BUT THEY'RE SO BITTER ...
POU KWEE!
KA (SNAP)

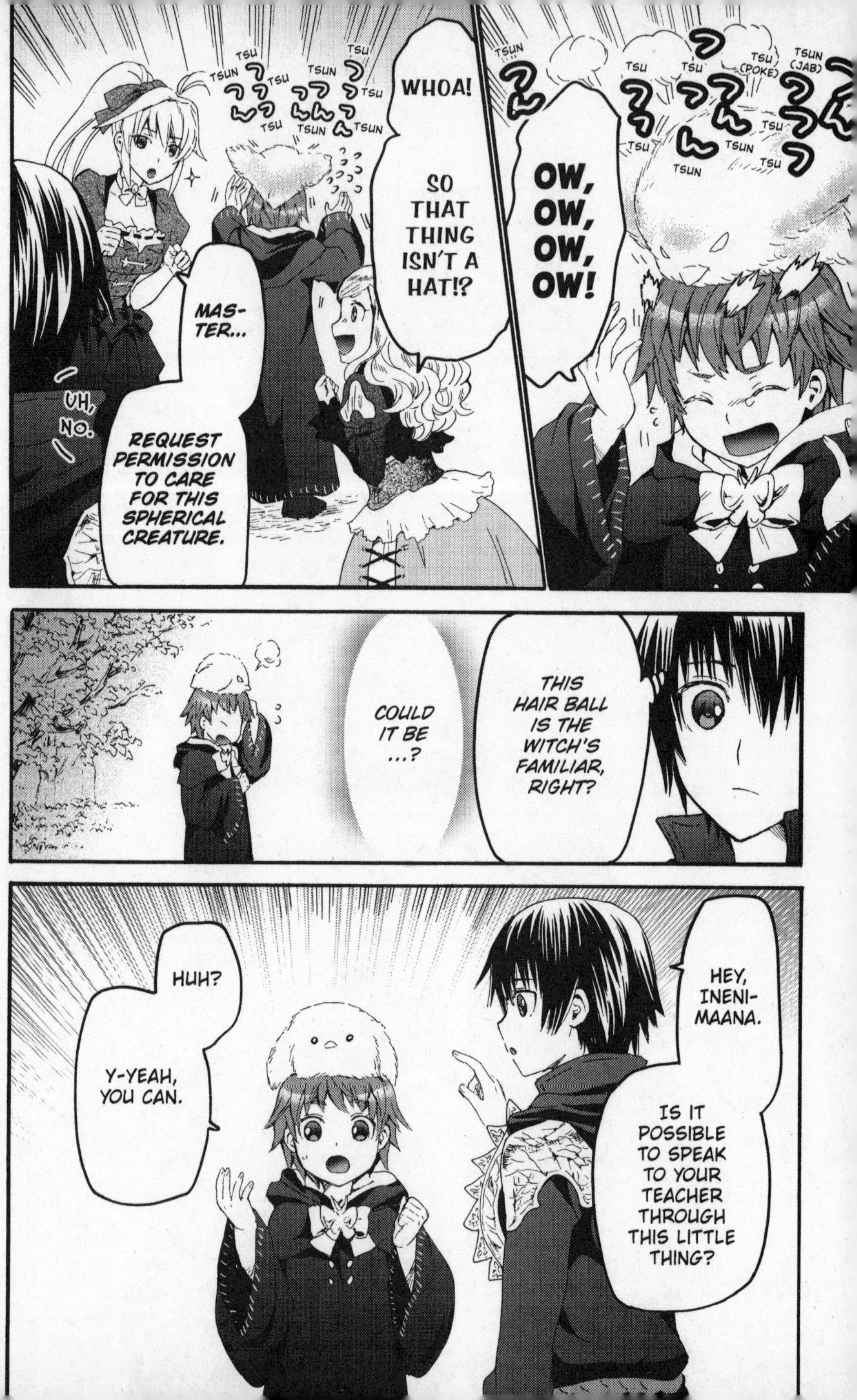
TSUN
TSU
TSU (POKE)
TSUN (JAB)
TSU
TSU
TSUN
TSU
TSUN
TSU
OW, OW, OW, OW!
TSU
TSUN
TSU
TSUN
TSU
TSU
TSUN
TSU
TSUN
WHOA!
SO THAT THING ISN'T A HAT!?
MASTER...
REQUEST PERMISSION TO CARE FOR THIS SPHERICAL CREATURE.
UH, NO.
THIS HAIR BALL IS THE WITCH'S FAMILIAR, RIGHT?
COULD IT BE ...?
HEY, INENI-MAANA.
IS IT POSSIBLE TO SPEAK TO YOUR TEACHER THROUGH THIS LITTLE THING?
HUH?
Y-YEAH, YOU CAN.

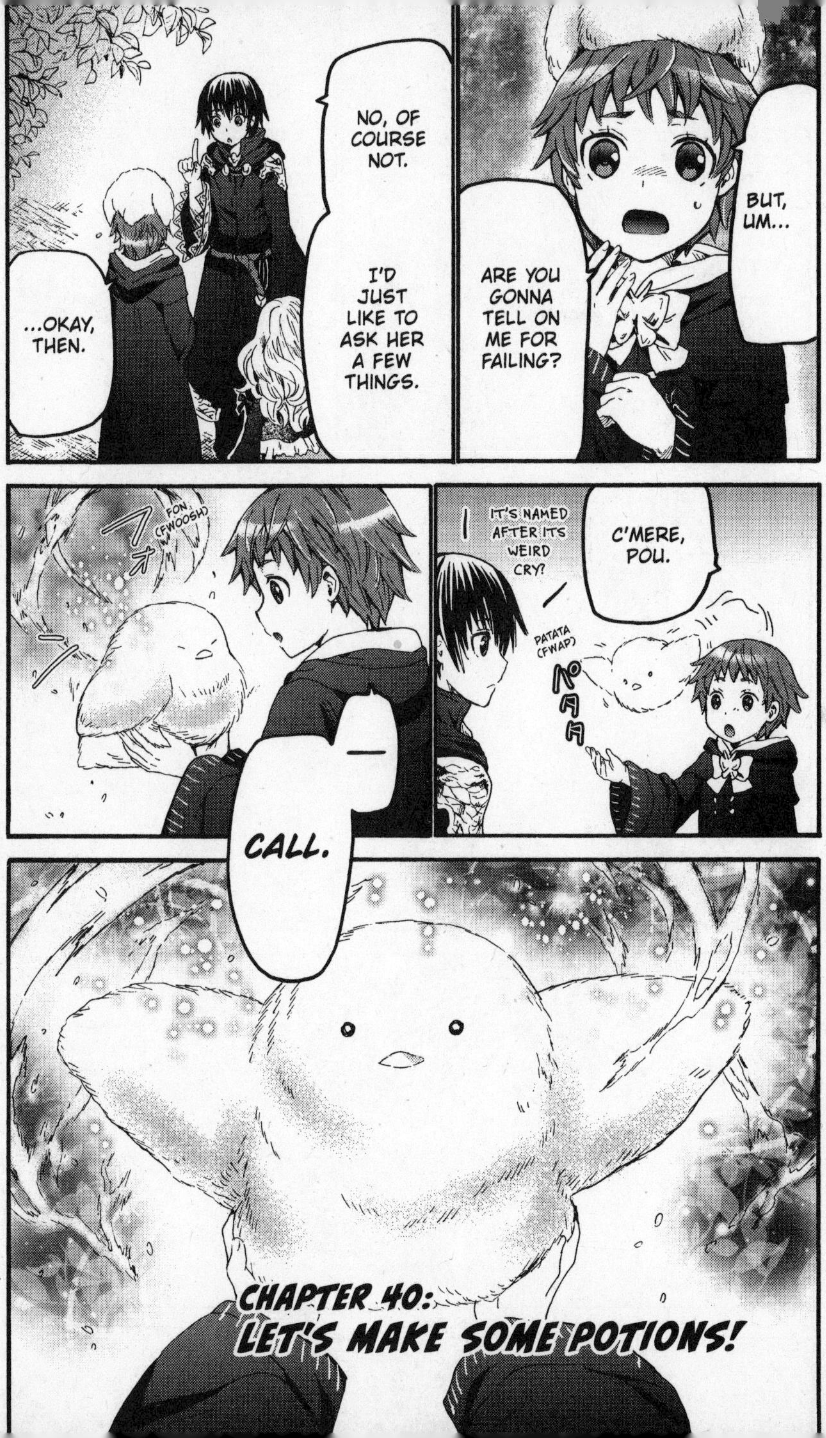
BUT, UM...
ARE YOU GONNA TELL ON ME FOR FAILING?
NO, OF COURSE NOT.
I'D JUST LIKE TO ASK HER A FEW THINGS.
...OKAY, THEN.
C'MERE, POU.
PATATA (FWAP)
IT'S NAMED AFTER ITS WEIRD CRY?
FON (FWOOSH)
CALL.
CHAPTER 40:
LET'S MAKE SOME POTIONS!

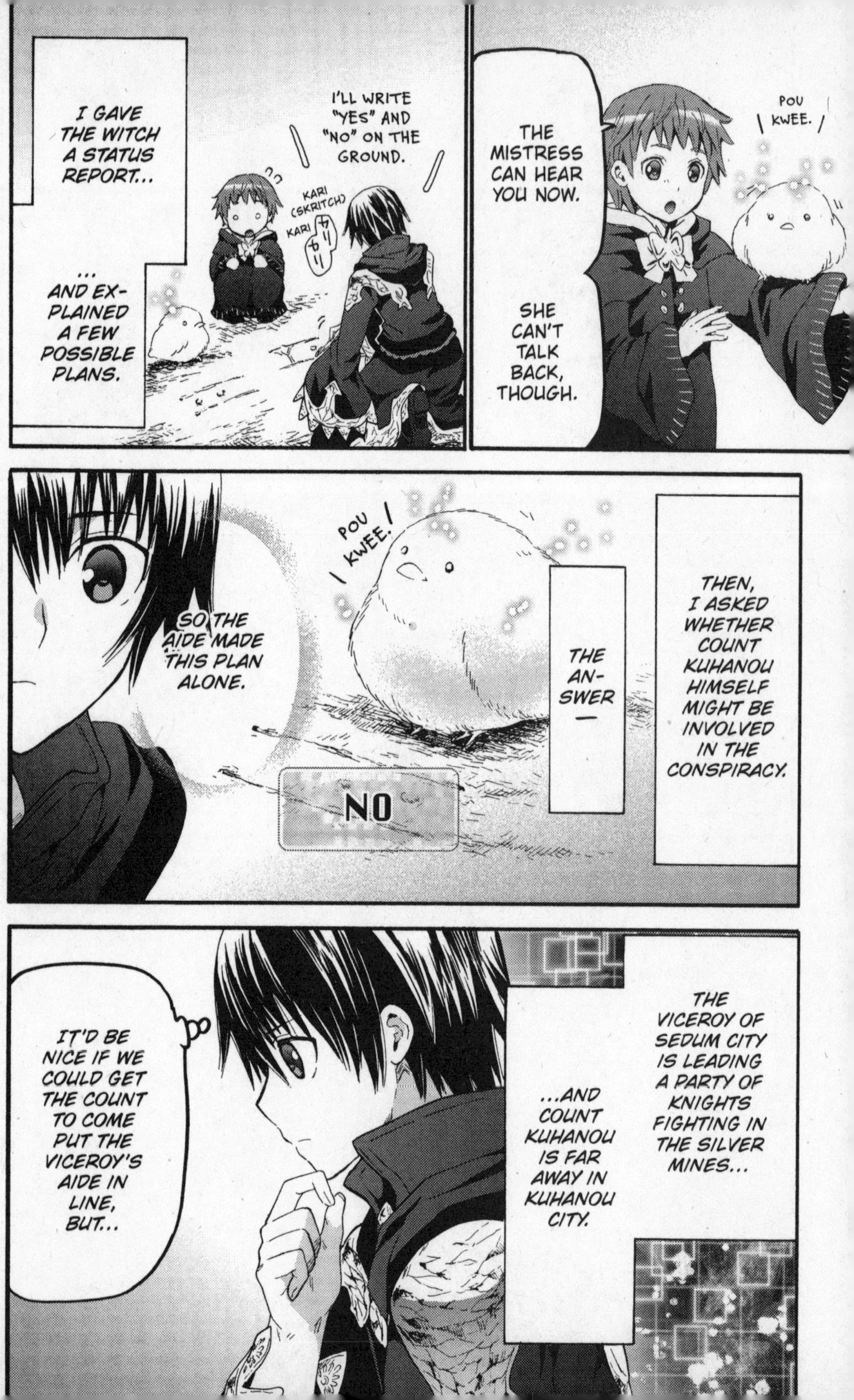
THE MISTRESS CAN HEAR YOU NOW.
SHE CAN'T TALK BACK, THOUGH.
POU KWEE.
I'LL WRITE "YES" AND "NO" ON THE GROUND.
KARI (SKRITCH) KARI
I GAVE THE WITCH A STATUS REPORT...
... AND EXPLAINED A FEW POSSIBLE PLANS.
THEN, I ASKED WHETHER COUNT KUHANOU HIMSELF MIGHT BE INVOLVED IN THE CONSPIRACY.
THE ANSWER —
POU KWEE!
NO
SO THE AIDE MADE THIS PLAN ALONE.
THE VICEROY OF SEDUM CITY IS LEADING A PARTY OF KNIGHTS FIGHTING IN THE SILVER MINES...
...AND COUNT KUHANOU IS FAR AWAY IN KUHANOU CITY.
IT'D BE NICE IF WE COULD GET THE COUNT TO COME PUT THE VICEROY'S AIDE IN LINE, BUT...

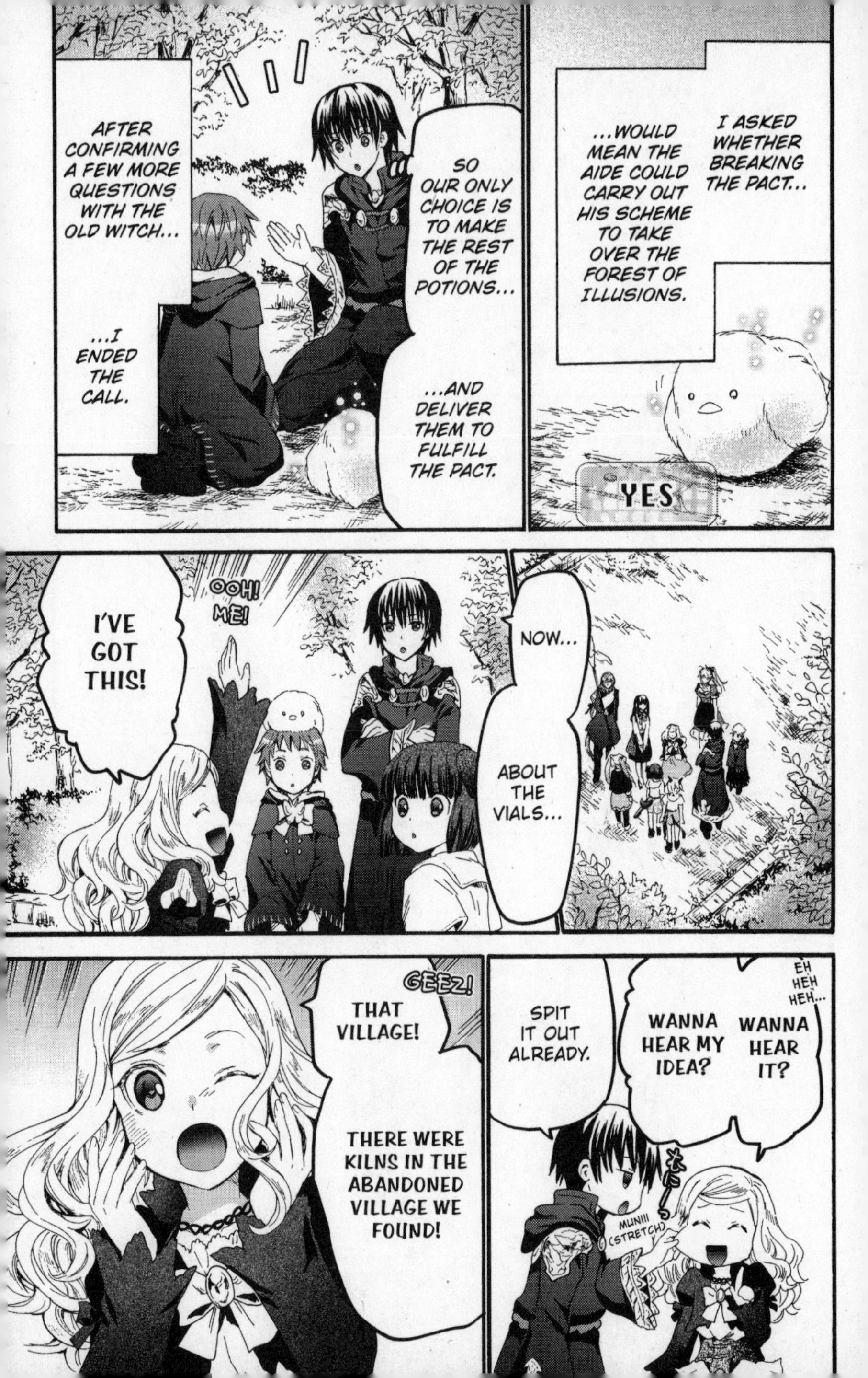
I ASKED WHETHER BREAKING THE PACT...
...WOULD MEAN THE AIDE COULD CARRY OUT HIS SCHEME TO TAKE OVER THE FOREST OF ILLUSIONS.
YES
SO OUR ONLY CHOICE IS TO MAKE THE REST OF THE POTIONS...
...AND DELIVER THEM TO FULFILL THE PACT.
AFTER CONFIRMING A FEW MORE QUESTIONS WITH THE OLD WITCH...
...I ENDED THE CALL.
NOW...
ABOUT THE VIALS...
OOH! ME!
I'VE GOT THIS!
EH HEH HEH...
WANNA HEAR IT?
WANNA HEAR MY IDEA?
SPIT IT OUT ALREADY.
MUNIII (STRETCH)
GEEZ!
THAT VILLAGE!
THERE WERE KILNS IN THE ABANDONED VILLAGE WE FOUND!

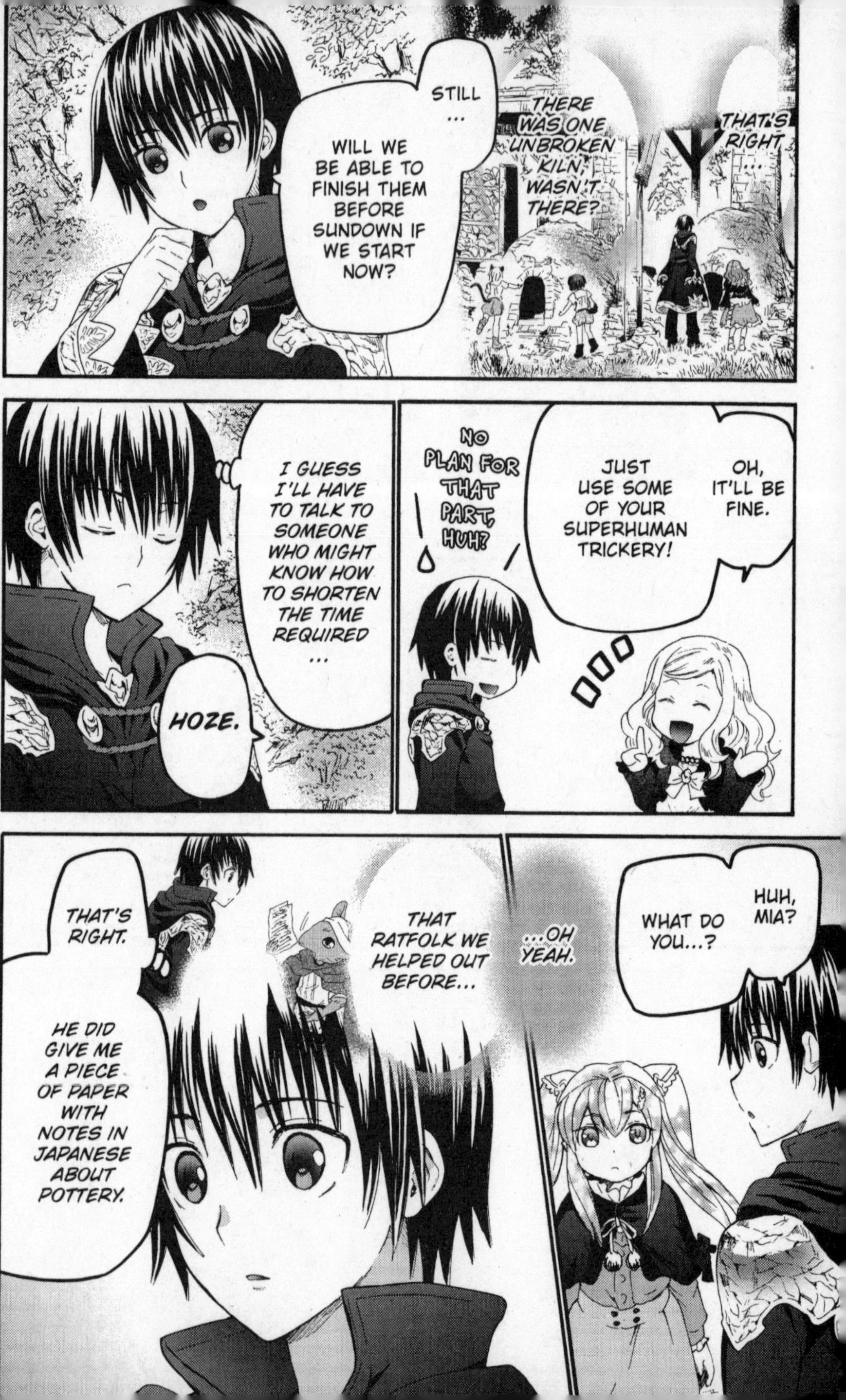
THAT'S RIGHT...
THERE WAS ONE UNBROKEN KILN, WASN'T THERE?
STILL...
WILL WE BE ABLE TO FINISH THEM BEFORE SUNDOWN IF WE START NOW?
OH, IT'LL BE FINE.
JUST USE SOME OF YOUR SUPERHUMAN TRICKERY!
NO PLAN FOR THAT PART, HUH?
I GUESS I'LL HAVE TO TALK TO SOMEONE WHO MIGHT KNOW HOW TO SHORTEN THE TIME REQUIRED...
HOZE.
HUH, MIA?
WHAT DO YOU...?
...OH YEAH.
THAT RATFOLK WE HELPED OUT BEFORE...
THAT'S RIGHT.
HE DID GIVE ME A PIECE OF PAPER WITH NOTES IN JAPANESE ABOUT POTTERY.

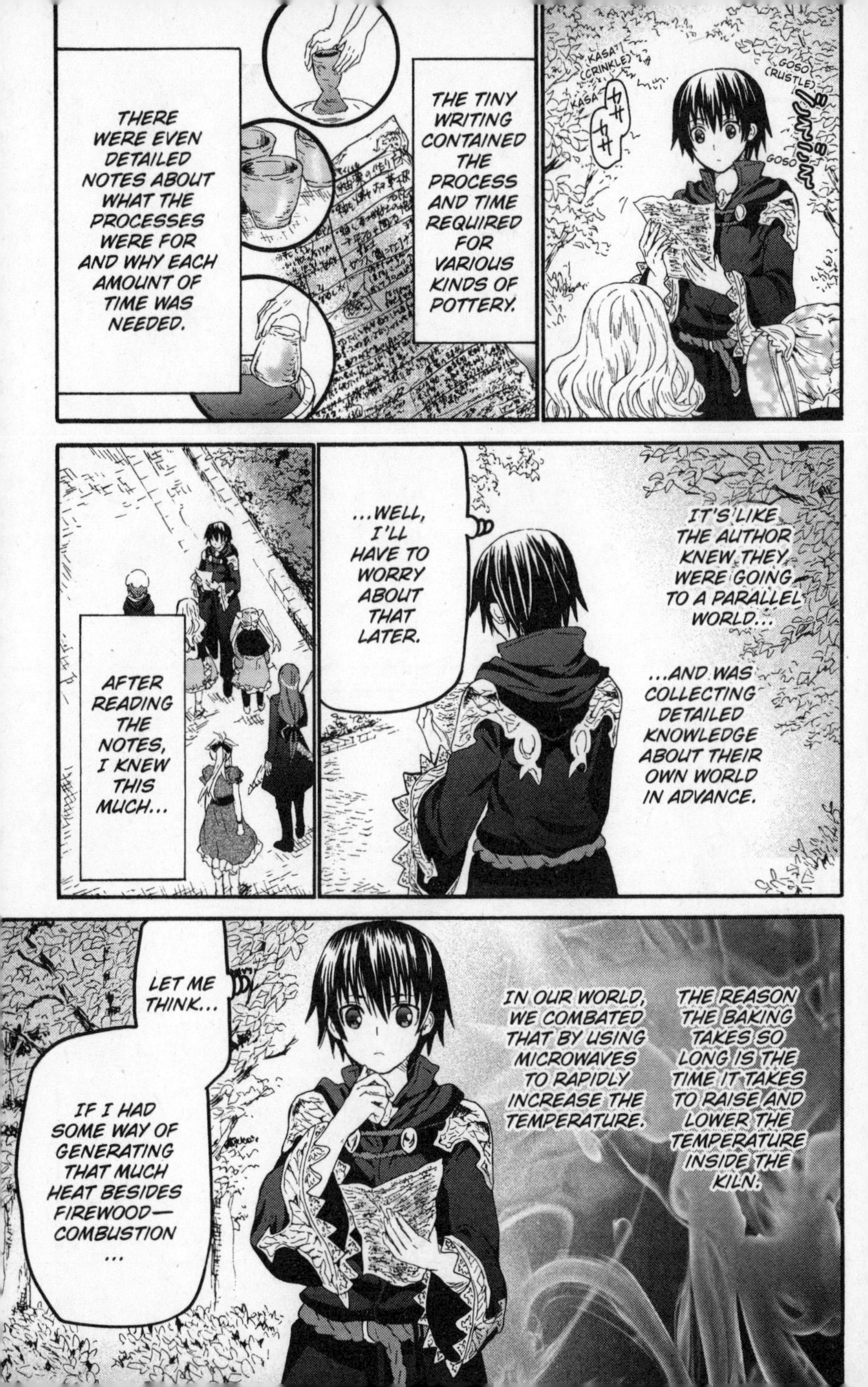
KASA (CRINKLE)
KASA
GOSO (RUSTLE)
GOSO
THE TINY WRITING CONTAINED THE PROCESS AND TIME REQUIRED FOR VARIOUS KINDS OF POTTERY.
THERE WERE EVEN DETAILED NOTES ABOUT WHAT THE PROCESSES WERE FOR AND WHY EACH AMOUNT OF TIME WAS NEEDED.
IT'S LIKE THE AUTHOR KNEW THEY WERE GOING TO A PARALLEL WORLD...
...AND WAS COLLECTING DETAILED KNOWLEDGE ABOUT THEIR OWN WORLD IN ADVANCE.
...WELL, I'LL HAVE TO WORRY ABOUT THAT LATER.
AFTER READING THE NOTES, I KNEW THIS MUCH...
THE REASON THE BAKING TAKES SO LONG IS THE TIME IT TAKES TO RAISE AND LOWER THE TEMPERATURE INSIDE THE KILN.
IN OUR WORLD, WE COMBATED THAT BY USING MICROWAVES TO RAPIDLY INCREASE THE TEMPERATURE.
LET ME THINK...
IF I HAD SOME WAY OF GENERATING THAT MUCH HEAT BESIDES FIREWOOD—COMBUSTION ...

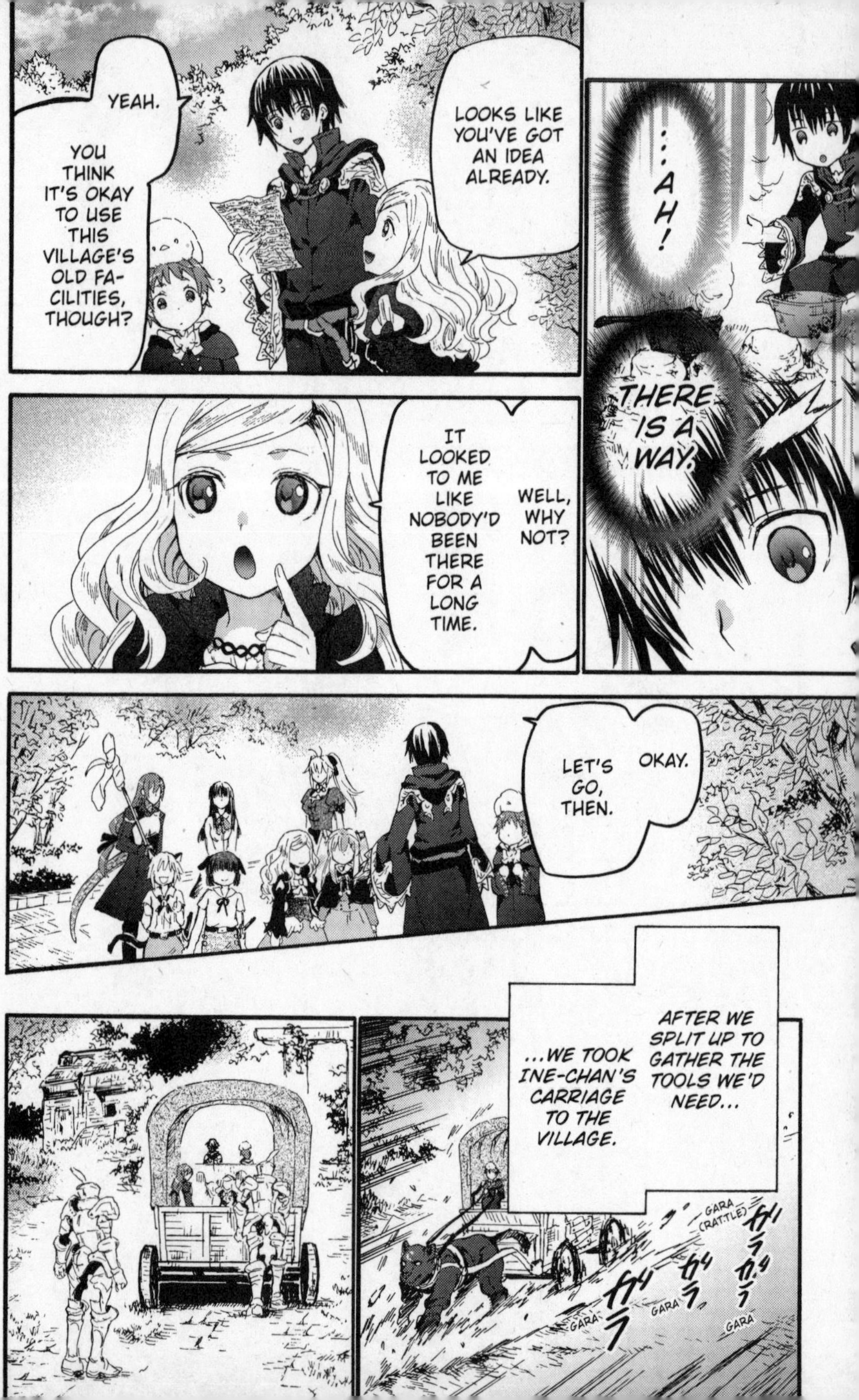
...AH!
THERE IS A WAY.
LOOKS LIKE YOU'VE GOT AN IDEA ALREADY.
YEAH.
YOU THINK IT'S OKAY TO USE THIS VILLAGE'S OLD FA-CILITIES, THOUGH?
WELL, WHY NOT?
IT LOOKED TO ME LIKE NOBODY'D BEEN THERE FOR A LONG TIME.
OKAY.
LET'S GO, THEN.
AFTER WE SPLIT UP TO GATHER THE TOOLS WE'D NEED...
...WE TOOK INE-CHAN'S CARRIAGE TO THE VILLAGE.
GARA (RATTLE)
GARA
GARA
GARA

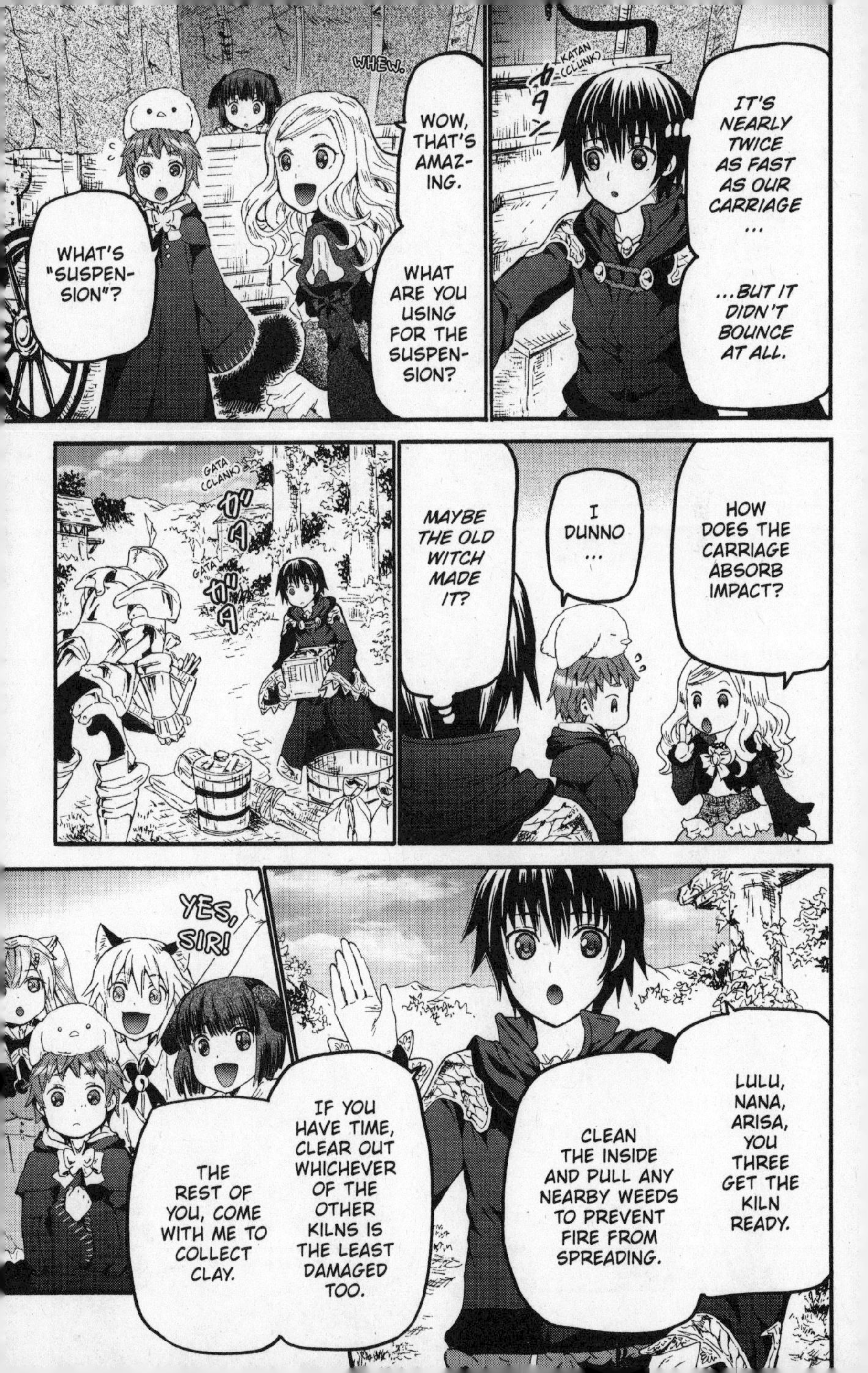
KATAN (CLUNK)
IT'S NEARLY TWICE AS FAST AS OUR CARRIAGE...
...BUT IT DIDN'T BOUNCE AT ALL.
WHEW.
WOW, THAT'S AMAZ-ING.
WHAT ARE YOU USING FOR THE SUSPEN-SION?
WHAT'S "SUSPEN-SION"?
HOW DOES THE CARRIAGE ABSORB IMPACT?
I DUNNO...
MAYBE THE OLD WITCH MADE IT?
GATA (CLANK)
GATA
LULU, NANA, ARISA, YOU THREE GET THE KILN READY.
CLEAN THE INSIDE AND PULL ANY NEARBY WEEDS TO PREVENT FIRE FROM SPREADING.
IF YOU HAVE TIME, CLEAR OUT WHICHEVER OF THE OTHER KILNS IS THE LEAST DAMAGED TOO.
THE REST OF YOU, COME WITH ME TO COLLECT CLAY.
YES, SIR!

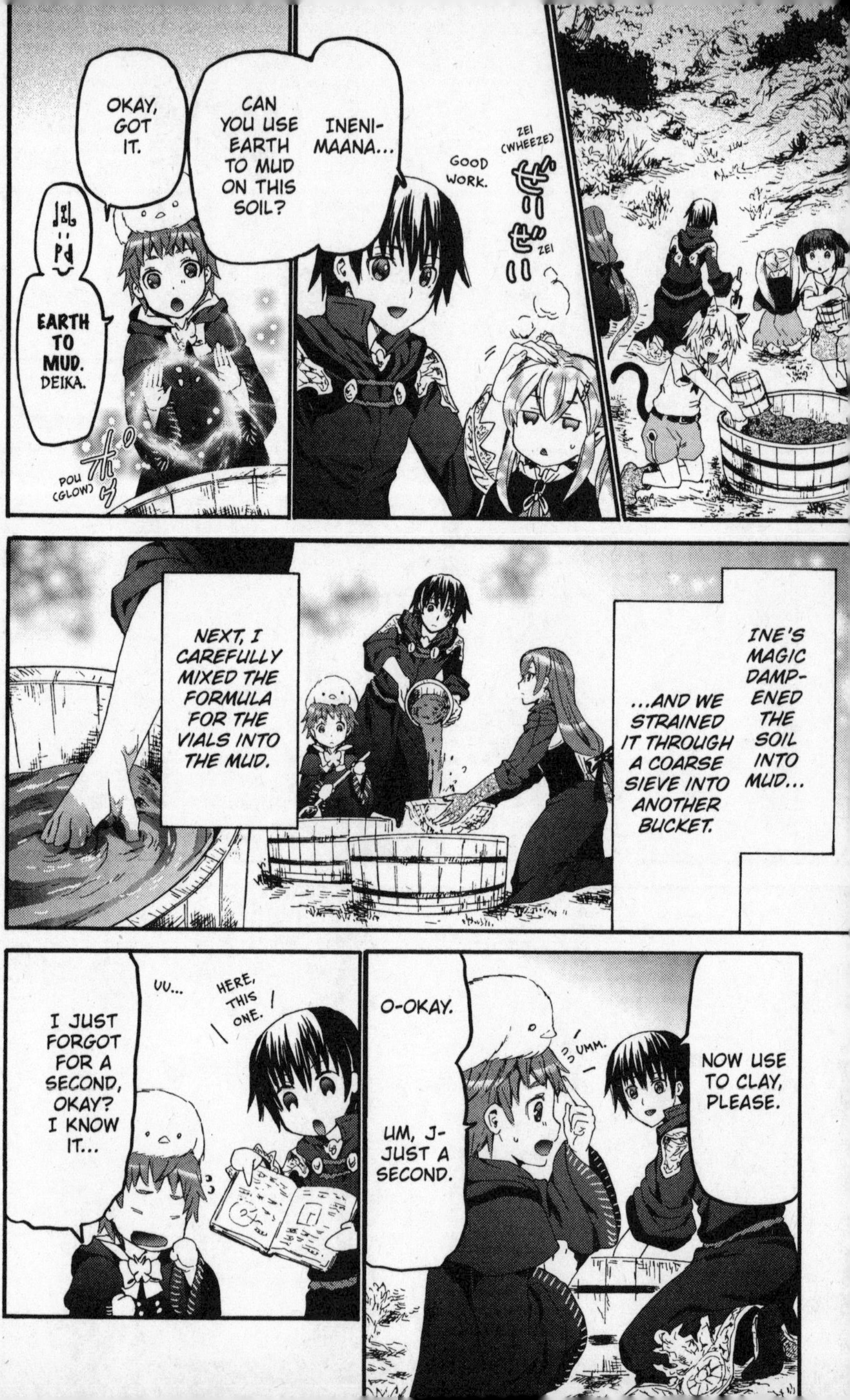
ZEI (WHEEZE)
ZEI
GOOD WORK.
INENI-MAANA...
CAN YOU USE EARTH TO MUD ON THIS SOIL?
OKAY, GOT IT.
EARTH TO MUD. DEIKA.
POU (GLOW)
INE'S MAGIC DAMPENED THE SOIL INTO MUD...
...AND WE STRAINED IT THROUGH A COARSE SIEVE INTO ANOTHER BUCKET.
NEXT, I CAREFULLY MIXED THE FORMULA FOR THE VIALS INTO THE MUD.
NOW USE TO CLAY, PLEASE.
UMM.
O-OKAY.
UM, J-JUST A SECOND.
HERE, THIS ONE.
UU...
I JUST FORGOT FOR A SECOND, OKAY? I KNOW IT...

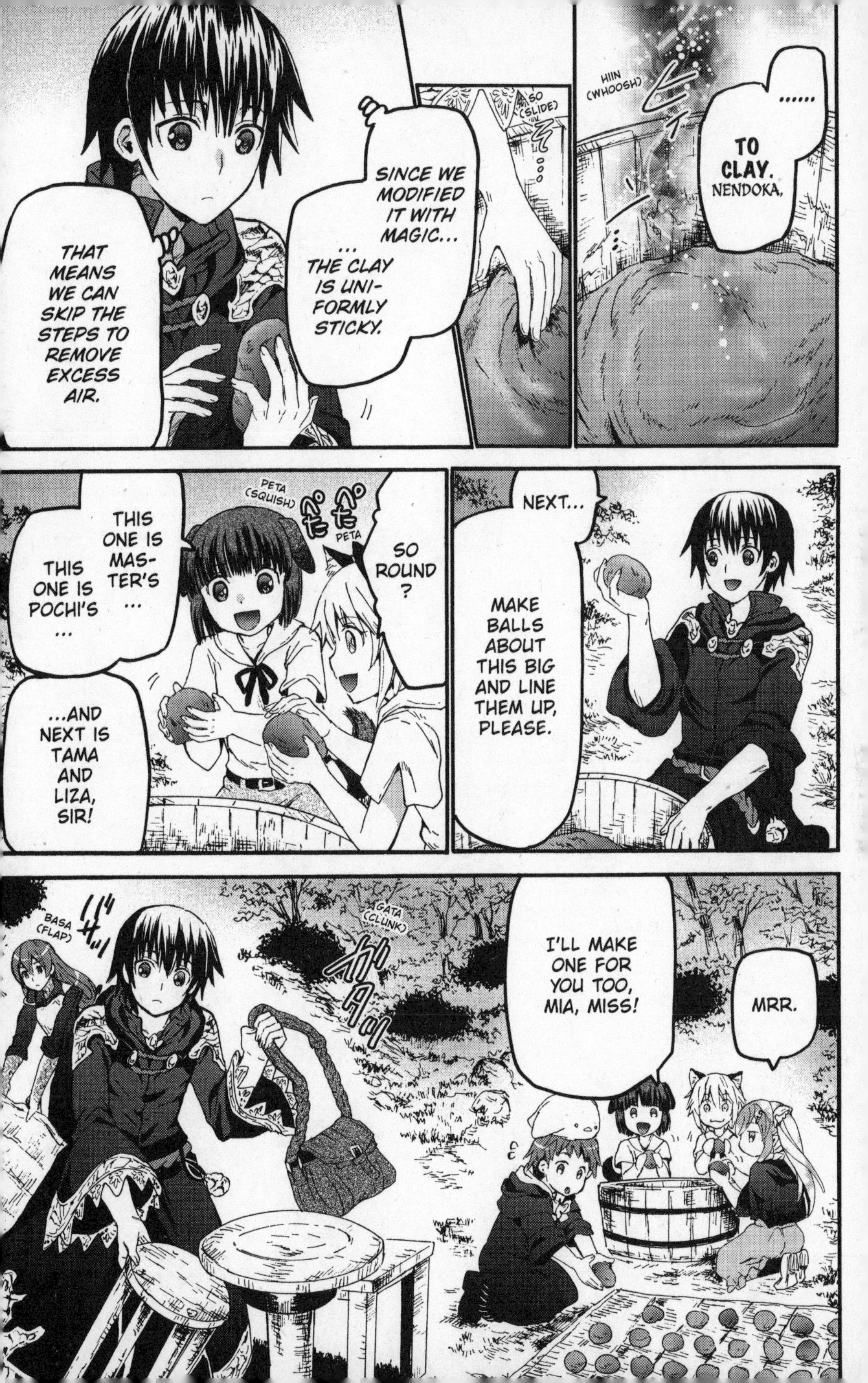
......
TO CLAY. NENDOKA,
HIIN (WHOOSH)
SO (SLIDE)
SINCE WE MODIFIED IT WITH MAGIC...
... THE CLAY IS UNIFORMLY STICKY.
THAT MEANS WE CAN SKIP THE STEPS TO REMOVE EXCESS AIR.
NEXT...
MAKE BALLS ABOUT THIS BIG AND LINE THEM UP, PLEASE.
SO ROUND?
PETA (SQUISH)
PETA
THIS ONE IS MASTER'S...
THIS ONE IS POCHI'S...
...AND NEXT IS TAMA AND LIZA, SIR!
MRR.
I'LL MAKE ONE FOR YOU TOO, MIA, MISS!
GATA (CLUNK)
BASA (FLAP)

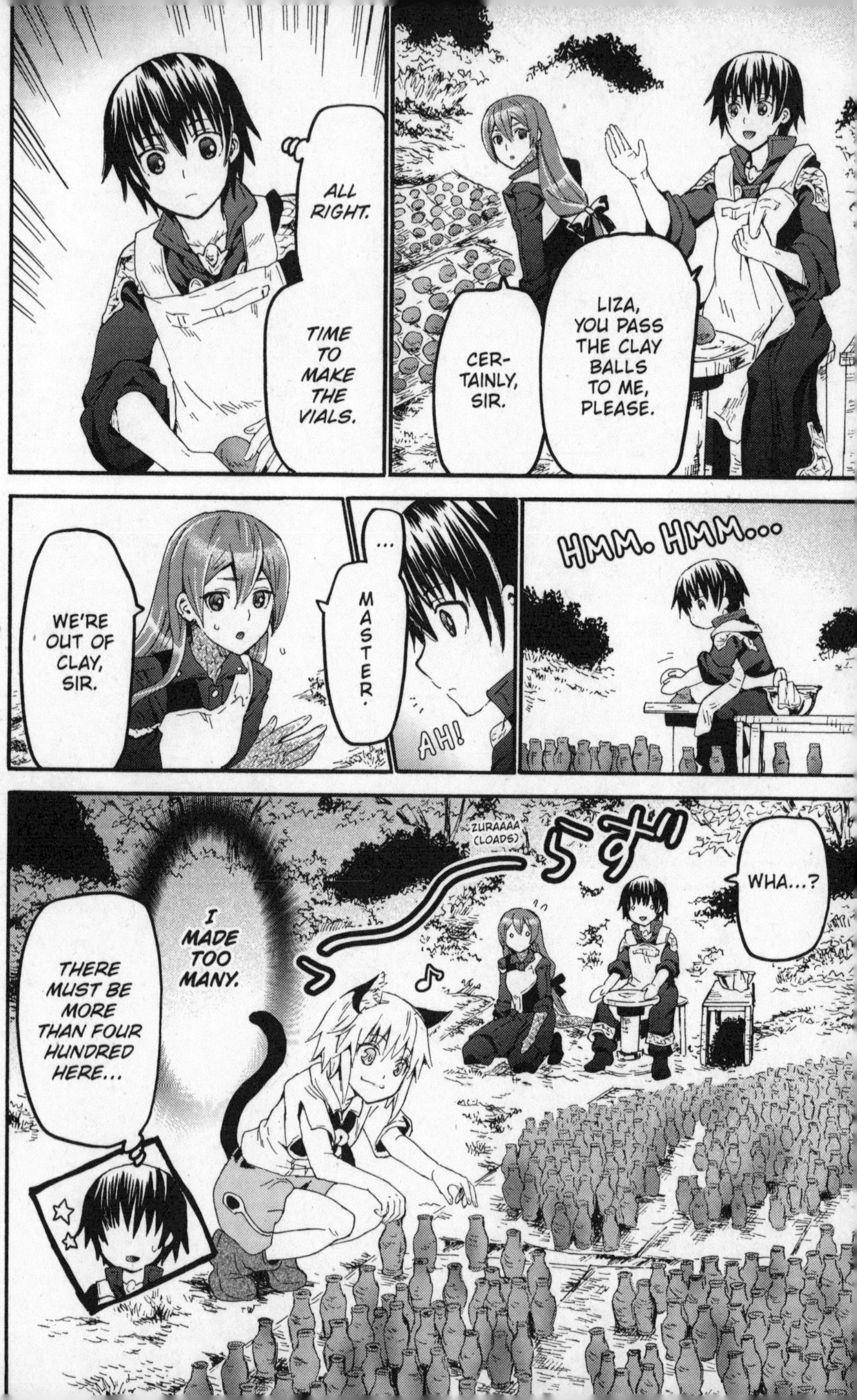
LIZA, YOU PASS THE CLAY BALLS TO ME, PLEASE.
CER-TAINLY, SIR.
ALL RIGHT.
TIME TO MAKE THE VIALS.
HMM. HMM...
... MASTER.
AH!
WE'RE OUT OF CLAY, SIR.
WHA...?
ZURAAAA (LOADS)
I MADE TOO MANY.
THERE MUST BE MORE THAN FOUR HUNDRED HERE...

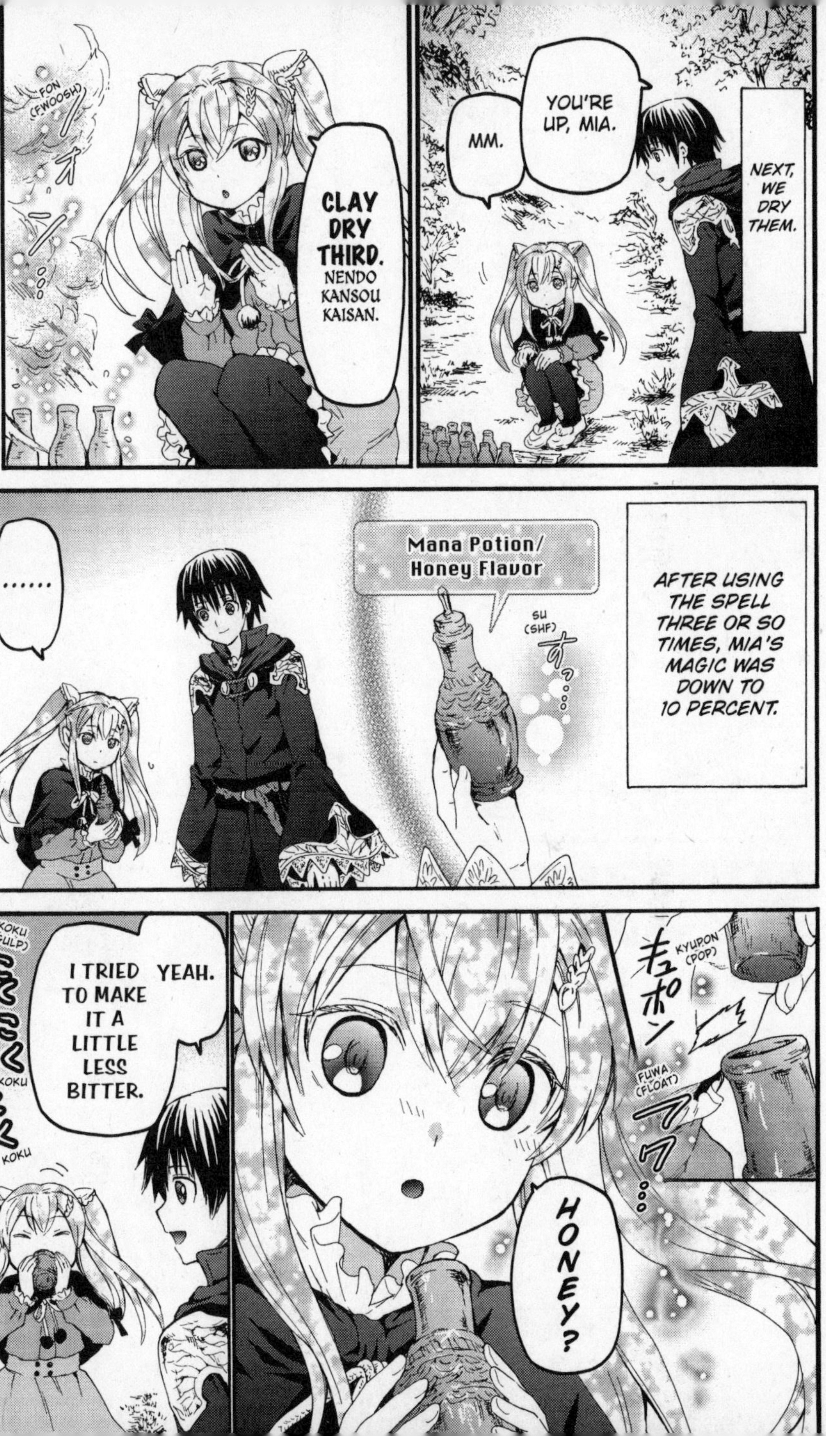
NEXT, WE DRY THEM.
YOU'RE UP, MIA.
MM.
FON (FWOOSH)
CLAY DRY THIRD.
NENDO KANSOU KAISAN.
AFTER USING THE SPELL THREE OR SO TIMES, MIA'S MAGIC WAS DOWN TO 10 PERCENT.
Mana Potion/ Honey Flavor
SU (SHF)
......
KYUPON (POP)
FUWA (FLOAT)
HONEY?
YEAH.
I TRIED TO MAKE IT A LITTLE LESS BITTER.
KOKU (GULP)
KOKU
KOKU
KOKU

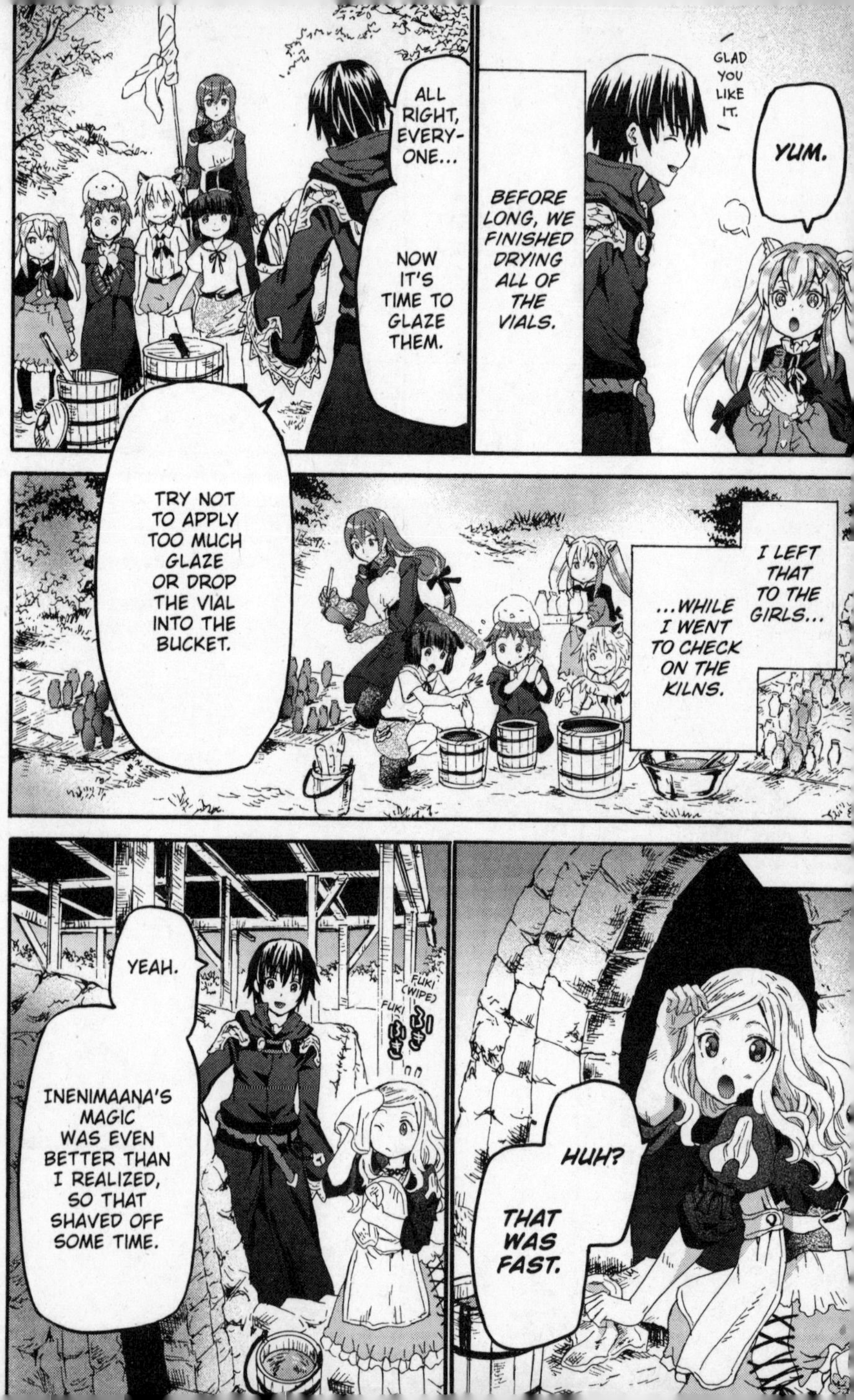

YUM.
GLAD YOU LIKE IT.
BEFORE LONG, WE FINISHED DRYING ALL OF THE VIALS.
ALL RIGHT, EVERYONE...
NOW IT'S TIME TO GLAZE THEM.
I LEFT THAT TO THE GIRLS...
...WHILE I WENT TO CHECK ON THE KILNS.
TRY NOT TO APPLY TOO MUCH GLAZE OR DROP THE VIAL INTO THE BUCKET.
HUH?
THAT WAS FAST.
YEAH.
ふき ふき
FUKI (WIPE)
FUKI
INENIMAANA'S MAGIC WAS EVEN BETTER THAN I REALIZED, SO THAT SHAVED OFF SOME TIME.

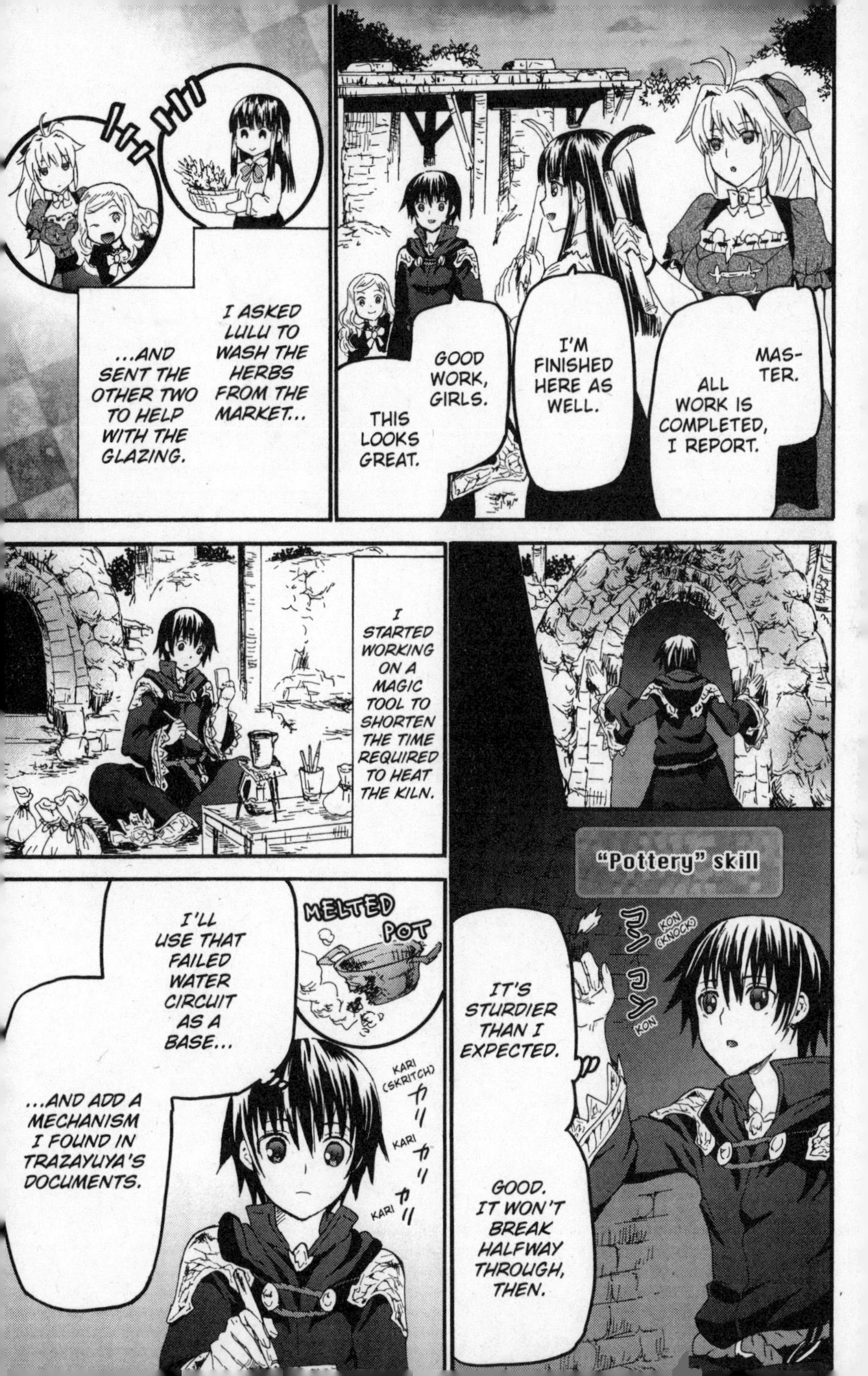
MAS-TER.
ALL WORK IS COMPLETED, I REPORT.
I'M FINISHED HERE AS WELL.
GOOD WORK, GIRLS.
THIS LOOKS GREAT.
I ASKED LULU TO WASH THE HERBS FROM THE MARKET...
...AND SENT THE OTHER TWO TO HELP WITH THE GLAZING.
“Pottery” skill
コン KON (KNOCK)
コン KON
IT'S STURDIER THAN I EXPECTED.
GOOD. IT WON'T BREAK HALFWAY THROUGH, THEN.
I STARTED WORKING ON A MAGIC TOOL TO SHORTEN THE TIME REQUIRED TO HEAT THE KILN.
MELTED POT
I'LL USE THAT FAILED WATER CIRCUIT AS A BASE...
カリ KARI (SKRITCH)
カリ KARI
カリ KARI
...AND ADD A MECHANISM I FOUND IN TRAZAYUYA'S DOCUMENTS.

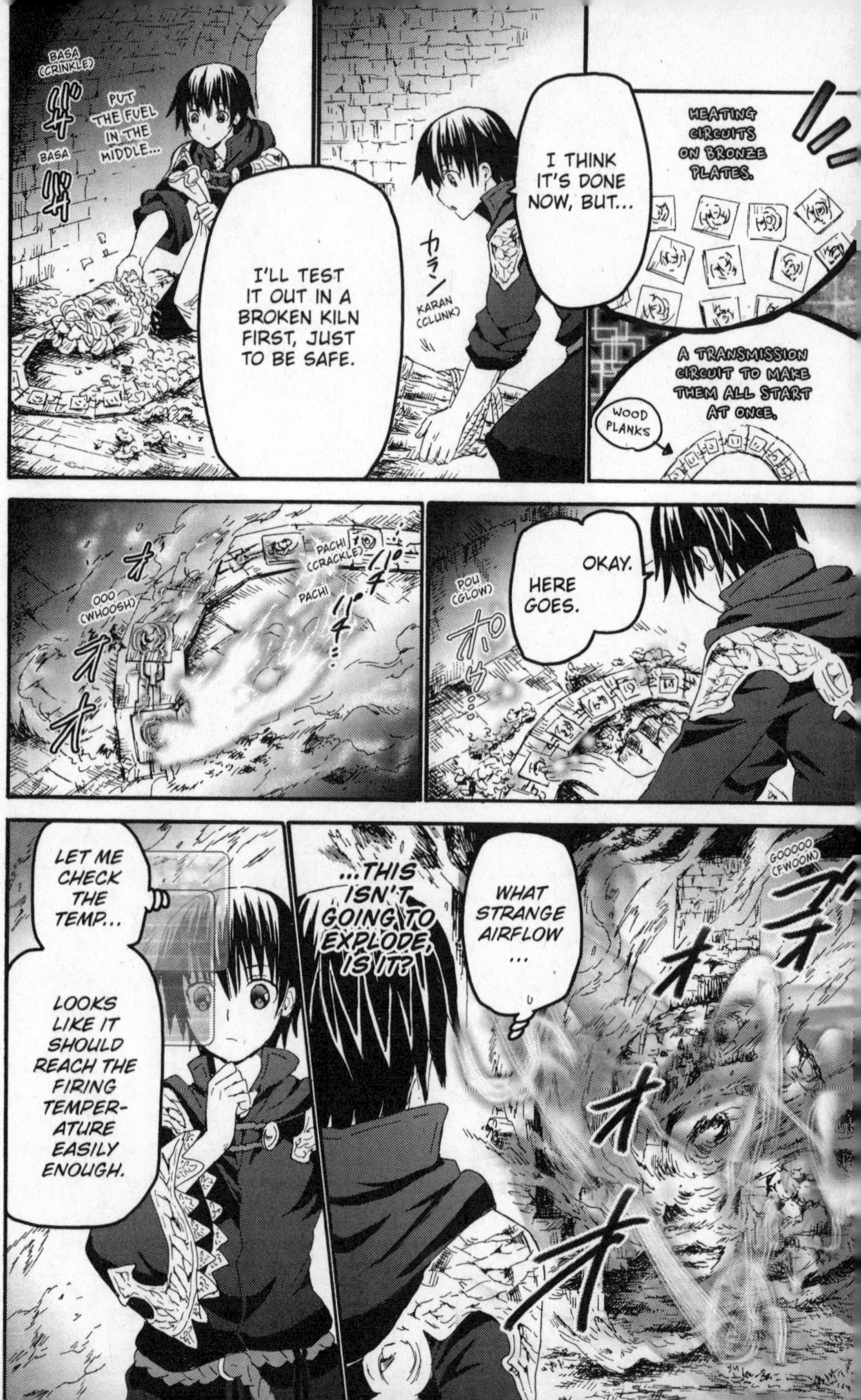
HEATING CIRCUITS ON BRONZE PLATES.
A TRANSMISSION CIRCUIT TO MAKE THEM ALL START AT ONCE.
WOOD PLANKS
I THINK IT'S DONE NOW, BUT...
カラン
KARAN (CLUNK)
I'LL TEST IT OUT IN A BROKEN KILN FIRST, JUST TO BE SAFE.
BASA (CRINKLE)
PUT THE FUEL IN THE MIDDLE...
BASA
OKAY. HERE GOES.
POU (GLOW)
PACHI (CRACKLE)
PACHI
OOO (WHOOSH)
GOOOOO (FWOOM)
WHAT STRANGE AIRFLOW...
...THIS ISN'T GOING TO EXPLODE, IS IT?
LET ME CHECK THE TEMP...
LOOKS LIKE IT SHOULD REACH THE FIRING TEMPERATURE EASILY ENOUGH.

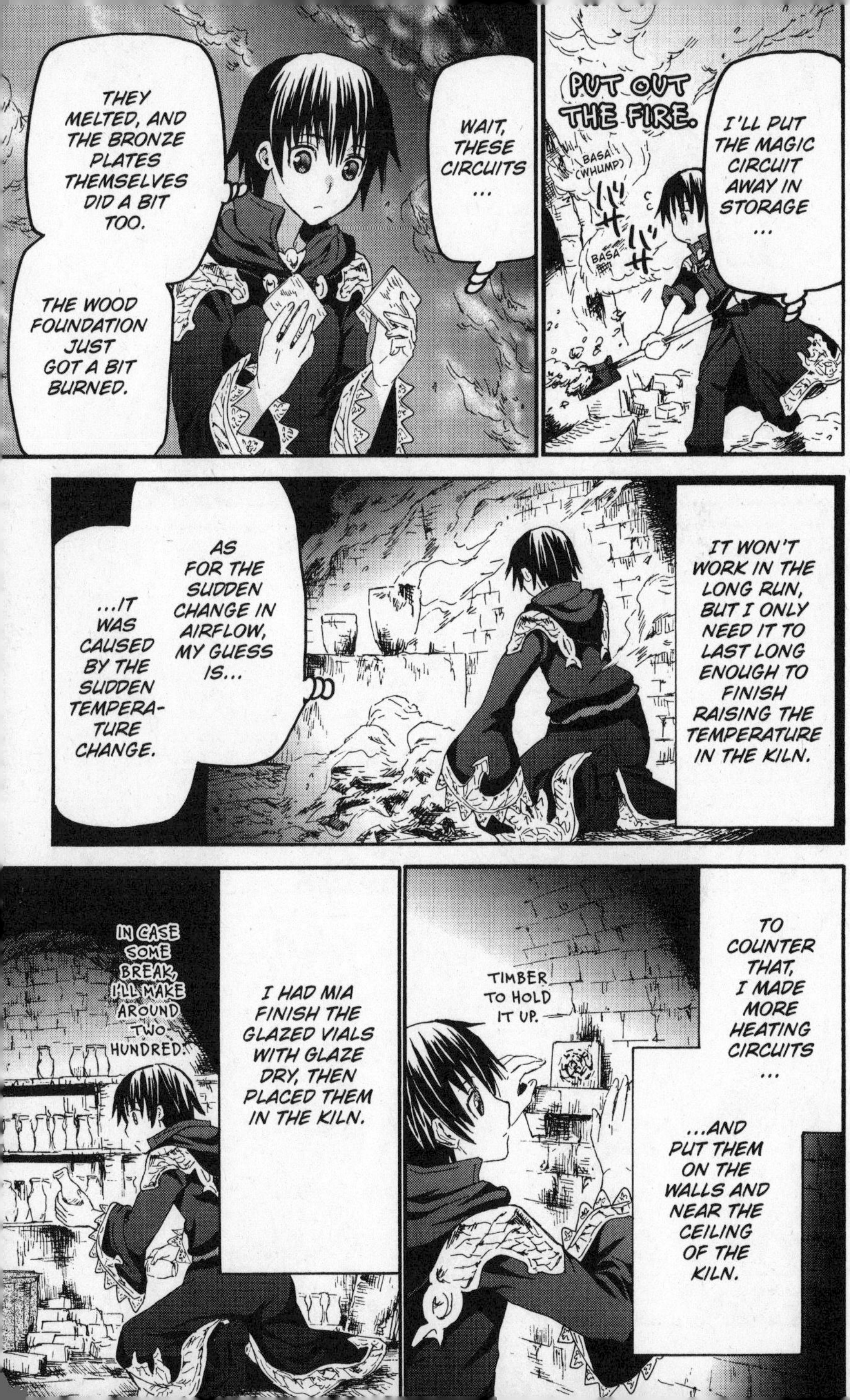
PUT OUT THE FIRE.
I'LL PUT THE MAGIC CIRCUIT AWAY IN STORAGE ...
BASA (WHUMP)
BASA
WAIT, THESE CIRCUITS ...
THEY MELTED, AND THE BRONZE PLATES THEMSELVES DID A BIT TOO.
THE WOOD FOUNDATION JUST GOT A BIT BURNED.
IT WON'T WORK IN THE LONG RUN, BUT I ONLY NEED IT TO LAST LONG ENOUGH TO FINISH RAISING THE TEMPERATURE IN THE KILN.
AS FOR THE SUDDEN CHANGE IN AIRFLOW, MY GUESS IS...
...IT WAS CAUSED BY THE SUDDEN TEMPERA-TURE CHANGE.
TO COUNTER THAT, I MADE MORE HEATING CIRCUITS ...
...AND PUT THEM ON THE WALLS AND NEAR THE CEILING OF THE KILN.
TIMBER TO HOLD IT UP.
I HAD MIA FINISH THE GLAZED VIALS WITH GLAZE DRY, THEN PLACED THEM IN THE KILN.
IN CASE SOME BREAK, I'LL MAKE AROUND TWO HUNDRED.

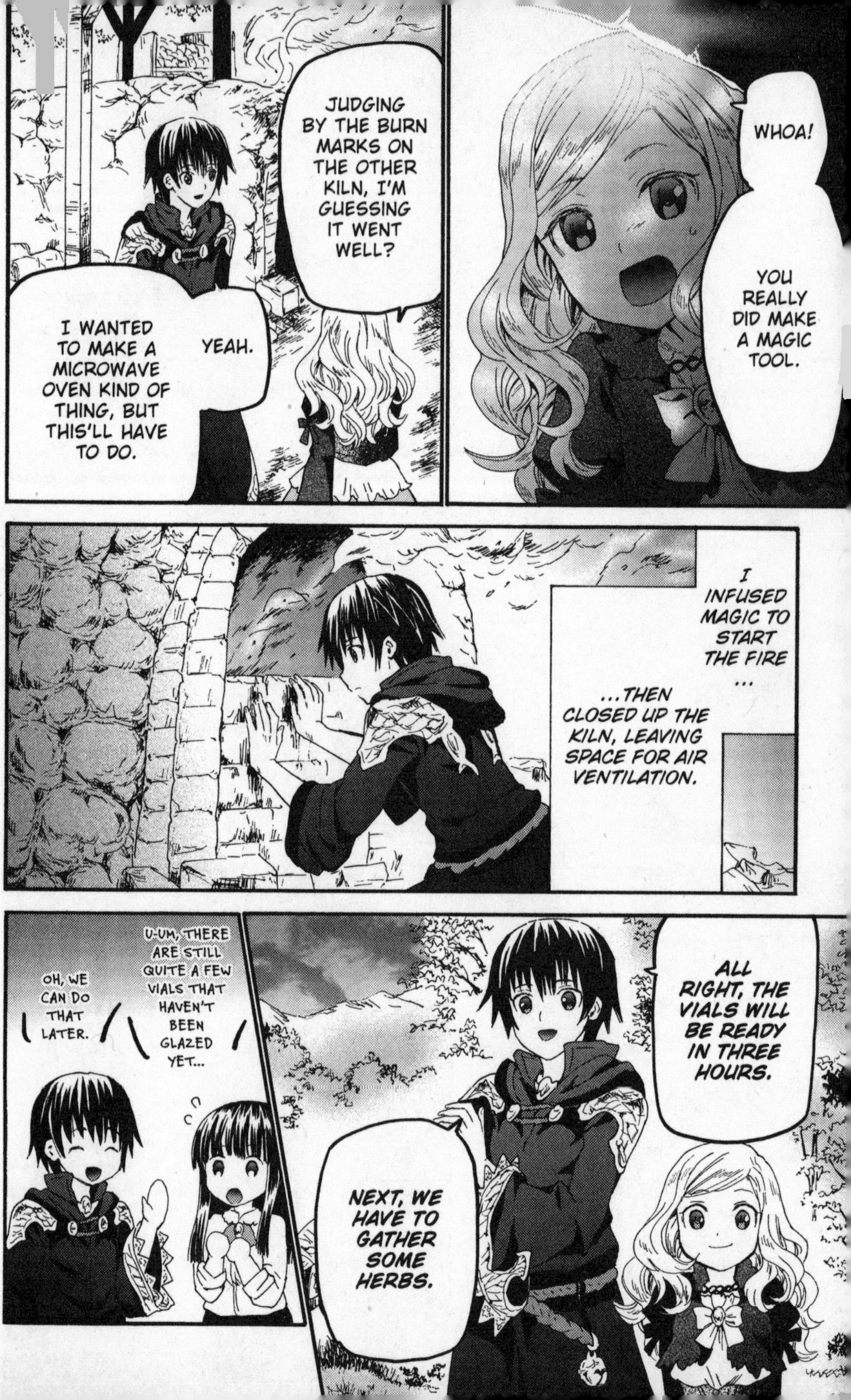
WHOA!
YOU REALLY DID MAKE A MAGIC TOOL.
JUDGING BY THE BURN MARKS ON THE OTHER KILN, I'M GUESSING IT WENT WELL?
YEAH.
I WANTED TO MAKE A MICROWAVE OVEN KIND OF THING, BUT THIS'LL HAVE TO DO.
I INFUSED MAGIC TO START THE FIRE...
...THEN CLOSED UP THE KILN, LEAVING SPACE FOR AIR VENTILATION.
ALL RIGHT, THE VIALS WILL BE READY IN THREE HOURS.
NEXT, WE HAVE TO GATHER SOME HERBS.
U-UM, THERE ARE STILL QUITE A FEW VIALS THAT HAVEN'T BEEN GLAZED YET...
OH, WE CAN DO THAT LATER.

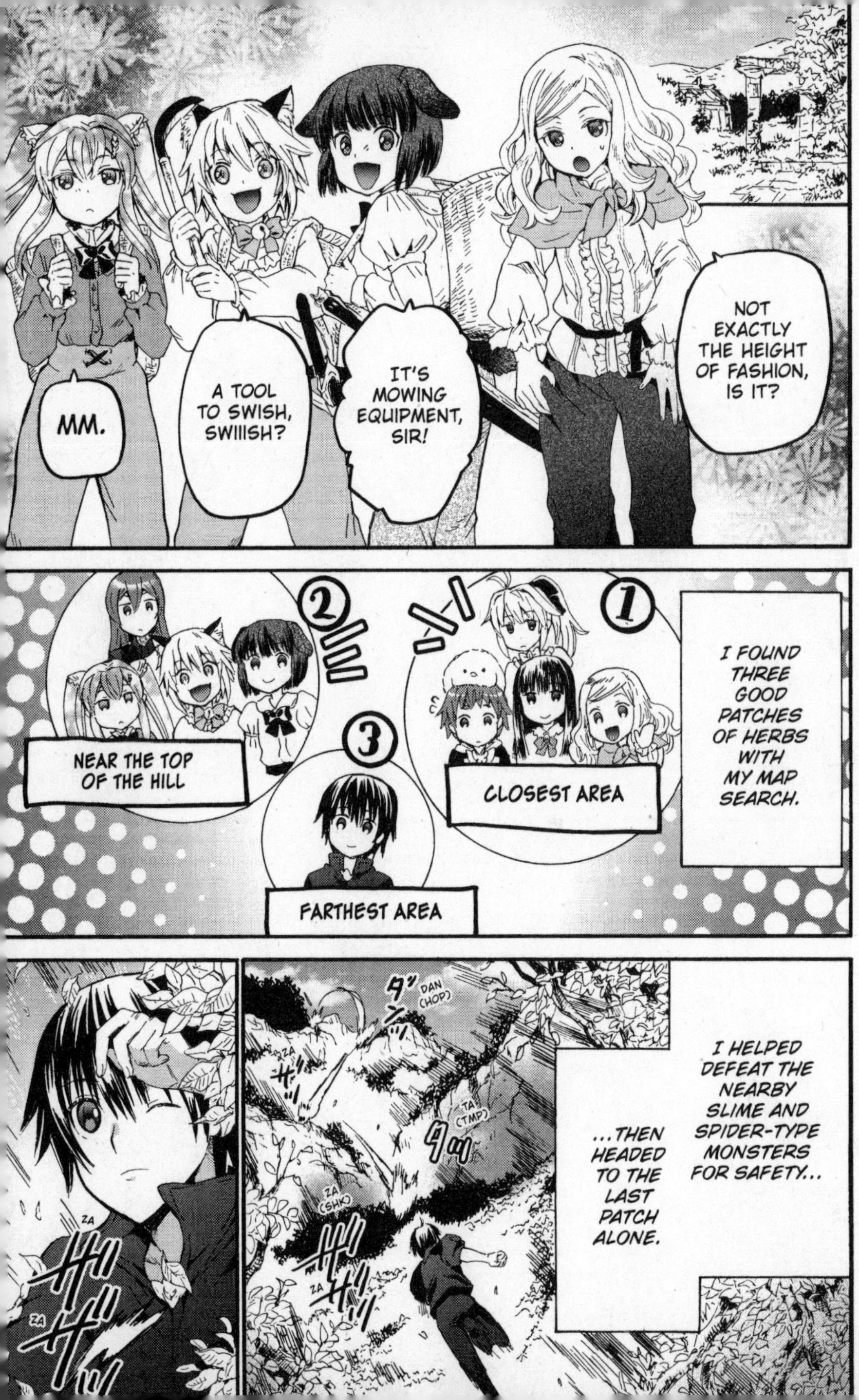
NOT EXACTLY THE HEIGHT OF FASHION, IS IT?
IT'S MOWING EQUIPMENT, SIR!
A TOOL TO SWISH, SWIIISH?
MM.
I FOUND THREE GOOD PATCHES OF HERBS WITH MY MAP SEARCH.
1
CLOSEST AREA
2
NEAR THE TOP OF THE HILL
3
FARTHEST AREA
I HELPED DEFEAT THE NEARBY SLIME AND SPIDER-TYPE MONSTERS FOR SAFETY...
...THEN HEADED TO THE LAST PATCH ALONE.
DAN (HOP)
ZA
TA (TMP)
ZA (SHK)
ZA
ZA
ZA

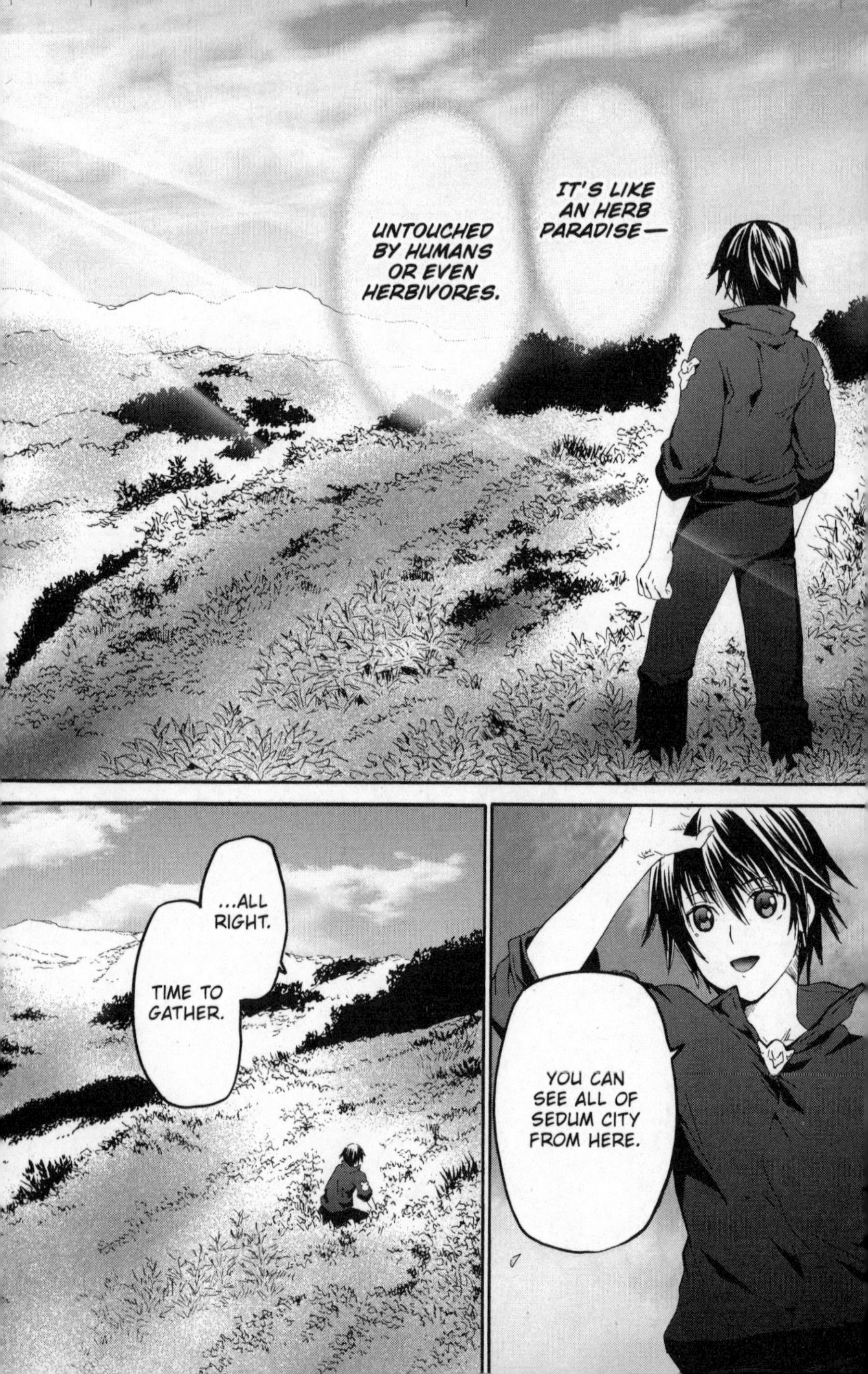
IT'S LIKE AN HERB PARADISE—
UNTOUCHED BY HUMANS OR EVEN HERBIVORES.
YOU CAN SEE ALL OF SEDUM CITY FROM HERE.
...ALL RIGHT.
TIME TO GATHER.

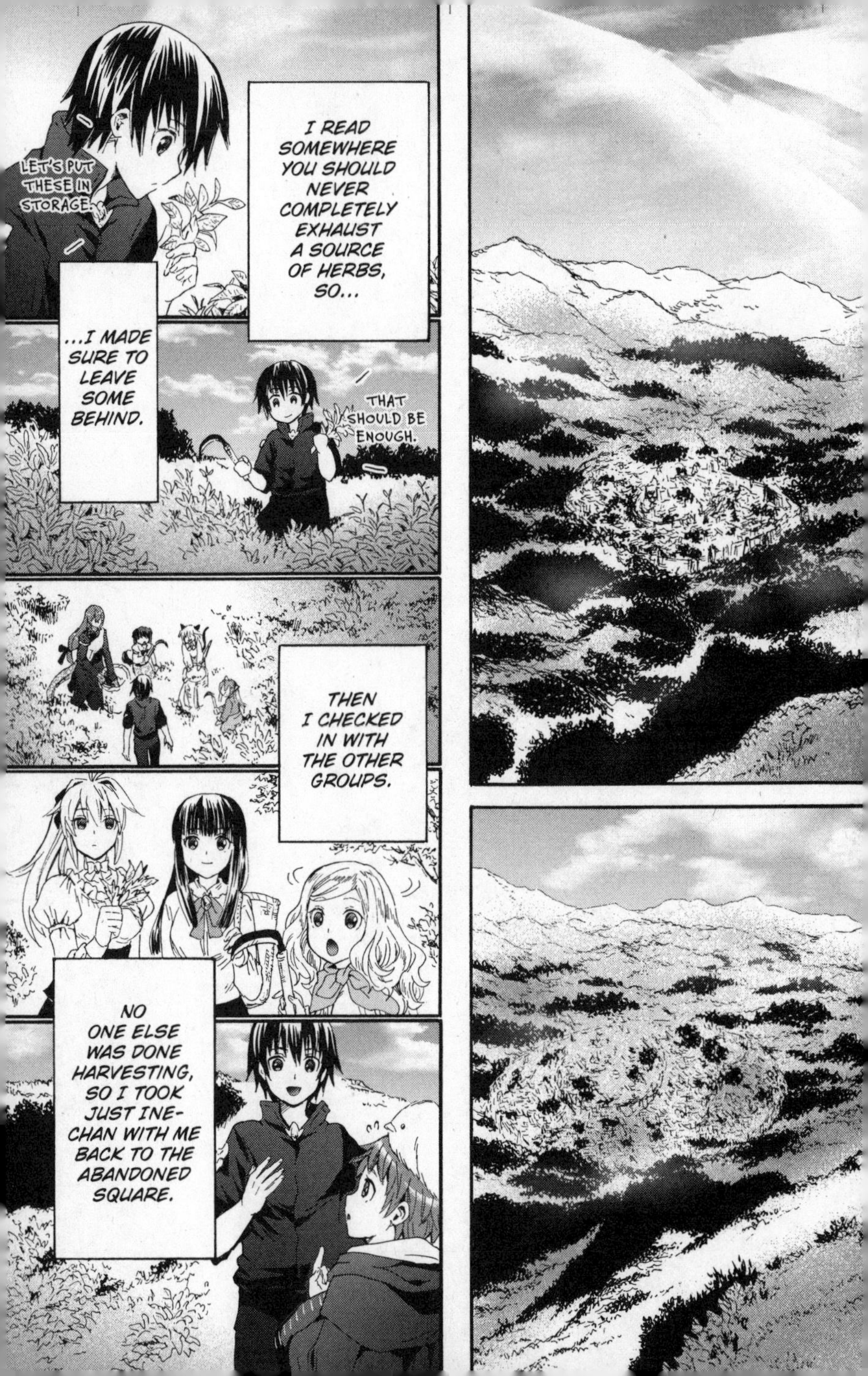
I READ SOMEWHERE YOU SHOULD NEVER COMPLETELY EXHAUST A SOURCE OF HERBS, SO...
LET'S PUT THESE IN STORAGE.
...I MADE SURE TO LEAVE SOME BEHIND.
THAT SHOULD BE ENOUGH.
THEN I CHECKED IN WITH THE OTHER GROUPS.
NO ONE ELSE WAS DONE HARVESTING, SO I TOOK JUST INE-CHAN WITH ME BACK TO THE ABANDONED SQUARE.

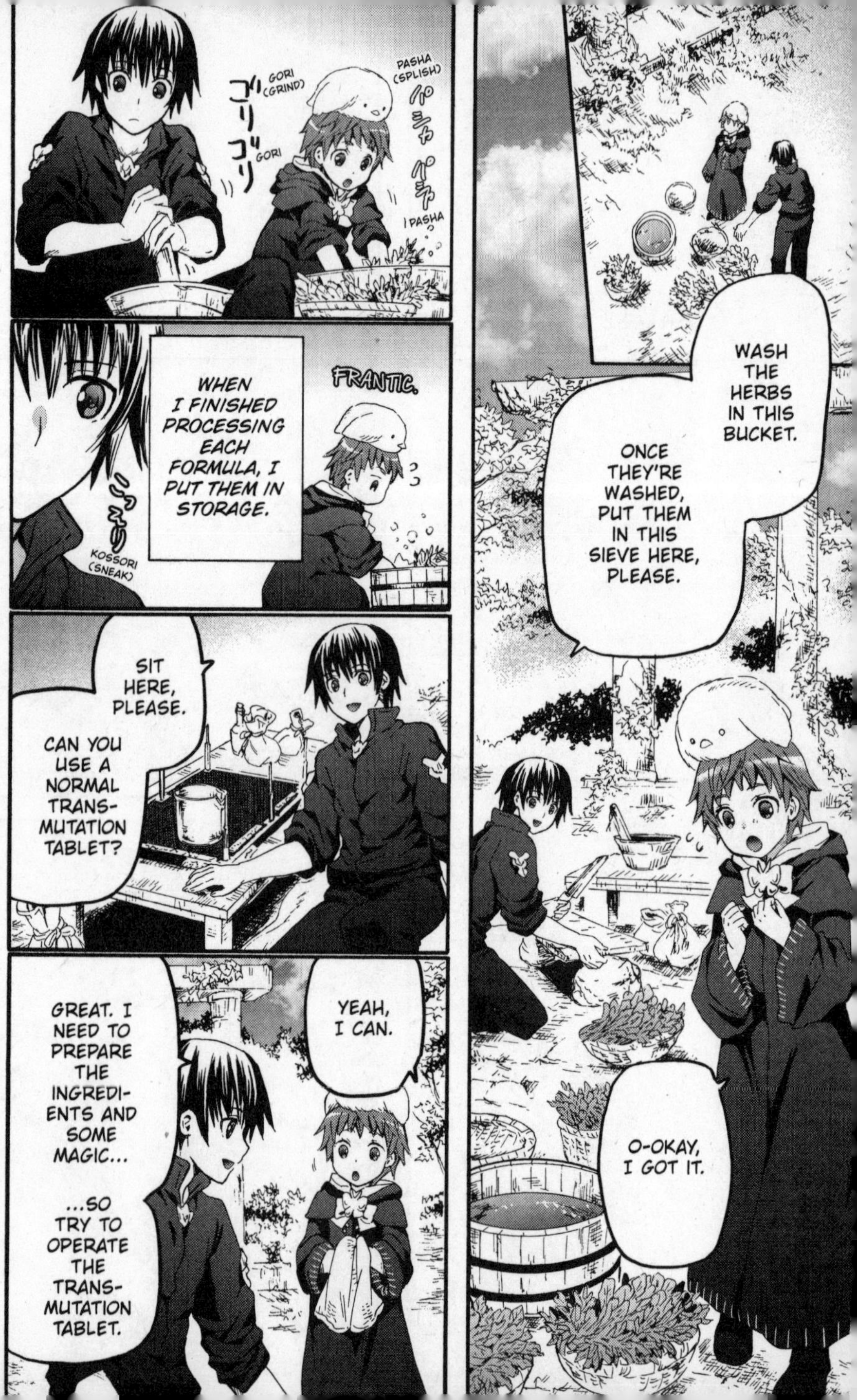
WASH THE HERBS IN THIS BUCKET.
ONCE THEY'RE WASHED, PUT THEM IN THIS SIEVE HERE, PLEASE.
O-OKAY, I GOT IT.
パシャ パシャ
PASHA (SPLISH)
PASHA
ゴリゴリ
GORI (GRIND)
GORI
FRANTIC.
WHEN I FINISHED PROCESSING EACH FORMULA, I PUT THEM IN STORAGE.
こっそり
KOSSORI (SNEAK)
SIT HERE, PLEASE.
CAN YOU USE A NORMAL TRANS-MUTATION TABLET?
YEAH, I CAN.
GREAT. I NEED TO PREPARE THE INGREDI-ENTS AND SOME MAGIC...
...SO TRY TO OPERATE THE TRANS-MUTATION TABLET.

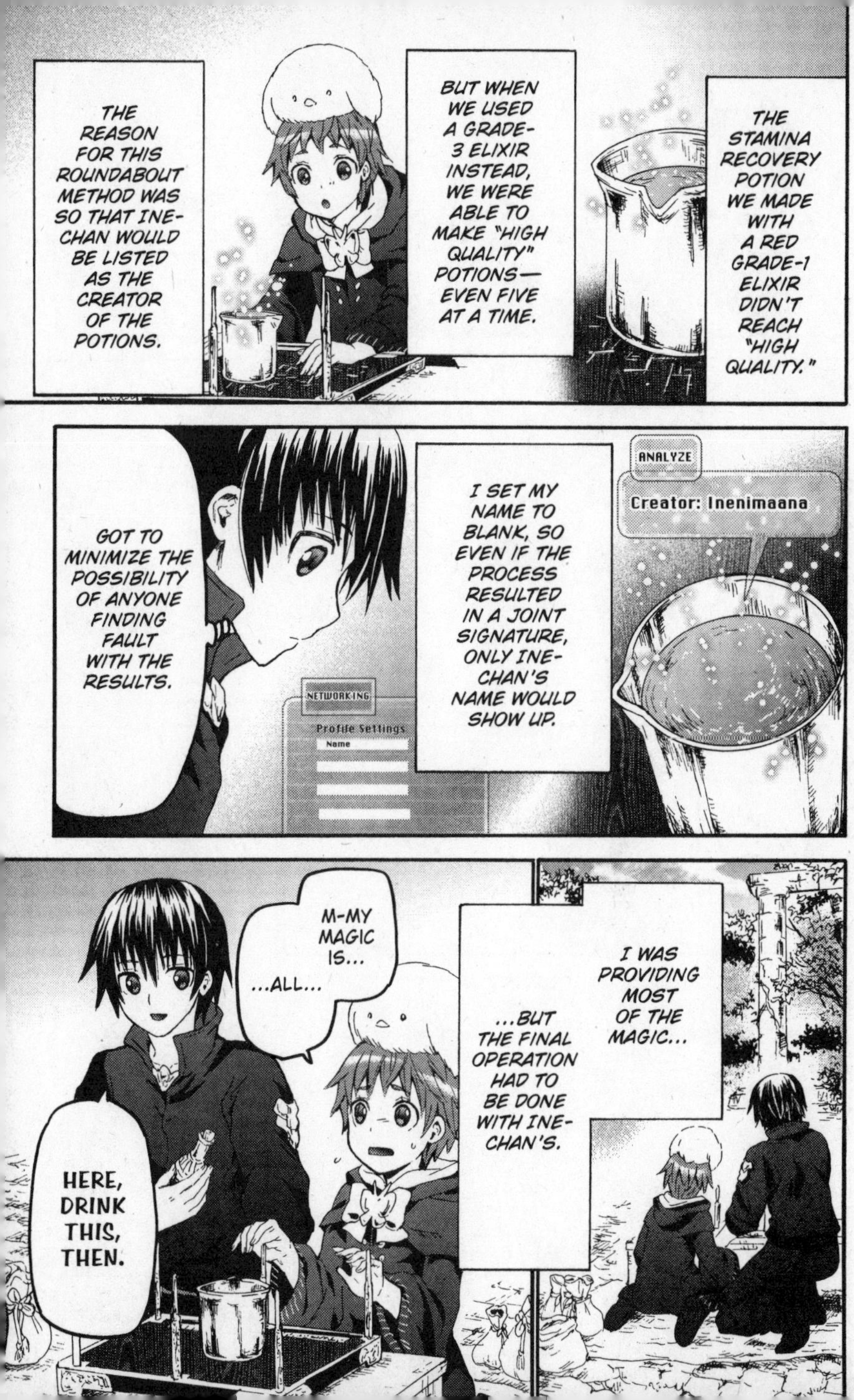
THE STAMINA RECOVERY POTION WE MADE WITH A RED GRADE-1 ELIXIR DIDN'T REACH "HIGH QUALITY."
BUT WHEN WE USED A GRADE-3 ELIXIR INSTEAD, WE WERE ABLE TO MAKE "HIGH QUALITY" POTIONS—EVEN FIVE AT A TIME.
THE REASON FOR THIS ROUNDABOUT METHOD WAS SO THAT INE-CHAN WOULD BE LISTED AS THE CREATOR OF THE POTIONS.
ANALYZE
Creator: Inenimaana
I SET MY NAME TO BLANK, SO EVEN IF THE PROCESS RESULTED IN A JOINT SIGNATURE, ONLY INE-CHAN'S NAME WOULD SHOW UP.
NETWORKING
Profile Settings
Name
GOT TO MINIMIZE THE POSSIBILITY OF ANYONE FINDING FAULT WITH THE RESULTS.
I WAS PROVIDING MOST OF THE MAGIC...
...BUT THE FINAL OPERATION HAD TO BE DONE WITH INE-CHAN'S.
M-MY MAGIC IS...
...ALL...
HERE, DRINK THIS, THEN.

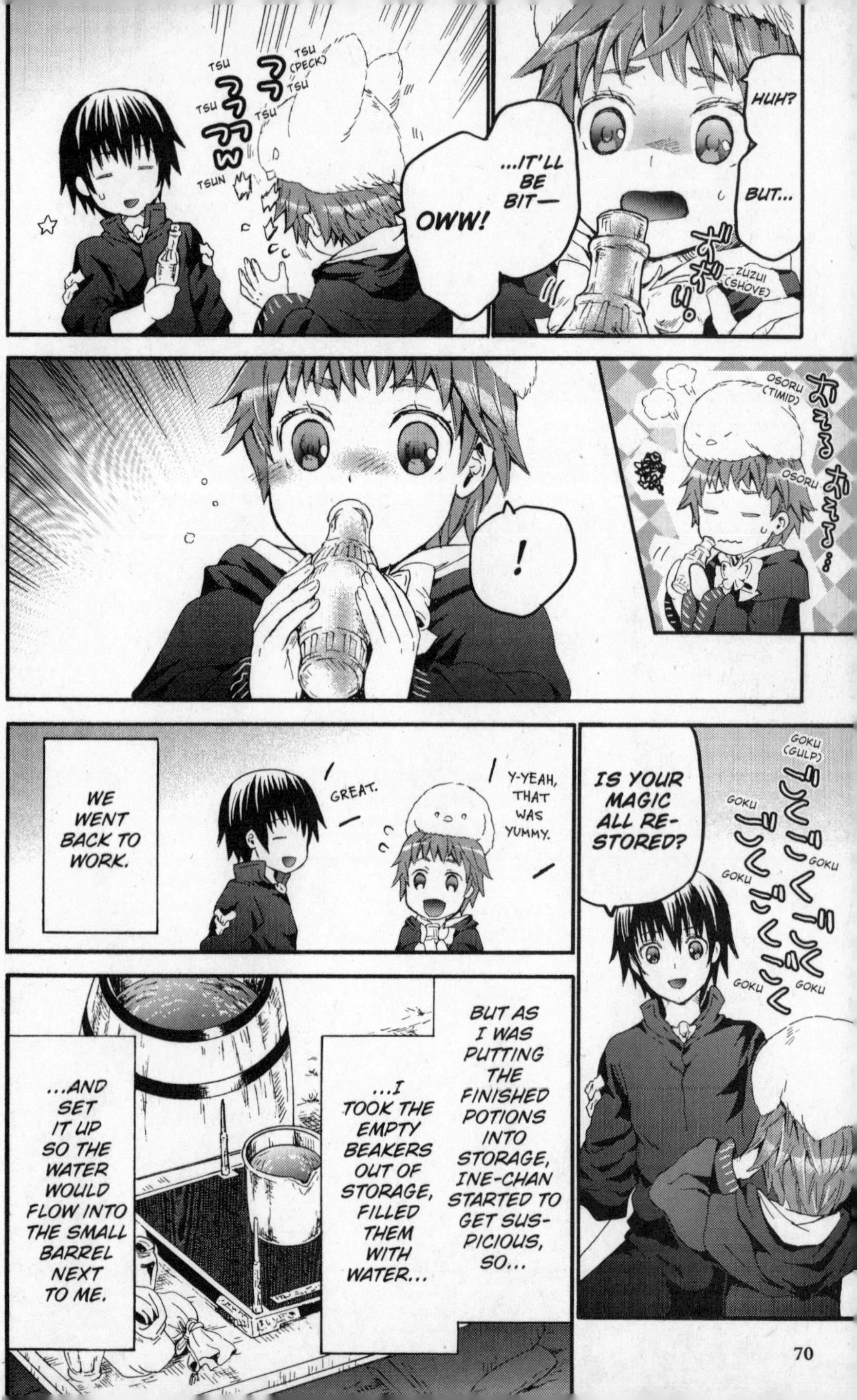
HUH?
BUT...
ZUZUI (SHOVE)
...IT'LL BE BIT—
OWW!
TSU (PECK)
TSU
TSU
TSU
TSU
TSUN
OSORU (TIMID)
OSORU
!
IS YOUR MAGIC ALL RE-STORED?
GOKU (GULP)
GOKU
GOKU
GOKU
GOKU
GOKU
Y-YEAH, THAT WAS YUMMY.
GREAT.
WE WENT BACK TO WORK.
BUT AS I WAS PUTTING THE FINISHED POTIONS INTO STORAGE, INE-CHAN STARTED TO GET SUS-PICIOUS, SO...
...I TOOK THE EMPTY BEAKERS OUT OF STORAGE, FILLED THEM WITH WATER...
...AND SET IT UP SO THE WATER WOULD FLOW INTO THE SMALL BARREL NEXT TO ME.

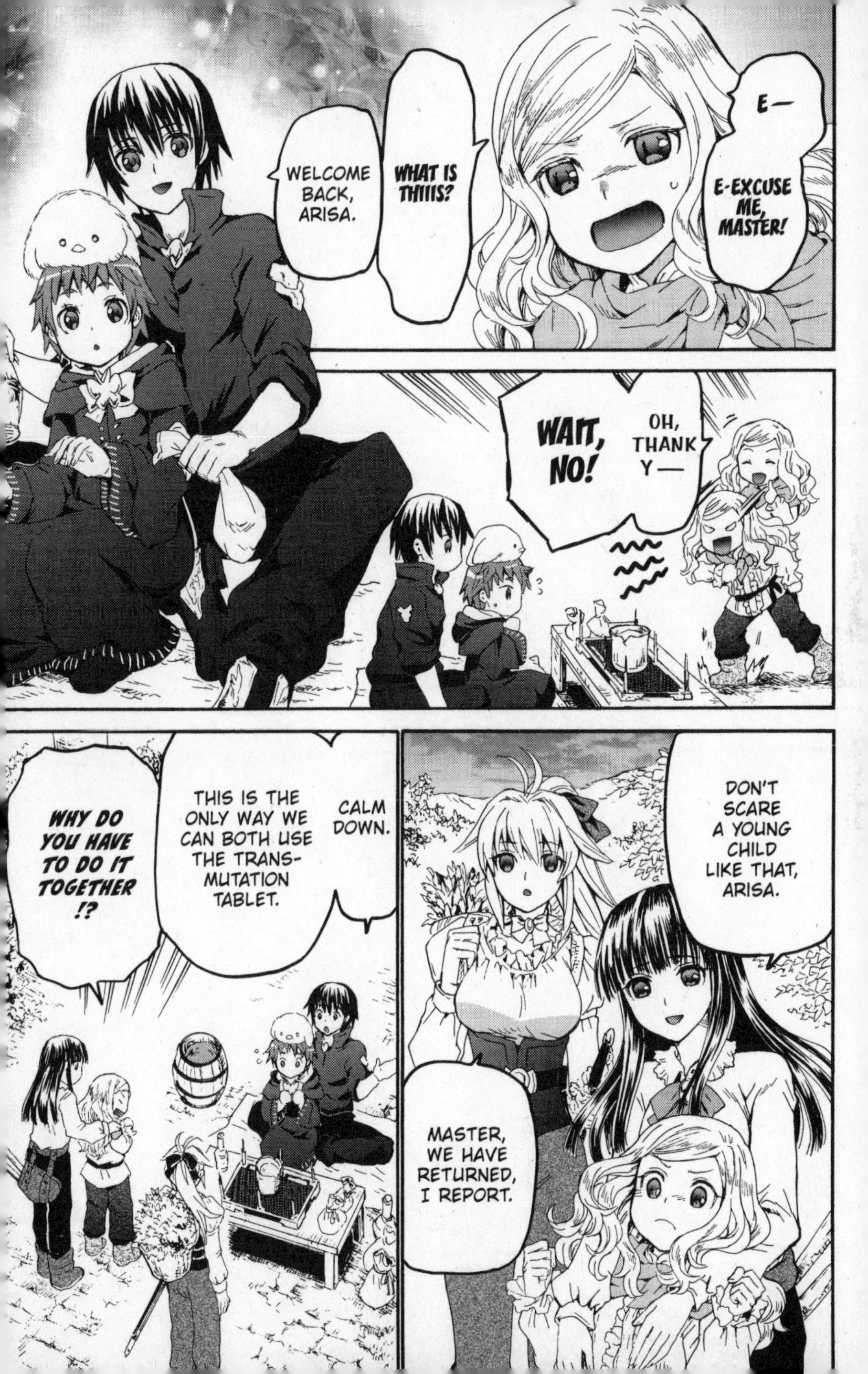
E—
E-EXCUSE ME, MASTER!
WHAT IS THIIIS?
WELCOME BACK, ARISA.
OH, THANK Y—
WAIT, NO!
DON'T SCARE A YOUNG CHILD LIKE THAT, ARISA.
MASTER, WE HAVE RETURNED, I REPORT.
CALM DOWN.
THIS IS THE ONLY WAY WE CAN BOTH USE THE TRANS-MUTATION TABLET.
WHY DO YOU HAVE TO DO IT TOGETHER!?

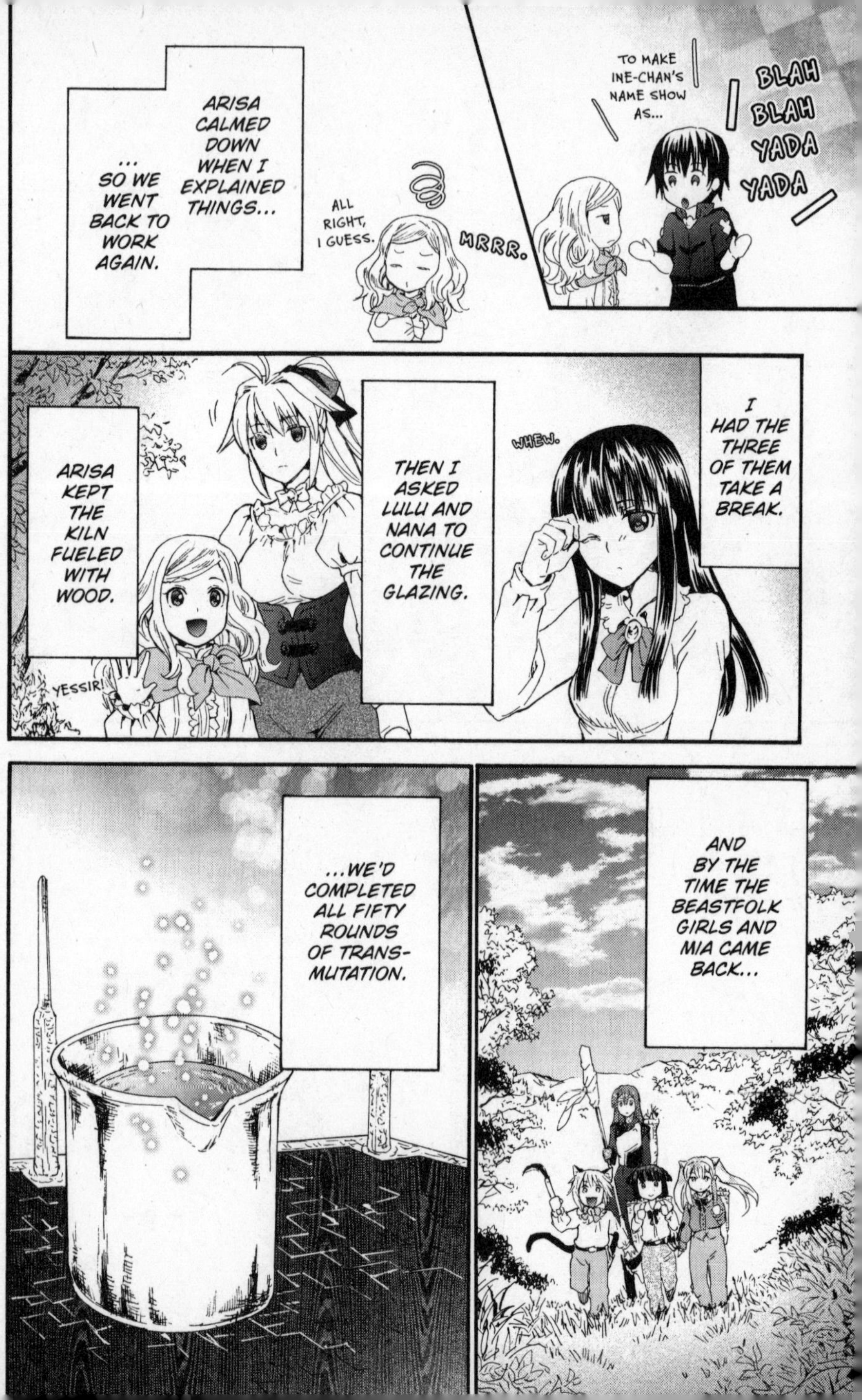
TO MAKE INE-CHAN'S NAME SHOW AS...
BLAH BLAH YADA YADA
ARISA CALMED DOWN WHEN I EXPLAINED THINGS...
ALL RIGHT, I GUESS.
MRRR.
...SO WE WENT BACK TO WORK AGAIN.
I HAD THE THREE OF THEM TAKE A BREAK.
WHEW.
THEN I ASKED LULU AND NANA TO CONTINUE THE GLAZING.
ARISA KEPT THE KILN FUELED WITH WOOD.
YESSIR!
AND BY THE TIME THE BEASTFOLK GIRLS AND MIA CAME BACK...
...WE'D COMPLETED ALL FIFTY ROUNDS OF TRANS-MUTATION.

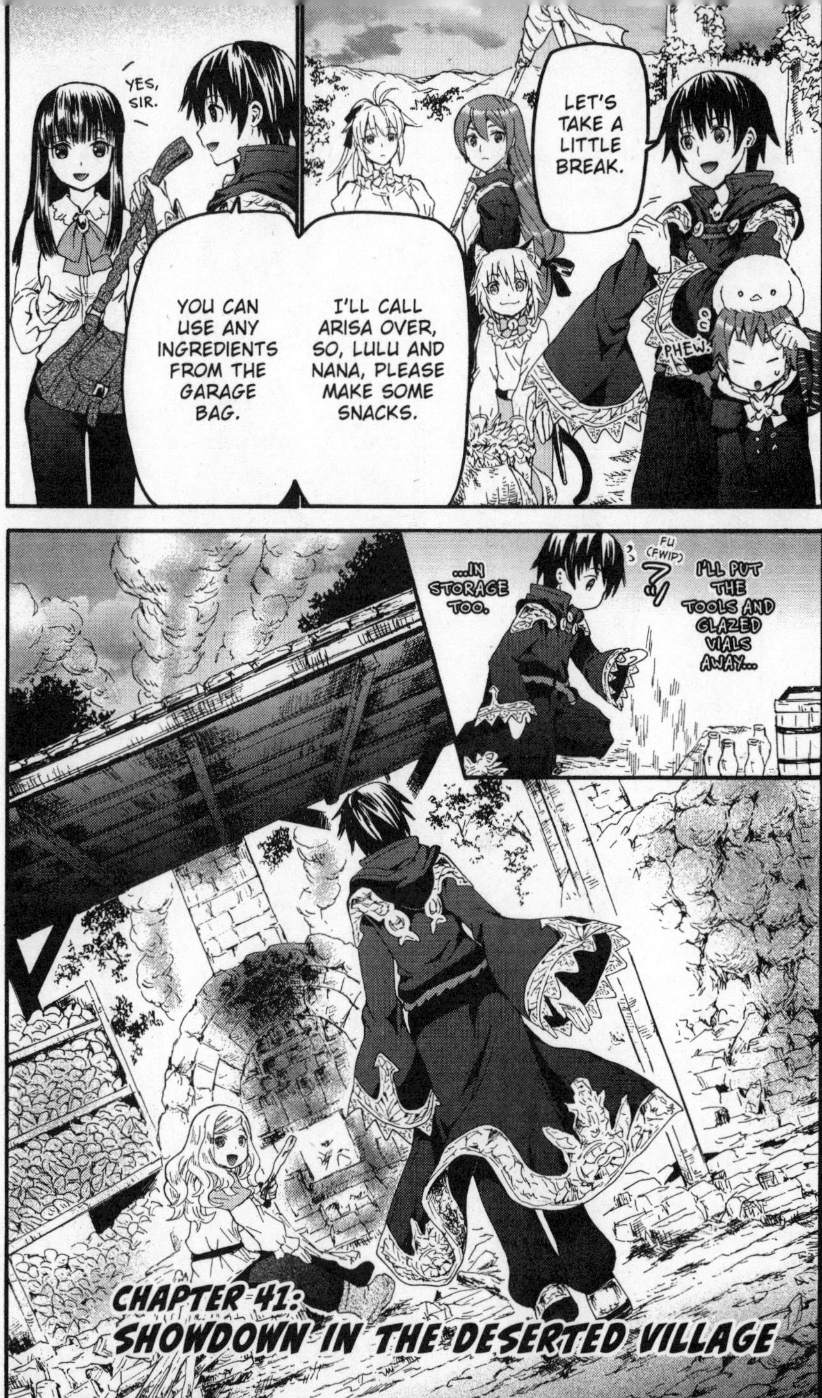
LET'S TAKE A LITTLE BREAK.
PHEW.
I'LL CALL ARISA OVER, SO, LULU AND NANA, PLEASE MAKE SOME SNACKS.
YOU CAN USE ANY INGREDIENTS FROM THE GARAGE BAG.
YES, SIR.
I'LL PUT THE TOOLS AND GLAZED VIALS AWAY...
FU (FWIP)
...IN STORAGE TOO.
CHAPTER 41: SHOWDOWN IN THE DESERTED VILLAGE

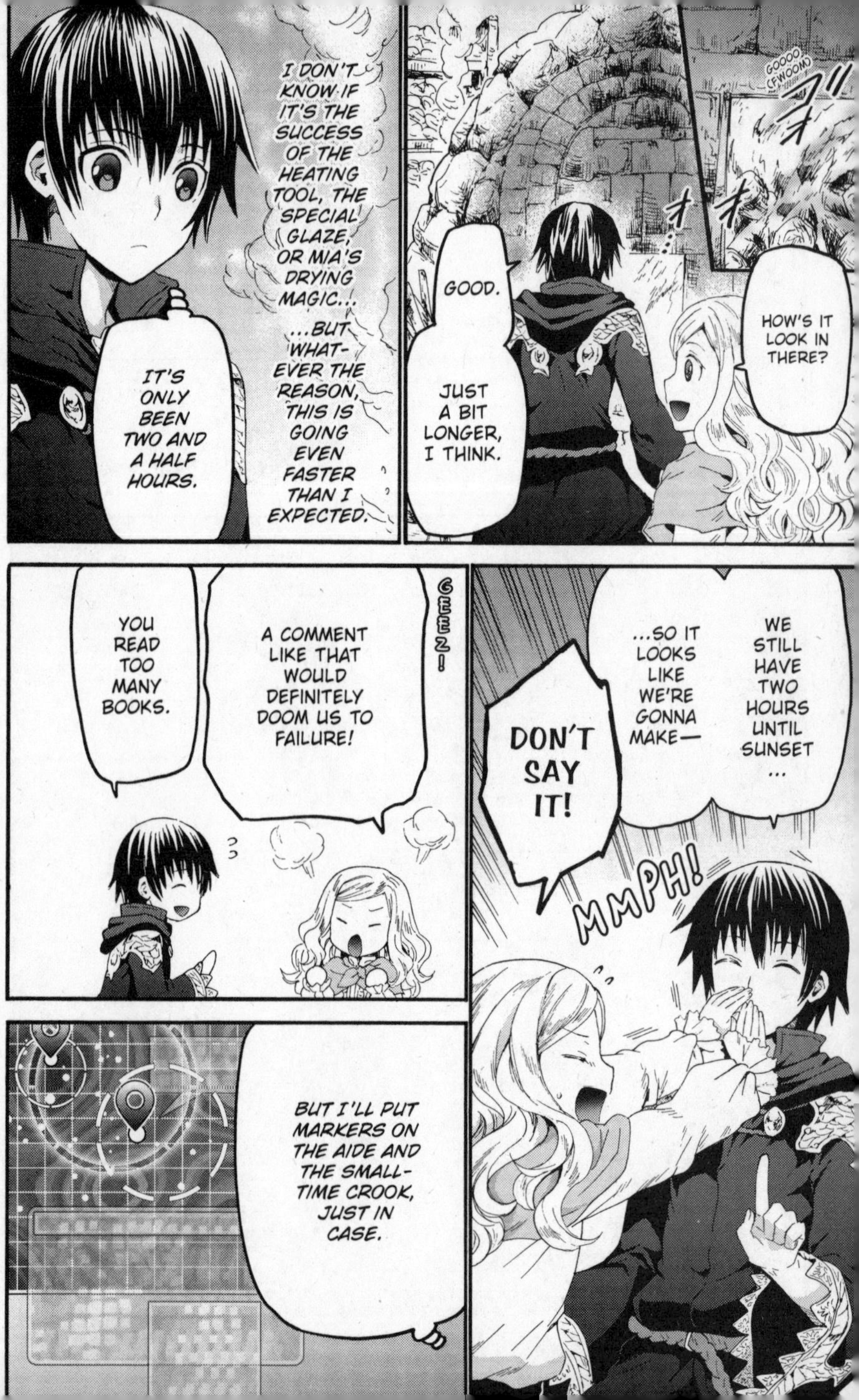
GOOOO (FWOOM)
HOW'S IT LOOK IN THERE?
GOOD.
JUST A BIT LONGER, I THINK.
I DON'T KNOW IF IT'S THE SUCCESS OF THE HEATING TOOL, THE SPECIAL GLAZE, OR MIA'S DRYING MAGIC...
...BUT WHAT-EVER THE REASON, THIS IS GOING EVEN FASTER THAN I EXPECTED.
IT'S ONLY BEEN TWO AND A HALF HOURS.
WE STILL HAVE TWO HOURS UNTIL SUNSET...
...SO IT LOOKS LIKE WE'RE GONNA MAKE—
DON'T SAY IT!
MMPH!
GEEZ!
A COMMENT LIKE THAT WOULD DEFINITELY DOOM US TO FAILURE!
YOU READ TOO MANY BOOKS.
BUT I'LL PUT MARKERS ON THE AIDE AND THE SMALL-TIME CROOK, JUST IN CASE.

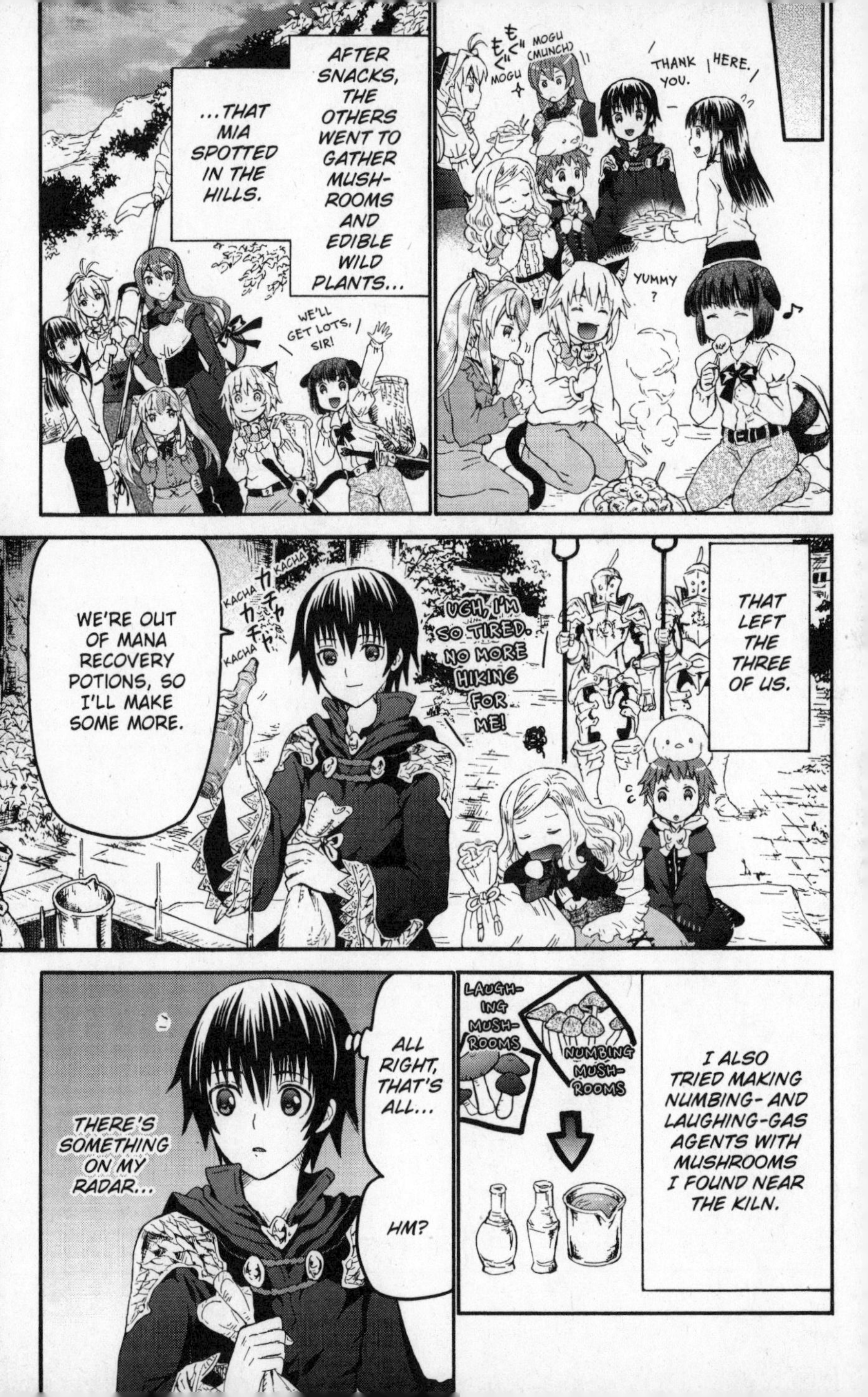

もぐもぐ
MOGU (MUNCH)
MOGU
HERE.
THANK YOU.
YUMMY?
AFTER SNACKS, THE OTHERS WENT TO GATHER MUSHROOMS AND EDIBLE WILD PLANTS...
...THAT MIA SPOTTED IN THE HILLS.
WE'LL GET LOTS, SIR!
THAT LEFT THE THREE OF US.
UGH, I'M SO TIRED. NO MORE HIKING FOR ME!
カチャカチャ
KACHA KACHA
WE'RE OUT OF MANA RECOVERY POTIONS, SO I'LL MAKE SOME MORE.
I ALSO TRIED MAKING NUMBING- AND LAUGHING-GAS AGENTS WITH MUSHROOMS I FOUND NEAR THE KILN.
LAUGHING MUSHROOMS
NUMBING MUSHROOMS
ALL RIGHT, THAT'S ALL...
HM?
THERE'S SOMETHING ON MY RADAR...

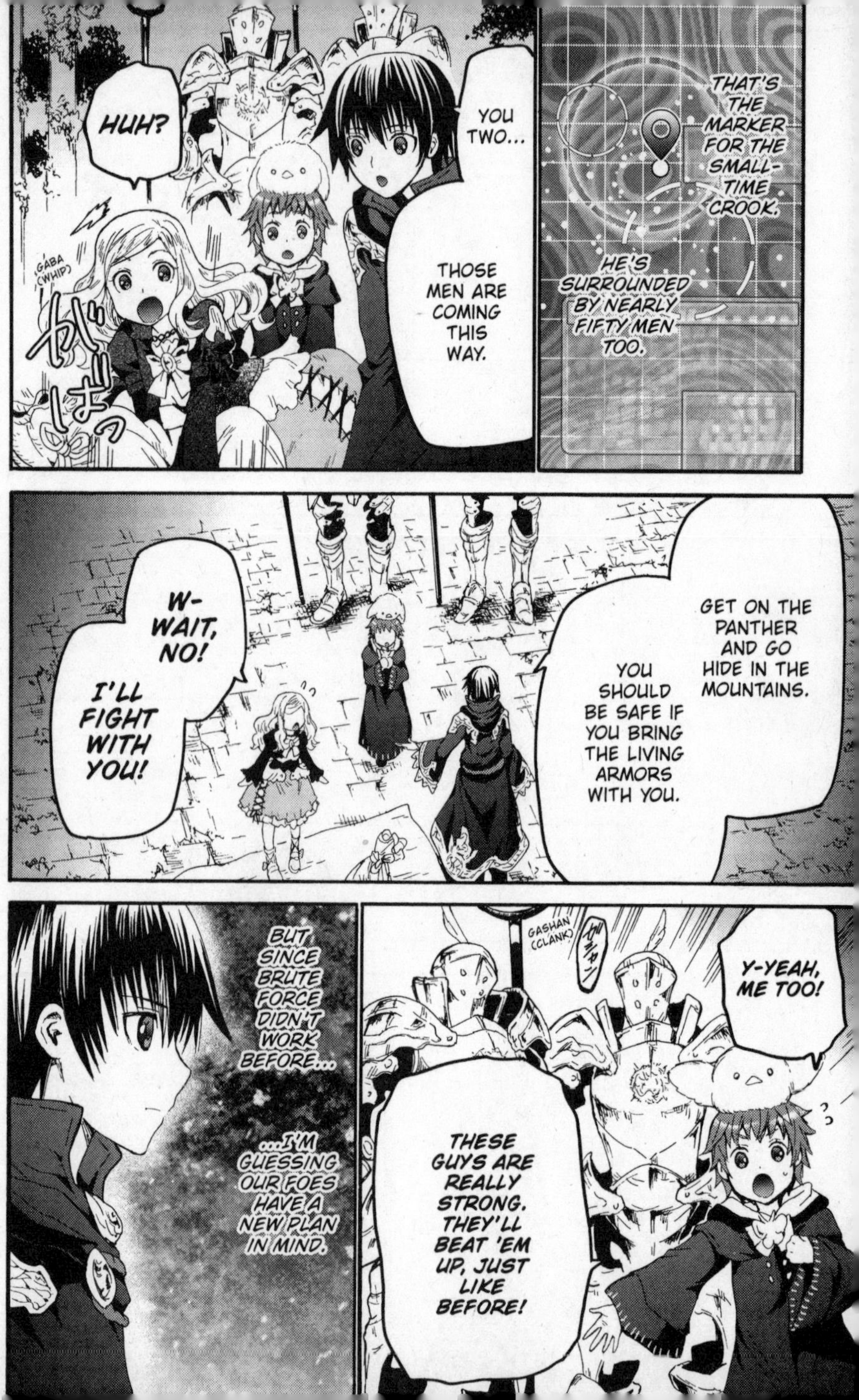
THAT'S THE MARKER FOR THE SMALL-TIME CROOK.
HE'S SURROUNDED BY NEARLY FIFTY MEN TOO.
YOU TWO...
THOSE MEN ARE COMING THIS WAY.
HUH?
GABA (WHIP)
GET ON THE PANTHER AND GO HIDE IN THE MOUNTAINS.
YOU SHOULD BE SAFE IF YOU BRING THE LIVING ARMORS WITH YOU.
W-WAIT, NO!
I'LL FIGHT WITH YOU!
Y-YEAH, ME TOO!
GASHAN (CLANK)
THESE GUYS ARE REALLY STRONG. THEY'LL BEAT 'EM UP, JUST LIKE BEFORE!
BUT SINCE BRUTE FORCE DIDN'T WORK BEFORE...
...I'M GUESSING OUR FOES HAVE A NEW PLAN IN MIND.

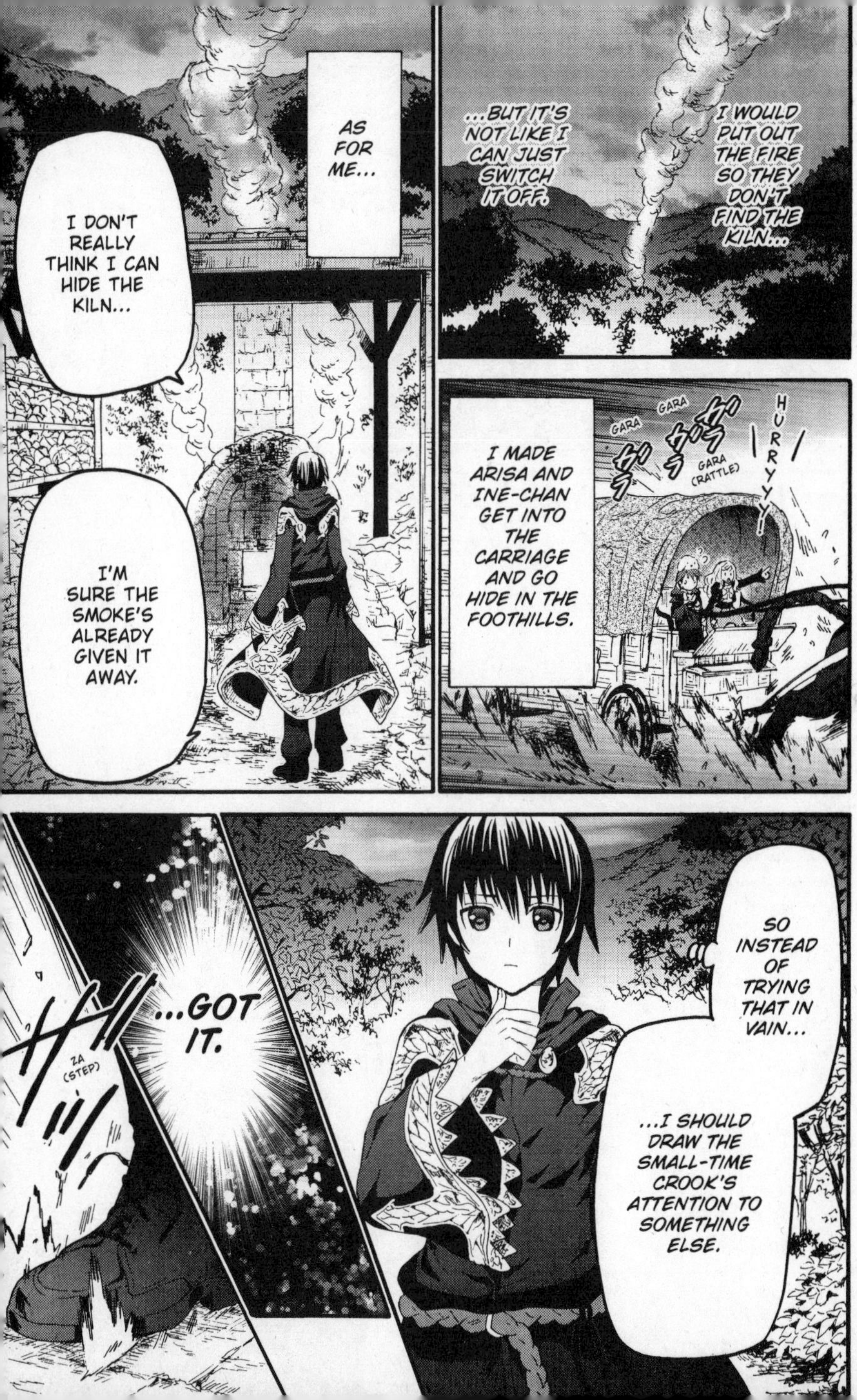
I WOULD PUT OUT THE FIRE SO THEY DON'T FIND THE KILN...
...BUT IT'S NOT LIKE I CAN JUST SWITCH IT OFF.
HURRYYY!
GARA
GARA
GARA (RATTLE)
I MADE ARISA AND INE-CHAN GET INTO THE CARRIAGE AND GO HIDE IN THE FOOTHILLS.
AS FOR ME...
I DON'T REALLY THINK I CAN HIDE THE KILN...
I'M SURE THE SMOKE'S ALREADY GIVEN IT AWAY.
SO INSTEAD OF TRYING THAT IN VAIN...
...I SHOULD DRAW THE SMALL-TIME CROOK'S ATTENTION TO SOMETHING ELSE.
...GOT IT.
ZA (STEP)

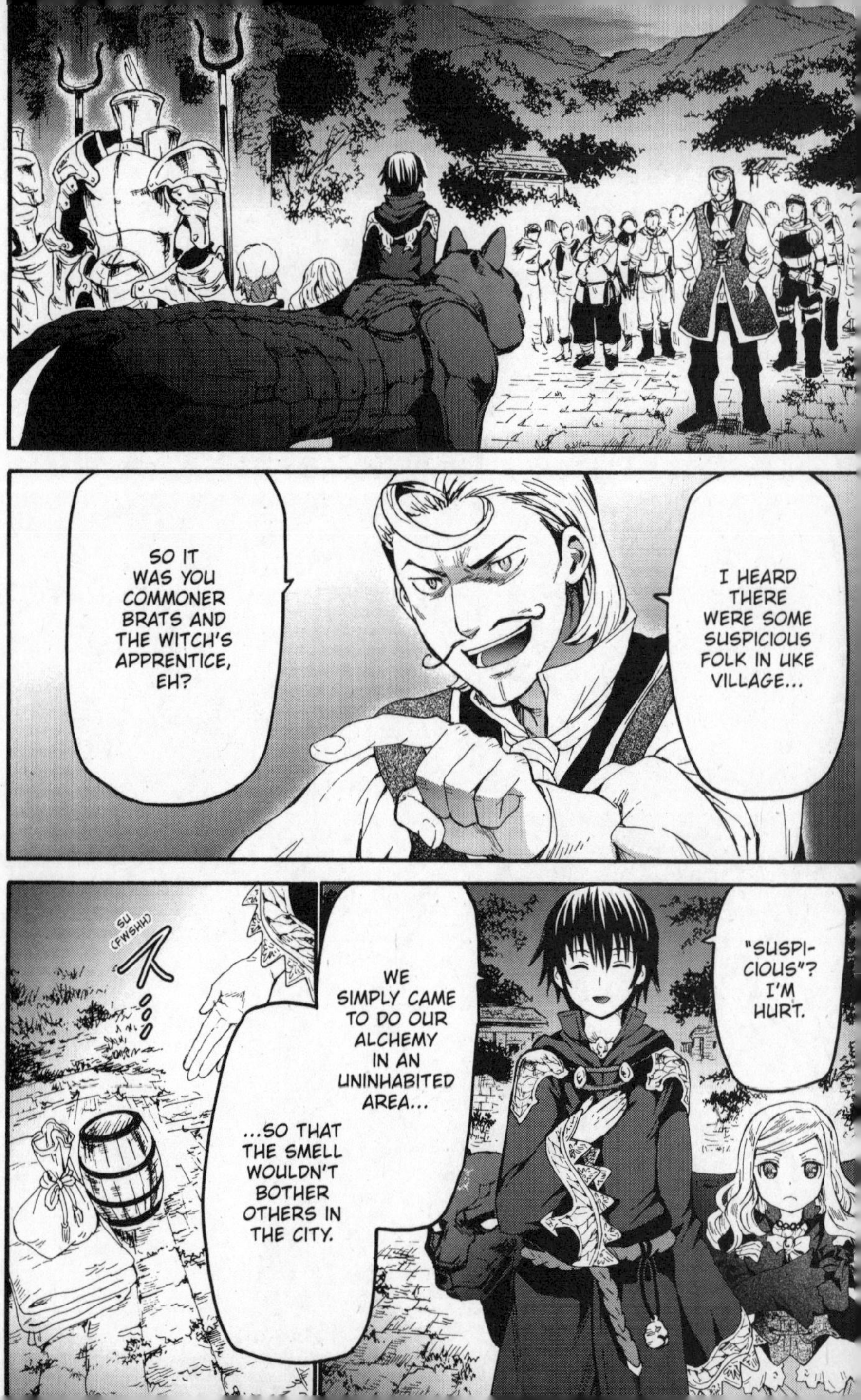
I HEARD THERE WERE SOME SUSPICIOUS FOLK IN UKE VILLAGE...
SO IT WAS YOU COMMONER BRATS AND THE WITCH'S APPRENTICE, EH?
"SUSPI-CIOUS"? I'M HURT.
WE SIMPLY CAME TO DO OUR ALCHEMY IN AN UNINHABITED AREA...
...SO THAT THE SMELL WOULDN'T BOTHER OTHERS IN THE CITY.
SU (FWSHH)

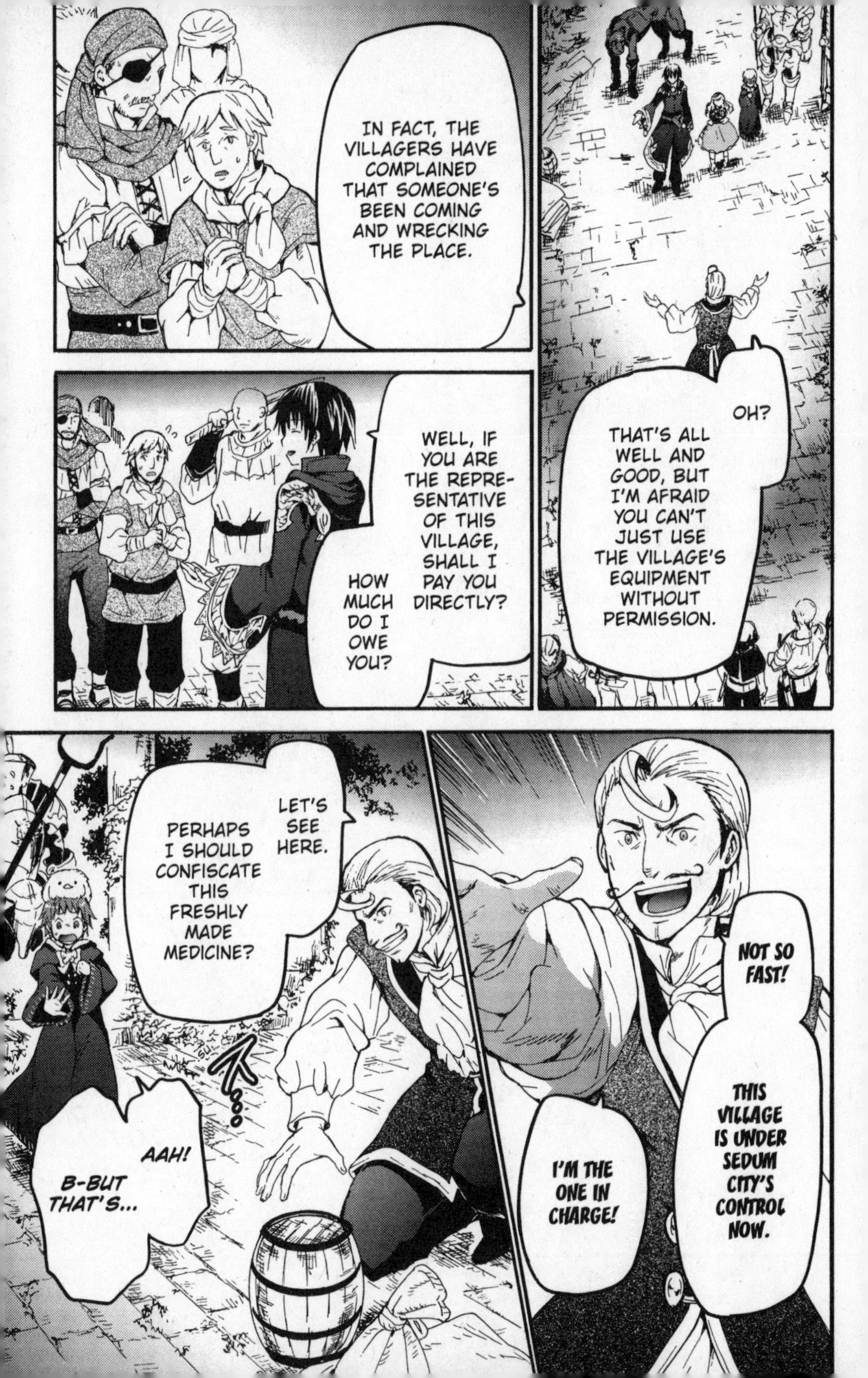
OH?
THAT'S ALL WELL AND GOOD, BUT I'M AFRAID YOU CAN'T JUST USE THE VILLAGE'S EQUIPMENT WITHOUT PERMISSION.
IN FACT, THE VILLAGERS HAVE COMPLAINED THAT SOMEONE'S BEEN COMING AND WRECKING THE PLACE.
WELL, IF YOU ARE THE REPRE-SENTATIVE OF THIS VILLAGE, SHALL I PAY YOU DIRECTLY?
HOW MUCH DO I OWE YOU?
NOT SO FAST!
THIS VILLAGE IS UNDER SEDUM CITY'S CONTROL NOW.
I'M THE ONE IN CHARGE!
LET'S SEE HERE.
PERHAPS I SHOULD CONFISCATE THIS FRESHLY MADE MEDICINE?
AAH!
B-BUT THAT'S...

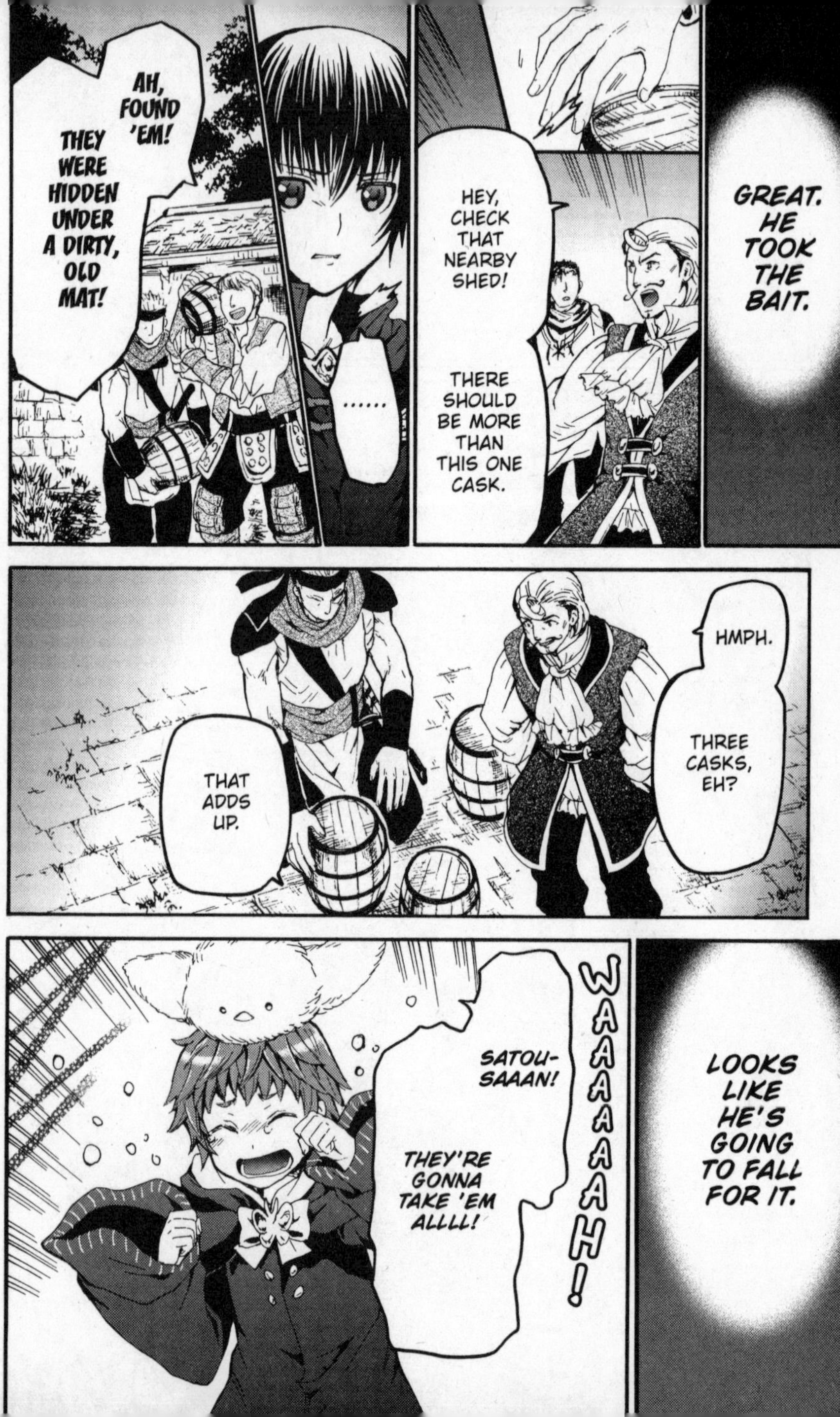
GREAT. HE TOOK THE BAIT.
HEY, CHECK THAT NEARBY SHED!
THERE SHOULD BE MORE THAN THIS ONE CASK.
......
AH, FOUND 'EM!
THEY WERE HIDDEN UNDER A DIRTY, OLD MAT!
HMPH.
THREE CASKS, EH?
THAT ADDS UP.
LOOKS LIKE HE'S GOING TO FALL FOR IT.
WAAAAAAAAH!
SATOU-SAAAN!
THEY'RE GONNA TAKE 'EM ALLLL!

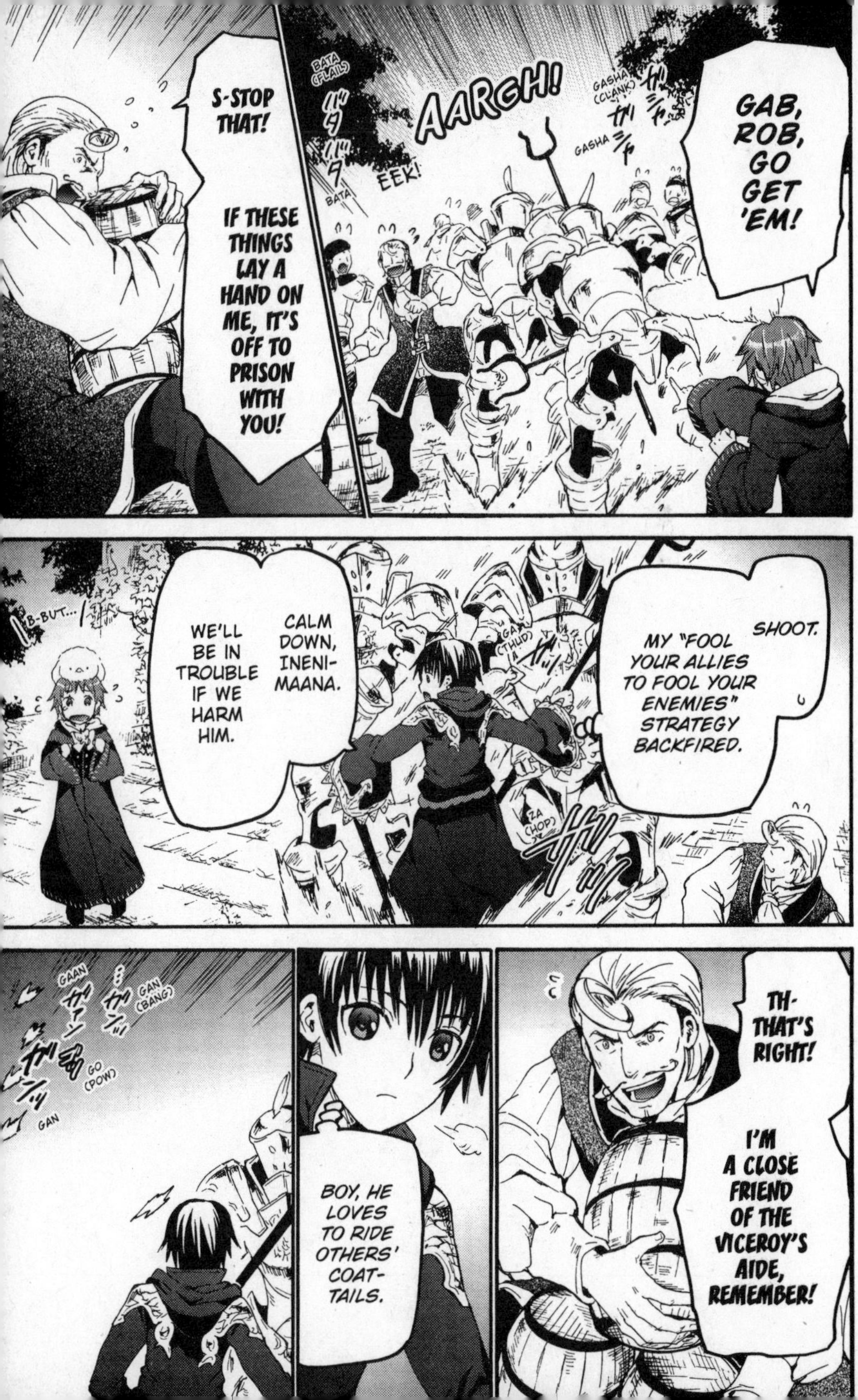
GAB, ROB, GO GET 'EM!
GASHA (CLANK)
GASHA
AARGH!
BATA (FLAIL)
EEK!
BATA
S-STOP THAT!
IF THESE THINGS LAY A HAND ON ME, IT'S OFF TO PRISON WITH YOU!
SHOOT.
MY "FOOL YOUR ALLIES TO FOOL YOUR ENEMIES" STRATEGY BACKFIRED.
GAN (THUD)
ZA (HOP)
CALM DOWN, INENI-MAANA.
WE'LL BE IN TROUBLE IF WE HARM HIM.
B-BUT...
TH-THAT'S RIGHT!
I'M A CLOSE FRIEND OF THE VICEROY'S AIDE, REMEMBER!
BOY, HE LOVES TO RIDE OTHERS' COAT-TAILS.
GAAN
GAN (BANG)
GO (POW)
GAN

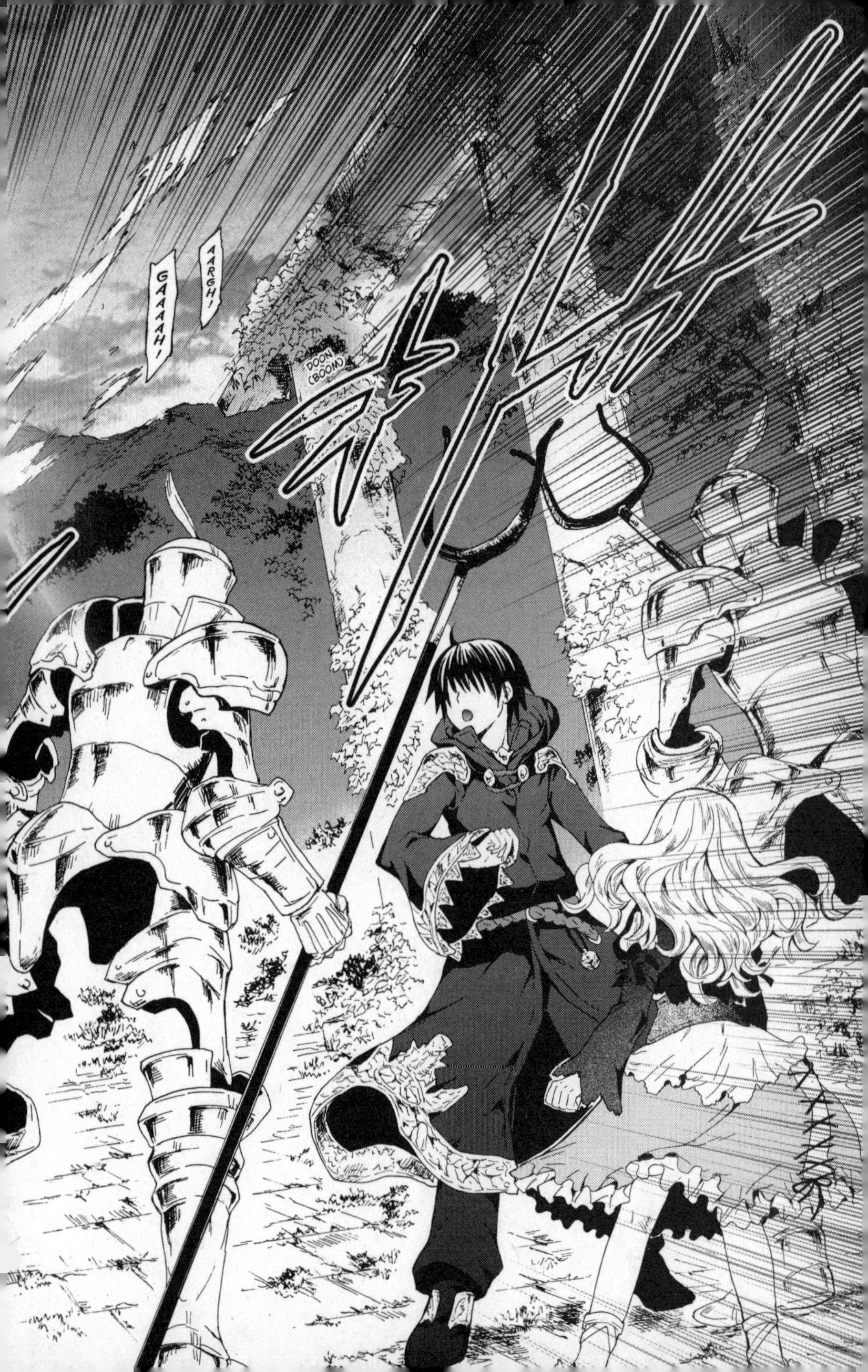
DOON (BOOM)
AARGH!
GAAAAAH!

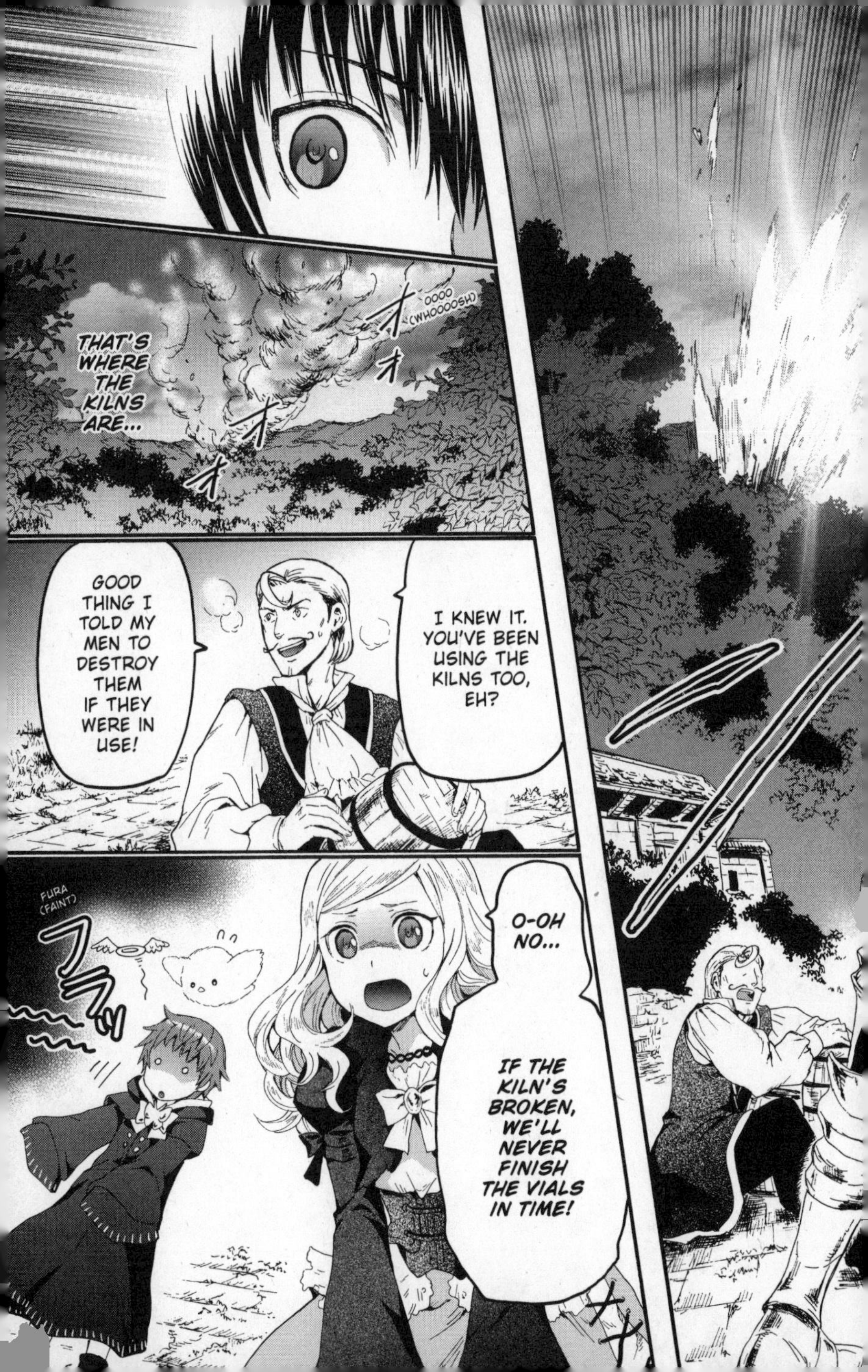
OOOO (WHOOOOSH)
THAT'S WHERE THE KILNS ARE...
I KNEW IT. YOU'VE BEEN USING THE KILNS TOO, EH?
GOOD THING I TOLD MY MEN TO DESTROY THEM IF THEY WERE IN USE!
O-OH NO...
IF THE KILN'S BROKEN, WE'LL NEVER FINISH THE VIALS IN TIME!
FURA (FAINT)

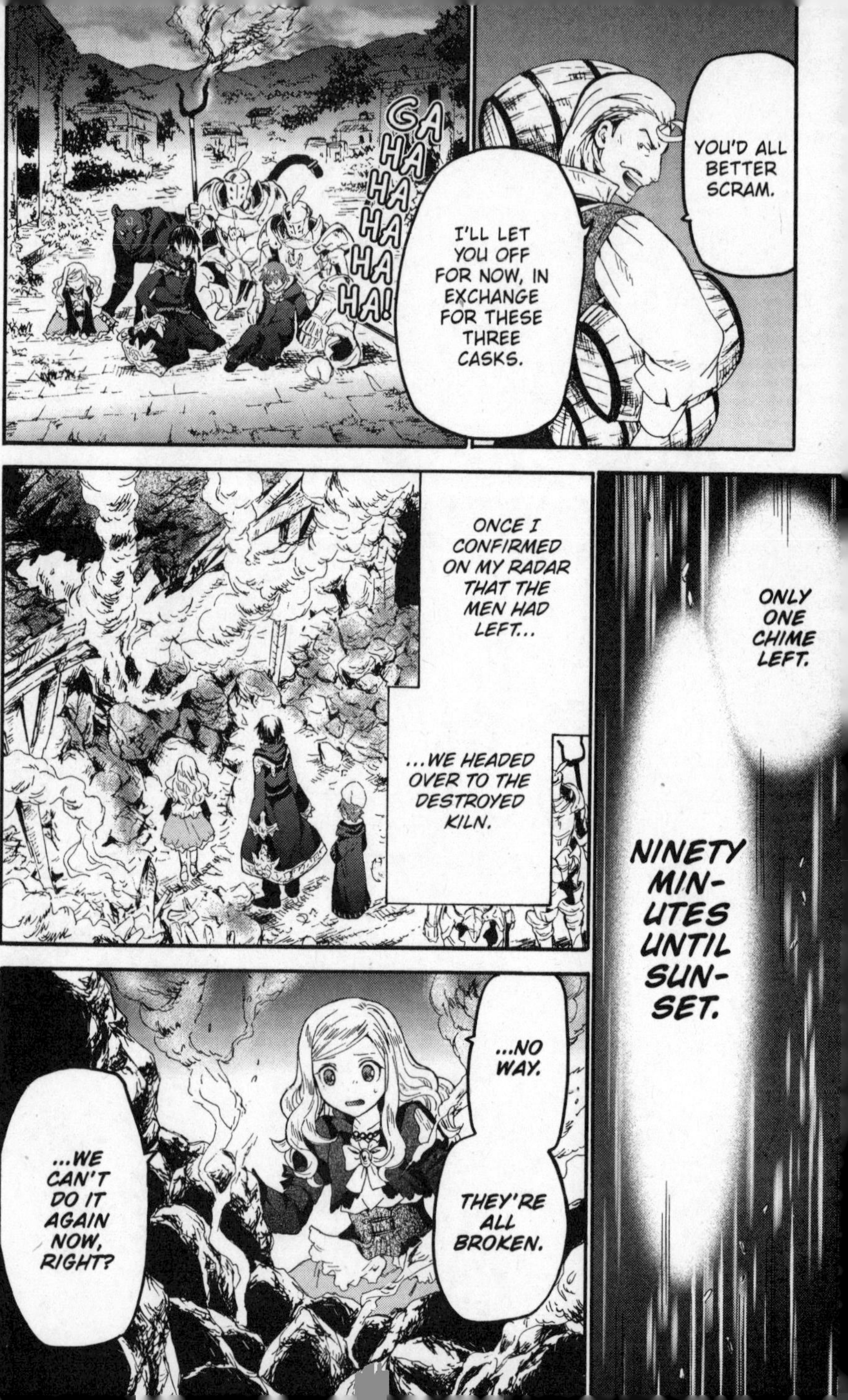
YOU'D ALL BETTER SCRAM.
I'LL LET YOU OFF FOR NOW, IN EXCHANGE FOR THESE THREE CASKS.
GAHAHAHAHAHA!
ONLY ONE CHIME LEFT.
NINETY MIN-UTES UNTIL SUN-SET.
ONCE I CONFIRMED ON MY RADAR THAT THE MEN HAD LEFT...
...WE HEADED OVER TO THE DESTROYED KILN.
...NO WAY.
THEY'RE ALL BROKEN.
...WE CAN'T DO IT AGAIN NOW, RIGHT?

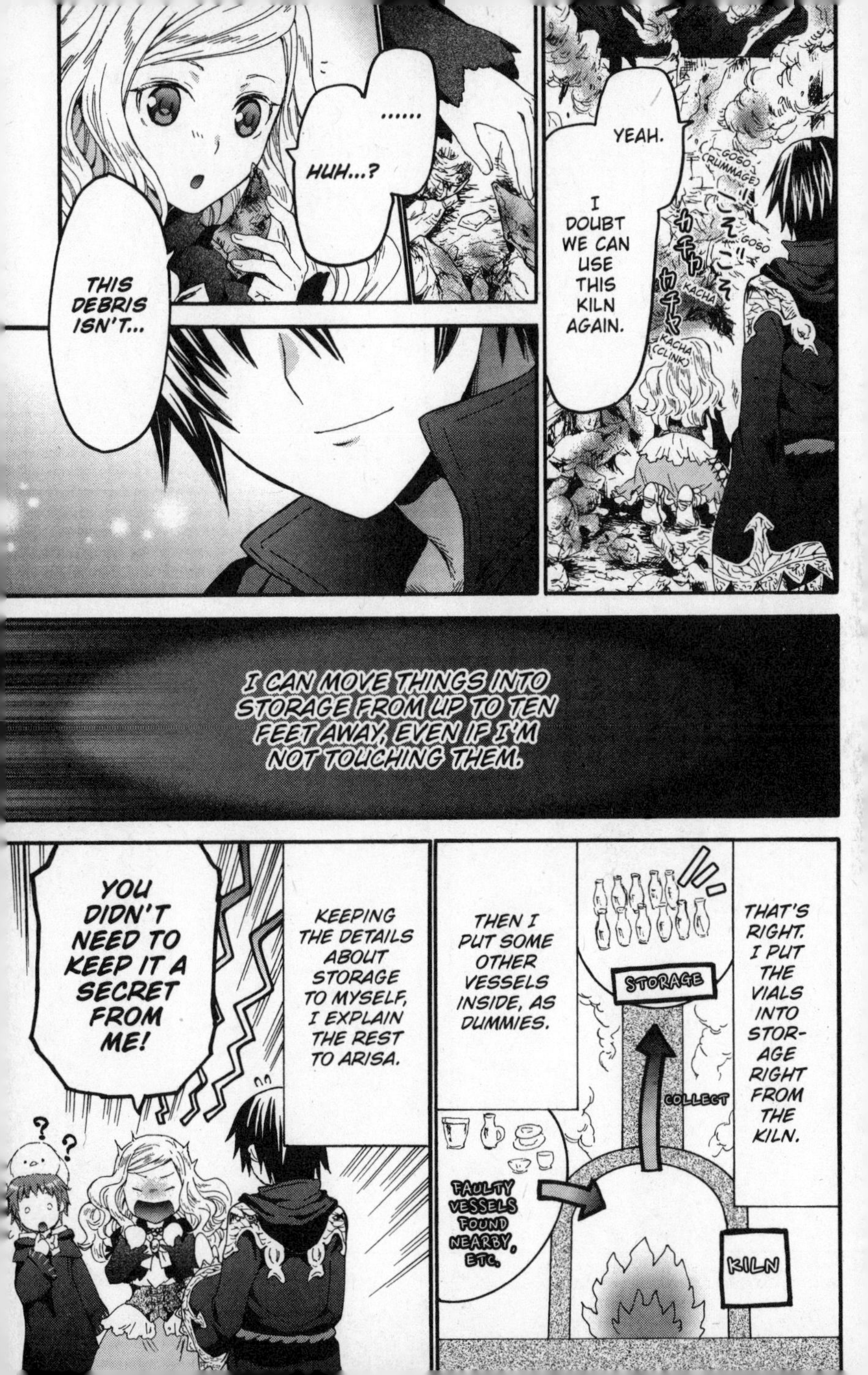
YEAH.
I DOUBT WE CAN USE THIS KILN AGAIN.
GOSO (RUMMAGE)
GOSO
KACHA
KACHA (CLINK)
......
HUH...?
THIS DEBRIS ISN'T...
I CAN MOVE THINGS INTO STORAGE FROM UP TO TEN FEET AWAY, EVEN IF I'M NOT TOUCHING THEM.
THAT'S RIGHT. I PUT THE VIALS INTO STORAGE RIGHT FROM THE KILN.
THEN I PUT SOME OTHER VESSELS INSIDE, AS DUMMIES.
STORAGE
COLLECT
FAULTY VESSELS FOUND NEARBY, ETC.
KILN
KEEPING THE DETAILS ABOUT STORAGE TO MYSELF, I EXPLAIN THE REST TO ARISA.
YOU DIDN'T NEED TO KEEP IT A SECRET FROM ME!

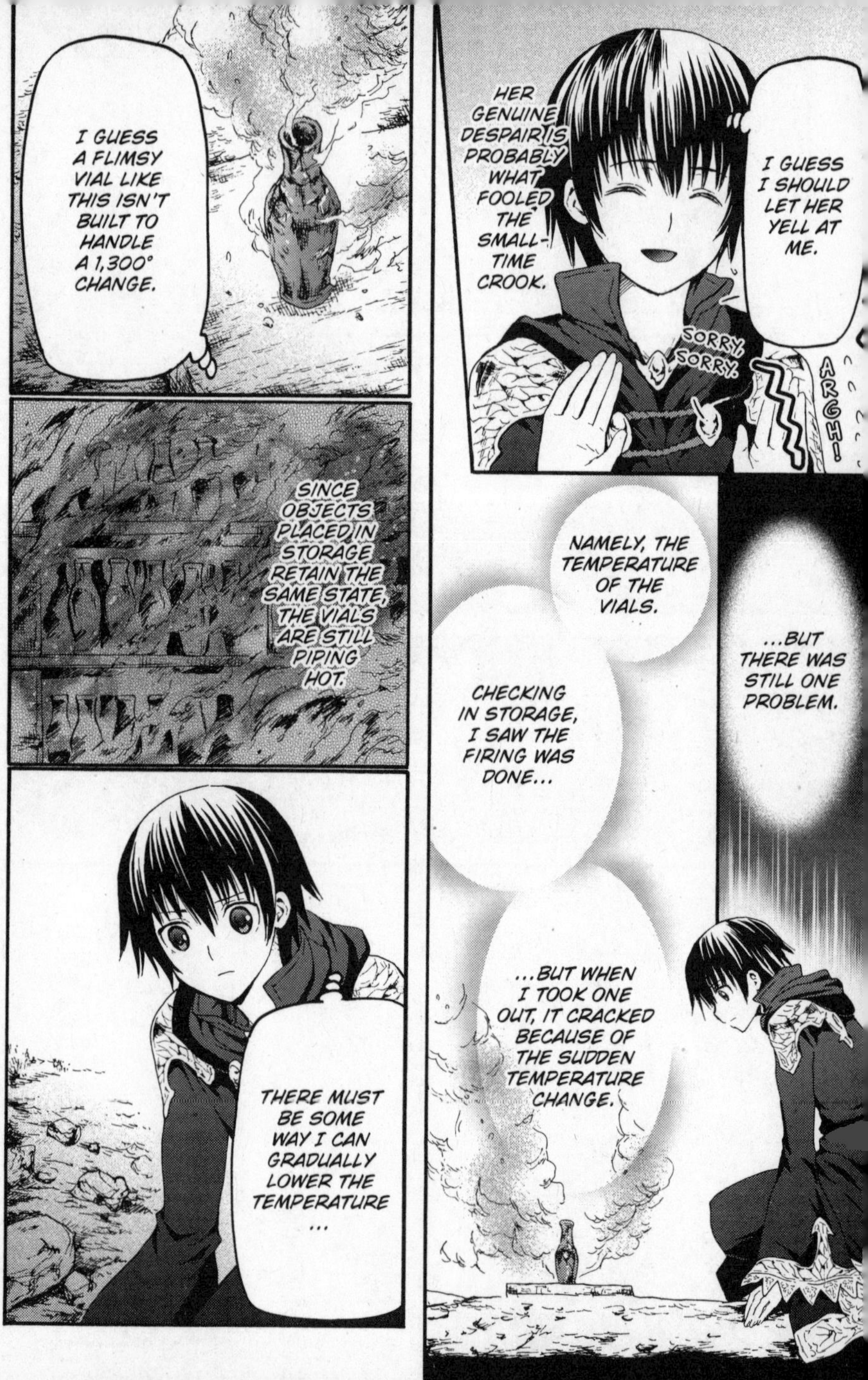
I GUESS I SHOULD LET HER YELL AT ME.
HER GENUINE DESPAIR IS PROBABLY WHAT FOOLED THE SMALL-TIME CROOK.
ARGH!
SORRY, SORRY.
...BUT THERE WAS STILL ONE PROBLEM.
NAMELY, THE TEMPERATURE OF THE VIALS.
CHECKING IN STORAGE, I SAW THE FIRING WAS DONE...
...BUT WHEN I TOOK ONE OUT, IT CRACKED BECAUSE OF THE SUDDEN TEMPERATURE CHANGE.
I GUESS A FLIMSY VIAL LIKE THIS ISN'T BUILT TO HANDLE A 1,300° CHANGE.
SINCE OBJECTS PLACED IN STORAGE RETAIN THE SAME STATE, THE VIALS ARE STILL PIPING HOT.
THERE MUST BE SOME WAY I CAN GRADUALLY LOWER THE TEMPERATURE ...

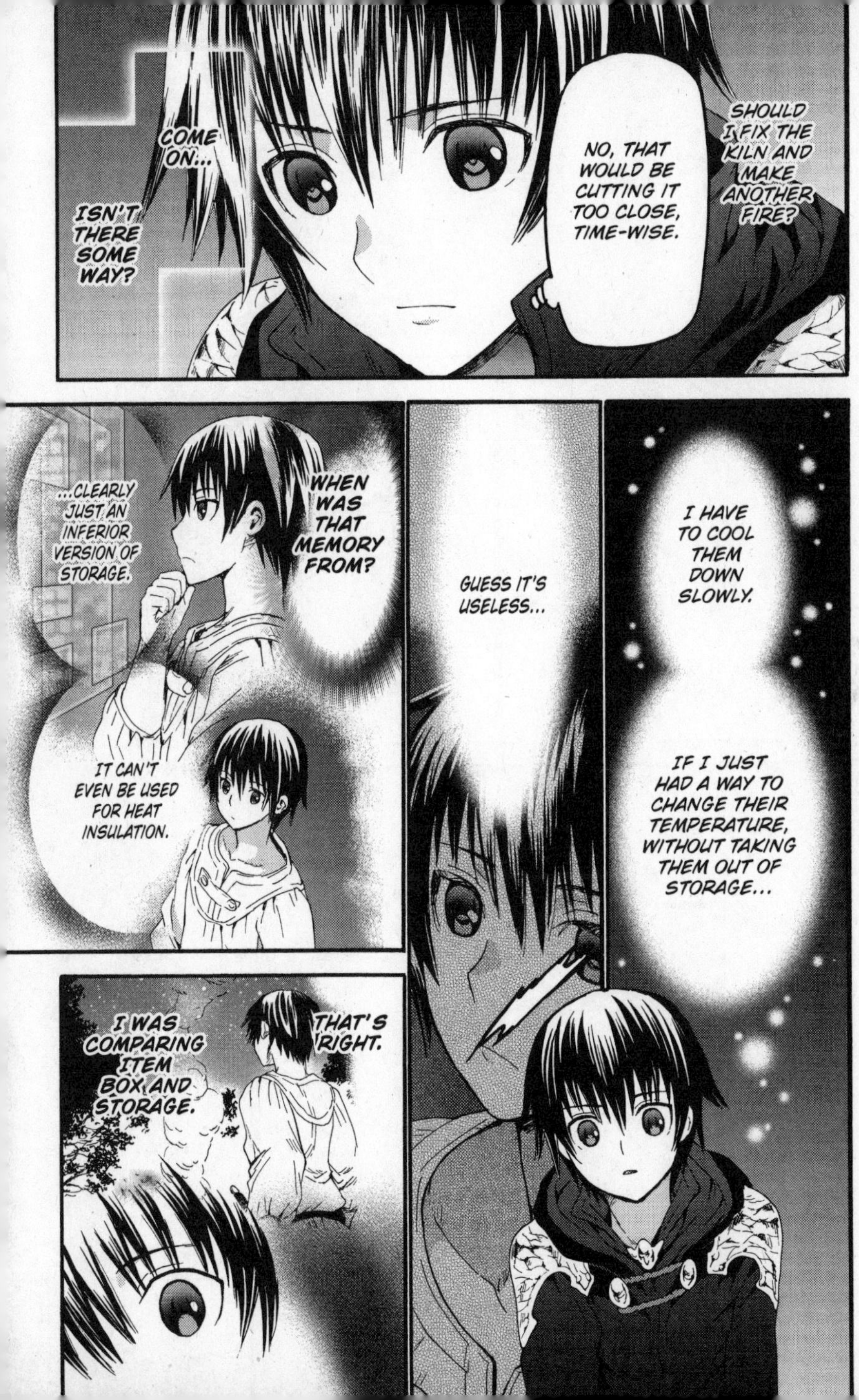
SHOULD I FIX THE KILN AND MAKE ANOTHER FIRE?
NO, THAT WOULD BE CUTTING IT TOO CLOSE, TIME-WISE.
COME ON...
ISN'T THERE SOME WAY?
I HAVE TO COOL THEM DOWN SLOWLY.
IF I JUST HAD A WAY TO CHANGE THEIR TEMPERATURE, WITHOUT TAKING THEM OUT OF STORAGE...
GUESS IT'S USELESS...
WHEN WAS THAT MEMORY FROM?
...CLEARLY JUST AN INFERIOR VERSION OF STORAGE.
IT CAN'T EVEN BE USED FOR HEAT INSULATION.
THAT'S RIGHT.
I WAS COMPARING ITEM BOX AND STORAGE.

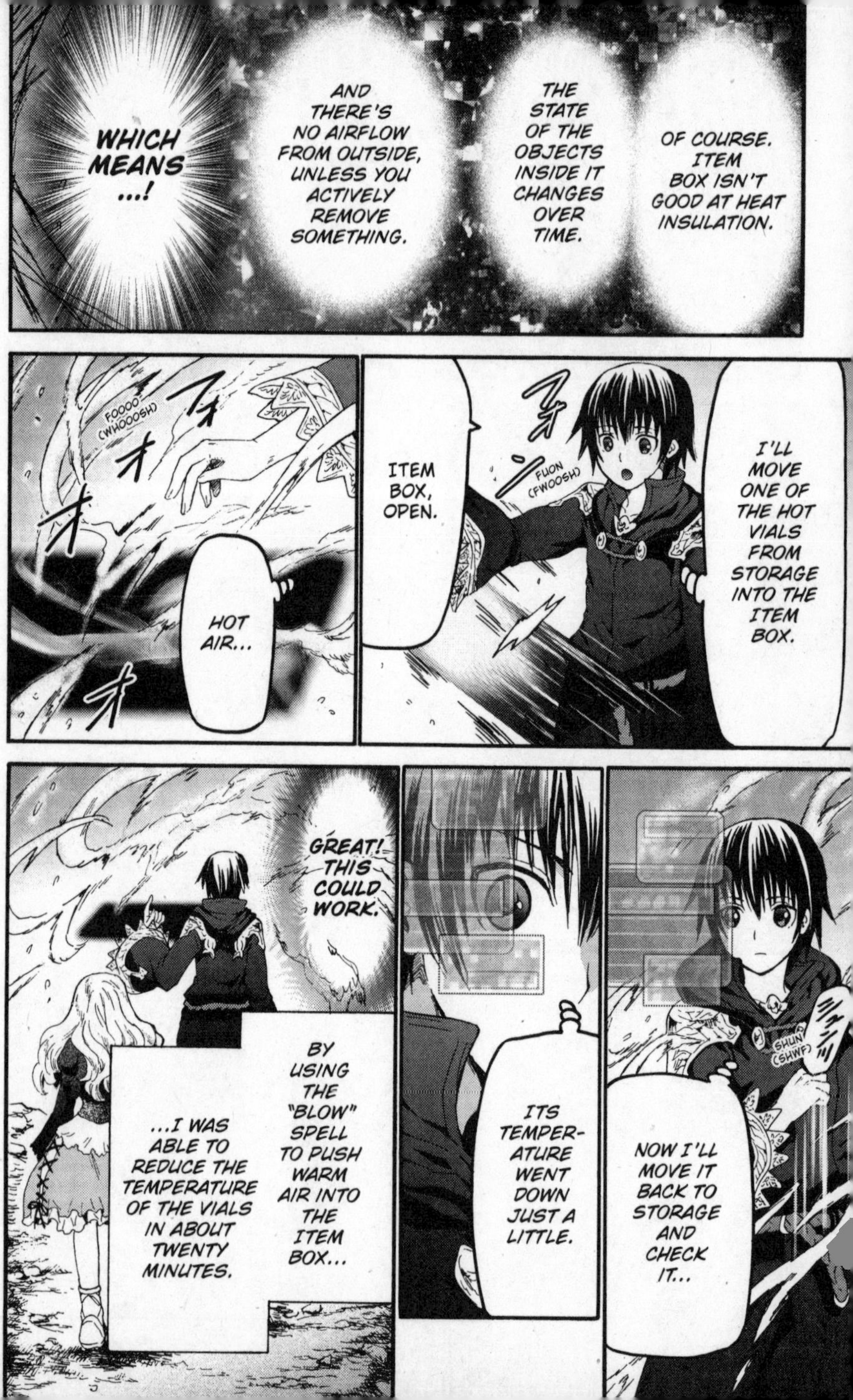
OF COURSE. ITEM BOX ISN'T GOOD AT HEAT INSULATION.
THE STATE OF THE OBJECTS INSIDE IT CHANGES OVER TIME.
AND THERE'S NO AIRFLOW FROM OUTSIDE, UNLESS YOU ACTIVELY REMOVE SOMETHING.
WHICH MEANS ...!
I'LL MOVE ONE OF THE HOT VIALS FROM STORAGE INTO THE ITEM BOX.
FUON (FWOOSH)
ITEM BOX, OPEN.
FOOOO (WHOOOSH)
HOT AIR...
SHUN (SHWF)
NOW I'LL MOVE IT BACK TO STORAGE AND CHECK IT...
ITS TEMPER-ATURE WENT DOWN JUST A LITTLE.
GREAT! THIS COULD WORK.
BY USING THE "BLOW" SPELL TO PUSH WARM AIR INTO THE ITEM BOX...
...I WAS ABLE TO REDUCE THE TEMPERATURE OF THE VIALS IN ABOUT TWENTY MINUTES.

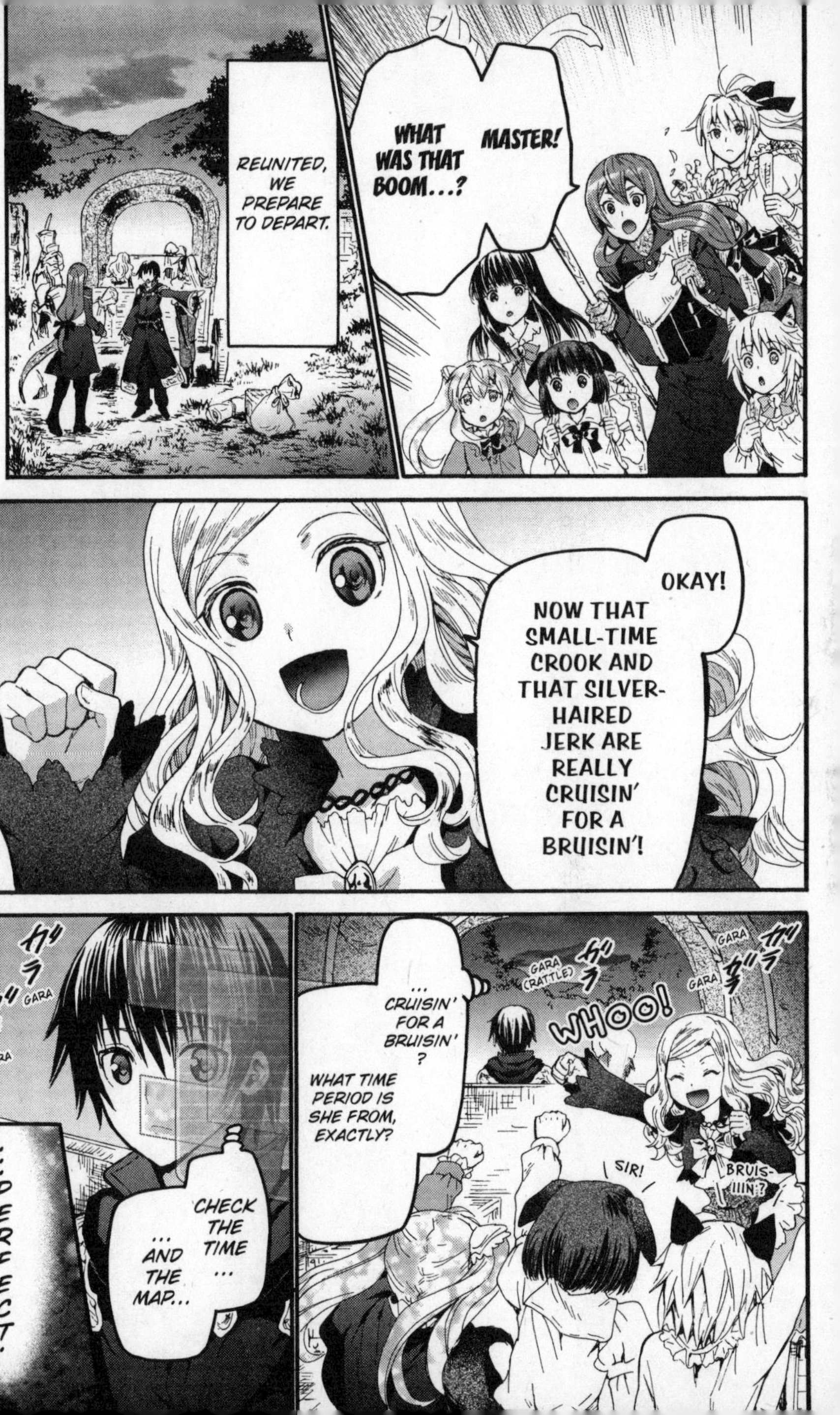
MASTER!
WHAT WAS THAT BOOM...?
REUNITED, WE PREPARE TO DEPART.
OKAY! NOW THAT SMALL-TIME CROOK AND THAT SILVER-HAIRED JERK ARE REALLY CRUISIN' FOR A BRUISIN'!
GARA
GARA
GARA (RATTLE)
... CRUISIN' FOR A BRUISIN'?
WHAT TIME PERIOD IS SHE FROM, EXACTLY?
WHOO!
SIR!
BRUIS-IIIN?
GARA
GARA
CHECK THE TIME...
... AND THE MAP...
...PERFECT.

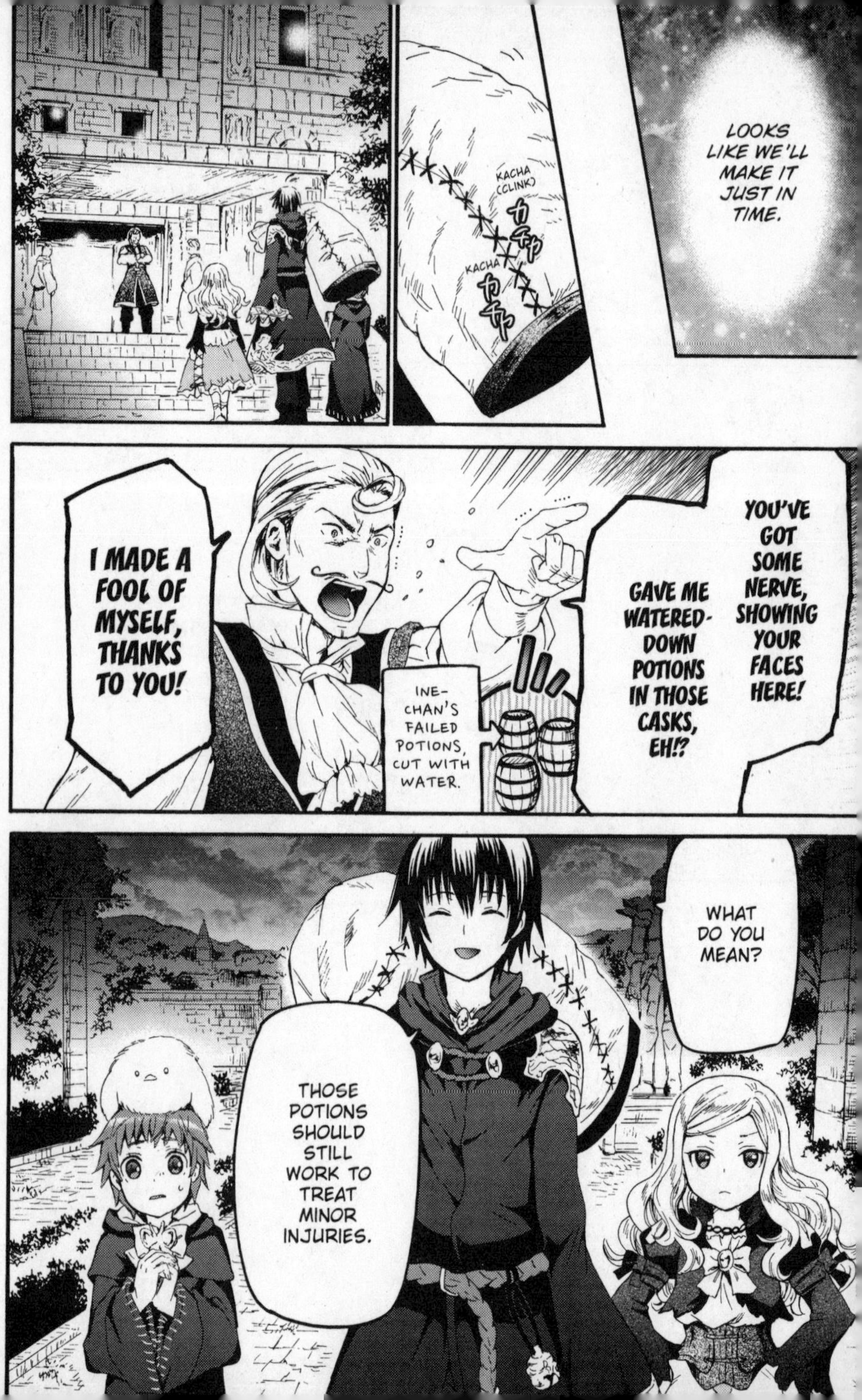
LOOKS LIKE WE'LL MAKE IT JUST IN TIME.
KACHA (CLINK)
カチャ
KACHA
カチャ
YOU'VE GOT SOME NERVE, SHOWING YOUR FACES HERE!
GAVE ME WATERED-DOWN POTIONS IN THOSE CASKS, EH!?
INE-CHAN'S FAILED POTIONS, CUT WITH WATER.
I MADE A FOOL OF MYSELF, THANKS TO YOU!
WHAT DO YOU MEAN?
THOSE POTIONS SHOULD STILL WORK TO TREAT MINOR INJURIES.

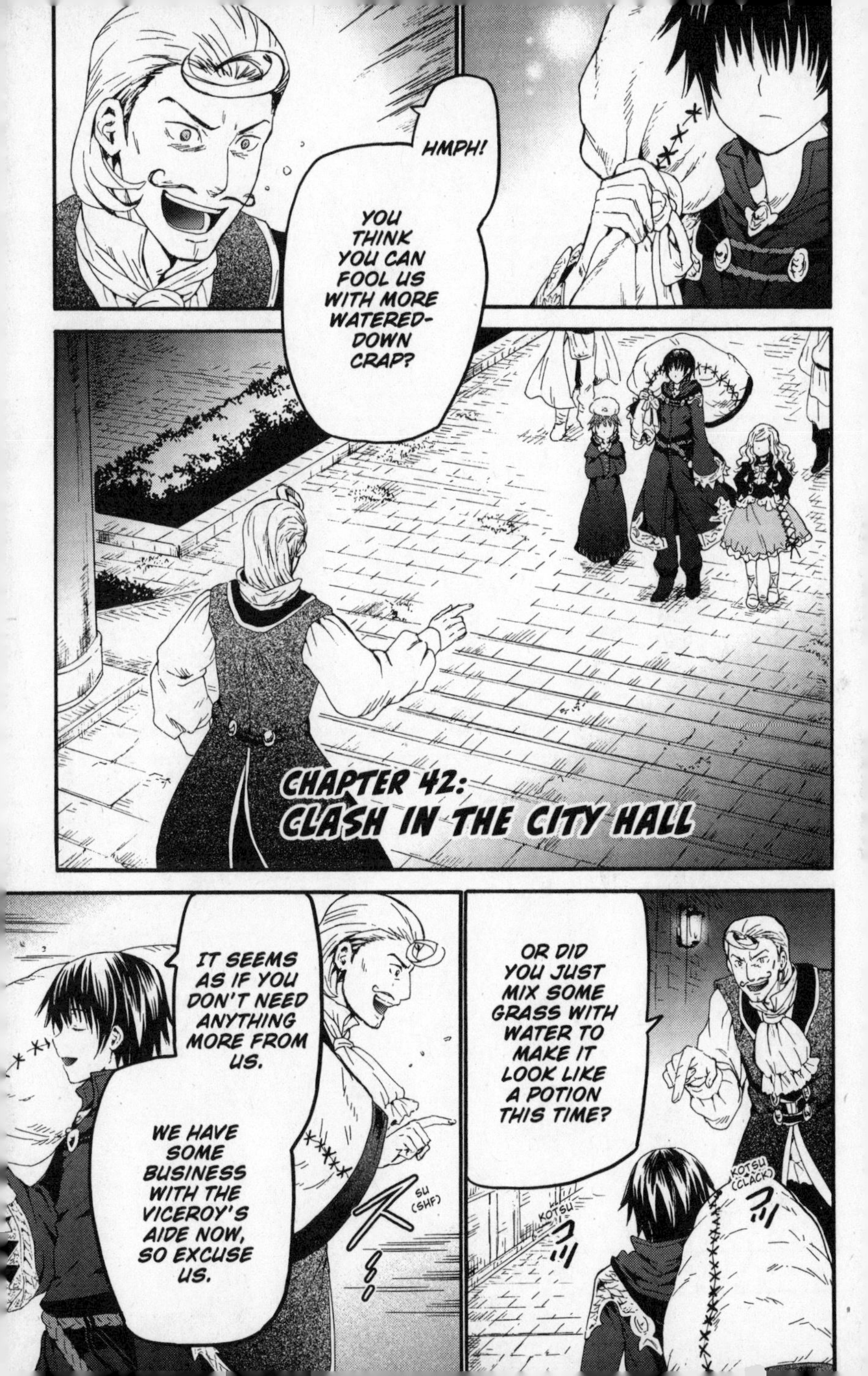
HMPH!
YOU THINK YOU CAN FOOL US WITH MORE WATERED-DOWN CRAP?
CHAPTER 42:
CLASH IN THE CITY HALL
OR DID YOU JUST MIX SOME GRASS WITH WATER TO MAKE IT LOOK LIKE A POTION THIS TIME?
KOTSU (CLACK)
KOTSU
IT SEEMS AS IF YOU DON'T NEED ANYTHING MORE FROM US.
WE HAVE SOME BUSINESS WITH THE VICEROY'S AIDE NOW, SO EXCUSE US.
SU (SHF)

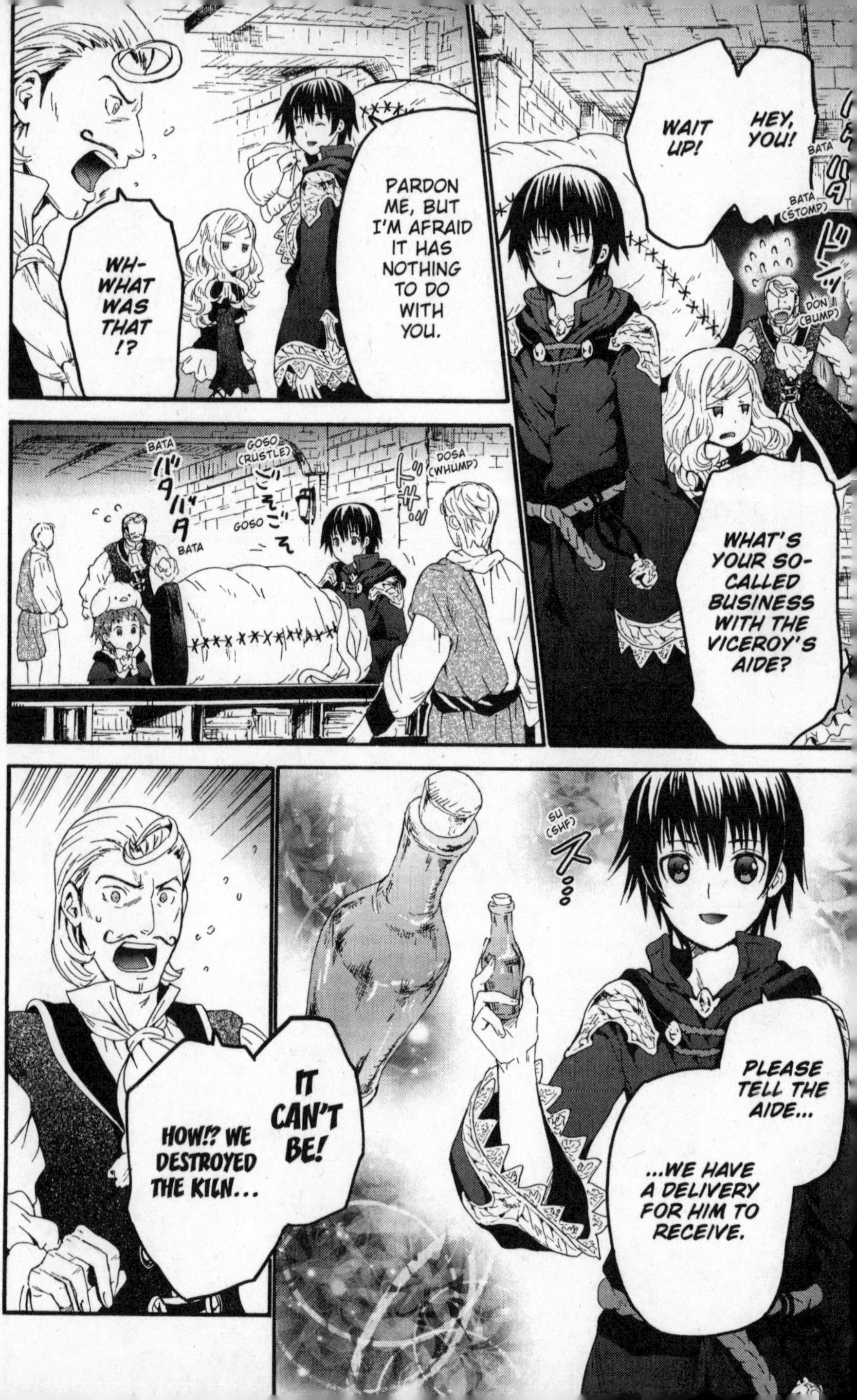
HEY, YOU!
WAIT UP!
BATA
BATA (STOMP)
DON (BUMP)
WHAT'S YOUR SO-CALLED BUSINESS WITH THE VICEROY'S AIDE?
PARDON ME, BUT I'M AFRAID IT HAS NOTHING TO DO WITH YOU.
WH-WHAT WAS THAT!?
DOSA (WHUMP)
GOSO (RUSTLE)
GOSO
BATA
BATA
SU (SHF)
PLEASE TELL THE AIDE...
...WE HAVE A DELIVERY FOR HIM TO RECEIVE.
IT CAN'T BE!
HOW!? WE DESTROYED THE KILN...

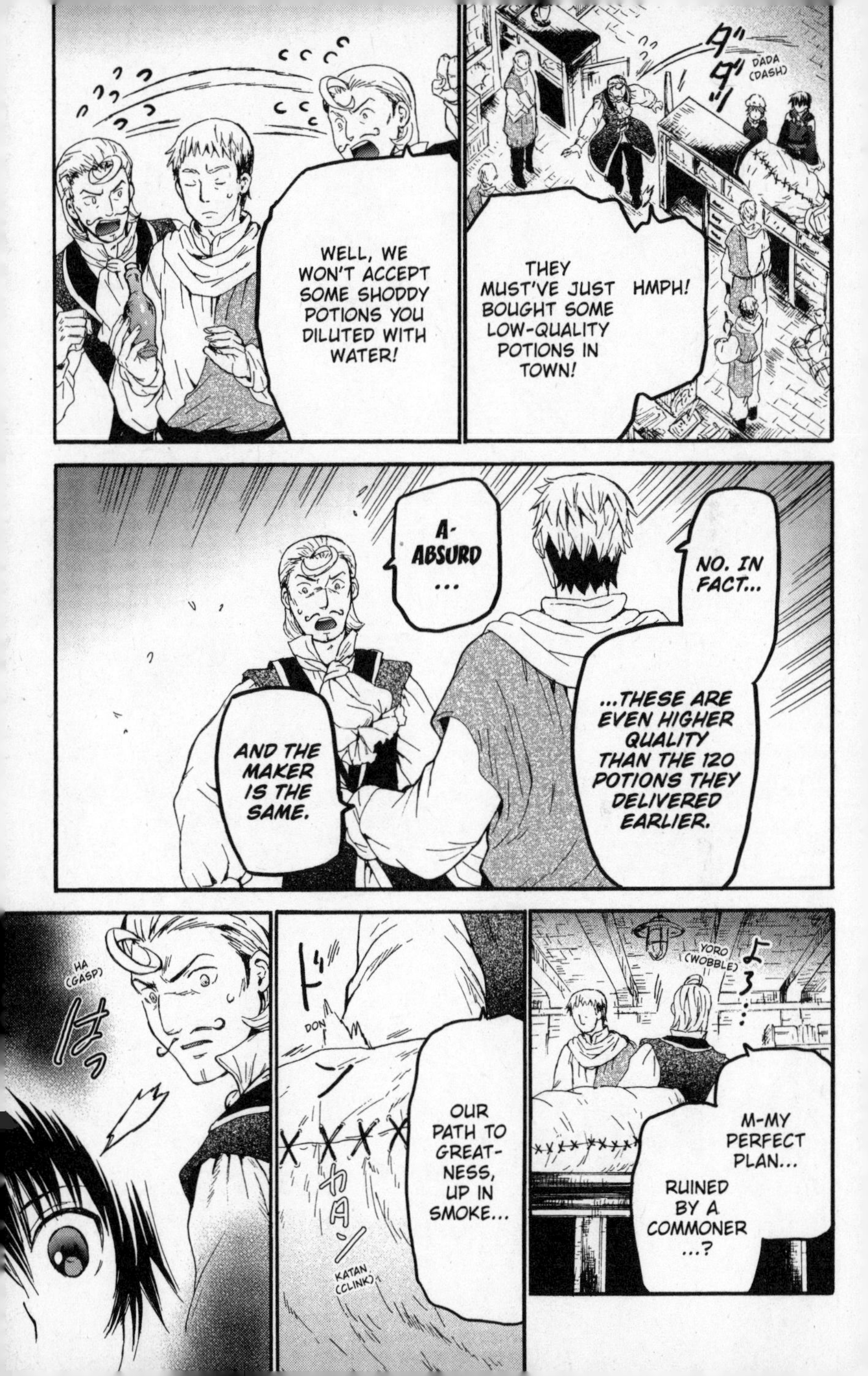
DADA (DASH)
HMPH!
THEY MUST'VE JUST BOUGHT SOME LOW-QUALITY POTIONS IN TOWN!
WELL, WE WON'T ACCEPT SOME SHODDY POTIONS YOU DILUTED WITH WATER!
NO. IN FACT...
...THESE ARE EVEN HIGHER QUALITY THAN THE 120 POTIONS THEY DELIVERED EARLIER.
A-ABSURD...
AND THE MAKER IS THE SAME.
YORO (WOBBLE)
M-MY PERFECT PLAN...
RUINED BY A COMMONER...?
DON
OUR PATH TO GREATNESS, UP IN SMOKE...
KATAN (CLINK)
HA (GASP)

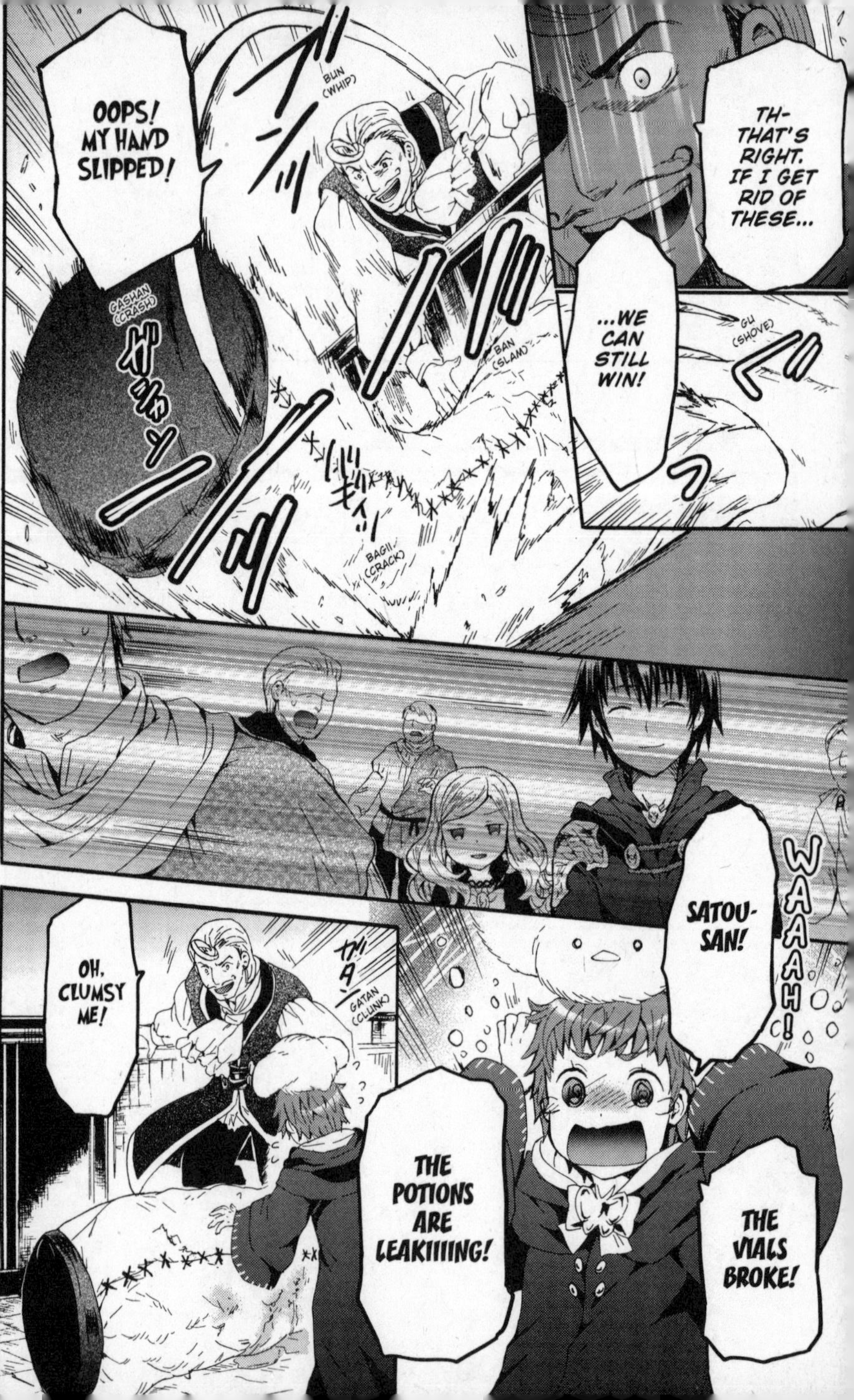
TH-THAT'S RIGHT. IF I GET RID OF THESE...
...WE CAN STILL WIN!
GU (SHOVE)
BUN (WHIP)
OOPS! MY HAND SLIPPED!
BAN (SLAM)
GASHAN (CRASH)
BAGII (CRACK)
WAAAAH!
SATOU-SAN!
THE VIALS BROKE!
THE POTIONS ARE LEAKIIIING!
GATAN (CLUNK)
OH, CLUMSY ME!

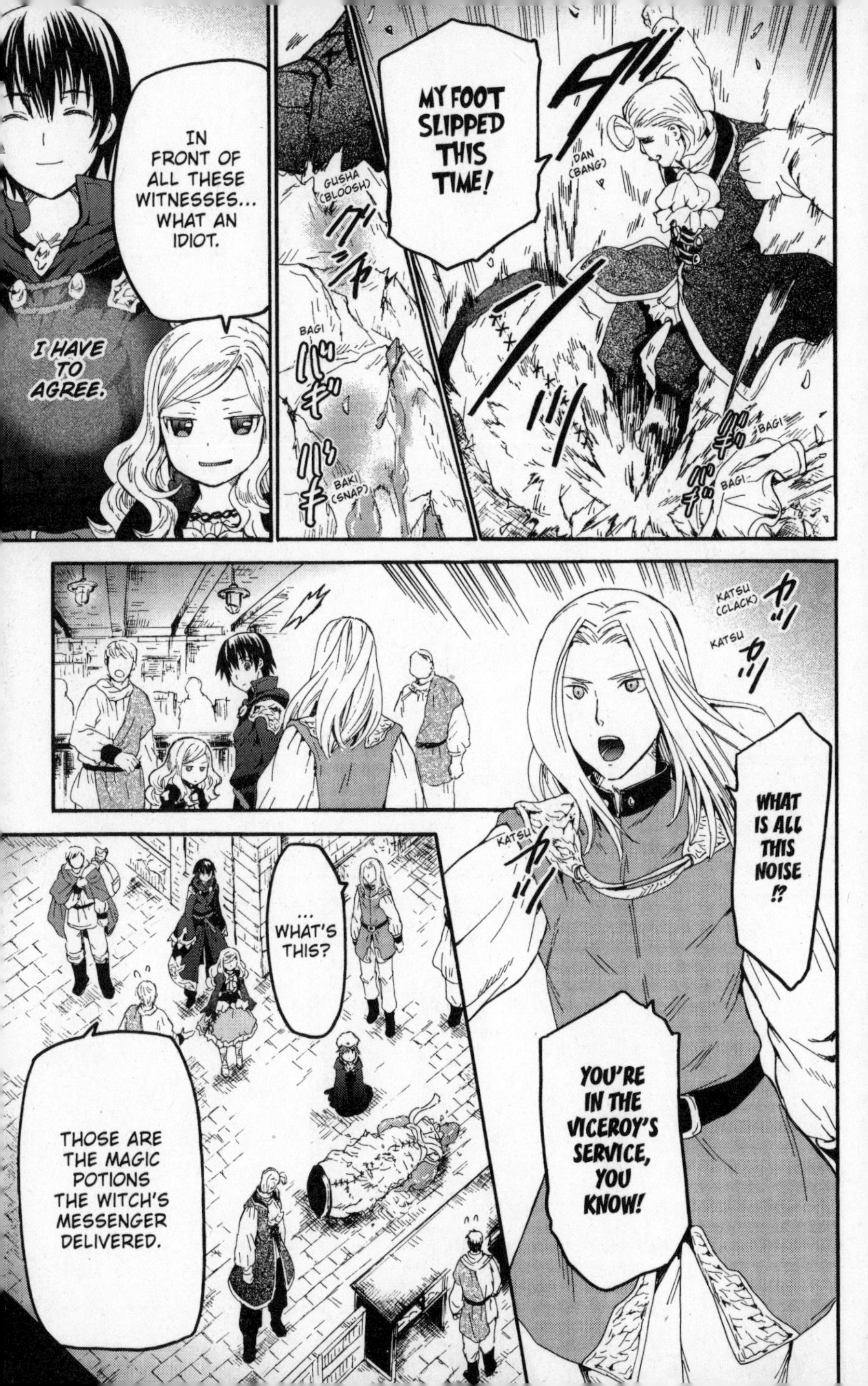
DAN (BANG)
BAGI
BAGI
MY FOOT SLIPPED THIS TIME!
GUSHA (BLOOSH)
BAGI
BAKI (SNAP)
IN FRONT OF ALL THESE WITNESSES... WHAT AN IDIOT.
I HAVE TO AGREE.
KATSU (CLACK)
KATSU
KATSU
WHAT IS ALL THIS NOISE!?
YOU'RE IN THE VICEROY'S SERVICE, YOU KNOW!
...WHAT'S THIS?
THOSE ARE THE MAGIC POTIONS THE WITCH'S MESSENGER DELIVERED.

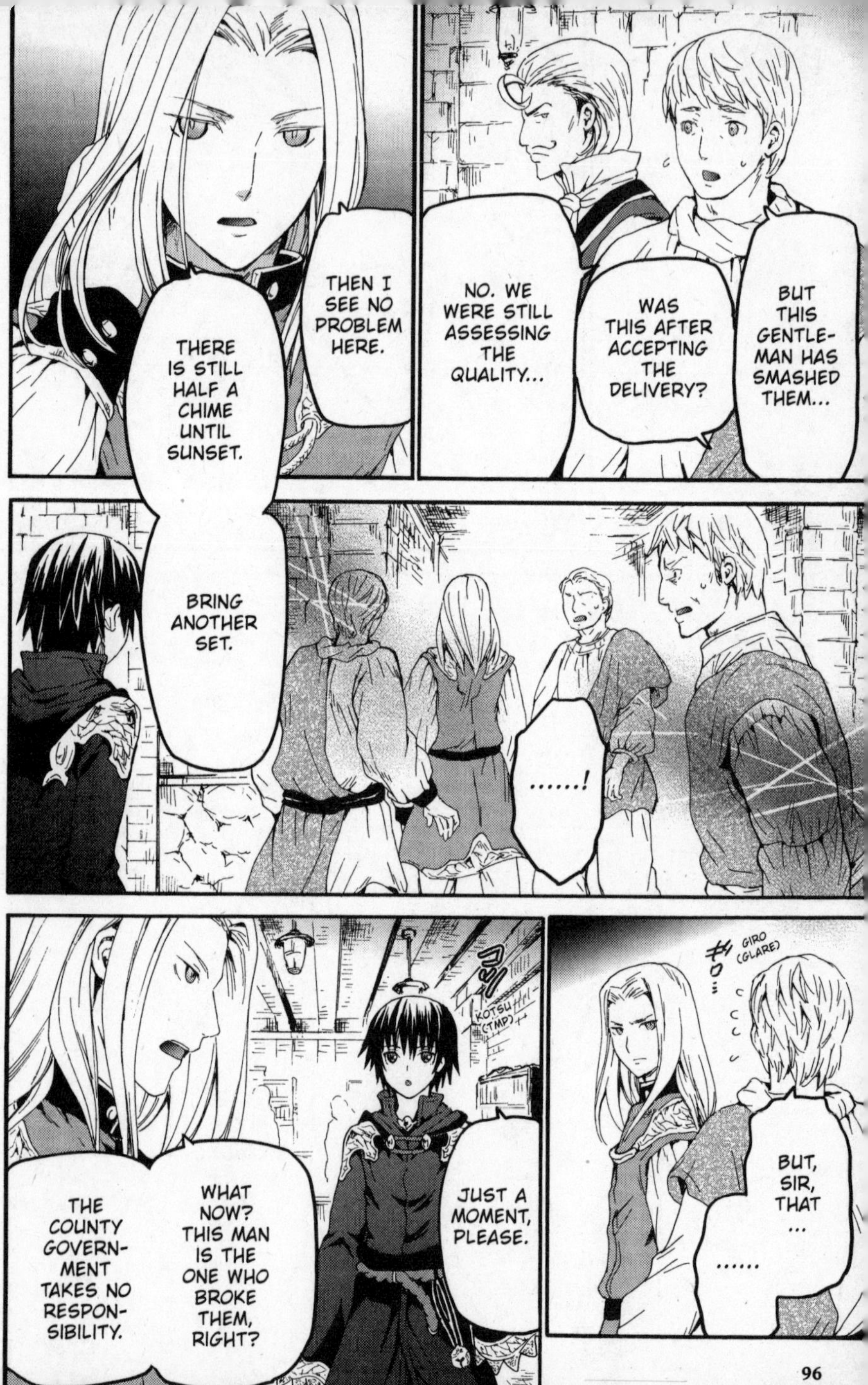
BUT THIS GENTLEMAN HAS SMASHED THEM...
WAS THIS AFTER ACCEPTING THE DELIVERY?
NO. WE WERE STILL ASSESSING THE QUALITY...
THEN I SEE NO PROBLEM HERE.
THERE IS STILL HALF A CHIME UNTIL SUNSET.
BRING ANOTHER SET.
......!
GIRO (GLARE)
BUT, SIR, THAT ...
......
KOTSU (TMP)
JUST A MOMENT, PLEASE.
WHAT NOW? THIS MAN IS THE ONE WHO BROKE THEM, RIGHT?
THE COUNTY GOVERNMENT TAKES NO RESPONSIBILITY.

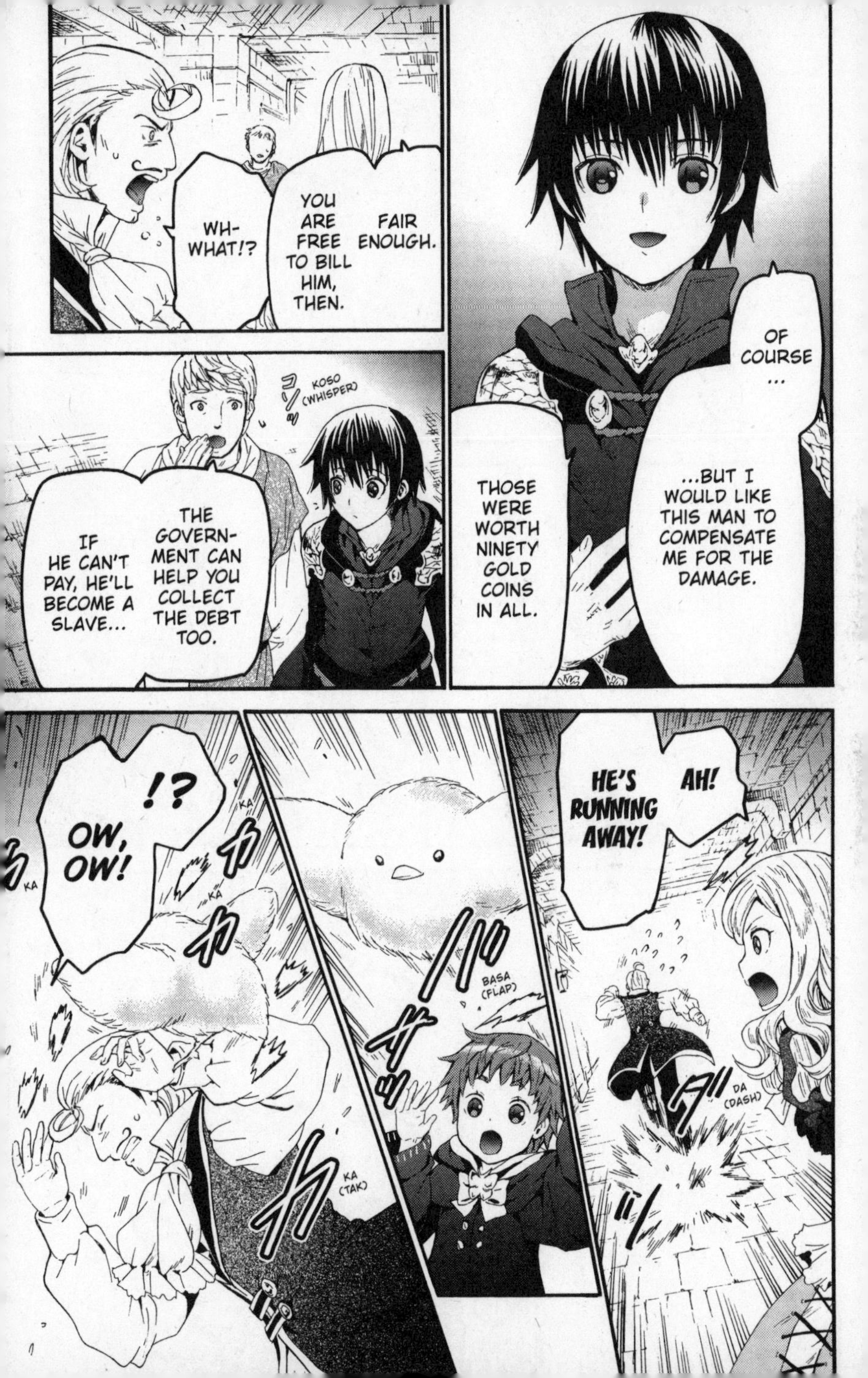
OF COURSE ...
...BUT I WOULD LIKE THIS MAN TO COMPENSATE ME FOR THE DAMAGE.
THOSE WERE WORTH NINETY GOLD COINS IN ALL.
FAIR ENOUGH.
YOU ARE FREE TO BILL HIM, THEN.
WH-WHAT!?
KOSO (WHISPER)
THE GOVERNMENT CAN HELP YOU COLLECT THE DEBT TOO.
IF HE CAN'T PAY, HE'LL BECOME A SLAVE...
AH!
HE'S RUNNING AWAY!
DA (DASH)
BASA (FLAP)
KA (TAK)
!?
OW, OW!
KA
KA
KA

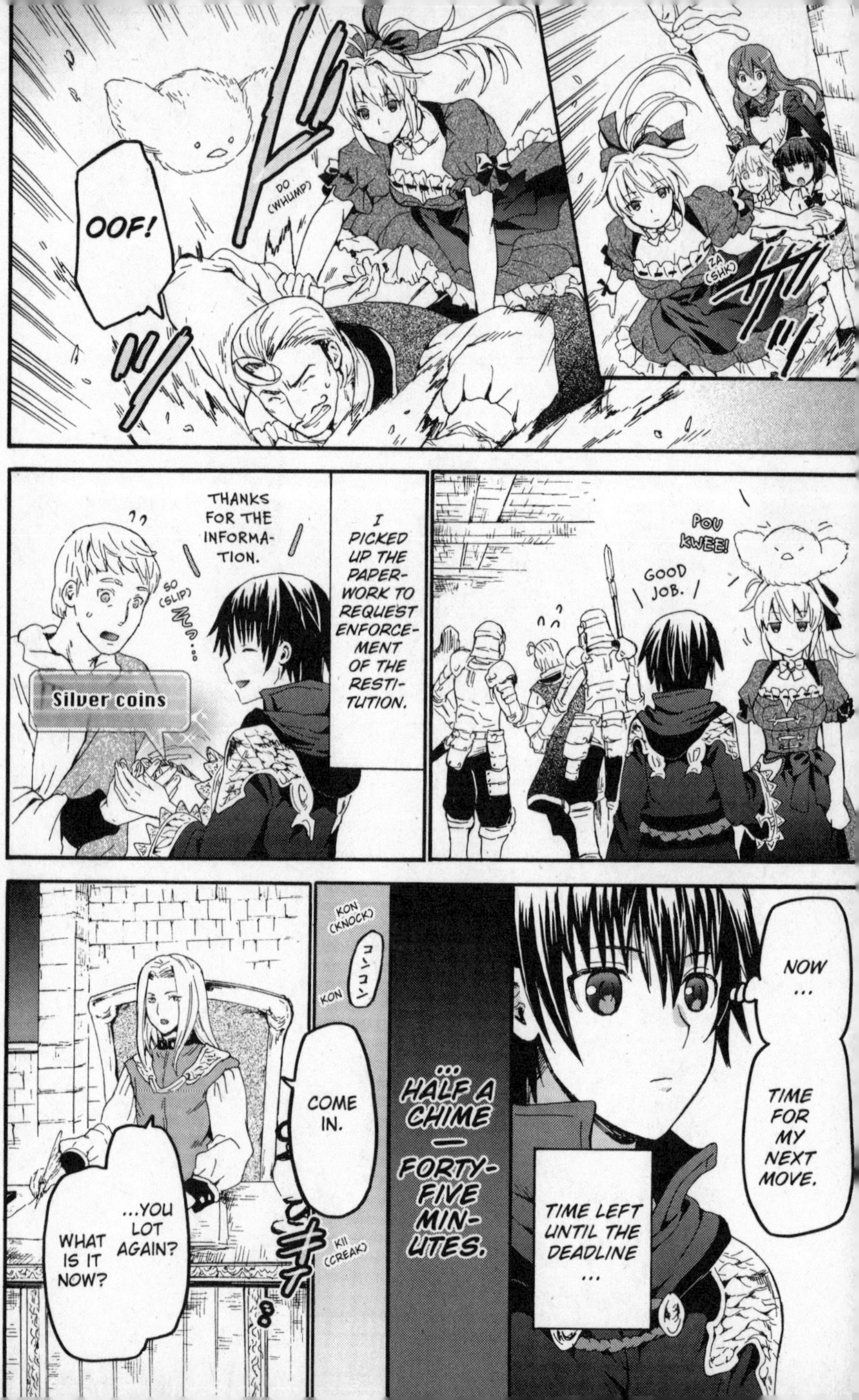
ZA (SHK)
DO (WHUMP)
OOF!
POU KWEE!
GOOD JOB.
I PICKED UP THE PAPER-WORK TO REQUEST ENFORCE-MENT OF THE RESTI-TUTION.
THANKS FOR THE INFORMA-TION.
SO (SLIP)
Silver coins
NOW ...
TIME FOR MY NEXT MOVE.
TIME LEFT UNTIL THE DEADLINE ...
...HALF A CHIME — FORTY-FIVE MIN-UTES.
KON (KNOCK)
コンコン
KON
COME IN.
KII (CREAK)
...YOU LOT AGAIN?
WHAT IS IT NOW?

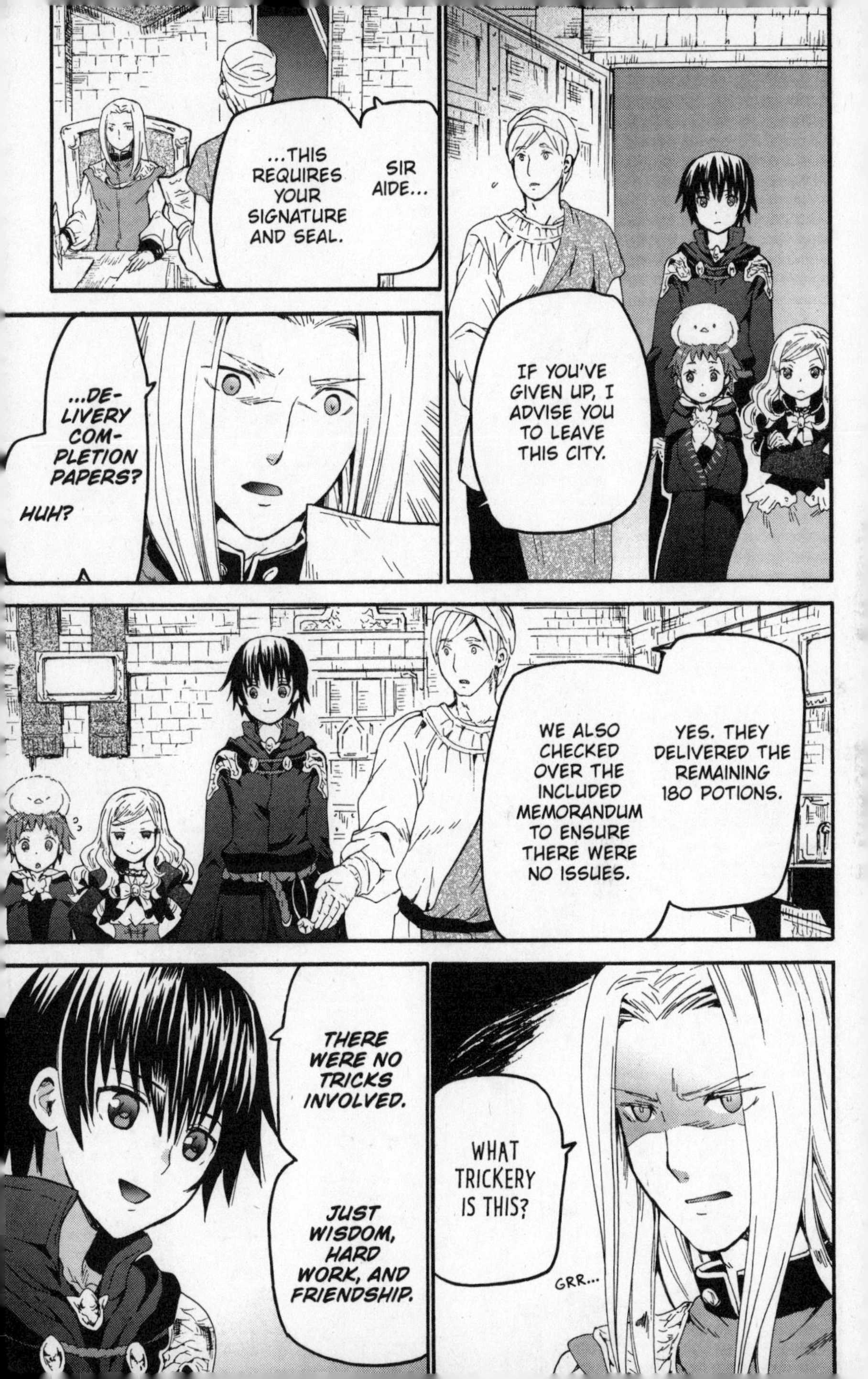
IF YOU'VE GIVEN UP, I ADVISE YOU TO LEAVE THIS CITY.
SIR AIDE...
...THIS REQUIRES YOUR SIGNATURE AND SEAL.
...DE-LIVERY COM-PLETION PAPERS?
HUH?
YES. THEY DELIVERED THE REMAINING 180 POTIONS.
WE ALSO CHECKED OVER THE INCLUDED MEMORANDUM TO ENSURE THERE WERE NO ISSUES.
WHAT TRICKERY IS THIS?
GRR...
THERE WERE NO TRICKS INVOLVED.
JUST WISDOM, HARD WORK, AND FRIENDSHIP.

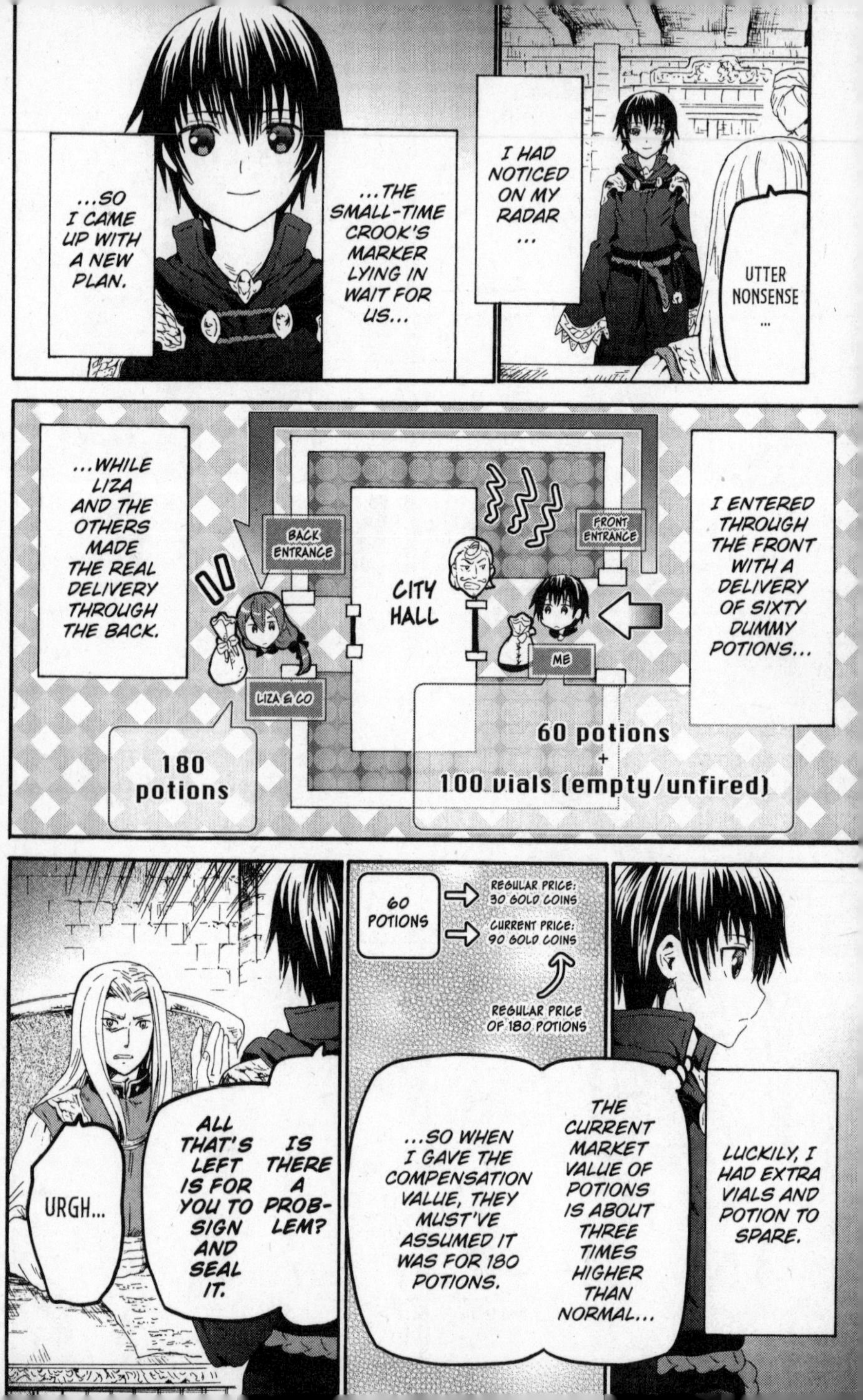
I HAD NOTICED ON MY RADAR ...
UTTER NONSENSE ...
...THE SMALL-TIME CROOK'S MARKER LYING IN WAIT FOR US...
...SO I CAME UP WITH A NEW PLAN.
I ENTERED THROUGH THE FRONT WITH A DELIVERY OF SIXTY DUMMY POTIONS...
FRONT ENTRANCE
CITY HALL
ME
60 potions + 100 vials (empty/unfired)
BACK ENTRANCE
LIZA & CO
180 potions
...WHILE LIZA AND THE OTHERS MADE THE REAL DELIVERY THROUGH THE BACK.
LUCKILY, I HAD EXTRA VIALS AND POTION TO SPARE.
60 POTIONS
REGULAR PRICE: 30 GOLD COINS
CURRENT PRICE: 90 GOLD COINS
REGULAR PRICE OF 180 POTIONS
THE CURRENT MARKET VALUE OF POTIONS IS ABOUT THREE TIMES HIGHER THAN NORMAL...
...SO WHEN I GAVE THE COMPENSATION VALUE, THEY MUST'VE ASSUMED IT WAS FOR 180 POTIONS.
IS THERE A PROBLEM?
ALL THAT'S LEFT IS FOR YOU TO SIGN AND SEAL IT.
URGH...

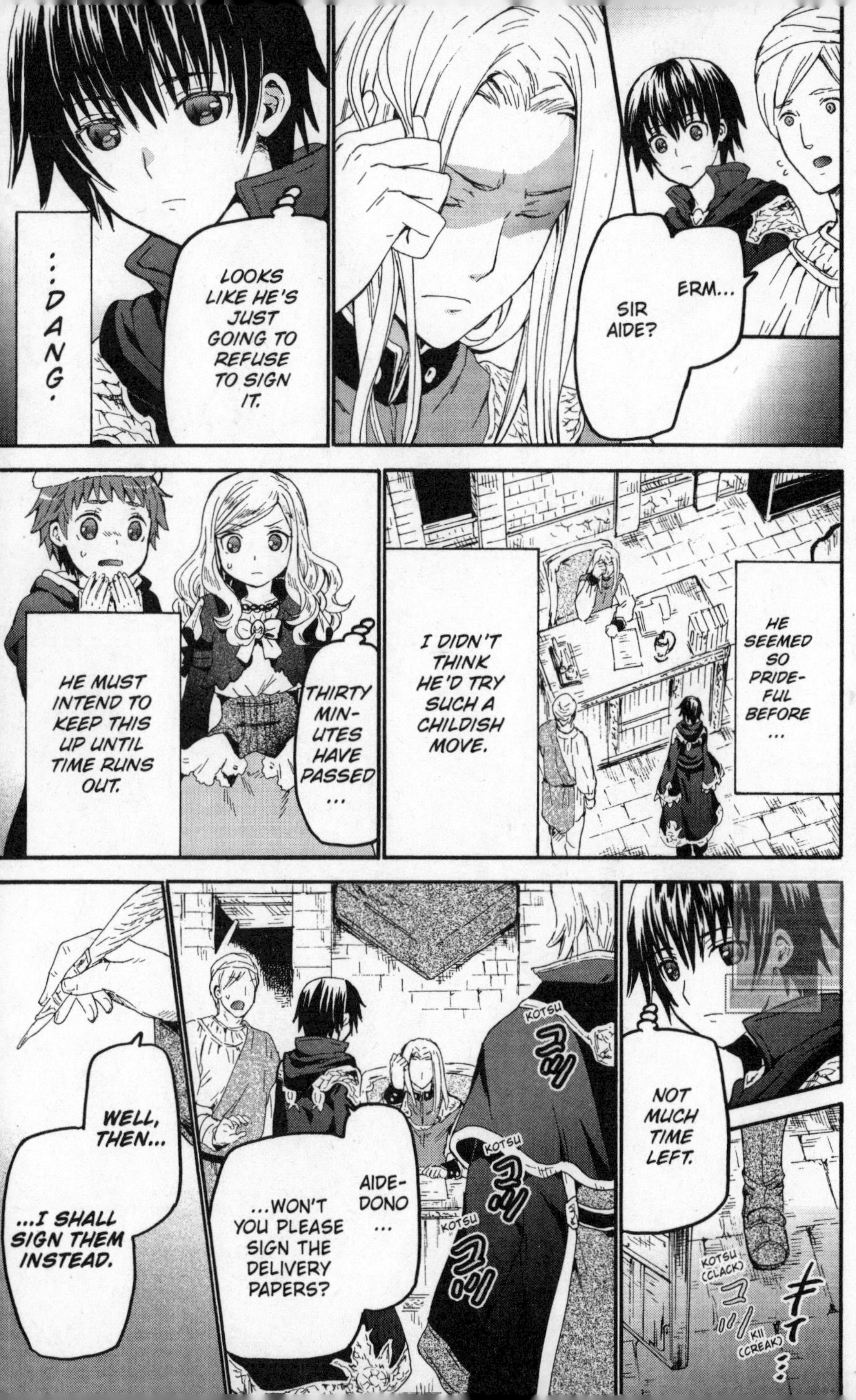
ERM...
SIR AIDE?
LOOKS LIKE HE'S JUST GOING TO REFUSE TO SIGN IT.
...DANG.
HE SEEMED SO PRIDE-FUL BEFORE...
I DIDN'T THINK HE'D TRY SUCH A CHILDISH MOVE.
THIRTY MIN-UTES HAVE PASSED...
HE MUST INTEND TO KEEP THIS UP UNTIL TIME RUNS OUT.
NOT MUCH TIME LEFT.
KOTSU (CLACK)
KII (CREAK)
KOTSU
KOTSU
KOTSU
AIDE-DONO...
...WON'T YOU PLEASE SIGN THE DELIVERY PAPERS?
WELL, THEN...
...I SHALL SIGN THEM INSTEAD.

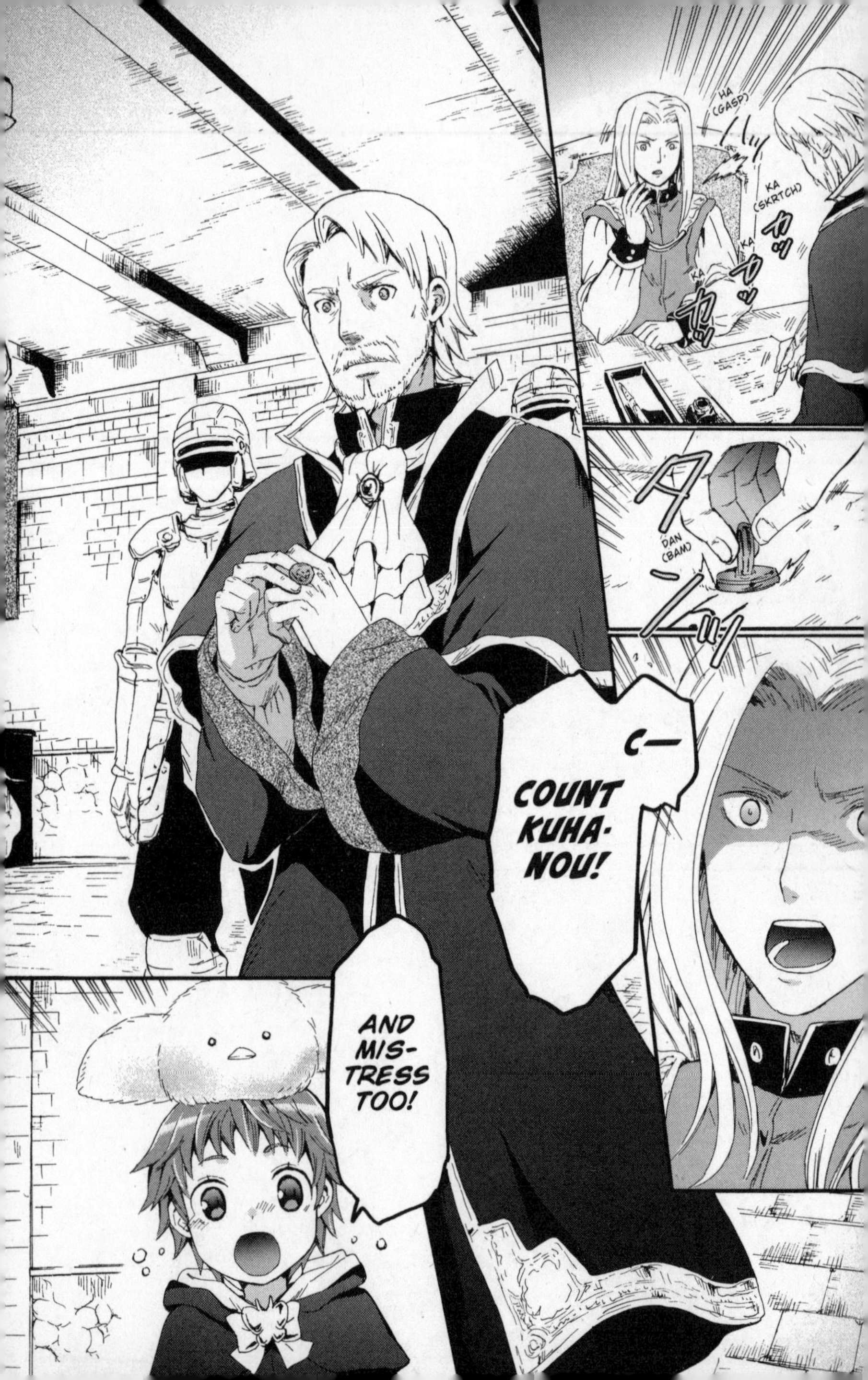
HA (GASP)
KA (SKRTCH)
KA
KA
DAN (BAM)
C— COUNT KUHA-NOU!
AND MIS-TRESS TOO!

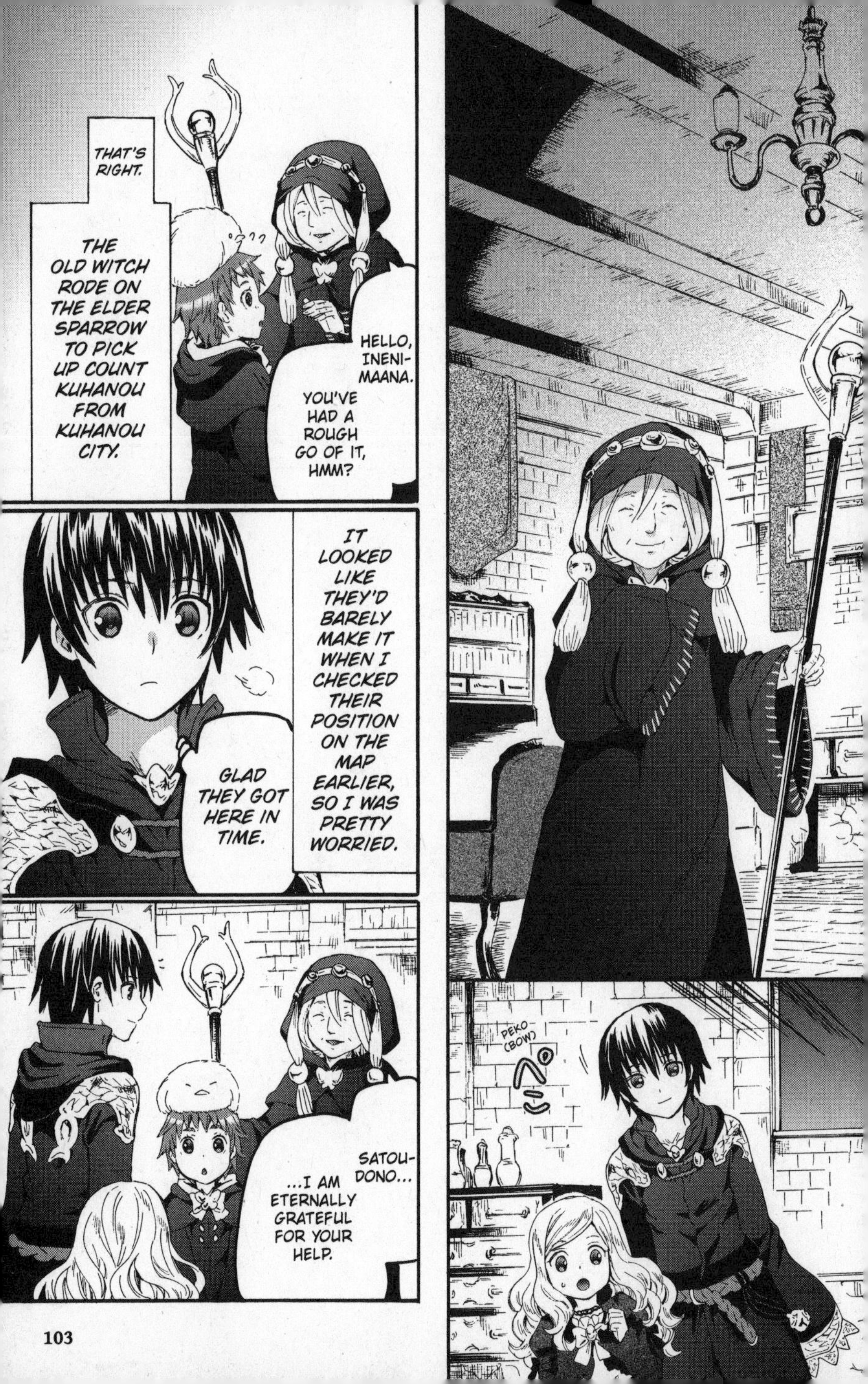
THAT'S RIGHT.
THE OLD WITCH RODE ON THE ELDER SPARROW TO PICK UP COUNT KUHANOU FROM KUHANOU CITY.
HELLO, INENI-MAANA.
YOU'VE HAD A ROUGH GO OF IT, HMM?
IT LOOKED LIKE THEY'D BARELY MAKE IT WHEN I CHECKED THEIR POSITION ON THE MAP EARLIER, SO I WAS PRETTY WORRIED.
GLAD THEY GOT HERE IN TIME.
SATOU-DONO...
...I AM ETERNALLY GRATEFUL FOR YOUR HELP.
PEKO (BOW)

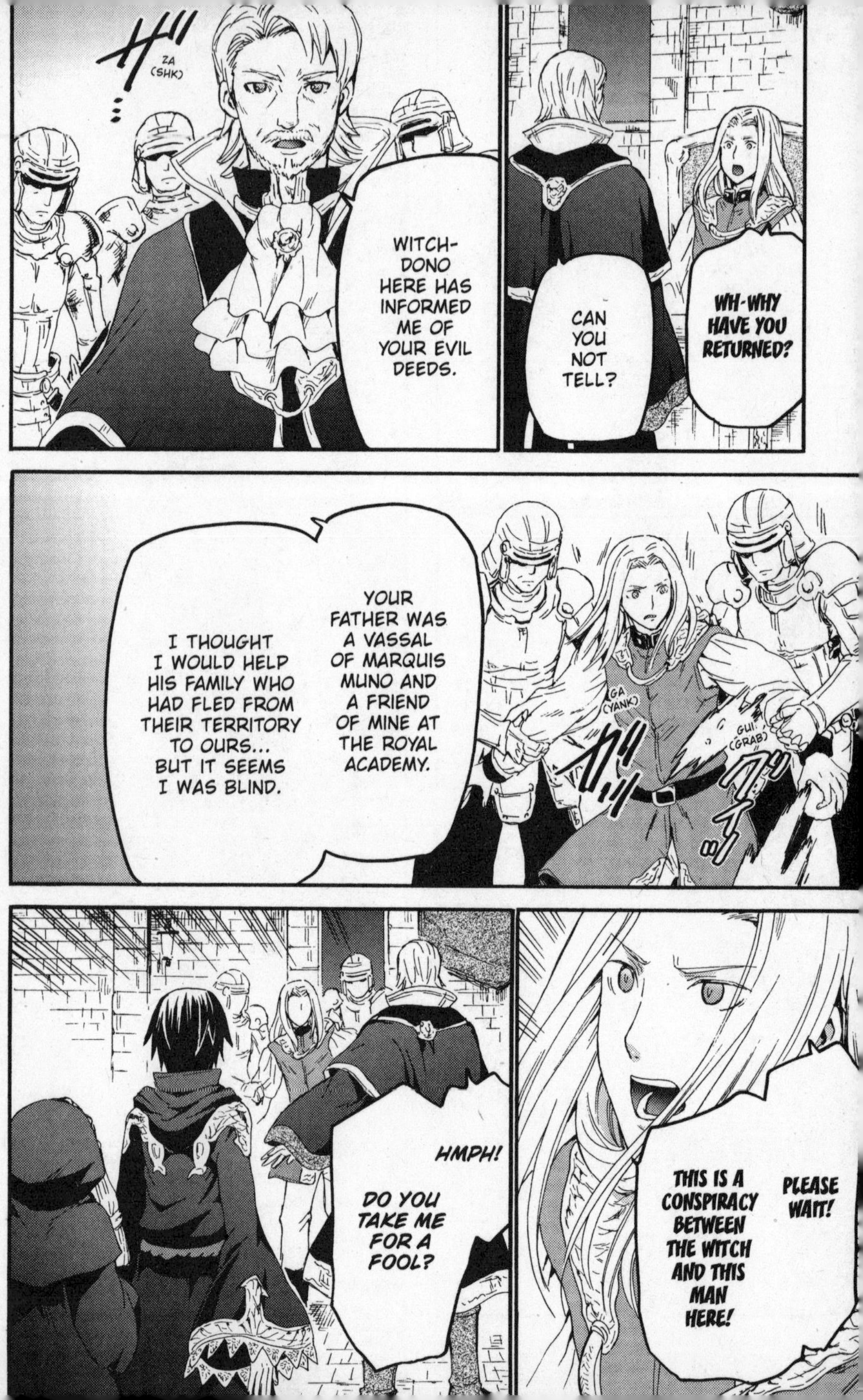
WH-WHY HAVE YOU RETURNED?
CAN YOU NOT TELL?
ZA (SHK)
WITCH-DONO HERE HAS INFORMED ME OF YOUR EVIL DEEDS.
GUI (GRAB)
GA (YANK)
YOUR FATHER WAS A VASSAL OF MARQUIS MUNO AND A FRIEND OF MINE AT THE ROYAL ACADEMY.
I THOUGHT I WOULD HELP HIS FAMILY WHO HAD FLED FROM THEIR TERRITORY TO OURS... BUT IT SEEMS I WAS BLIND.
PLEASE WAIT!
THIS IS A CONSPIRACY BETWEEN THE WITCH AND THIS MAN HERE!
HMPH!
DO YOU TAKE ME FOR A FOOL?

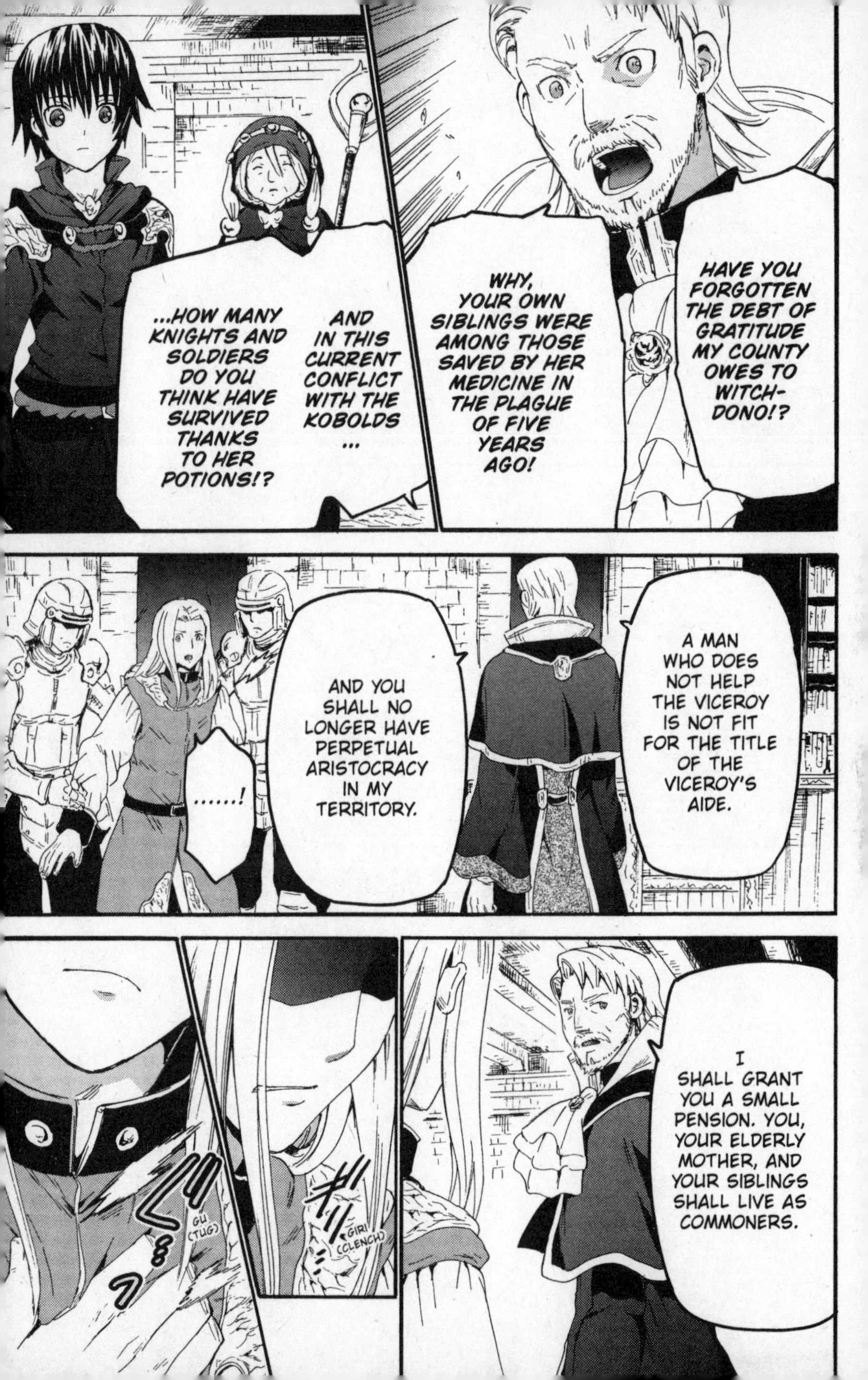
HAVE YOU FORGOTTEN THE DEBT OF GRATITUDE MY COUNTY OWES TO WITCH-DONO!?
WHY, YOUR OWN SIBLINGS WERE AMONG THOSE SAVED BY HER MEDICINE IN THE PLAGUE OF FIVE YEARS AGO!
AND IN THIS CURRENT CONFLICT WITH THE KOBOLDS ...
...HOW MANY KNIGHTS AND SOLDIERS DO YOU THINK HAVE SURVIVED THANKS TO HER POTIONS!?
A MAN WHO DOES NOT HELP THE VICEROY IS NOT FIT FOR THE TITLE OF THE VICEROY'S AIDE.
AND YOU SHALL NO LONGER HAVE PERPETUAL ARISTOCRACY IN MY TERRITORY.
......!
I SHALL GRANT YOU A SMALL PENSION. YOU, YOUR ELDERLY MOTHER, AND YOUR SIBLINGS SHALL LIVE AS COMMONERS.
GIRI (CLENCH)
GU (TUG)

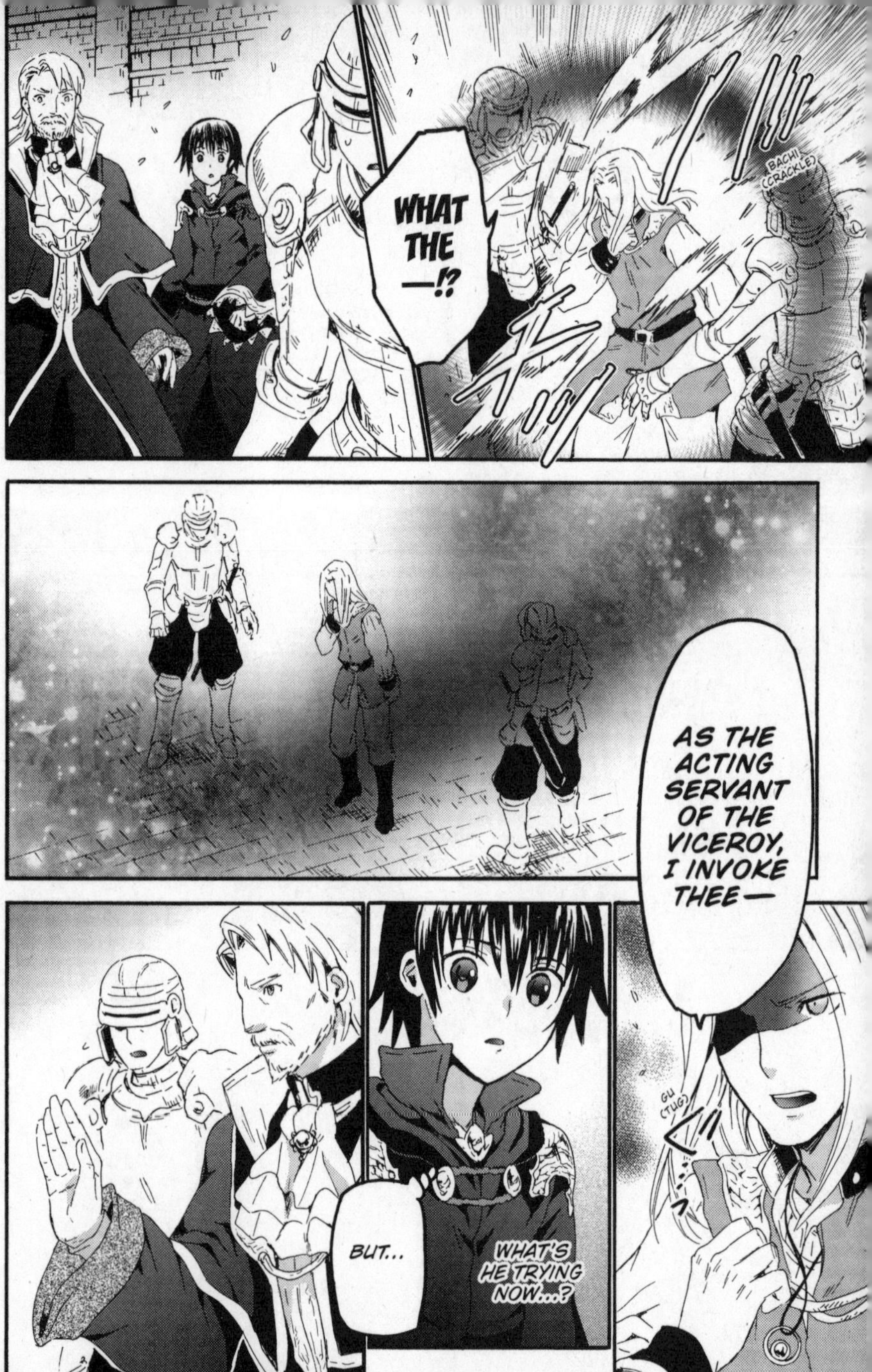
BACHI (CRACKLE)
WHAT THE—!?
AS THE ACTING SERVANT OF THE VICEROY, I INVOKE THEE—
GU (TUG)
WHAT'S HE TRYING NOW...?
BUT...

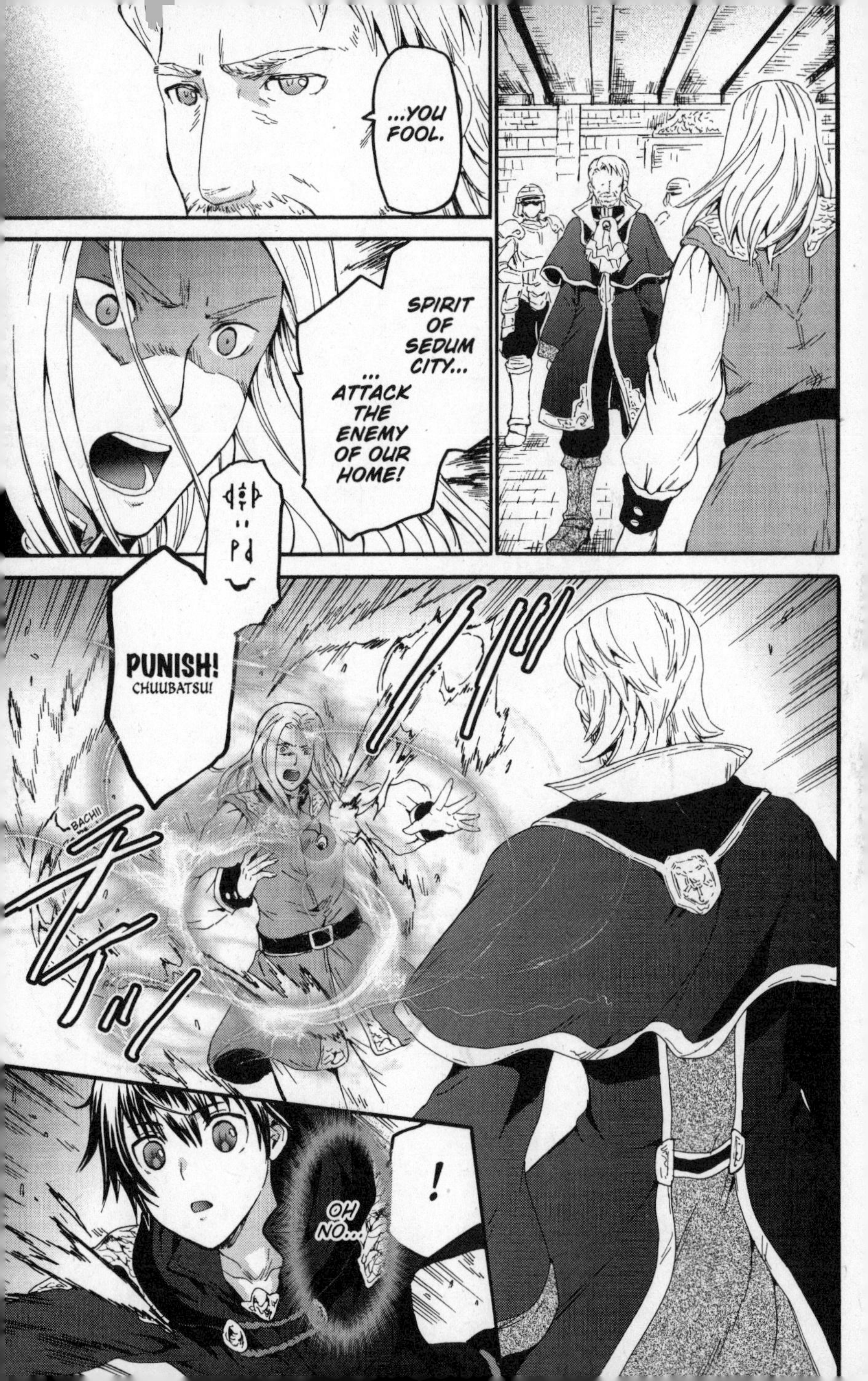

...YOU FOOL.
SPIRIT OF SEDUM CITY...
...ATTACK THE ENEMY OF OUR HOME!
PUNISH!
CHUUBATSU!
BACHII
!
OH NO...

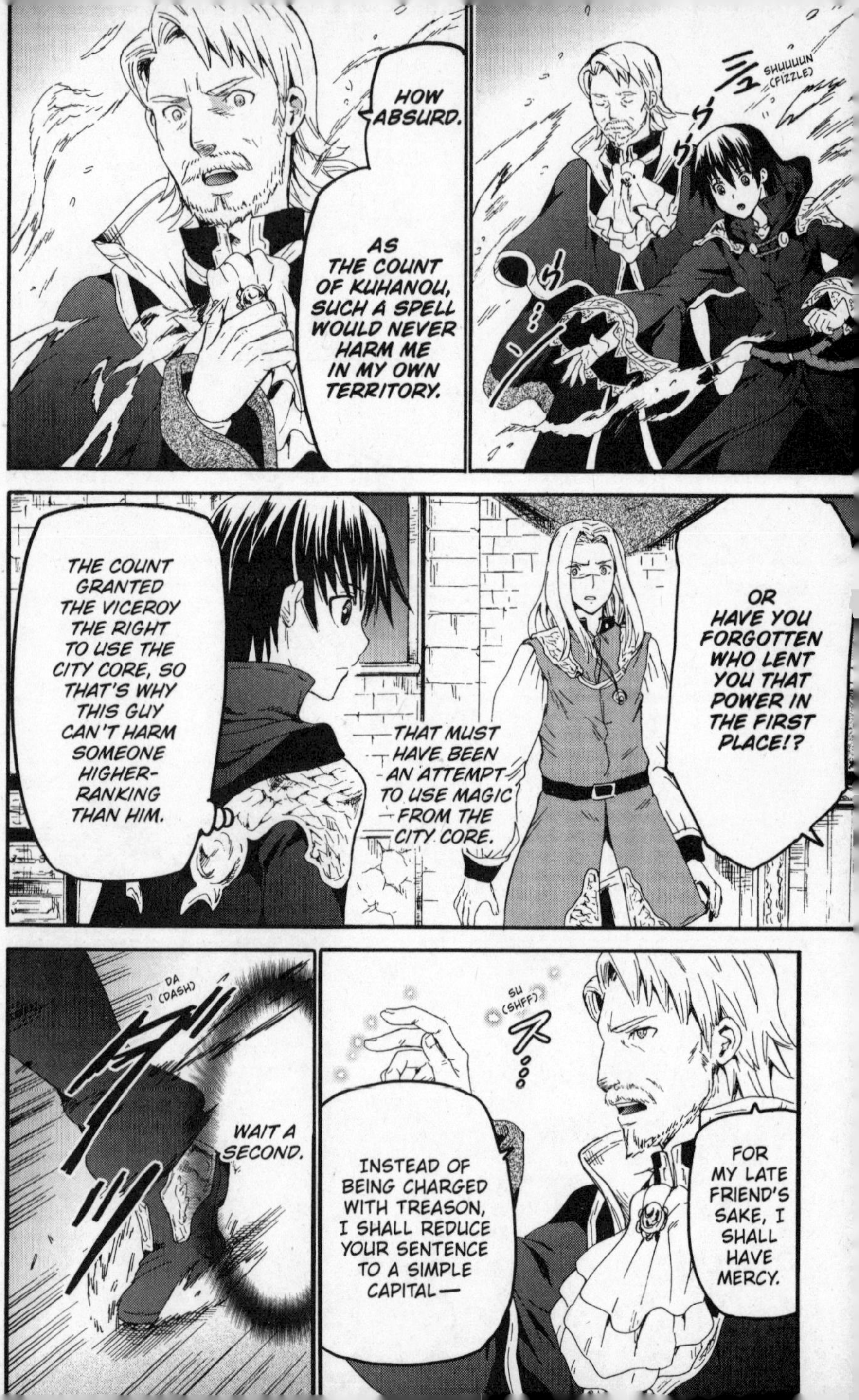
SHUUUUN (FIZZLE)
HOW ABSURD.
AS THE COUNT OF KUHANOU, SUCH A SPELL WOULD NEVER HARM ME IN MY OWN TERRITORY.
OR HAVE YOU FORGOTTEN WHO LENT YOU THAT POWER IN THE FIRST PLACE!?
THAT MUST HAVE BEEN AN ATTEMPT TO USE MAGIC FROM THE CITY CORE.
THE COUNT GRANTED THE VICEROY THE RIGHT TO USE THE CITY CORE, SO THAT'S WHY THIS GUY CAN'T HARM SOMEONE HIGHER-RANKING THAN HIM.
SU (SHFF)
FOR MY LATE FRIEND'S SAKE, I SHALL HAVE MERCY.
INSTEAD OF BEING CHARGED WITH TREASON, I SHALL REDUCE YOUR SENTENCE TO A SIMPLE CAPITAL—
DA (DASH)
WAIT A SECOND.

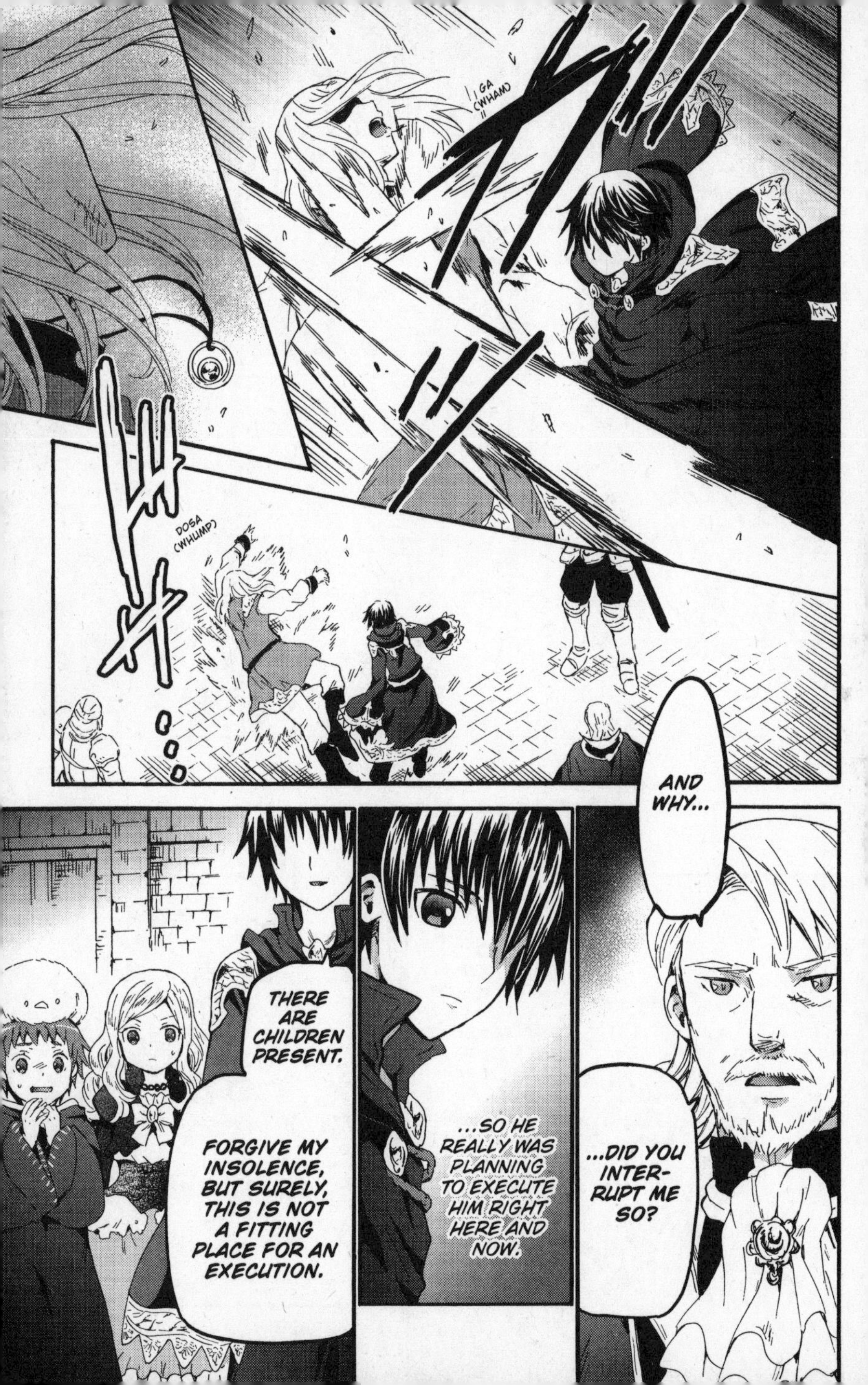
GA (WHAM)
DOSA (WHUMP)
AND WHY...
...DID YOU INTER-RUPT ME SO?
...SO HE REALLY WAS PLANNING TO EXECUTE HIM RIGHT HERE AND NOW.
THERE ARE CHILDREN PRESENT.
FORGIVE MY INSOLENCE, BUT SURELY, THIS IS NOT A FITTING PLACE FOR AN EXECUTION.

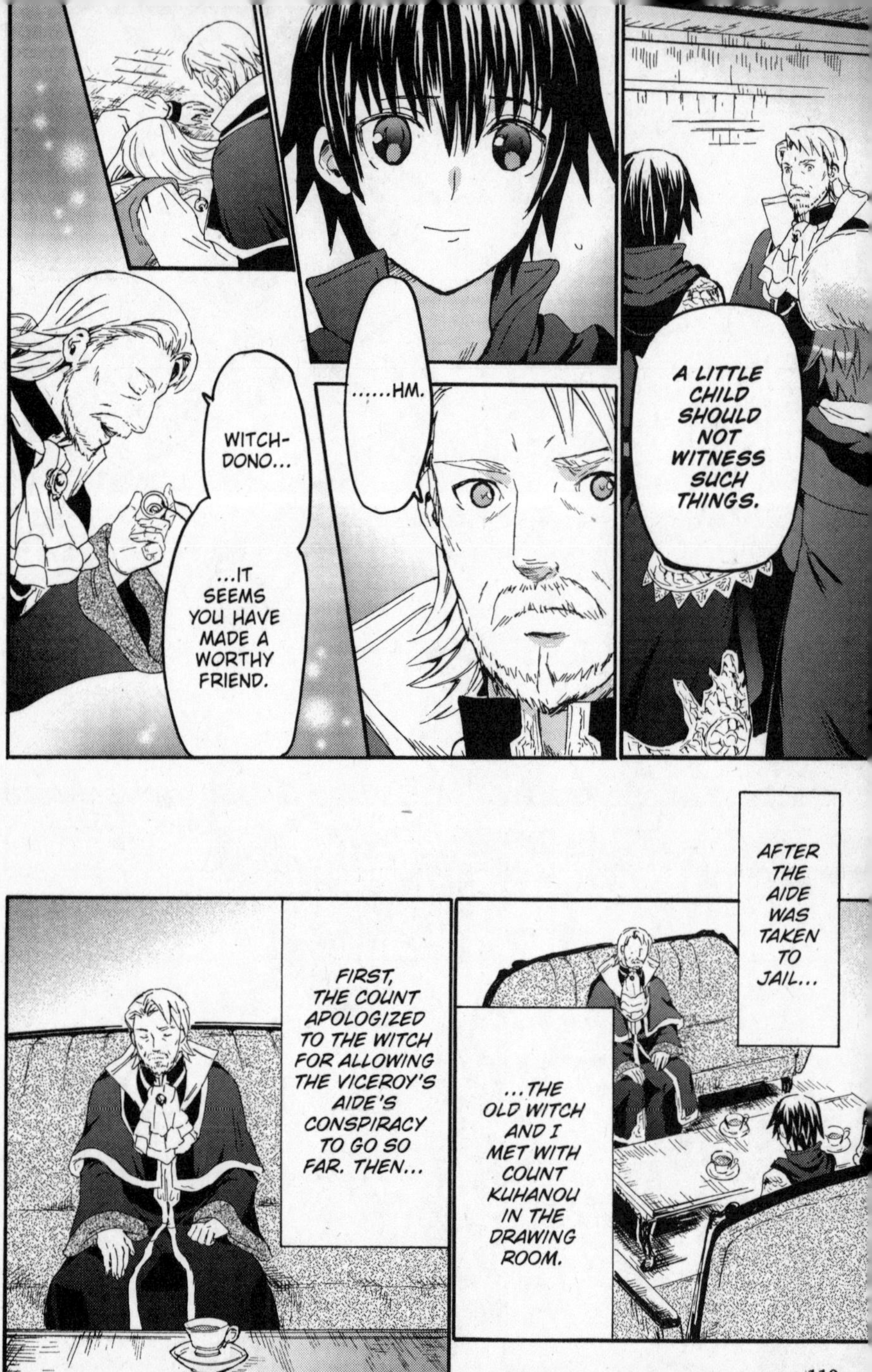
A LITTLE CHILD SHOULD NOT WITNESS SUCH THINGS.
......HM.
WITCH-DONO...
...IT SEEMS YOU HAVE MADE A WORTHY FRIEND.
AFTER THE AIDE WAS TAKEN TO JAIL...
...THE OLD WITCH AND I MET WITH COUNT KUHANOU IN THE DRAWING ROOM.
FIRST, THE COUNT APOLOGIZED TO THE WITCH FOR ALLOWING THE VICEROY'S AIDE'S CONSPIRACY TO GO SO FAR. THEN...

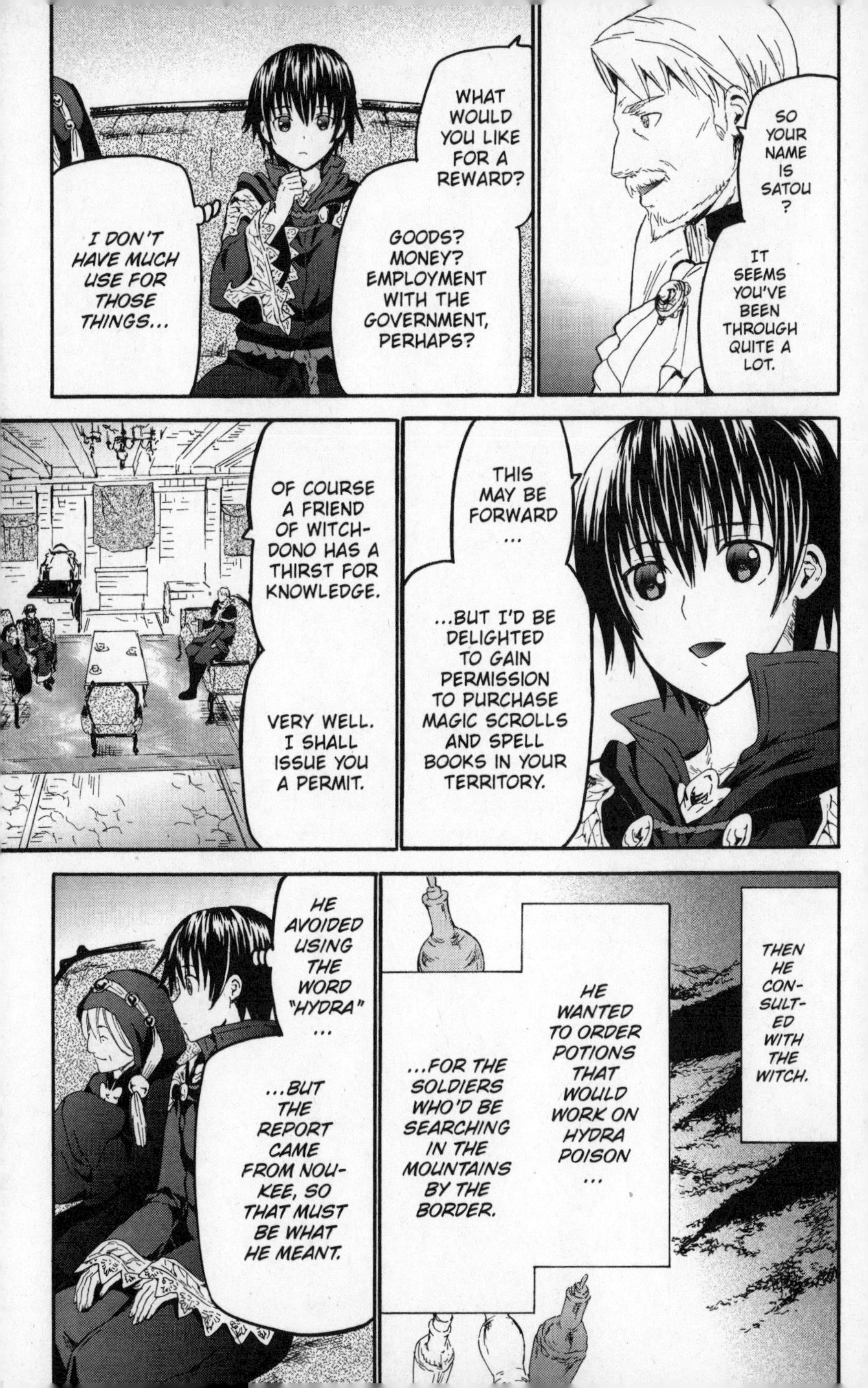
SO YOUR NAME IS SATOU?
IT SEEMS YOU'VE BEEN THROUGH QUITE A LOT.
WHAT WOULD YOU LIKE FOR A REWARD?
GOODS? MONEY? EMPLOYMENT WITH THE GOVERNMENT, PERHAPS?
I DON'T HAVE MUCH USE FOR THOSE THINGS...
THIS MAY BE FORWARD...
...BUT I'D BE DELIGHTED TO GAIN PERMISSION TO PURCHASE MAGIC SCROLLS AND SPELL BOOKS IN YOUR TERRITORY.
OF COURSE A FRIEND OF WITCH-DONO HAS A THIRST FOR KNOWLEDGE.
VERY WELL. I SHALL ISSUE YOU A PERMIT.
THEN HE CONSULTED WITH THE WITCH.
HE WANTED TO ORDER POTIONS THAT WOULD WORK ON HYDRA POISON...
...FOR THE SOLDIERS WHO'D BE SEARCHING IN THE MOUNTAINS BY THE BORDER.
HE AVOIDED USING THE WORD "HYDRA"...
...BUT THE REPORT CAME FROM NOUKEE, SO THAT MUST BE WHAT HE MEANT.

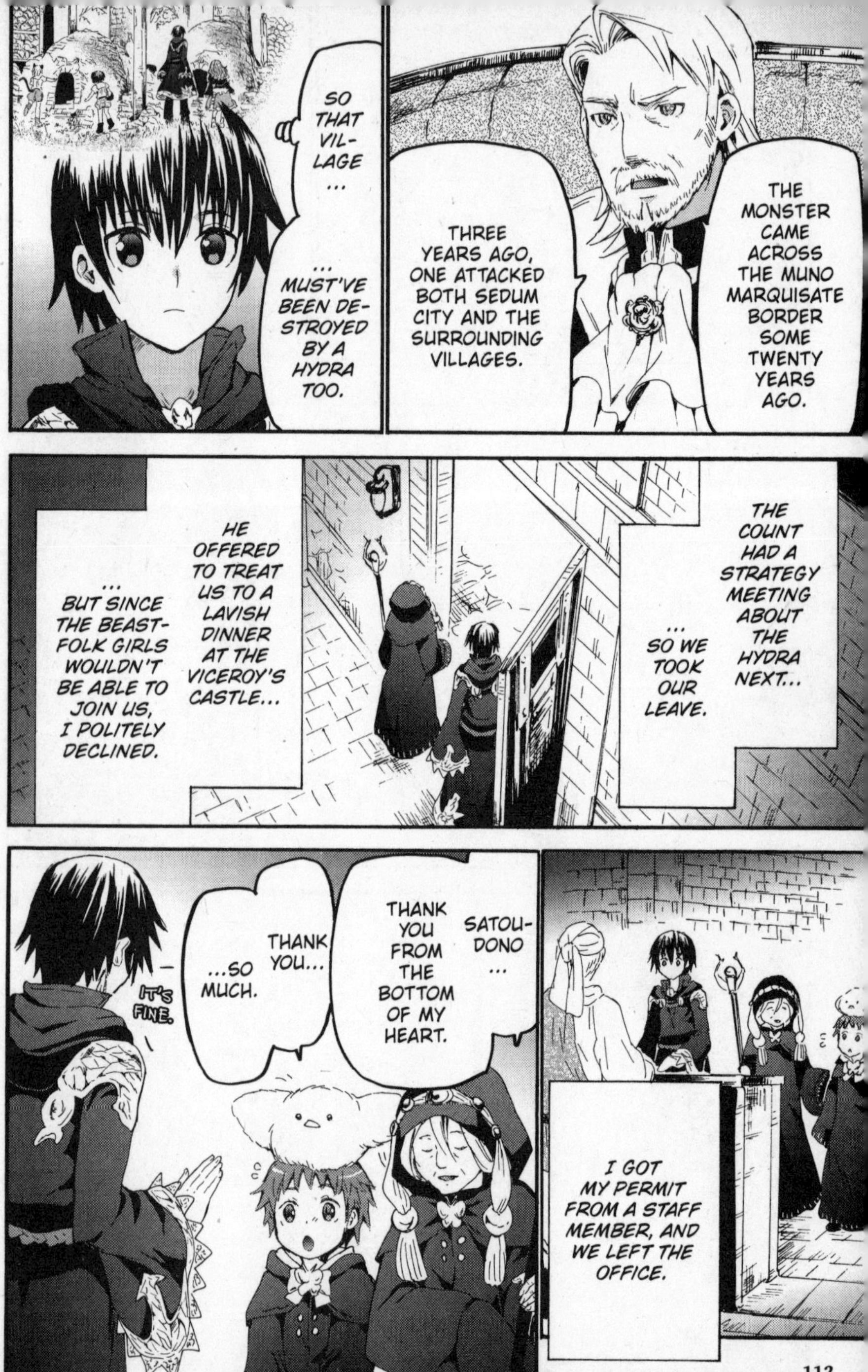
THE MONSTER CAME ACROSS THE MUNO MARQUISATE BORDER SOME TWENTY YEARS AGO.
THREE YEARS AGO, ONE ATTACKED BOTH SEDUM CITY AND THE SURROUNDING VILLAGES.
SO THAT VILLAGE...
...MUST'VE BEEN DESTROYED BY A HYDRA TOO.
THE COUNT HAD A STRATEGY MEETING ABOUT THE HYDRA NEXT...
...SO WE TOOK OUR LEAVE.
HE OFFERED TO TREAT US TO A LAVISH DINNER AT THE VICEROY'S CASTLE...
...BUT SINCE THE BEAST-FOLK GIRLS WOULDN'T BE ABLE TO JOIN US, I POLITELY DECLINED.
I GOT MY PERMIT FROM A STAFF MEMBER, AND WE LEFT THE OFFICE.
SATOU-DONO...
THANK YOU FROM THE BOTTOM OF MY HEART.
THANK YOU...
...SO MUCH.
IT'S FINE.

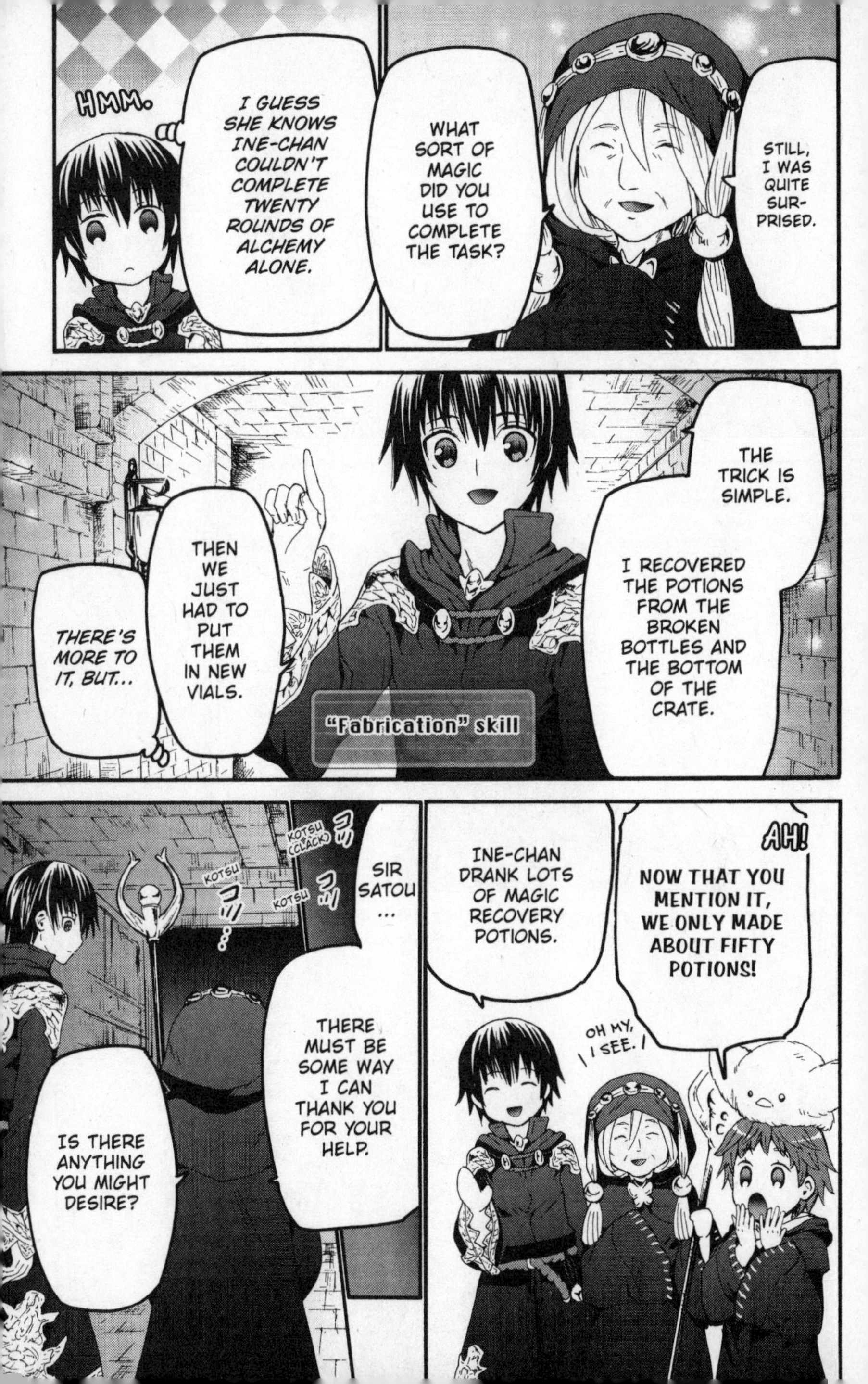
STILL, I WAS QUITE SUR-PRISED.
WHAT SORT OF MAGIC DID YOU USE TO COMPLETE THE TASK?
I GUESS SHE KNOWS INE-CHAN COULDN'T COMPLETE TWENTY ROUNDS OF ALCHEMY ALONE.
HMM.
THE TRICK IS SIMPLE.
I RECOVERED THE POTIONS FROM THE BROKEN BOTTLES AND THE BOTTOM OF THE CRATE.
"Fabrication" skill
THEN WE JUST HAD TO PUT THEM IN NEW VIALS.
THERE'S MORE TO IT, BUT...
AH!
NOW THAT YOU MENTION IT, WE ONLY MADE ABOUT FIFTY POTIONS!
INE-CHAN DRANK LOTS OF MAGIC RECOVERY POTIONS.
OH MY, I SEE.
KOTSU (CLACK)
KOTSU
KOTSU
SIR SATOU...
THERE MUST BE SOME WAY I CAN THANK YOU FOR YOUR HELP.
IS THERE ANYTHING YOU MIGHT DESIRE?

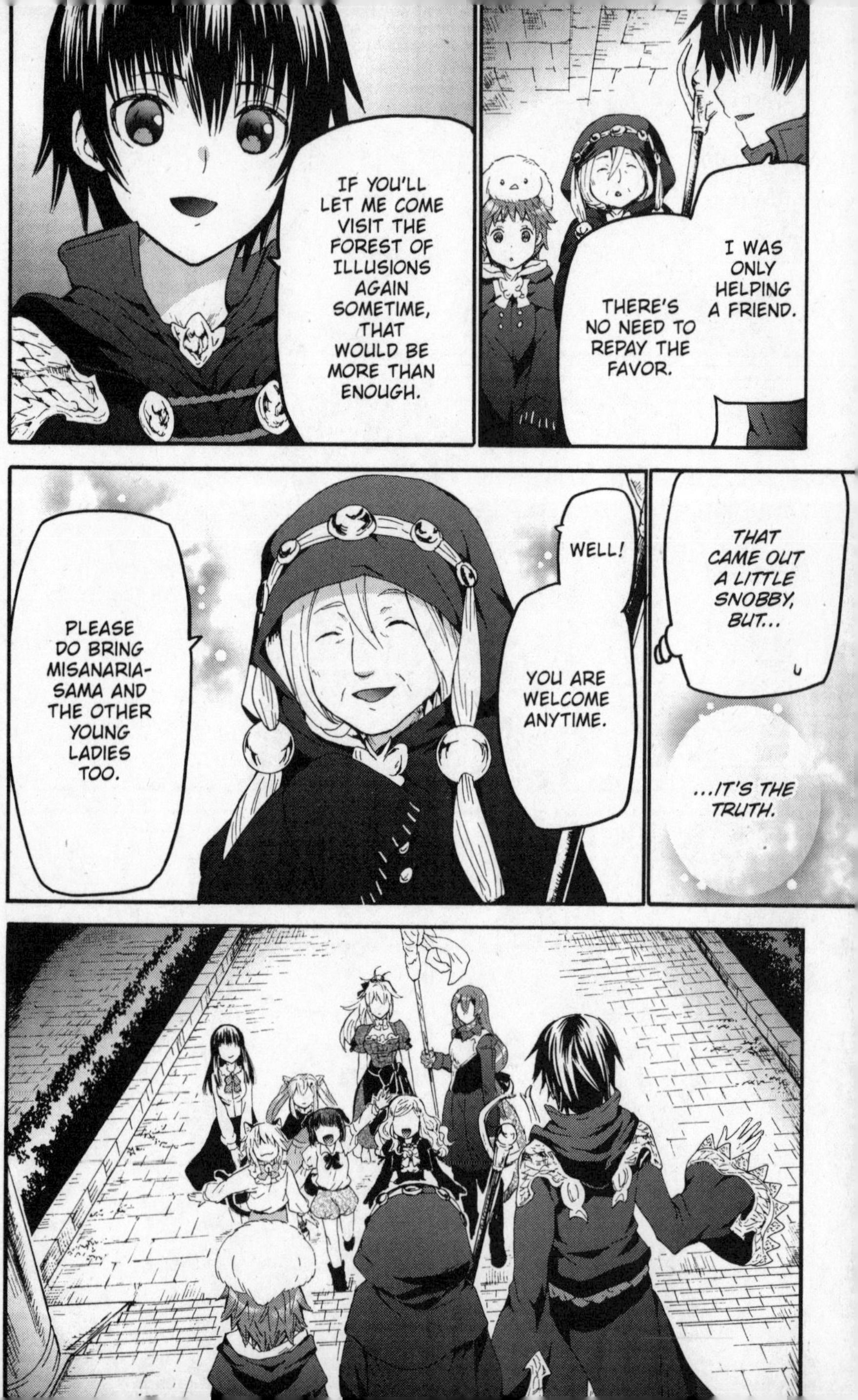
I WAS ONLY HELPING A FRIEND.
THERE'S NO NEED TO REPAY THE FAVOR.
IF YOU'LL LET ME COME VISIT THE FOREST OF ILLUSIONS AGAIN SOMETIME, THAT WOULD BE MORE THAN ENOUGH.
THAT CAME OUT A LITTLE SNOBBY, BUT...
...IT'S THE TRUTH.
WELL!
YOU ARE WELCOME ANYTIME.
PLEASE DO BRING MISANARIA-SAMA AND THE OTHER YOUNG LADIES TOO.

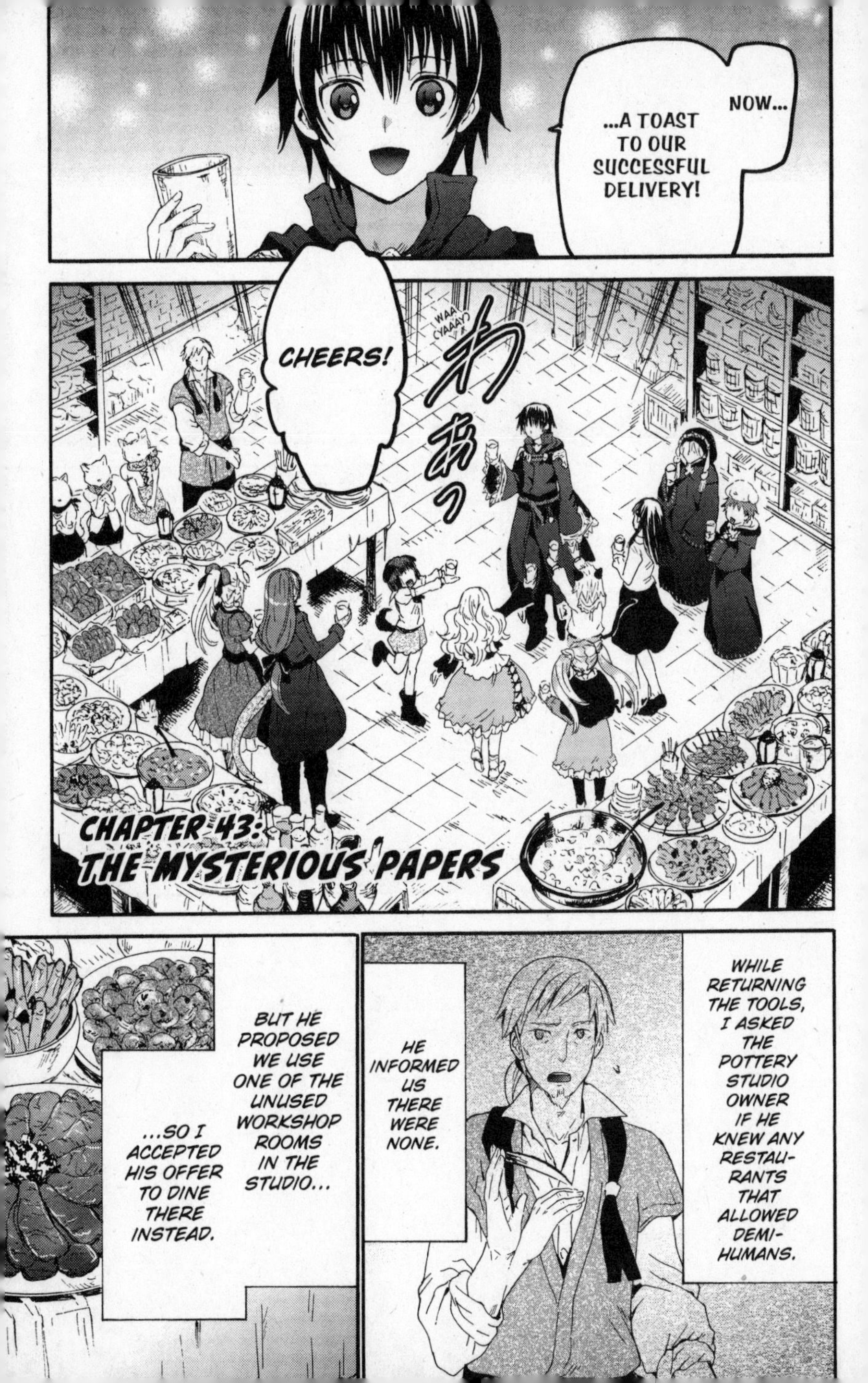
NOW...
...A TOAST TO OUR SUCCESSFUL DELIVERY!
CHEERS!
WAA (YAAAY)
わあっ
CHAPTER 43: THE MYSTERIOUS PAPERS
WHILE RETURNING THE TOOLS, I ASKED THE POTTERY STUDIO OWNER IF HE KNEW ANY RESTAU-RANTS THAT ALLOWED DEMI-HUMANS.
HE INFORMED US THERE WERE NONE.
BUT HE PROPOSED WE USE ONE OF THE UNUSED WORKSHOP ROOMS IN THE STUDIO...
...SO I ACCEPTED HIS OFFER TO DINE THERE INSTEAD.

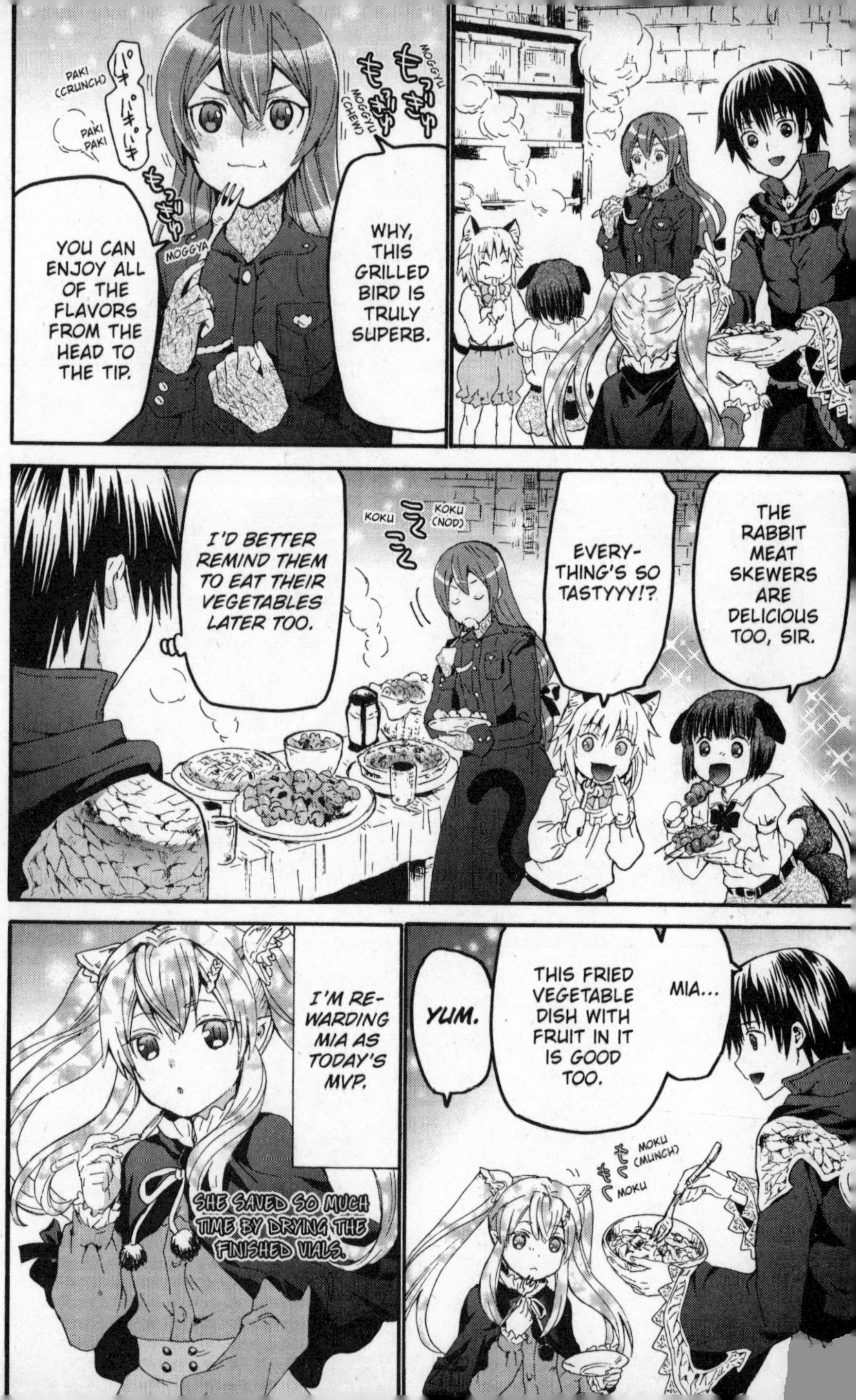

WHY, THIS GRILLED BIRD IS TRULY SUPERB.
もっぎゅ MOGGYU
もぎゅ MOGGYU (CHEW)
パキパキパキ PAKI (CRUNCH) PAKI PAKI
もっぎゅ MOGGYA
YOU CAN ENJOY ALL OF THE FLAVORS FROM THE HEAD TO THE TIP.
THE RABBIT MEAT SKEWERS ARE DELICIOUS TOO, SIR.
EVERY-THING'S SO TASTYYY!?
KOKU (NOD) KOKU
I'D BETTER REMIND THEM TO EAT THEIR VEGETABLES LATER TOO.
MIA...
THIS FRIED VEGETABLE DISH WITH FRUIT IN IT IS GOOD TOO.
YUM.
MOKU (MUNCH) MOKU
I'M RE-WARDING MIA AS TODAY'S MVP.
SHE SAVED SO MUCH TIME BY DRYING THE FINISHED VIALS.

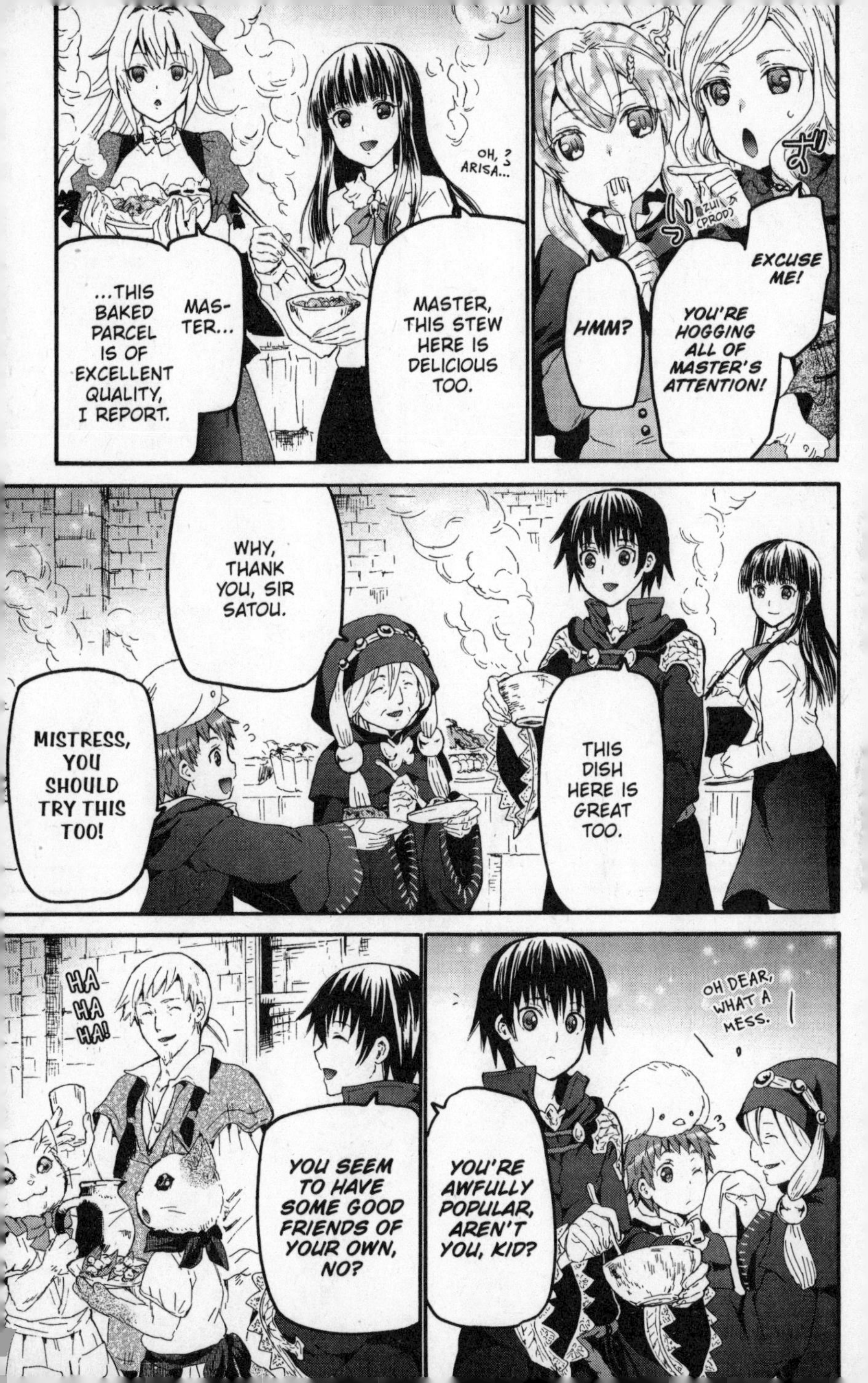
EXCUSE ME! YOU'RE HOGGING ALL OF MASTER'S ATTENTION!
ZUI (PROD)
HMM?
OH, ARISA...
MASTER, THIS STEW HERE IS DELICIOUS TOO.
MASTER...
...THIS BAKED PARCEL IS OF EXCELLENT QUALITY, I REPORT.
THIS DISH HERE IS GREAT TOO.
WHY, THANK YOU, SIR SATOU.
MISTRESS, YOU SHOULD TRY THIS TOO!
OH DEAR, WHAT A MESS.
YOU'RE AWFULLY POPULAR, AREN'T YOU, KID?
YOU SEEM TO HAVE SOME GOOD FRIENDS OF YOUR OWN, NO?
HA HA HA!

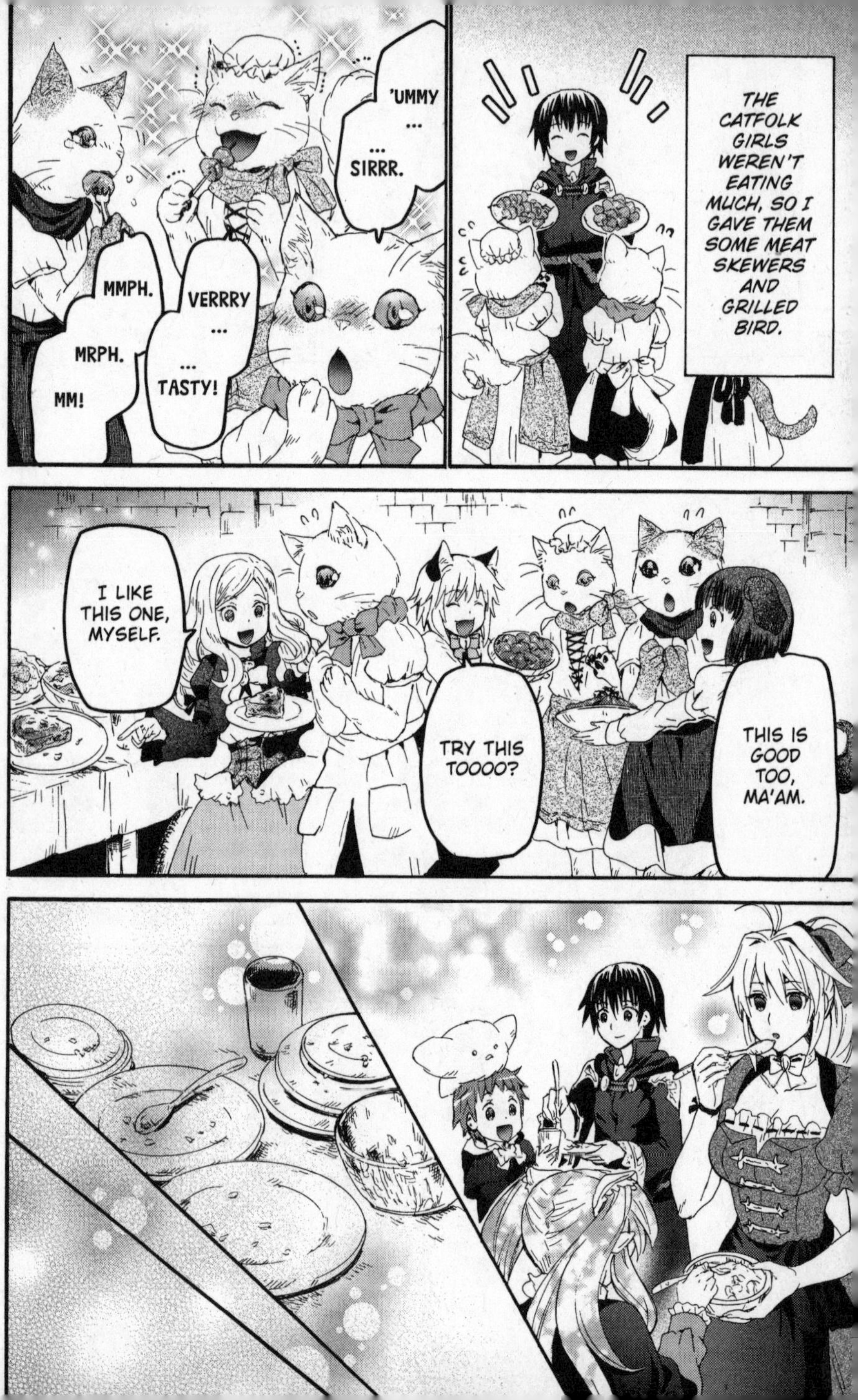
THE CATFOLK GIRLS WEREN'T EATING MUCH, SO I GAVE THEM SOME MEAT SKEWERS AND GRILLED BIRD.
'UMMY ... ... SIRRR.
VERRRY ... ... TASTY!
MMPH.
MRPH.
MM!
THIS IS GOOD TOO, MA'AM.
TRY THIS TOOOO?
I LIKE THIS ONE, MYSELF.

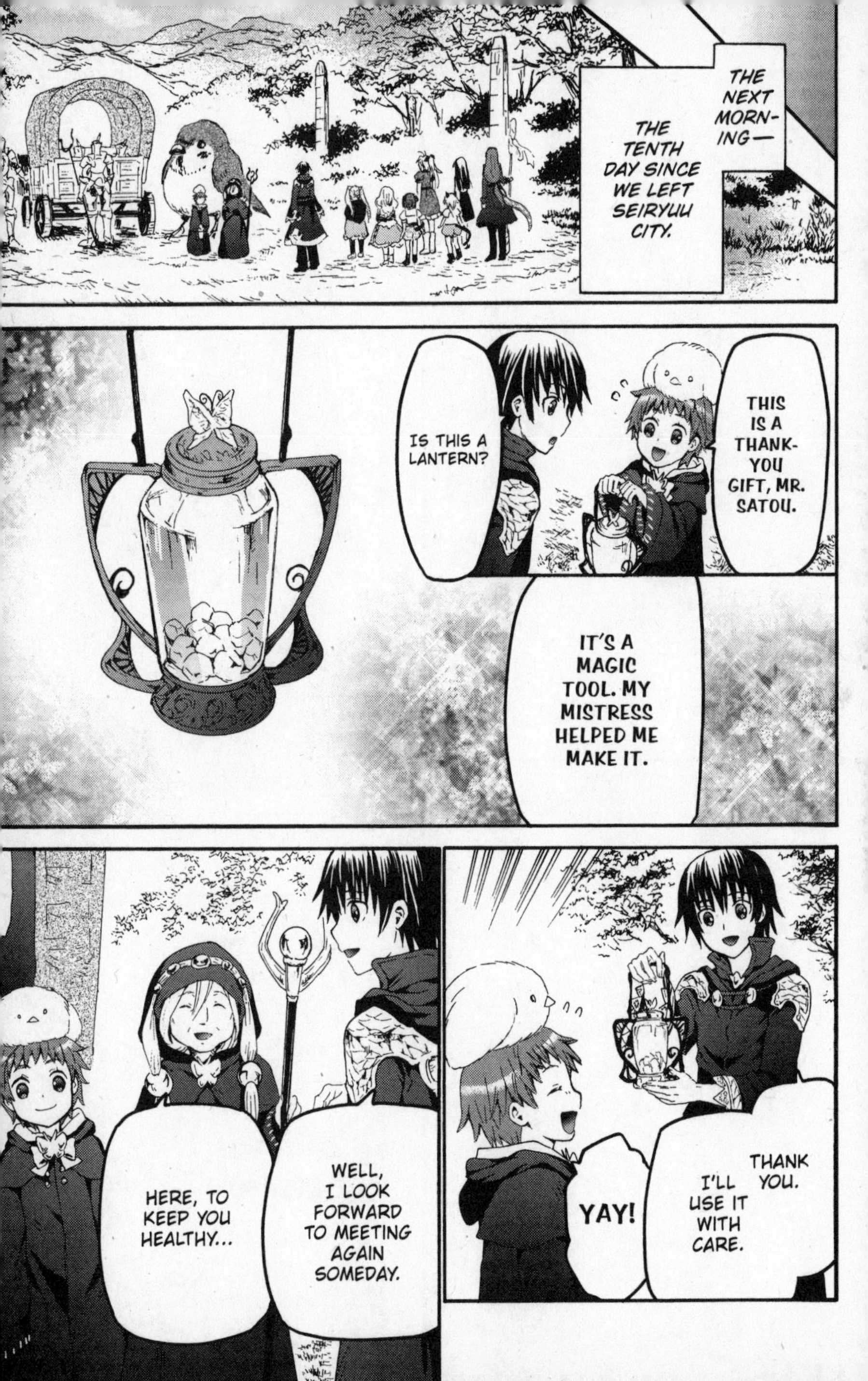
THE NEXT MORNING—
THE TENTH DAY SINCE WE LEFT SEIRYUU CITY.
THIS IS A THANK-YOU GIFT, MR. SATOU.
IS THIS A LANTERN?
IT'S A MAGIC TOOL. MY MISTRESS HELPED ME MAKE IT.
THANK YOU.
I'LL USE IT WITH CARE.
YAY!
WELL, I LOOK FORWARD TO MEETING AGAIN SOMEDAY.
HERE, TO KEEP YOU HEALTHY...

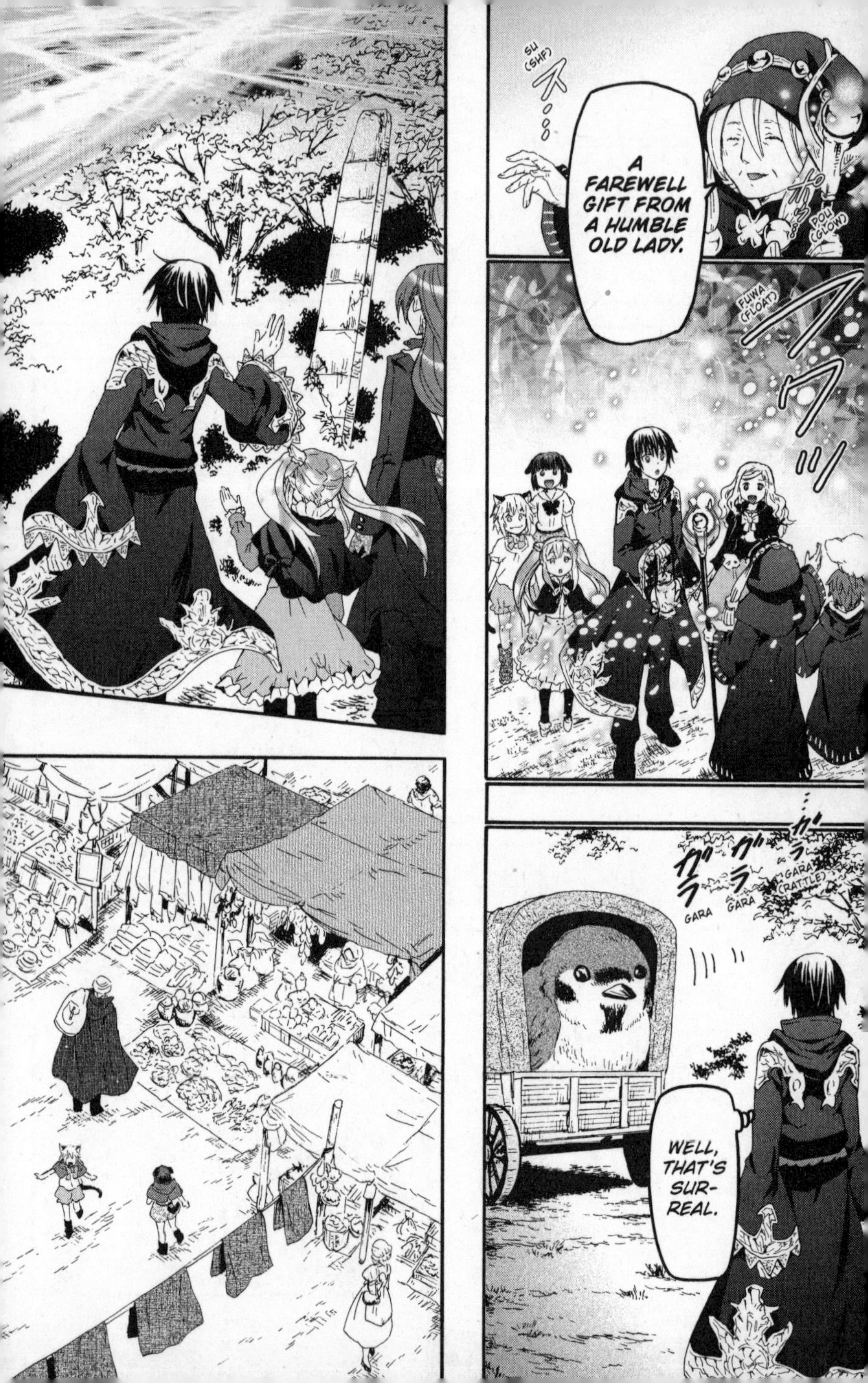
SU (SHF)
A FAREWELL GIFT FROM A HUMBLE OLD LADY.
POU (GLOW)
FUWA (FLOAT)
GARA (RATTLE)
GARA
GARA
WELL, THAT'S SUR-REAL.

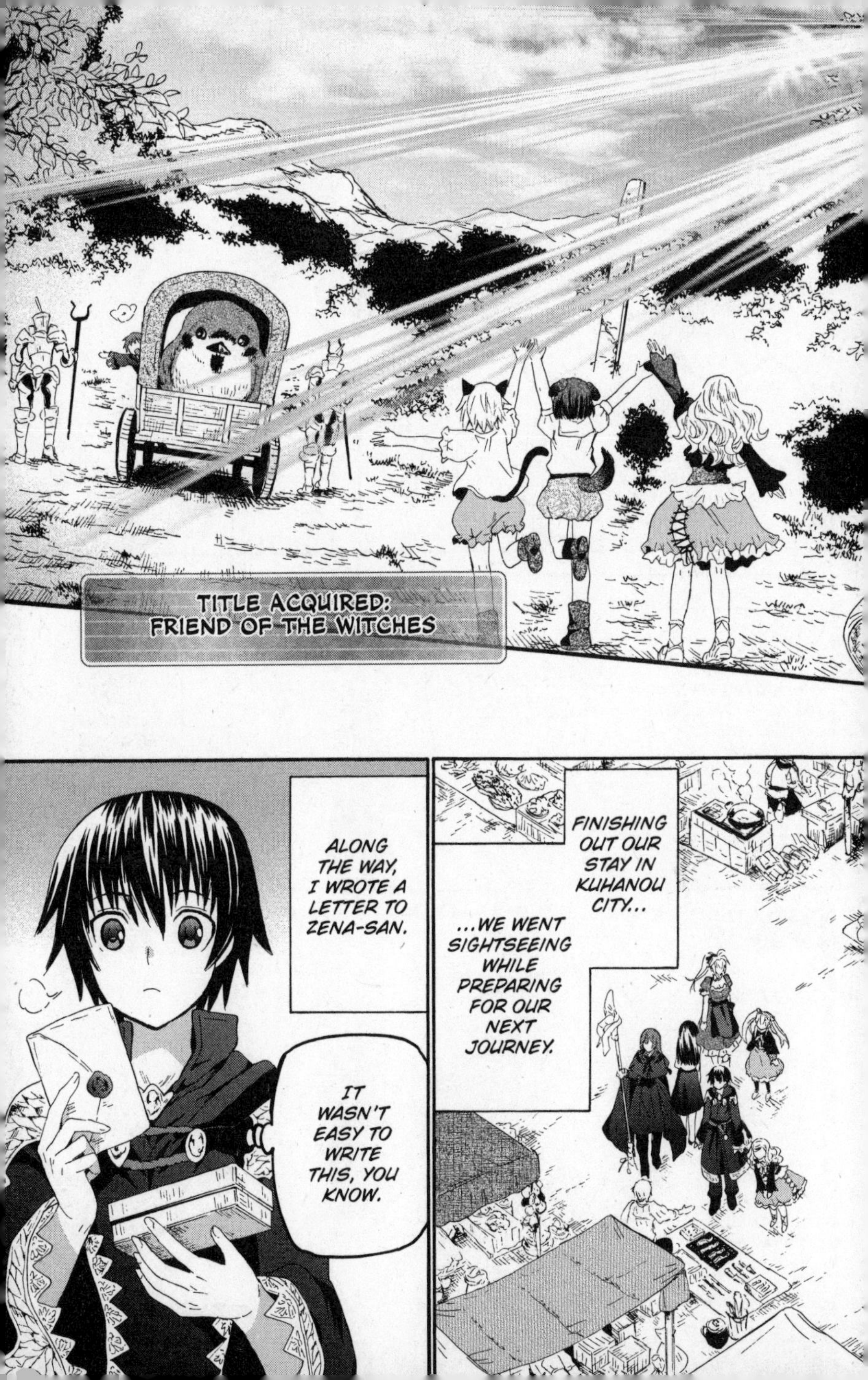
TITLE ACQUIRED: FRIEND OF THE WITCHES
FINISHING OUT OUR STAY IN KUHANOU CITY...
...WE WENT SIGHTSEEING WHILE PREPARING FOR OUR NEXT JOURNEY.
ALONG THE WAY, I WROTE A LETTER TO ZENA-SAN.
IT WASN'T EASY TO WRITE THIS, YOU KNOW.

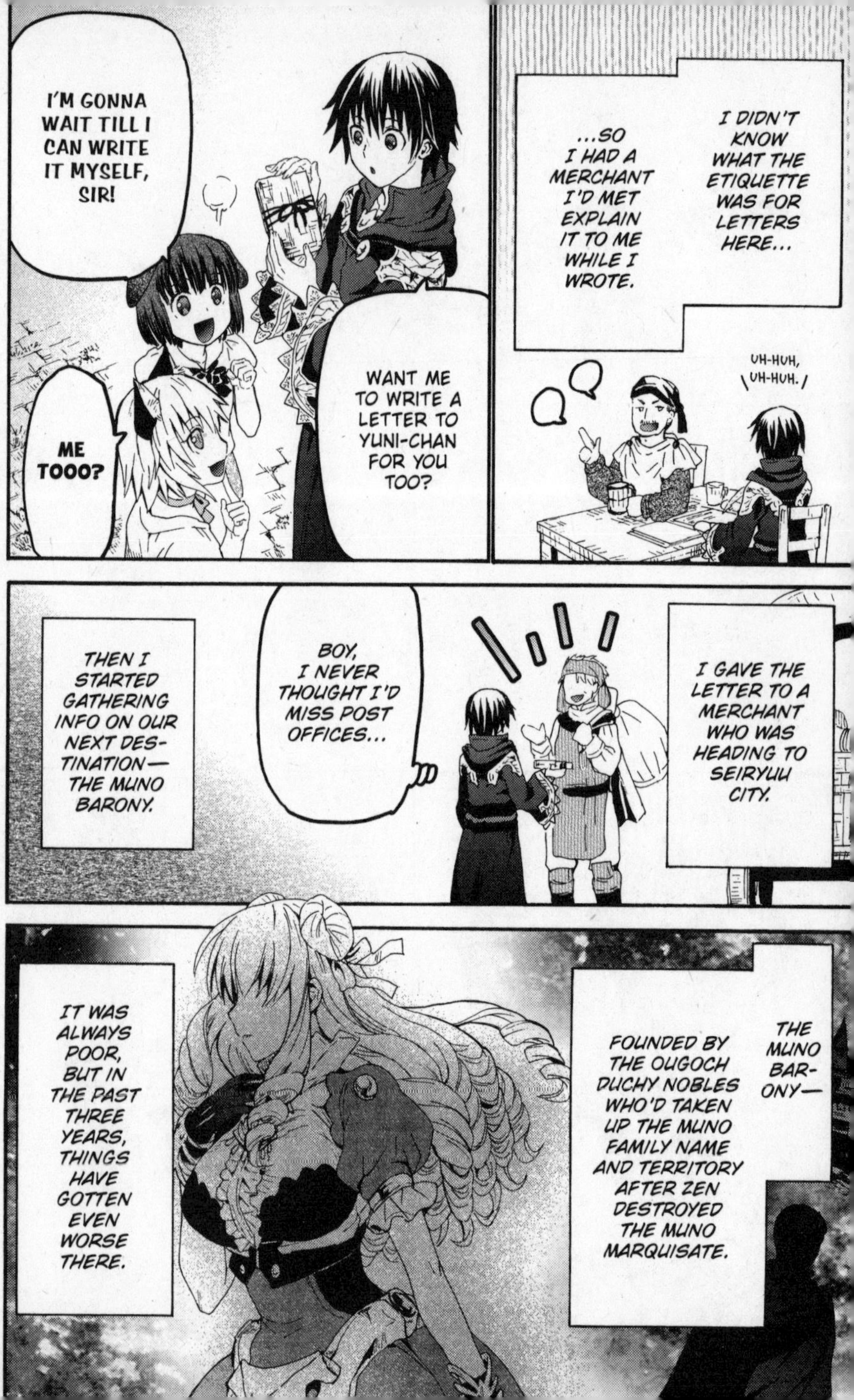
I DIDN'T KNOW WHAT THE ETIQUETTE WAS FOR LETTERS HERE...
...SO I HAD A MERCHANT I'D MET EXPLAIN IT TO ME WHILE I WROTE.
UH-HUH, UH-HUH.
WANT ME TO WRITE A LETTER TO YUNI-CHAN FOR YOU TOO?
ME TOOO?
I'M GONNA WAIT TILL I CAN WRITE IT MYSELF, SIR!
I GAVE THE LETTER TO A MERCHANT WHO WAS HEADING TO SEIRYUU CITY.
BOY, I NEVER THOUGHT I'D MISS POST OFFICES...
THEN I STARTED GATHERING INFO ON OUR NEXT DES-TINATION—THE MUNO BARONY.
THE MUNO BAR-ONY—
FOUNDED BY THE OUGOCH DUCHY NOBLES WHO'D TAKEN UP THE MUNO FAMILY NAME AND TERRITORY AFTER ZEN DESTROYED THE MUNO MARQUISATE.
IT WAS ALWAYS POOR, BUT IN THE PAST THREE YEARS, THINGS HAVE GOTTEN EVEN WORSE THERE.

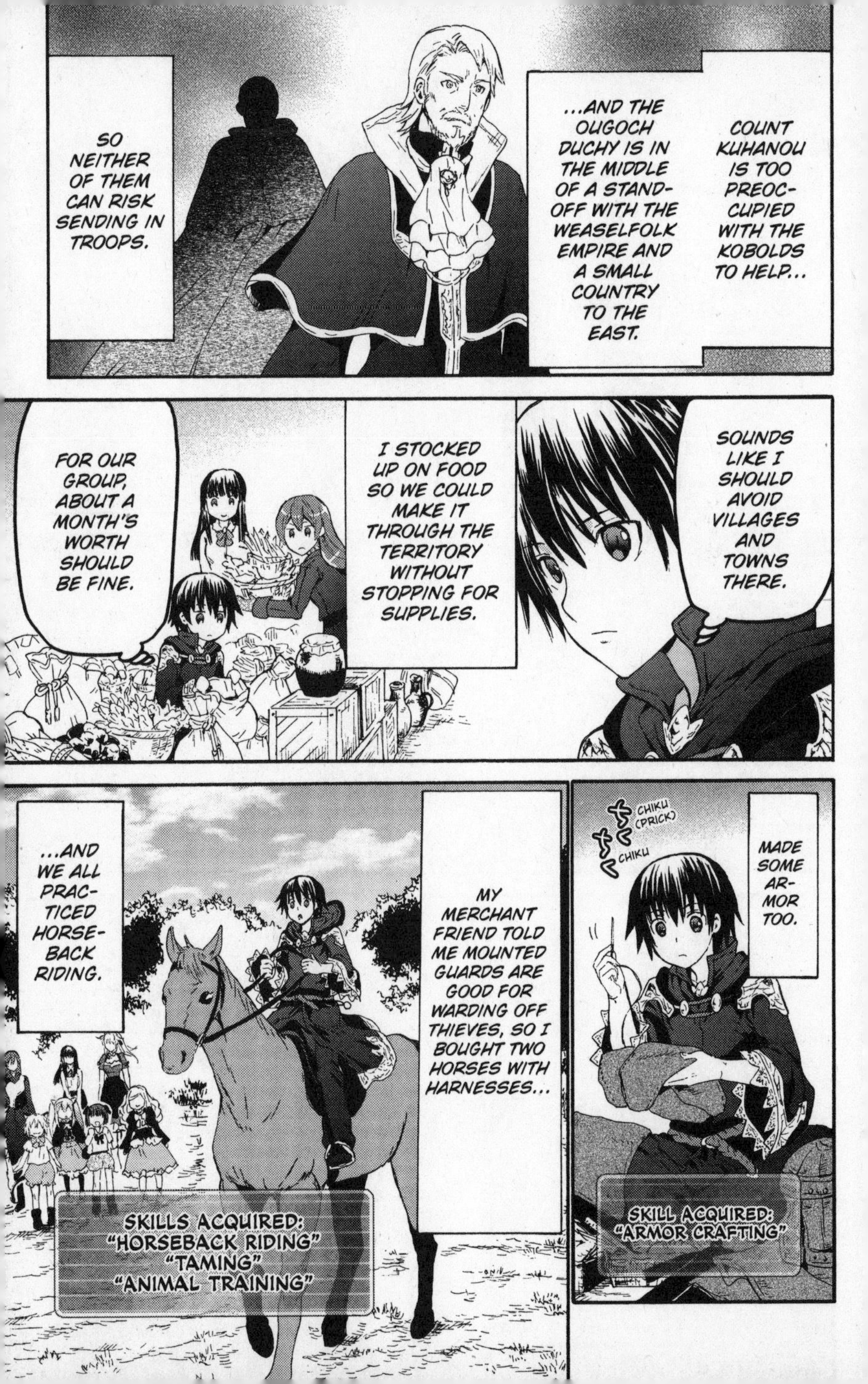
COUNT KUHANOU IS TOO PREOCCUPIED WITH THE KOBOLDS TO HELP...
...AND THE OUGOCH DUCHY IS IN THE MIDDLE OF A STAND-OFF WITH THE WEASELFOLK EMPIRE AND A SMALL COUNTRY TO THE EAST.
SO NEITHER OF THEM CAN RISK SENDING IN TROOPS.
SOUNDS LIKE I SHOULD AVOID VILLAGES AND TOWNS THERE.
I STOCKED UP ON FOOD SO WE COULD MAKE IT THROUGH THE TERRITORY WITHOUT STOPPING FOR SUPPLIES.
FOR OUR GROUP, ABOUT A MONTH'S WORTH SHOULD BE FINE.
ちく CHIKU (PRICK)
ちく CHIKU
MADE SOME ARMOR TOO.
SKILL ACQUIRED: "ARMOR CRAFTING"
MY MERCHANT FRIEND TOLD ME MOUNTED GUARDS ARE GOOD FOR WARDING OFF THIEVES, SO I BOUGHT TWO HORSES WITH HARNESSES...
...AND WE ALL PRACTICED HORSEBACK RIDING.
SKILLS ACQUIRED: "HORSEBACK RIDING" "TAMING" "ANIMAL TRAINING"

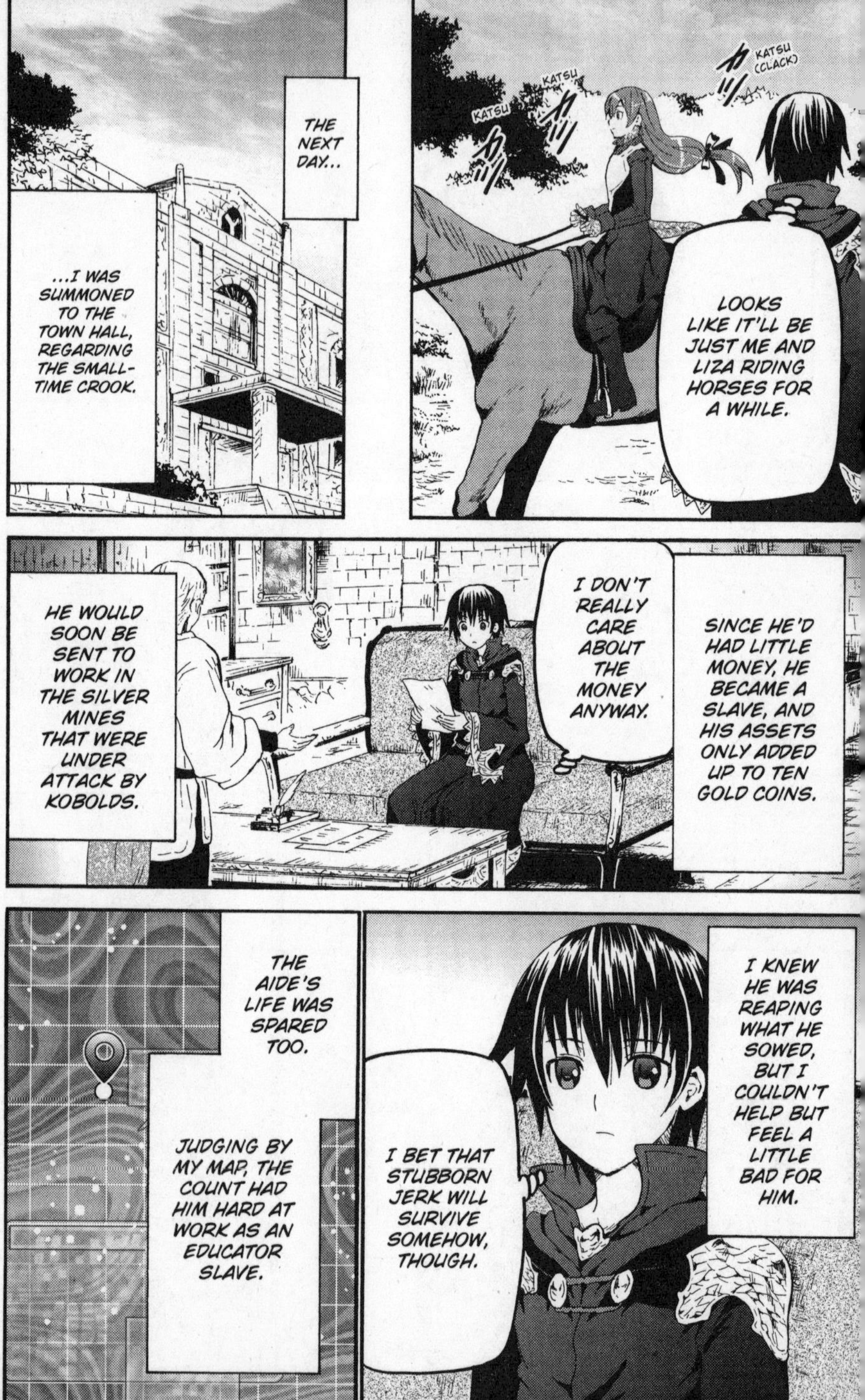
KATSU (CLACK)
KATSU
KATSU
LOOKS LIKE IT'LL BE JUST ME AND LIZA RIDING HORSES FOR A WHILE.
THE NEXT DAY...
...I WAS SUMMONED TO THE TOWN HALL, REGARDING THE SMALL-TIME CROOK.
SINCE HE'D HAD LITTLE MONEY, HE BECAME A SLAVE, AND HIS ASSETS ONLY ADDED UP TO TEN GOLD COINS.
I DON'T REALLY CARE ABOUT THE MONEY ANYWAY.
HE WOULD SOON BE SENT TO WORK IN THE SILVER MINES THAT WERE UNDER ATTACK BY KOBOLDS.
I KNEW HE WAS REAPING WHAT HE SOWED, BUT I COULDN'T HELP BUT FEEL A LITTLE BAD FOR HIM.
I BET THAT STUBBORN JERK WILL SURVIVE SOMEHOW, THOUGH.
THE AIDE'S LIFE WAS SPARED TOO.
JUDGING BY MY MAP, THE COUNT HAD HIM HARD AT WORK AS AN EDUCATOR SLAVE.

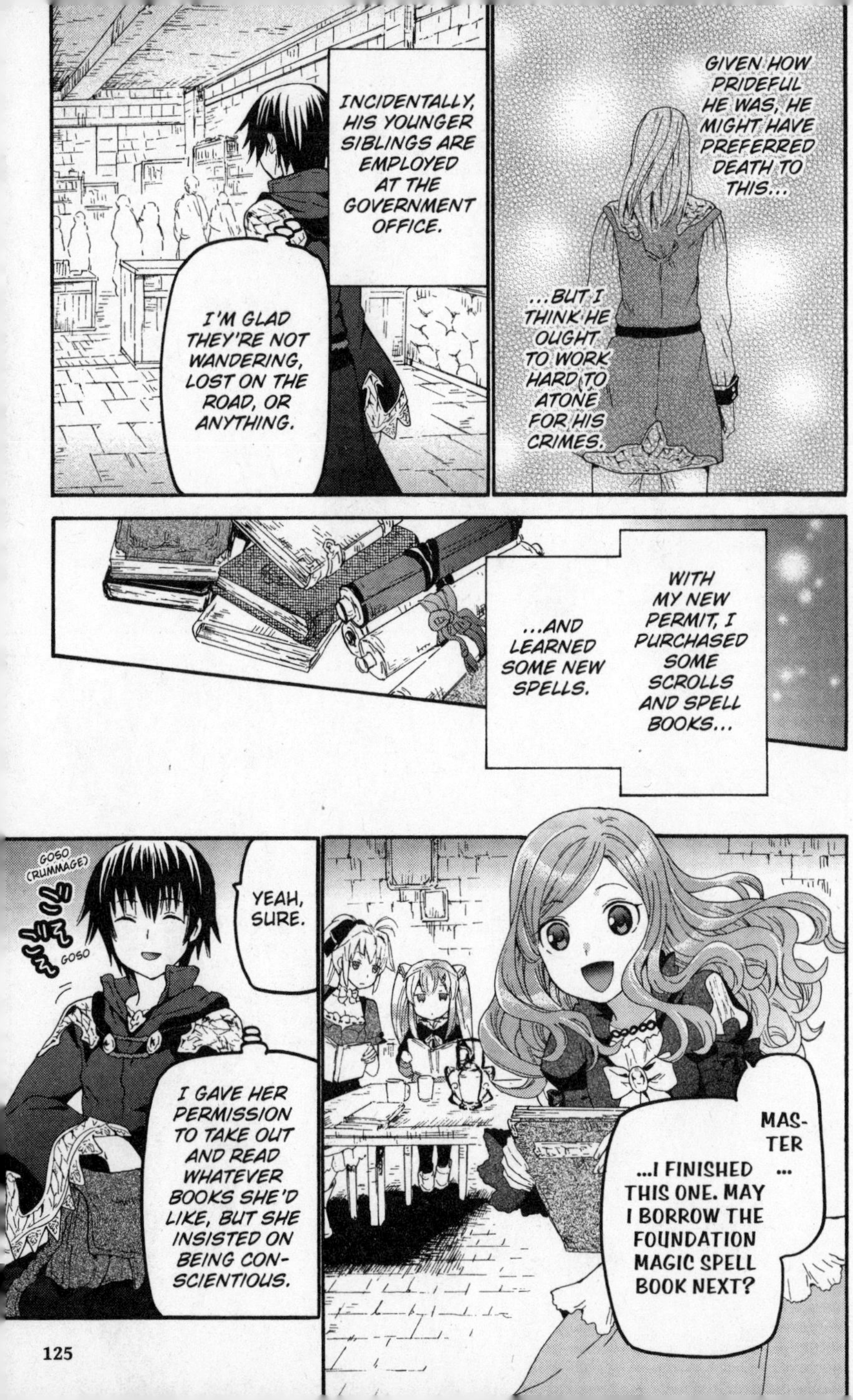
GIVEN HOW PRIDEFUL HE WAS, HE MIGHT HAVE PREFERRED DEATH TO THIS...
...BUT I THINK HE OUGHT TO WORK HARD TO ATONE FOR HIS CRIMES.
INCIDENTALLY, HIS YOUNGER SIBLINGS ARE EMPLOYED AT THE GOVERNMENT OFFICE.
I'M GLAD THEY'RE NOT WANDERING, LOST ON THE ROAD, OR ANYTHING.
WITH MY NEW PERMIT, I PURCHASED SOME SCROLLS AND SPELL BOOKS...
...AND LEARNED SOME NEW SPELLS.
MAS-TER...
...I FINISHED THIS ONE. MAY I BORROW THE FOUNDATION MAGIC SPELL BOOK NEXT?
YEAH, SURE.
GOSO (RUMMAGE)
GOSO
I GAVE HER PERMISSION TO TAKE OUT AND READ WHATEVER BOOKS SHE'D LIKE, BUT SHE INSISTED ON BEING CON-SCIENTIOUS.

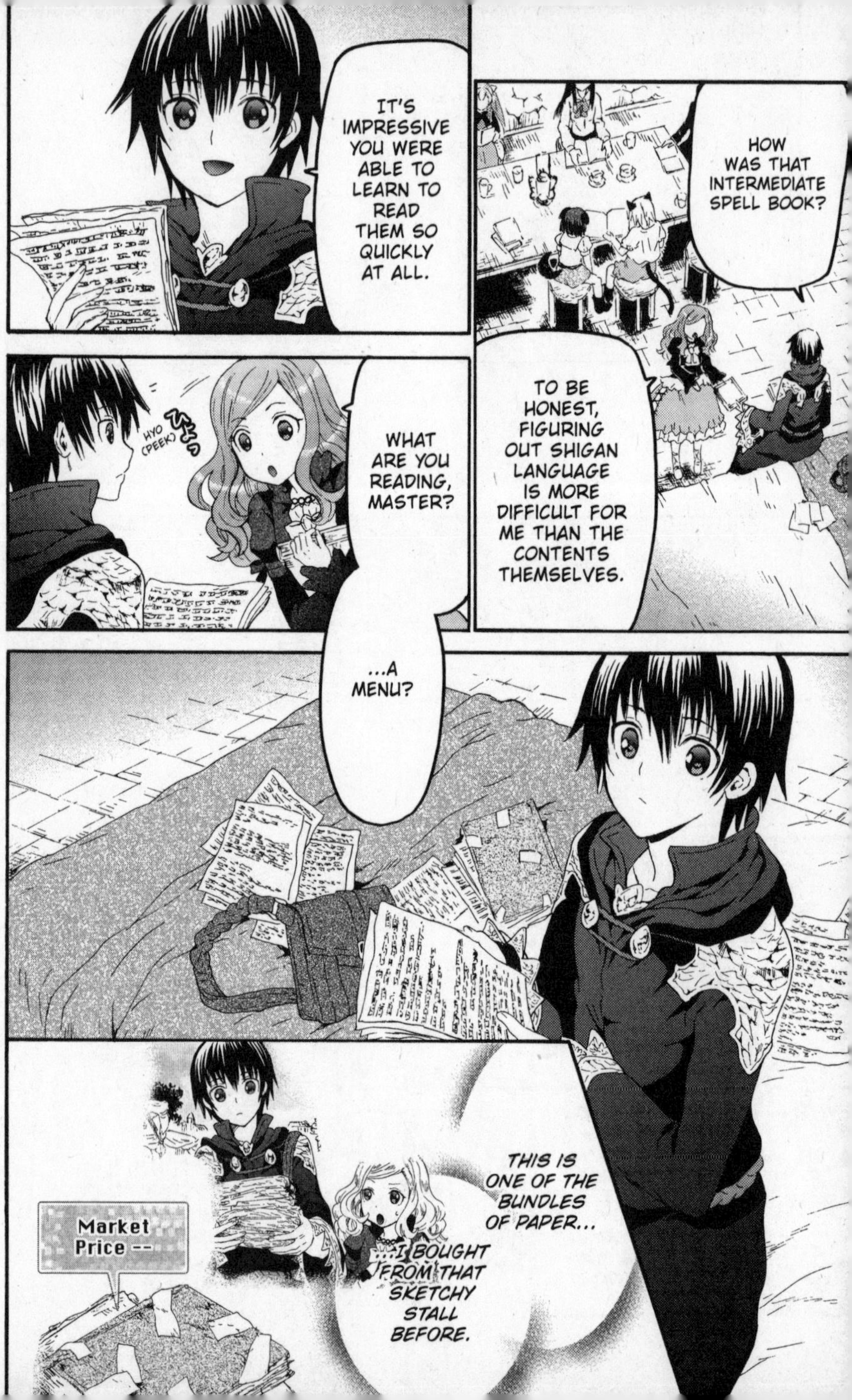

HOW WAS THAT INTERMEDIATE SPELL BOOK?
TO BE HONEST, FIGURING OUT SHIGAN LANGUAGE IS MORE DIFFICULT FOR ME THAN THE CONTENTS THEMSELVES.
IT'S IMPRESSIVE YOU WERE ABLE TO LEARN TO READ THEM SO QUICKLY AT ALL.
HYO (PEEK)
WHAT ARE YOU READING, MASTER?
...A MENU?
THIS IS ONE OF THE BUNDLES OF PAPER...
...I BOUGHT FROM THAT SKETCHY STALL BEFORE.
Market Price --

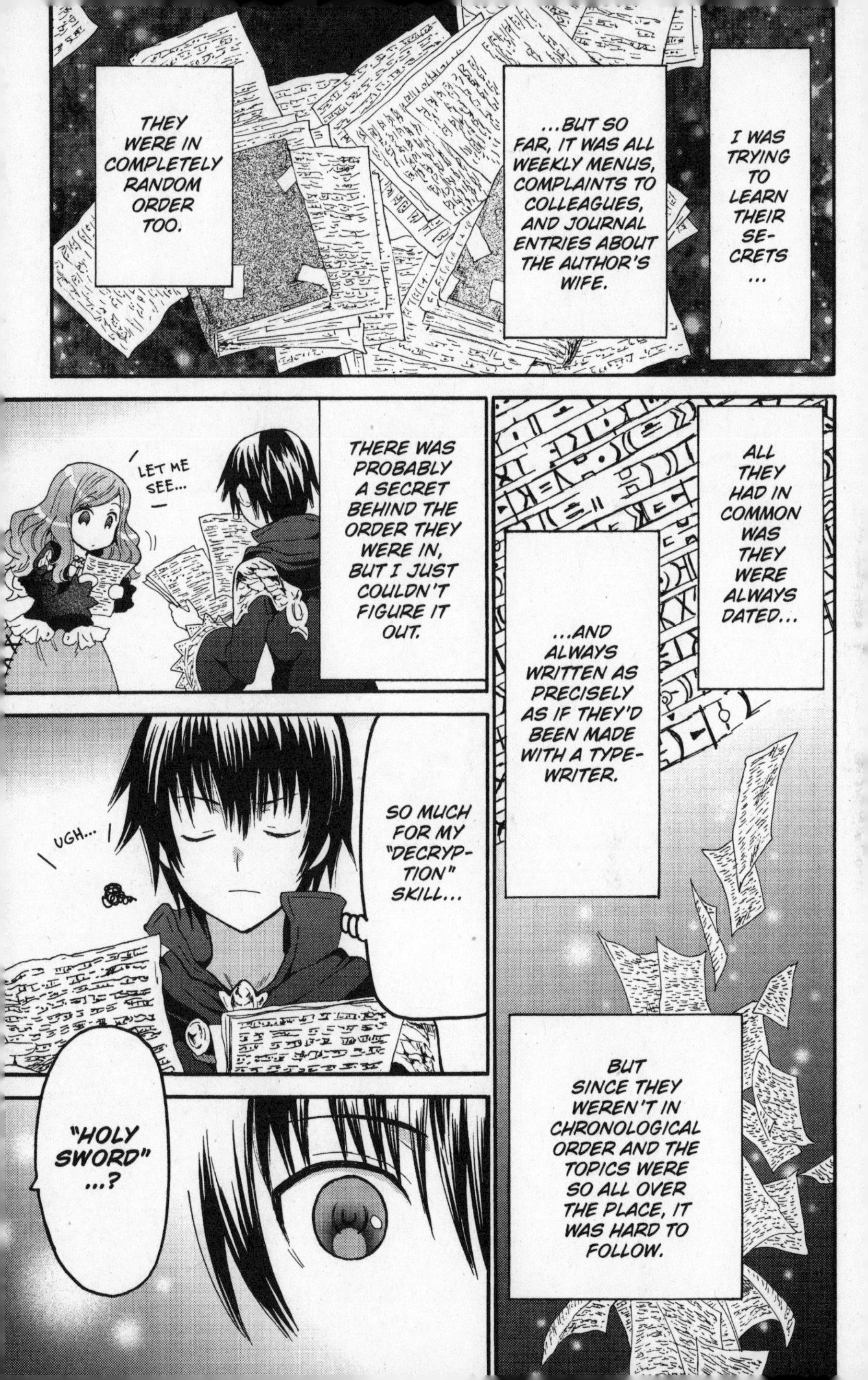
I WAS TRYING TO LEARN THEIR SECRETS...
...BUT SO FAR, IT WAS ALL WEEKLY MENUS, COMPLAINTS TO COLLEAGUES, AND JOURNAL ENTRIES ABOUT THE AUTHOR'S WIFE.
THEY WERE IN COMPLETELY RANDOM ORDER TOO.
ALL THEY HAD IN COMMON WAS THEY WERE ALWAYS DATED...
...AND ALWAYS WRITTEN AS PRECISELY AS IF THEY'D BEEN MADE WITH A TYPE-WRITER.
BUT SINCE THEY WEREN'T IN CHRONOLOGICAL ORDER AND THE TOPICS WERE SO ALL OVER THE PLACE, IT WAS HARD TO FOLLOW.
THERE WAS PROBABLY A SECRET BEHIND THE ORDER THEY WERE IN, BUT I JUST COULDN'T FIGURE IT OUT.
LET ME SEE...
SO MUCH FOR MY "DECRYP-TION" SKILL...
UGH...
"HOLY SWORD" ...?

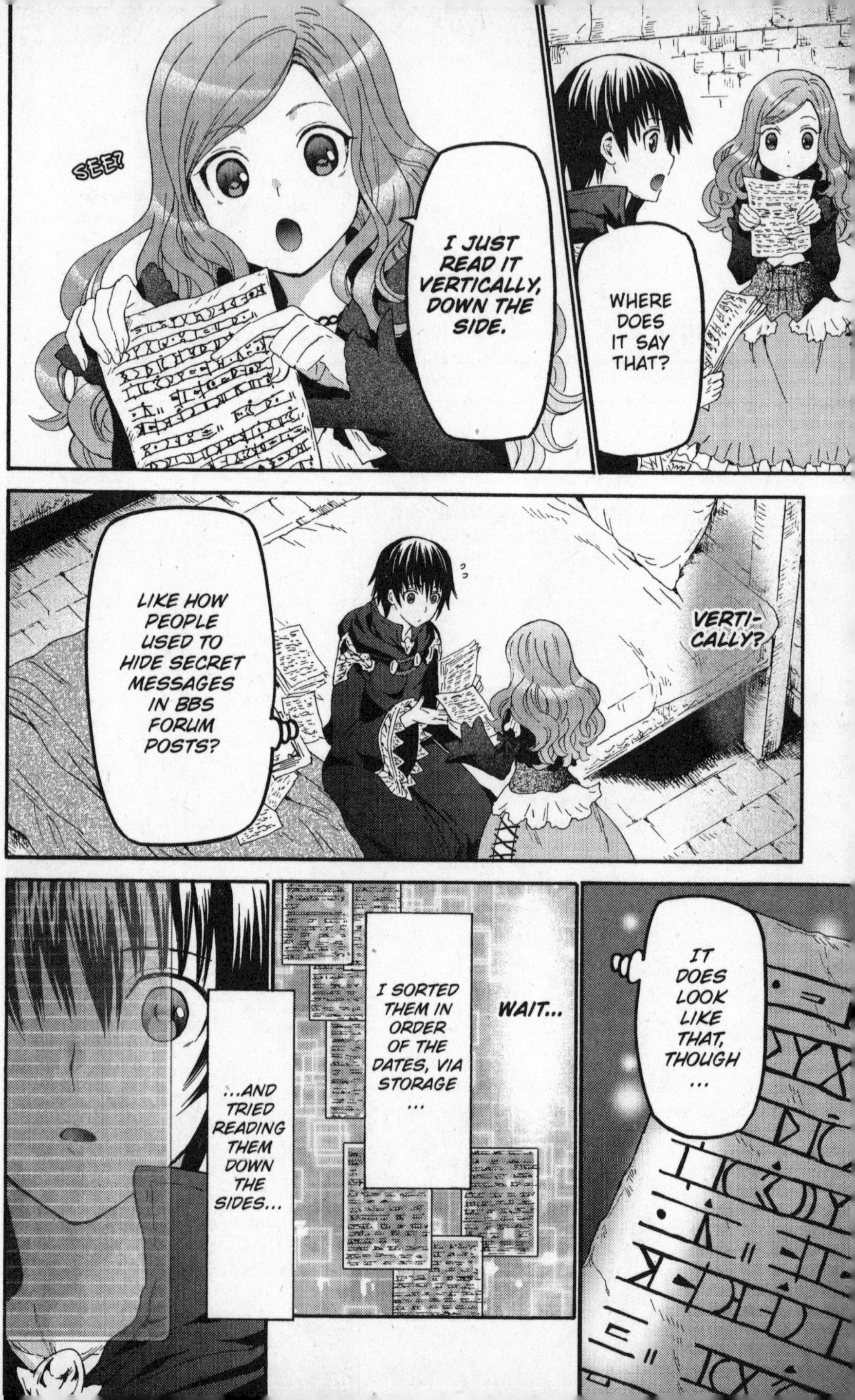
WHERE DOES IT SAY THAT?
I JUST READ IT VERTICALLY, DOWN THE SIDE.
SEE?
VERTI-CALLY?
LIKE HOW PEOPLE USED TO HIDE SECRET MESSAGES IN BBS FORUM POSTS?
IT DOES LOOK LIKE THAT, THOUGH...
WAIT...
I SORTED THEM IN ORDER OF THE DATES, VIA STORAGE...
...AND TRIED READING THEM DOWN THE SIDES...

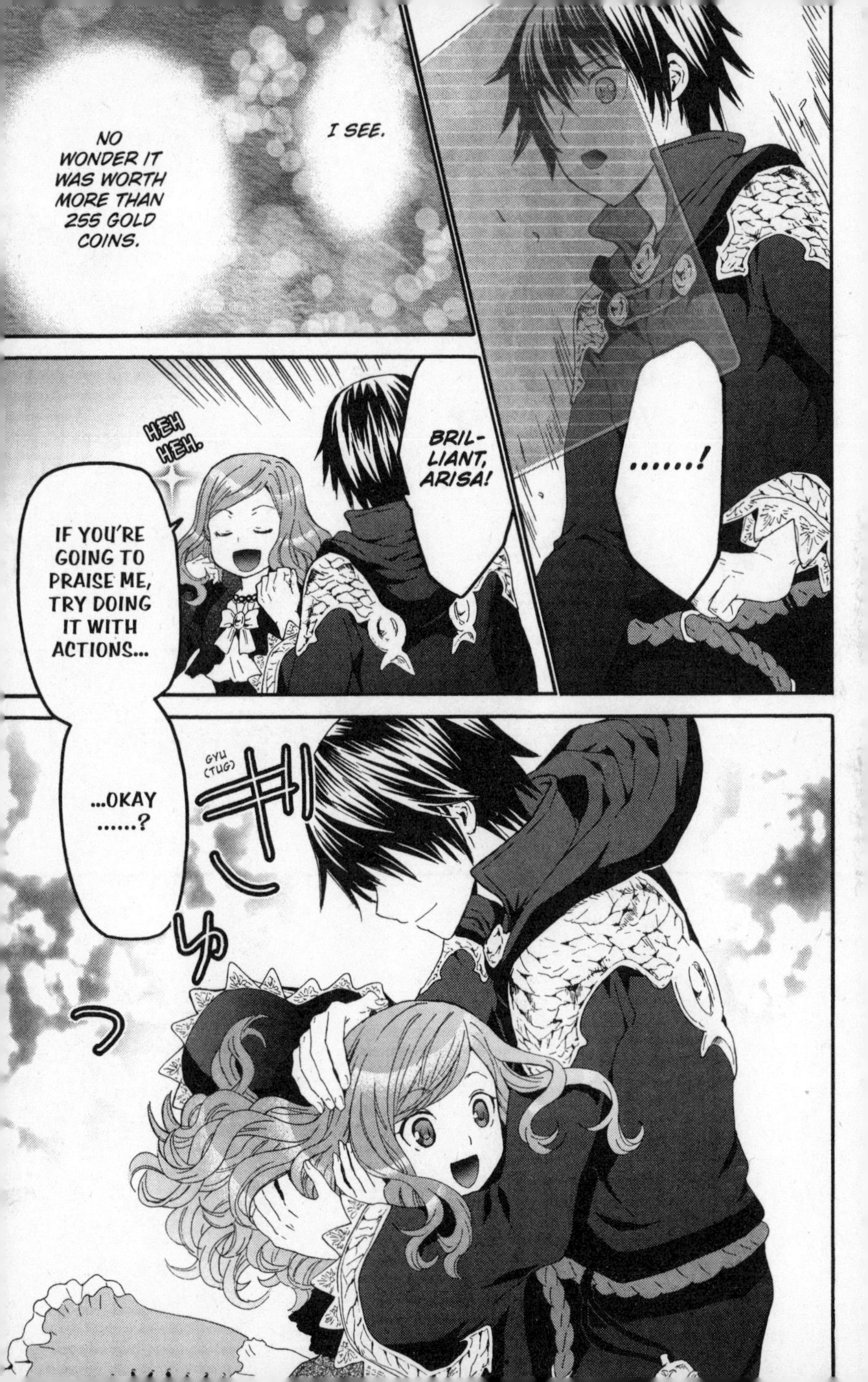

......!
I SEE.
NO WONDER IT WAS WORTH MORE THAN 255 GOLD COINS.
BRIL-LIANT, ARISA!
HEH HEH.
IF YOU'RE GOING TO PRAISE ME, TRY DOING IT WITH ACTIONS...
...OKAY ......?
GYU (TUG)

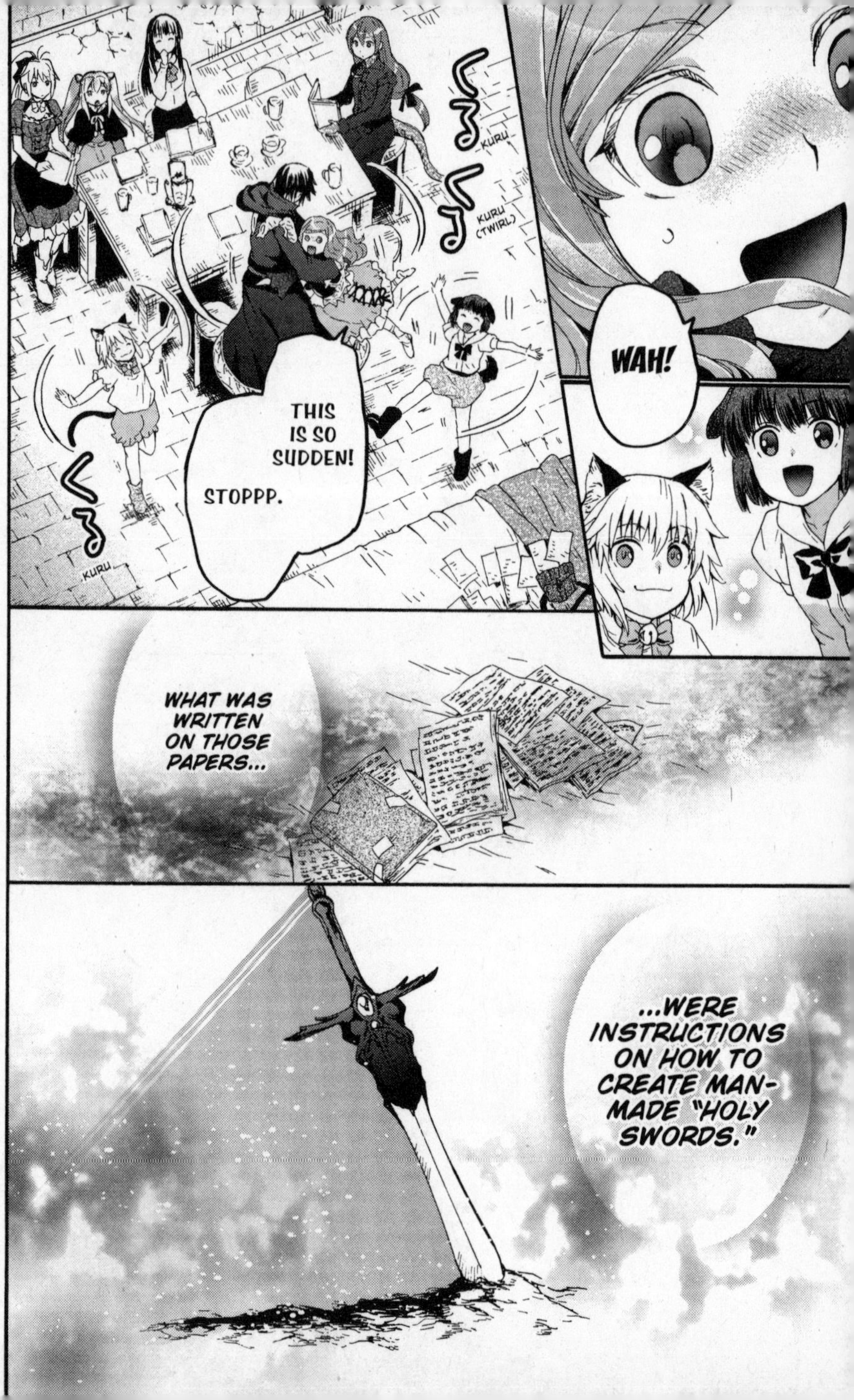
WAH!
KURU
KURU (TWIRL)
THIS IS SO SUDDEN!
STOPPP.
KURU
WHAT WAS WRITTEN ON THOSE PAPERS...
...WERE INSTRUCTIONS ON HOW TO CREATE MAN-MADE "HOLY SWORDS."

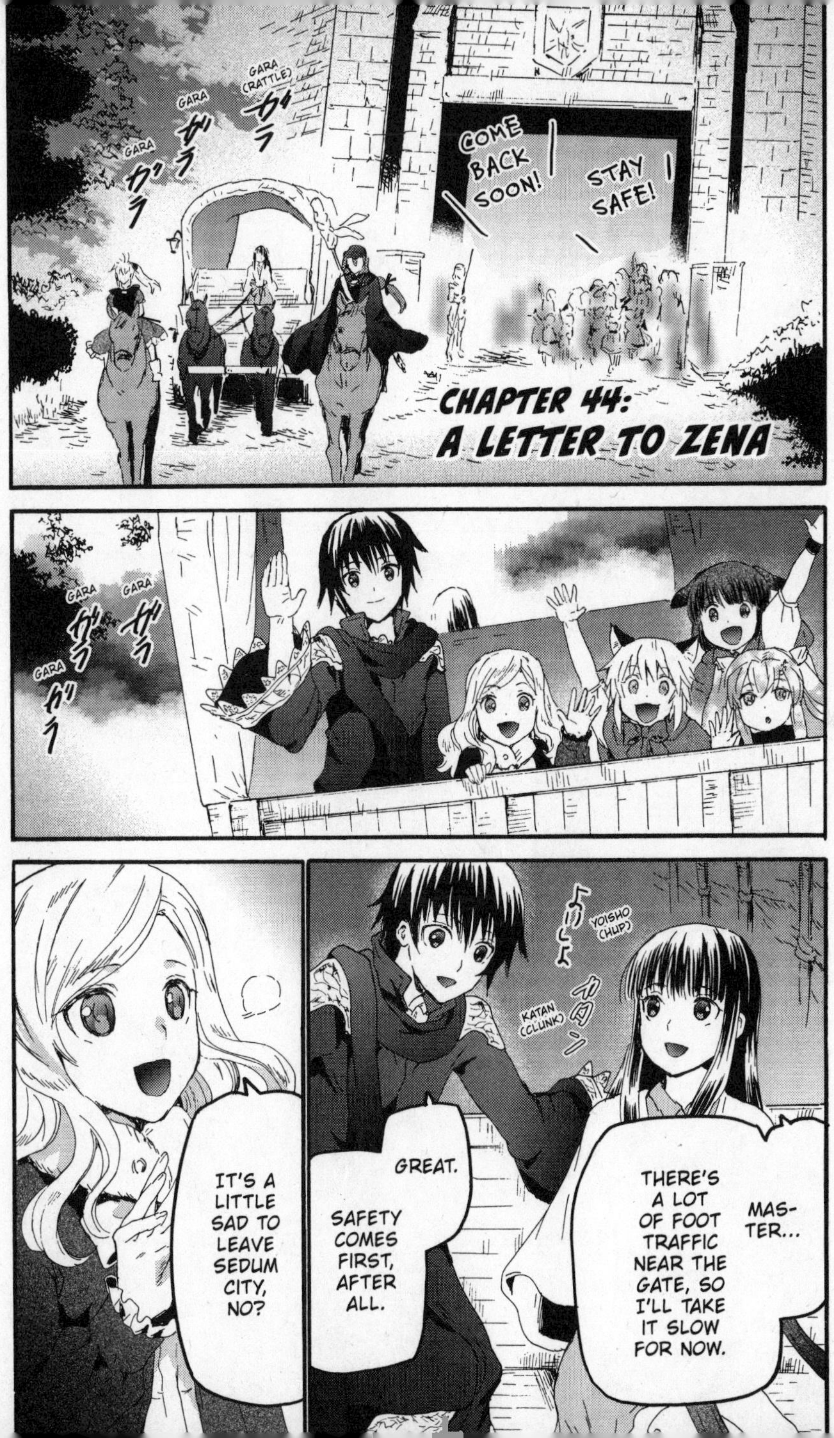
STAY SAFE!
COME BACK SOON!
GARA (RATTLE)
GARA
GARA
CHAPTER 44: A LETTER TO ZENA
GARA
GARA
GARA
YOISHO (HUP)
KATAN (CLUNK)
MAS-TER...
THERE'S A LOT OF FOOT TRAFFIC NEAR THE GATE, SO I'LL TAKE IT SLOW FOR NOW.
GREAT.
SAFETY COMES FIRST, AFTER ALL.
IT'S A LITTLE SAD TO LEAVE SEDUM CITY, NO?

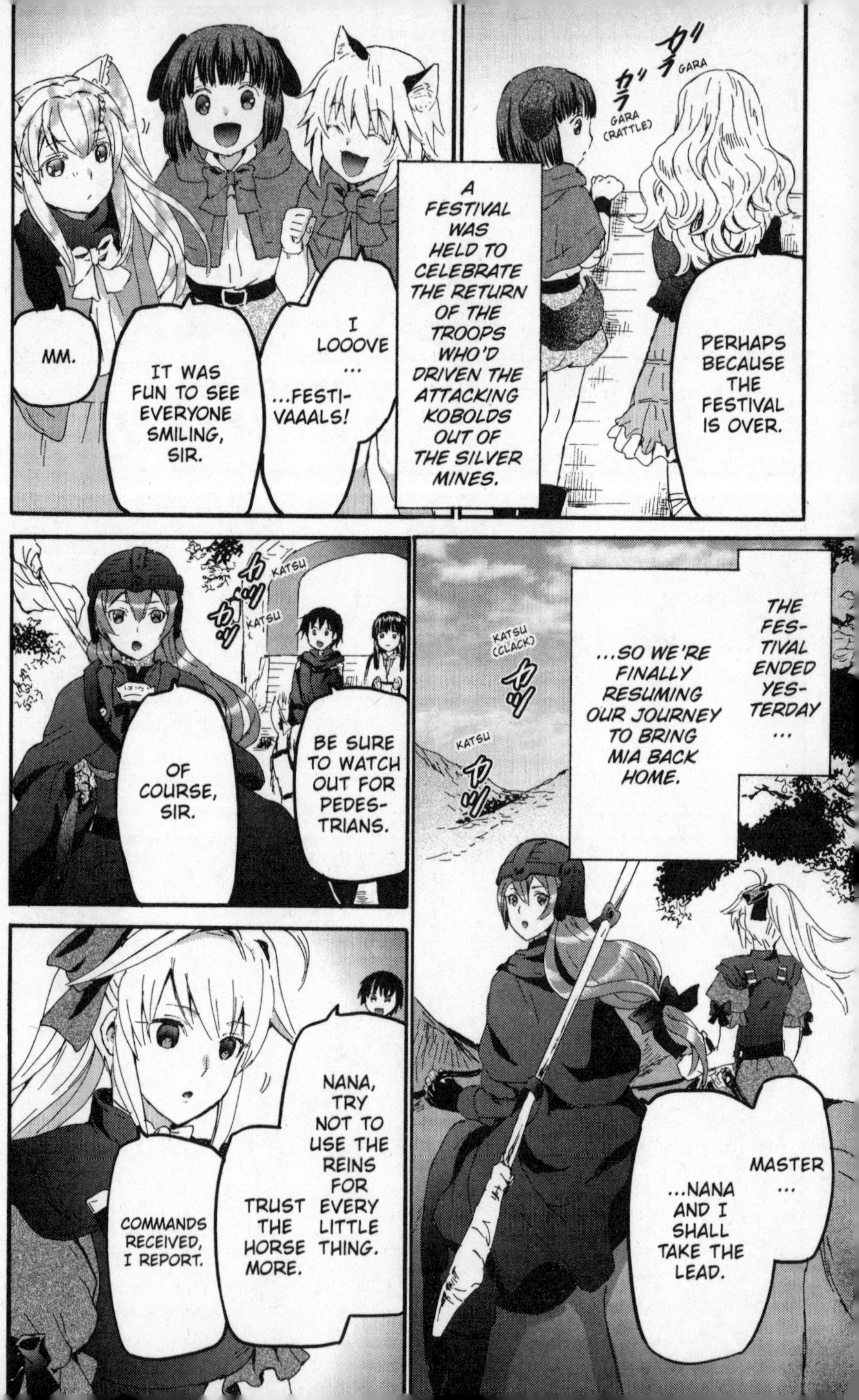
GARA
GARA (RATTLE)
PERHAPS BECAUSE THE FESTIVAL IS OVER.
A FESTIVAL WAS HELD TO CELEBRATE THE RETURN OF THE TROOPS WHO'D DRIVEN THE ATTACKING KOBOLDS OUT OF THE SILVER MINES.
I LOOOVE ...
...FESTI-VAAALS!
IT WAS FUN TO SEE EVERYONE SMILING, SIR.
MM.
THE FES-TIVAL ENDED YES-TERDAY ...
...SO WE'RE FINALLY RESUMING OUR JOURNEY TO BRING MIA BACK HOME.
KATSU (CLACK)
KATSU
KATSU
KATSU
BE SURE TO WATCH OUT FOR PEDES-TRIANS.
OF COURSE, SIR.
MASTER ...
...NANA AND I SHALL TAKE THE LEAD.
NANA, TRY NOT TO USE THE REINS FOR EVERY LITTLE THING.
TRUST THE HORSE MORE.
COMMANDS RECEIVED, I REPORT.

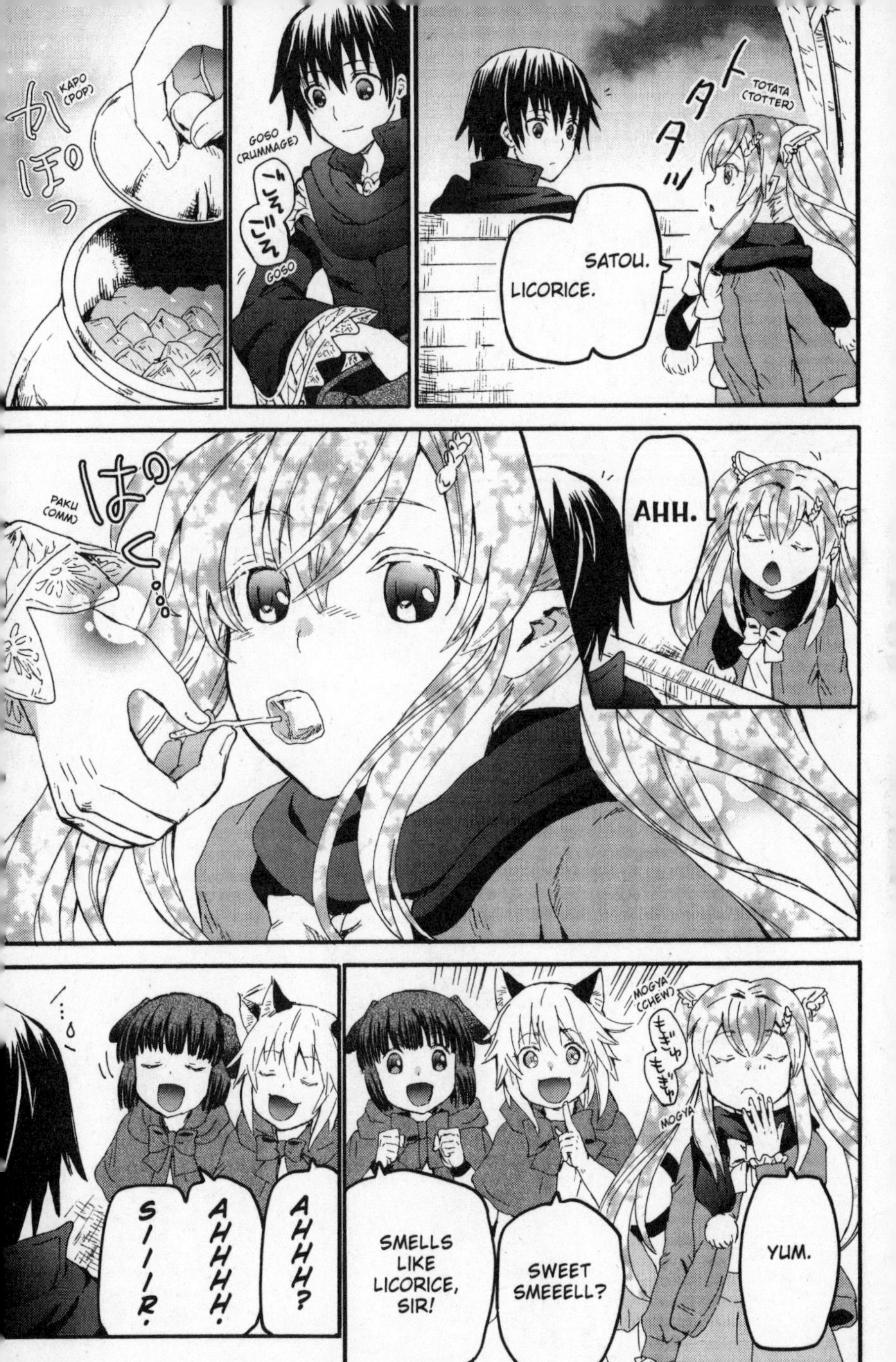
TOTATA (TOTTER)
トタタッ
SATOU. LICORICE.
GOSO (RUMMAGE)
ごそごそ
GOSO
KAPO (POP)
かぽっ
AHH.
PAKU (OMM)
MOGYA (CHEW)
MOGYA
YUM.
SWEET SMEEELL?
SMELLS LIKE LICORICE, SIR!
AHHH?
AHHHH.
SIIIR.
...

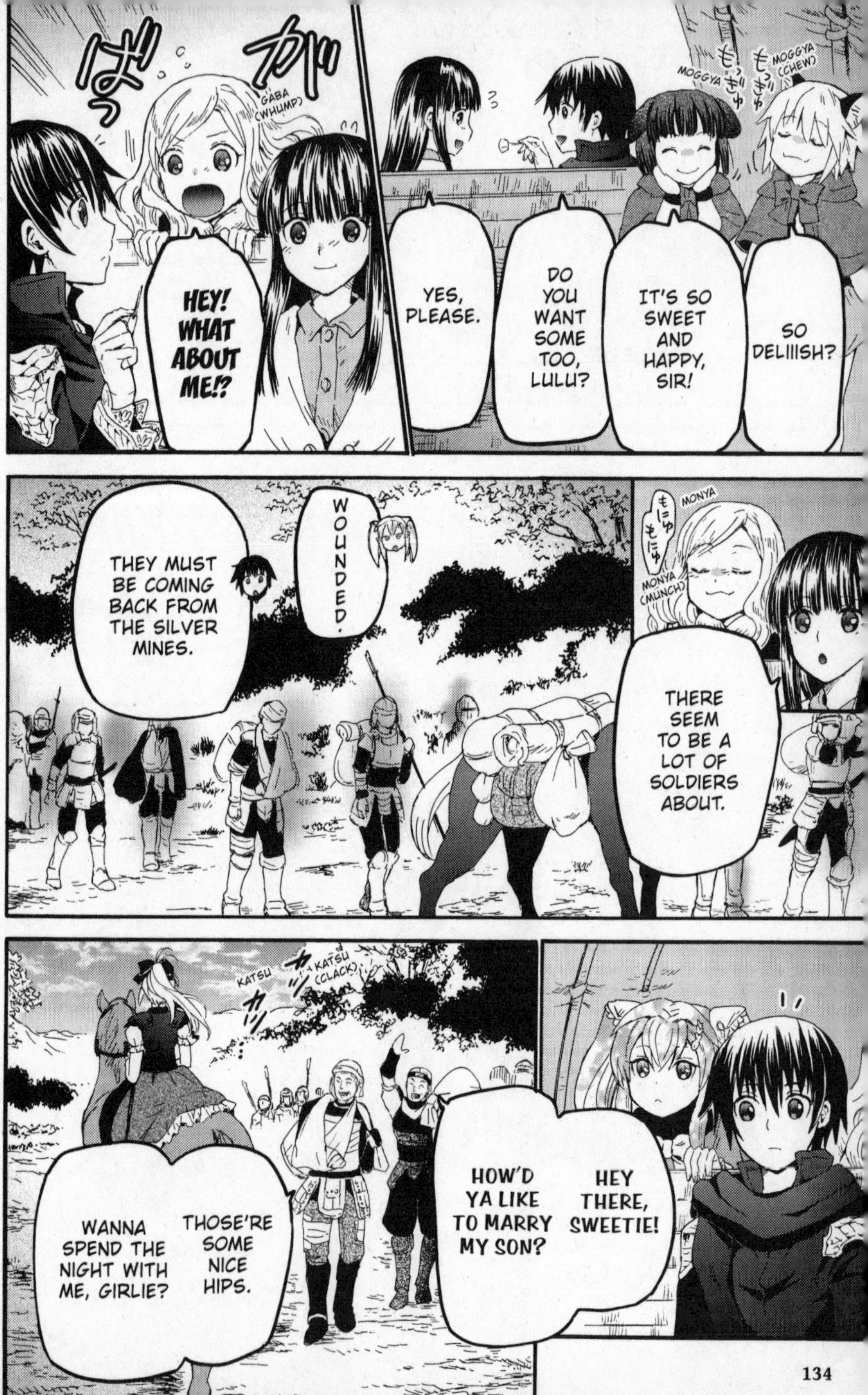
MOGGYA (CHEW)
MOGGYA
SO DELIIISH?
IT'S SO SWEET AND HAPPY, SIR!
DO YOU WANT SOME TOO, LULU?
YES, PLEASE.
GABA (WHUMP)
HEY! WHAT ABOUT ME!?
MONYA
MONYA (MUNCH)
THERE SEEM TO BE A LOT OF SOLDIERS ABOUT.
WOUNDED.
THEY MUST BE COMING BACK FROM THE SILVER MINES.
HEY THERE, SWEETIE!
HOW'D YA LIKE TO MARRY MY SON?
KATSU (CLACK)
KATSU
THOSE'RE SOME NICE HIPS.
WANNA SPEND THE NIGHT WITH ME, GIRLIE?

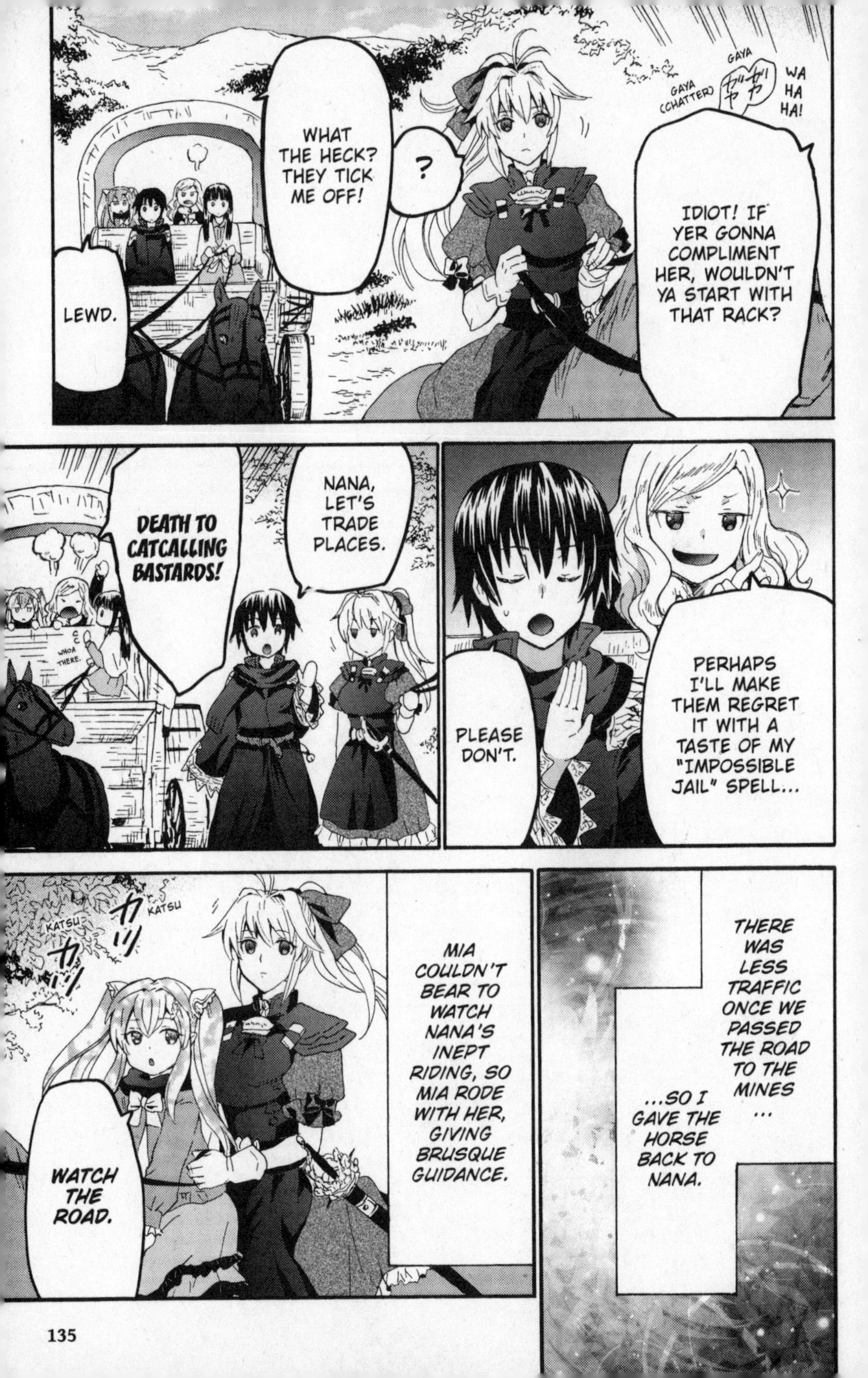
WA HA HA!
GAYA
GAYA (CHATTER)
IDIOT! IF YER GONNA COMPLIMENT HER, WOULDN'T YA START WITH THAT RACK?
?
WHAT THE HECK? THEY TICK ME OFF!
LEWD.
PERHAPS I'LL MAKE THEM REGRET IT WITH A TASTE OF MY "IMPOSSIBLE JAIL" SPELL...
PLEASE DON'T.
NANA, LET'S TRADE PLACES.
DEATH TO CATCALLING BASTARDS!
WHOA THERE.
THERE WAS LESS TRAFFIC ONCE WE PASSED THE ROAD TO THE MINES...
...SO I GAVE THE HORSE BACK TO NANA.
MIA COULDN'T BEAR TO WATCH NANA'S INEPT RIDING, SO MIA RODE WITH HER, GIVING BRUSQUE GUIDANCE.
KATSU
KATSU
WATCH THE ROAD.

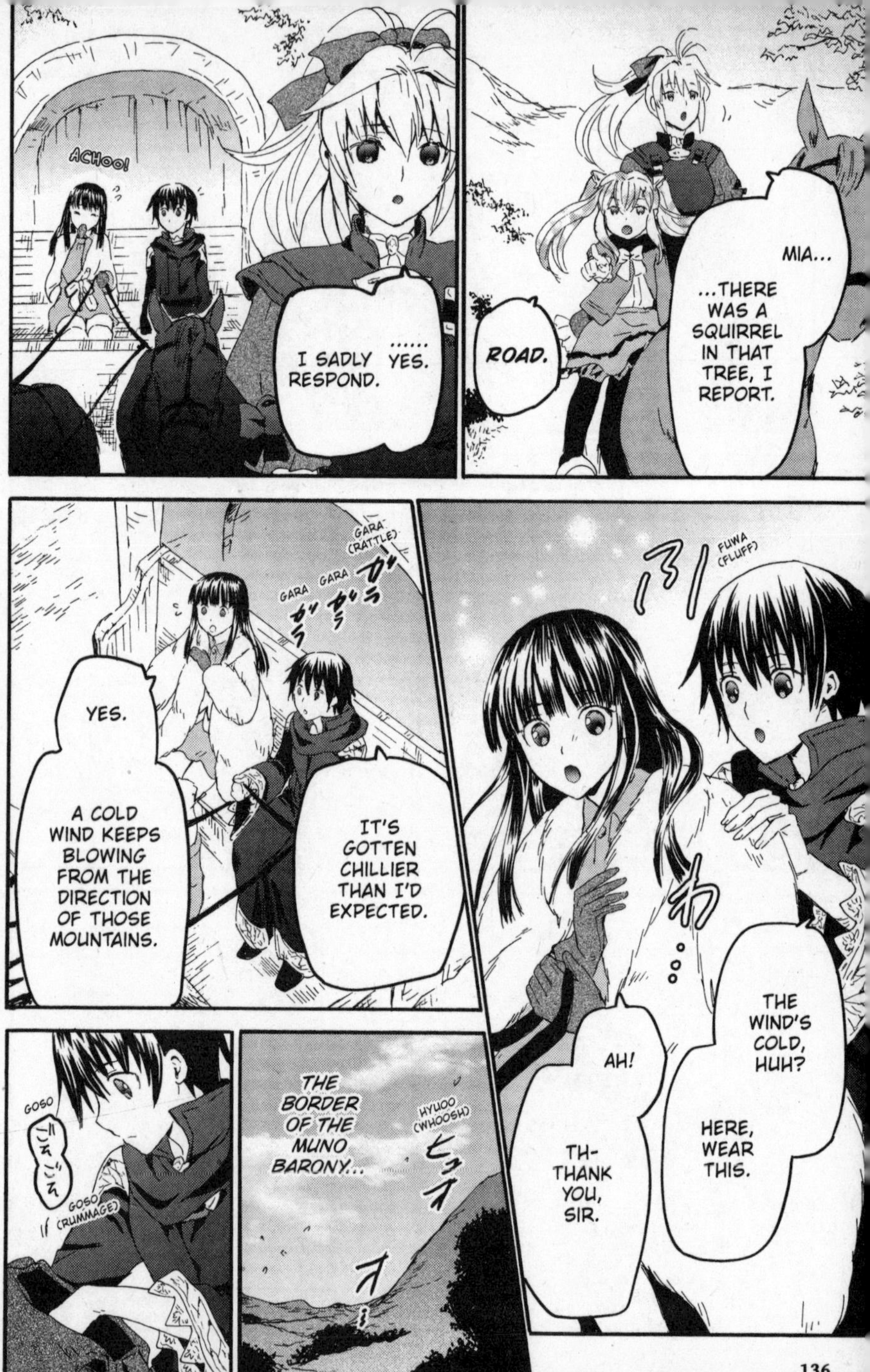
MIA...
...THERE WAS A SQUIRREL IN THAT TREE, I REPORT.
ROAD.
...... YES.
I SADLY RESPOND.
ACHOO!
FUWA (FLUFF)
THE WIND'S COLD, HUH?
HERE, WEAR THIS.
AH!
TH-THANK YOU, SIR.
GARA (RATTLE)
GARA GARA
IT'S GOTTEN CHILLIER THAN I'D EXPECTED.
YES.
A COLD WIND KEEPS BLOWING FROM THE DIRECTION OF THOSE MOUNTAINS.
HYUOO (WHOOSH)
THE BORDER OF THE MUNO BARONY...
GOSO
GOSO (RUMMAGE)

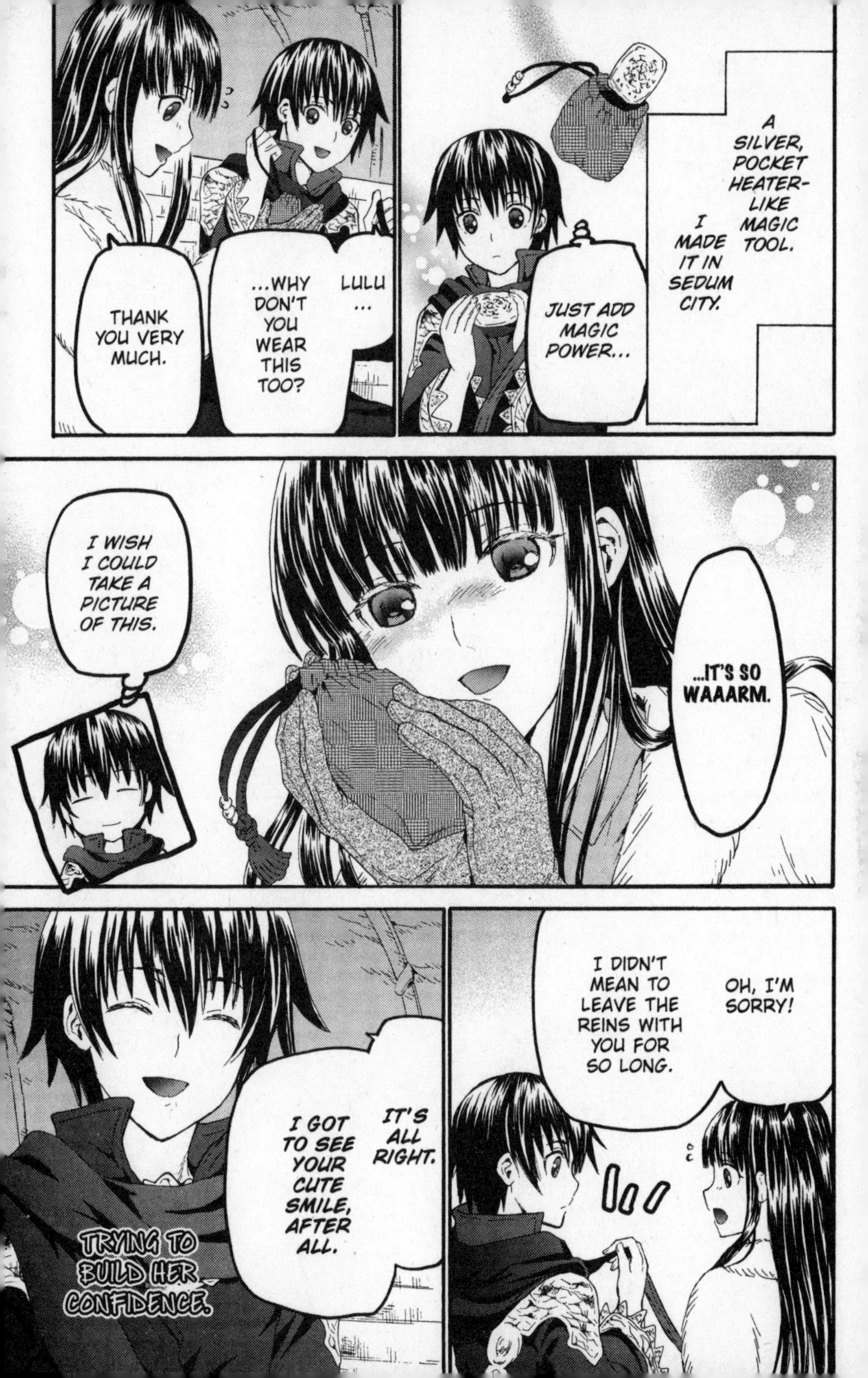
A SILVER, POCKET HEATER-LIKE MAGIC TOOL.
I MADE IT IN SEDUM CITY.
JUST ADD MAGIC POWER...
LULU...
...WHY DON'T YOU WEAR THIS TOO?
THANK YOU VERY MUCH.
...IT'S SO WAAARM.
I WISH I COULD TAKE A PICTURE OF THIS.
OH, I'M SORRY!
I DIDN'T MEAN TO LEAVE THE REINS WITH YOU FOR SO LONG.
IT'S ALL RIGHT.
I GOT TO SEE YOUR CUTE SMILE, AFTER ALL.
TRYING TO BUILD HER CONFIDENCE.

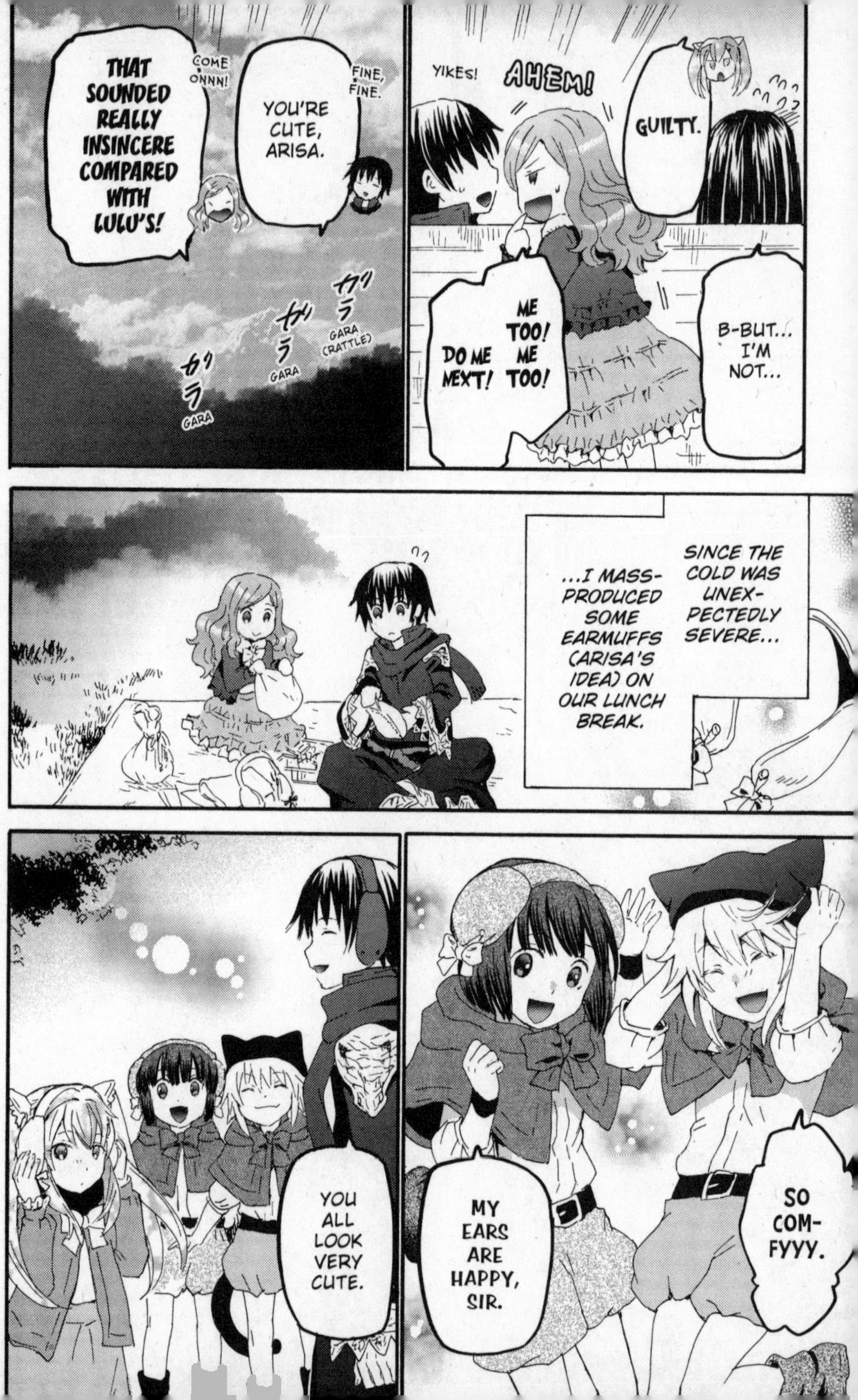
GUILTY.
AHEM!
YIKES!
B-BUT... I'M NOT...
ME TOO! ME TOO!
DO ME NEXT!
FINE, FINE.
YOU'RE CUTE, ARISA.
COME ONNN!
THAT SOUNDED REALLY INSINCERE COMPARED WITH LULU'S!
カラ
GARA (RATTLE)
カラ
GARA
カラ
GARA
SINCE THE COLD WAS UNEX-PECTEDLY SEVERE...
...I MASS-PRODUCED SOME EARMUFFS (ARISA'S IDEA) ON OUR LUNCH BREAK.
SO COM-FYYY.
MY EARS ARE HAPPY, SIR.
YOU ALL LOOK VERY CUTE.

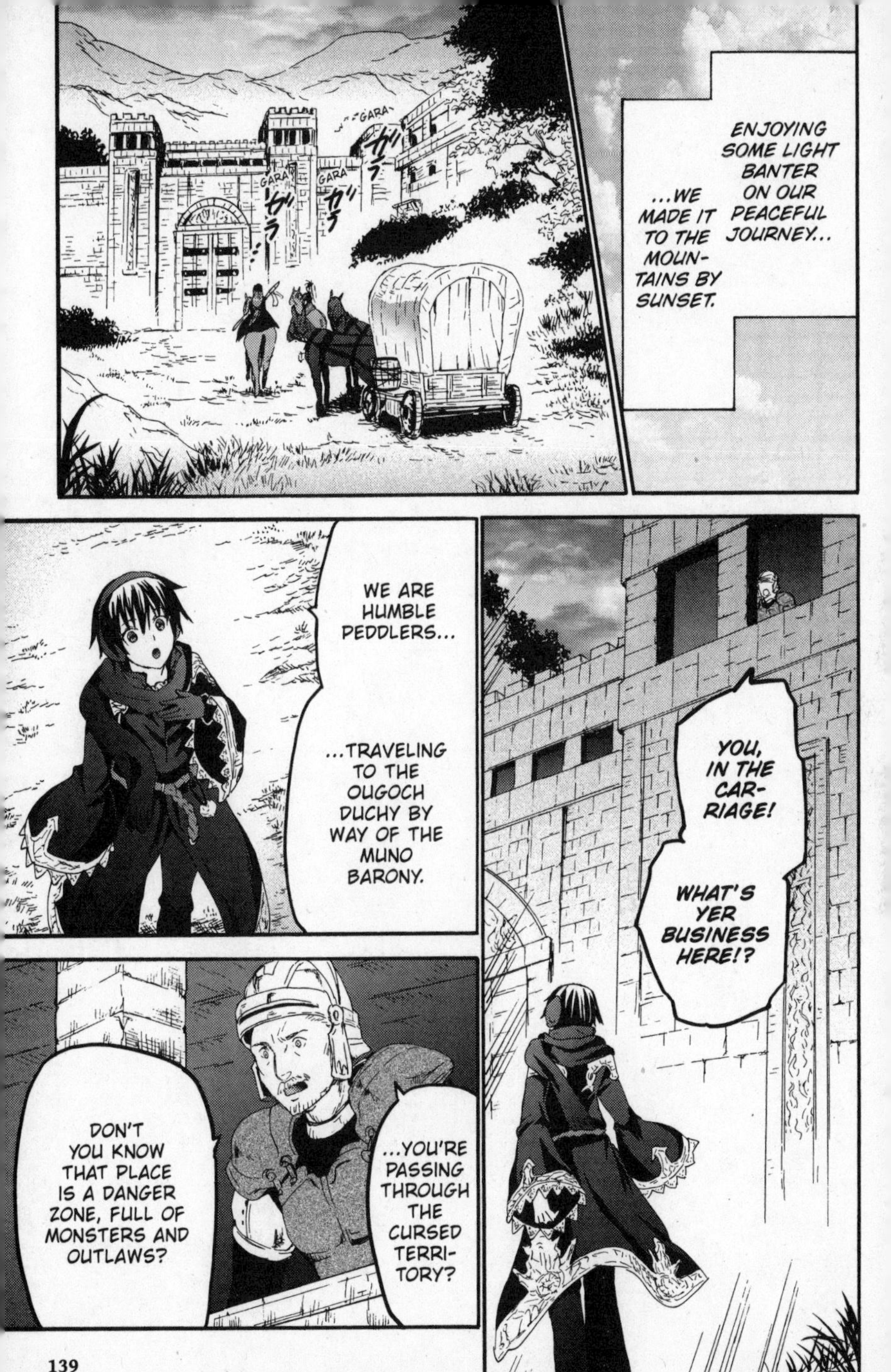
ENJOYING SOME LIGHT BANTER ON OUR PEACEFUL JOURNEY...
...WE MADE IT TO THE MOUNTAINS BY SUNSET.
GARA
GARA
GARA
YOU, IN THE CARRIAGE!
WHAT'S YER BUSINESS HERE!?
WE ARE HUMBLE PEDDLERS...
...TRAVELING TO THE OUGOCH DUCHY BY WAY OF THE MUNO BARONY.
...YOU'RE PASSING THROUGH THE CURSED TERRITORY?
DON'T YOU KNOW THAT PLACE IS A DANGER ZONE, FULL OF MONSTERS AND OUTLAWS?

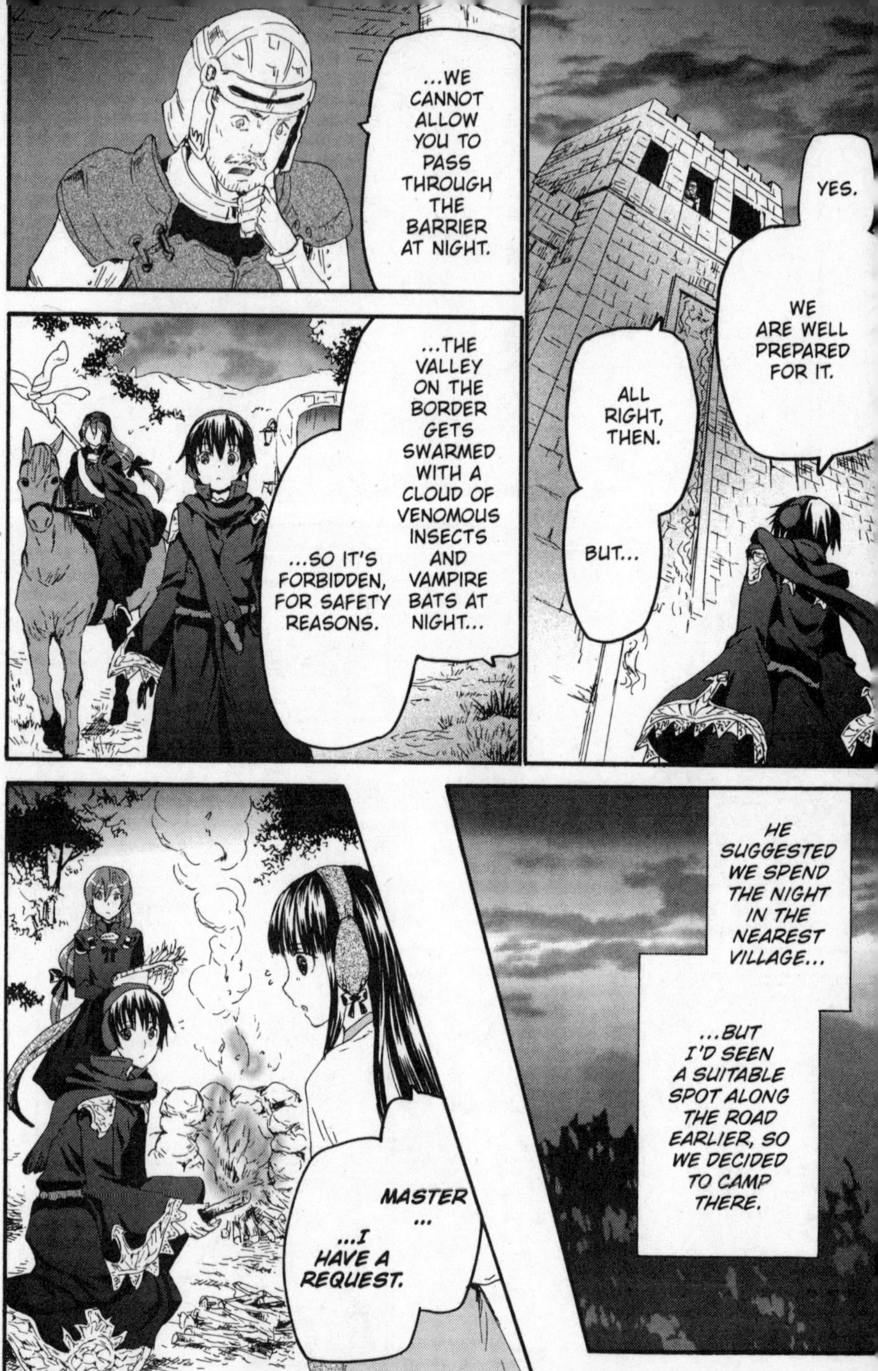
YES.
WE ARE WELL PREPARED FOR IT.
ALL RIGHT, THEN.
BUT...
...WE CANNOT ALLOW YOU TO PASS THROUGH THE BARRIER AT NIGHT.
...THE VALLEY ON THE BORDER GETS SWARMED WITH A CLOUD OF VENOMOUS INSECTS AND VAMPIRE BATS AT NIGHT...
...SO IT'S FORBIDDEN, FOR SAFETY REASONS.
HE SUGGESTED WE SPEND THE NIGHT IN THE NEAREST VILLAGE...
...BUT I'D SEEN A SUITABLE SPOT ALONG THE ROAD EARLIER, SO WE DECIDED TO CAMP THERE.
MASTER...
...I HAVE A REQUEST.

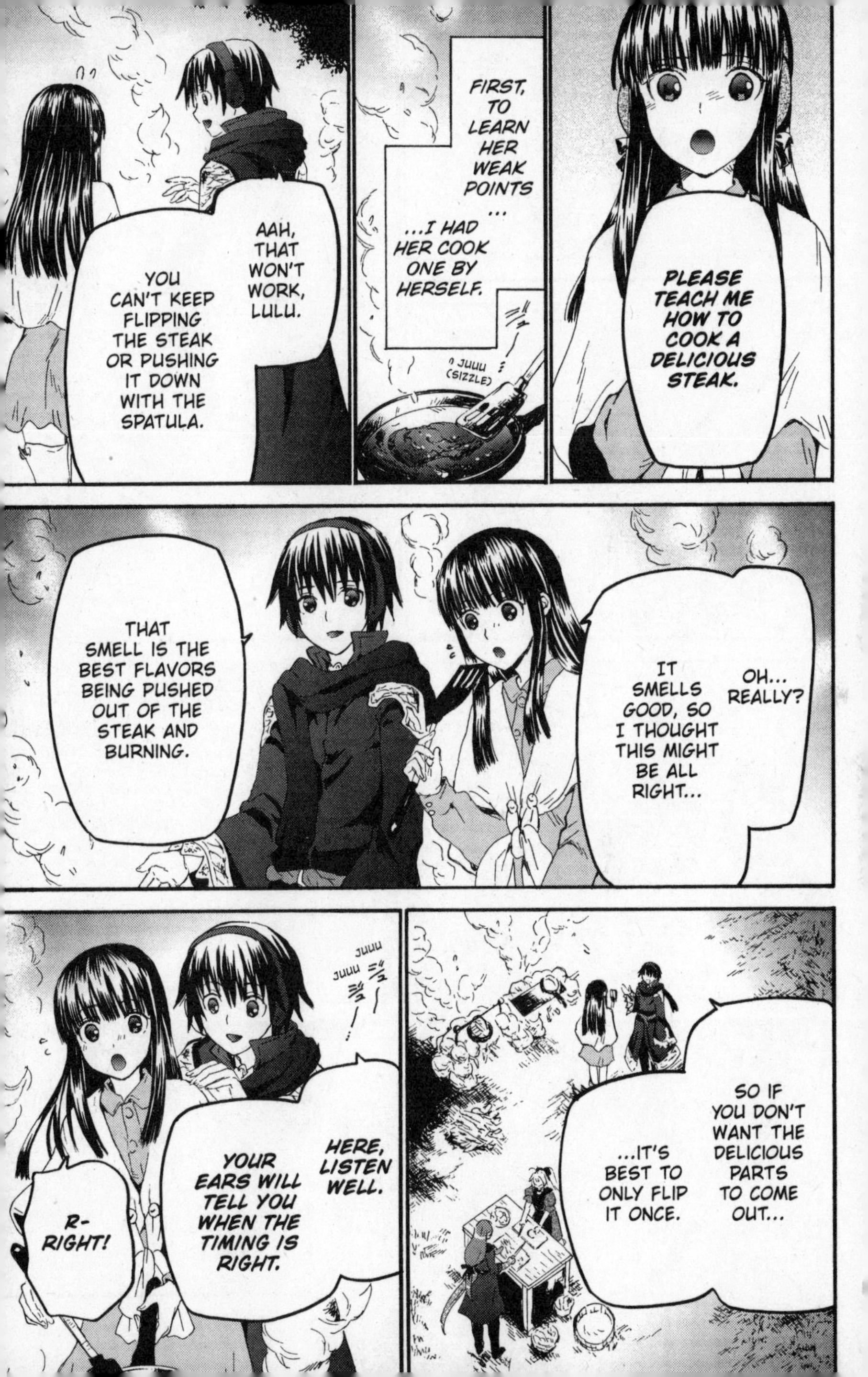
PLEASE TEACH ME HOW TO COOK A DELICIOUS STEAK.
FIRST, TO LEARN HER WEAK POINTS...
...I HAD HER COOK ONE BY HERSELF.
JUUU (SIZZLE)
AAH, THAT WON'T WORK, LULU.
YOU CAN'T KEEP FLIPPING THE STEAK OR PUSHING IT DOWN WITH THE SPATULA.
OH... REALLY?
IT SMELLS GOOD, SO I THOUGHT THIS MIGHT BE ALL RIGHT...
THAT SMELL IS THE BEST FLAVORS BEING PUSHED OUT OF THE STEAK AND BURNING.
SO IF YOU DON'T WANT THE DELICIOUS PARTS TO COME OUT...
...IT'S BEST TO ONLY FLIP IT ONCE.
JUUU
JUUU
HERE, LISTEN WELL.
YOUR EARS WILL TELL YOU WHEN THE TIMING IS RIGHT.
R-RIGHT!

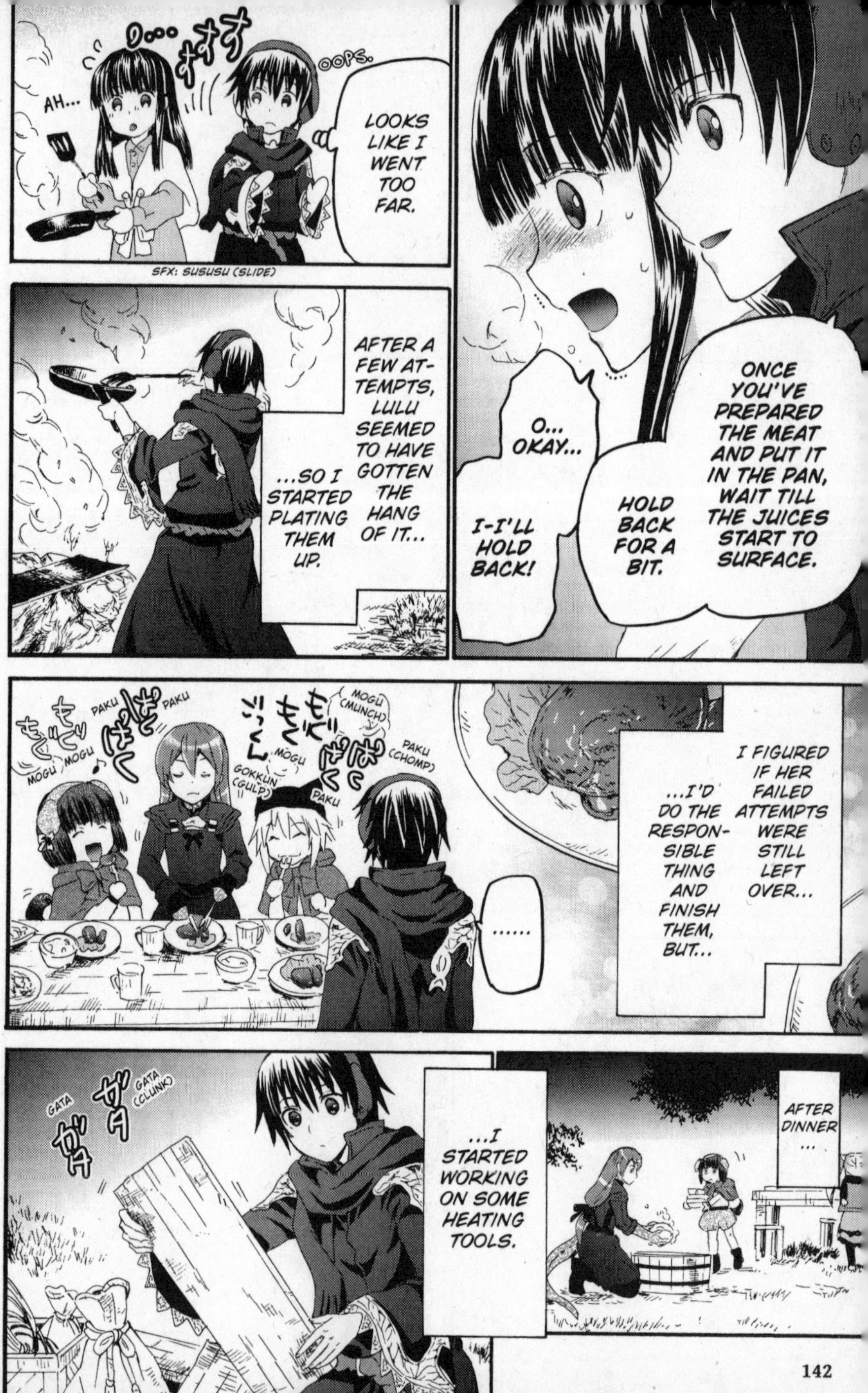
ONCE YOU'VE PREPARED THE MEAT AND PUT IT IN THE PAN, WAIT TILL THE JUICES START TO SURFACE.
HOLD BACK FOR A BIT.
O... OKAY...
I-I'LL HOLD BACK!
OOPS.
LOOKS LIKE I WENT TOO FAR.
AH...
SFX: SUSUSU (SLIDE)
AFTER A FEW AT-TEMPTS, LULU SEEMED TO HAVE GOTTEN THE HANG OF IT...
...SO I STARTED PLATING THEM UP.
I FIGURED IF HER FAILED ATTEMPTS WERE STILL LEFT OVER...
...I'D DO THE RESPON-SIBLE THING AND FINISH THEM, BUT...
......
MOGU (MUNCH)
PAKU (CHOMP)
PAKU
MOGU
GOKKUN (GULP)
PAKU
PAKU
MOGU
MOGU
MOGU
AFTER DINNER...
...I STARTED WORKING ON SOME HEATING TOOLS.
GATA (CLUNK)
GATA

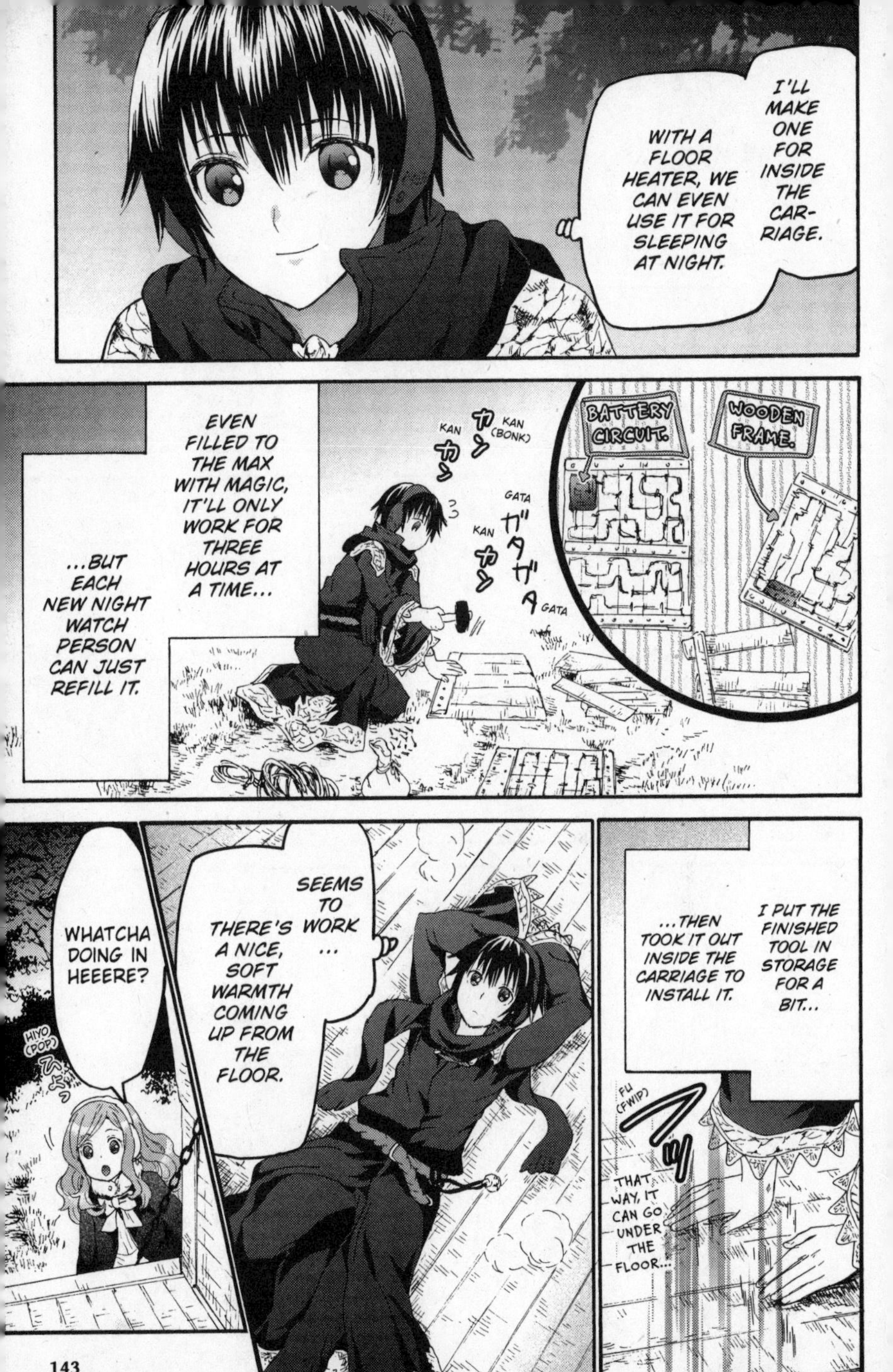

I'LL MAKE ONE FOR INSIDE THE CAR-RIAGE.
WITH A FLOOR HEATER, WE CAN EVEN USE IT FOR SLEEPING AT NIGHT.
WOODEN FRAME.
BATTERY CIRCUIT.
KAN (BONK)
カン
KAN
カン
GATA
ガタ
KAN
カン
ガタ
GATA
EVEN FILLED TO THE MAX WITH MAGIC, IT'LL ONLY WORK FOR THREE HOURS AT A TIME...
...BUT EACH NEW NIGHT WATCH PERSON CAN JUST REFILL IT.
I PUT THE FINISHED TOOL IN STORAGE FOR A BIT...
...THEN TOOK IT OUT INSIDE THE CARRIAGE TO INSTALL IT.
FU (FWIP)
フッ
THAT WAY, IT CAN GO UNDER THE FLOOR...
SEEMS TO WORK...
THERE'S A NICE, SOFT WARMTH COMING UP FROM THE FLOOR.
HIYO (POP)
ひょっ
WHATCHA DOING IN HEEERE?

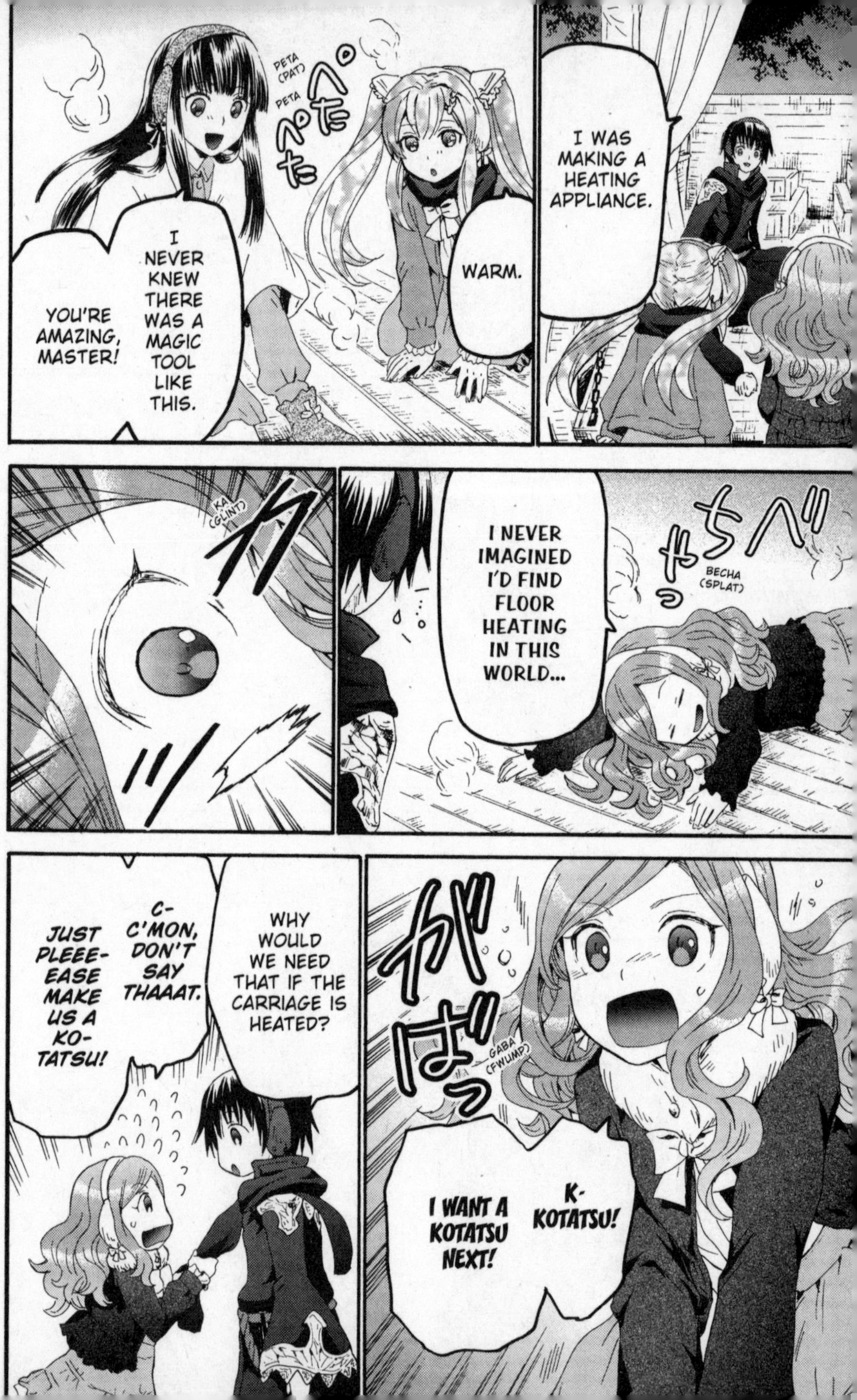
I WAS MAKING A HEATING APPLIANCE.
PETA (PAT) PETA
WARM.
I NEVER KNEW THERE WAS A MAGIC TOOL LIKE THIS.
YOU'RE AMAZING, MASTER!
BECHA (SPLAT)
I NEVER IMAGINED I'D FIND FLOOR HEATING IN THIS WORLD...
KA (GLINT)
GABA (FWUMP)
K-KOTATSU!
I WANT A KOTATSU NEXT!
WHY WOULD WE NEED THAT IF THE CARRIAGE IS HEATED?
C-C'MON, DON'T SAY THAAAT.
JUST PLEEE-EASE MAKE US A KO-TATSU!

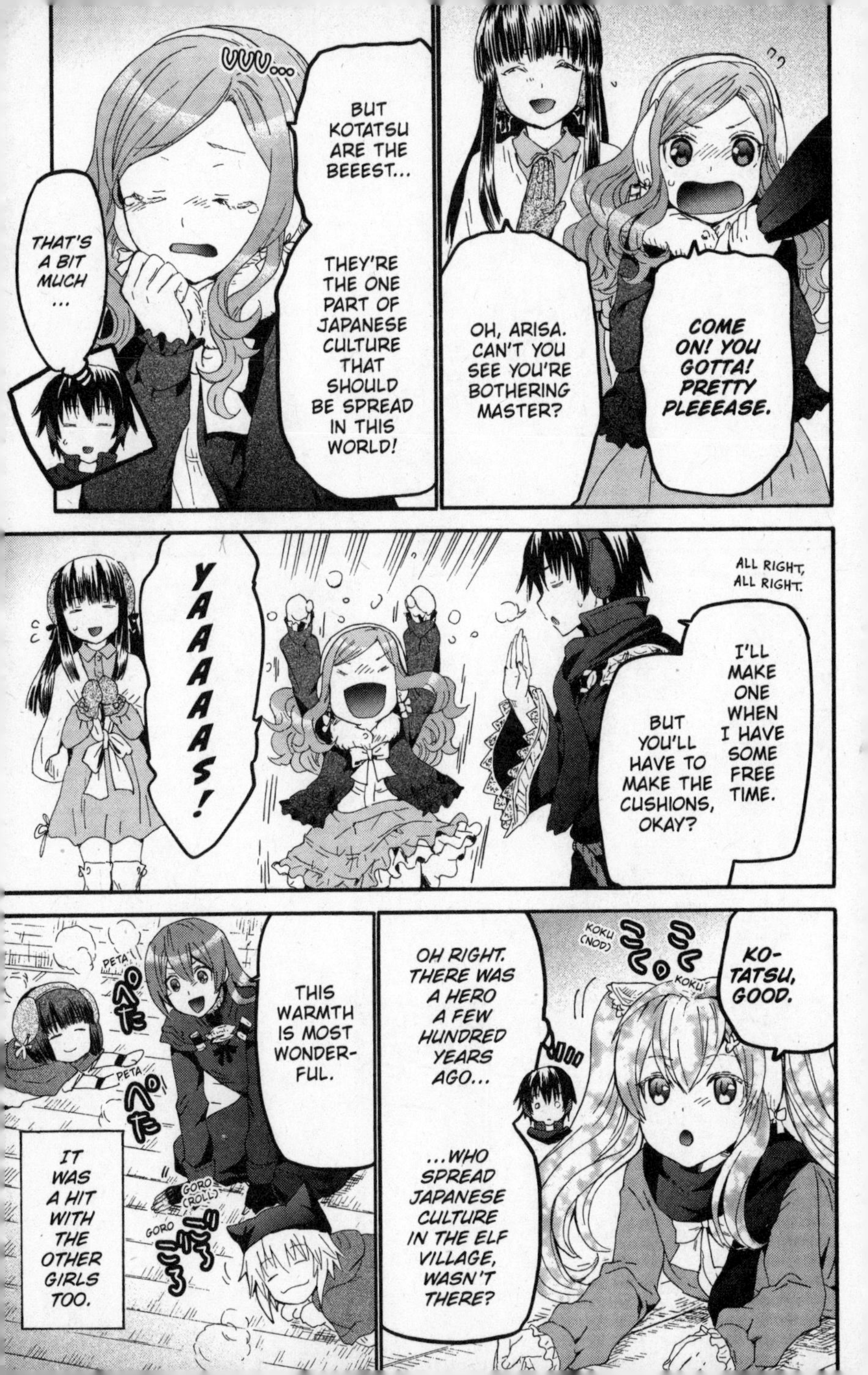
COME ON! YOU GOTTA! PRETTY PLEEEASE.
OH, ARISA. CAN'T YOU SEE YOU'RE BOTHERING MASTER?
UUU...
BUT KOTATSU ARE THE BEEEST...
THEY'RE THE ONE PART OF JAPANESE CULTURE THAT SHOULD BE SPREAD IN THIS WORLD!
THAT'S A BIT MUCH...
ALL RIGHT, ALL RIGHT.
I'LL MAKE ONE WHEN I HAVE SOME FREE TIME.
BUT YOU'LL HAVE TO MAKE THE CUSHIONS, OKAY?
YAAAAAAS!
KO-TATSU, GOOD.
KOKU (NOD)
KOKU
OH RIGHT. THERE WAS A HERO A FEW HUNDRED YEARS AGO...
...WHO SPREAD JAPANESE CULTURE IN THE ELF VILLAGE, WASN'T THERE?
THIS WARMTH IS MOST WONDERFUL.
PETA
PETA
GORO (ROLL)
GORO
IT WAS A HIT WITH THE OTHER GIRLS TOO.

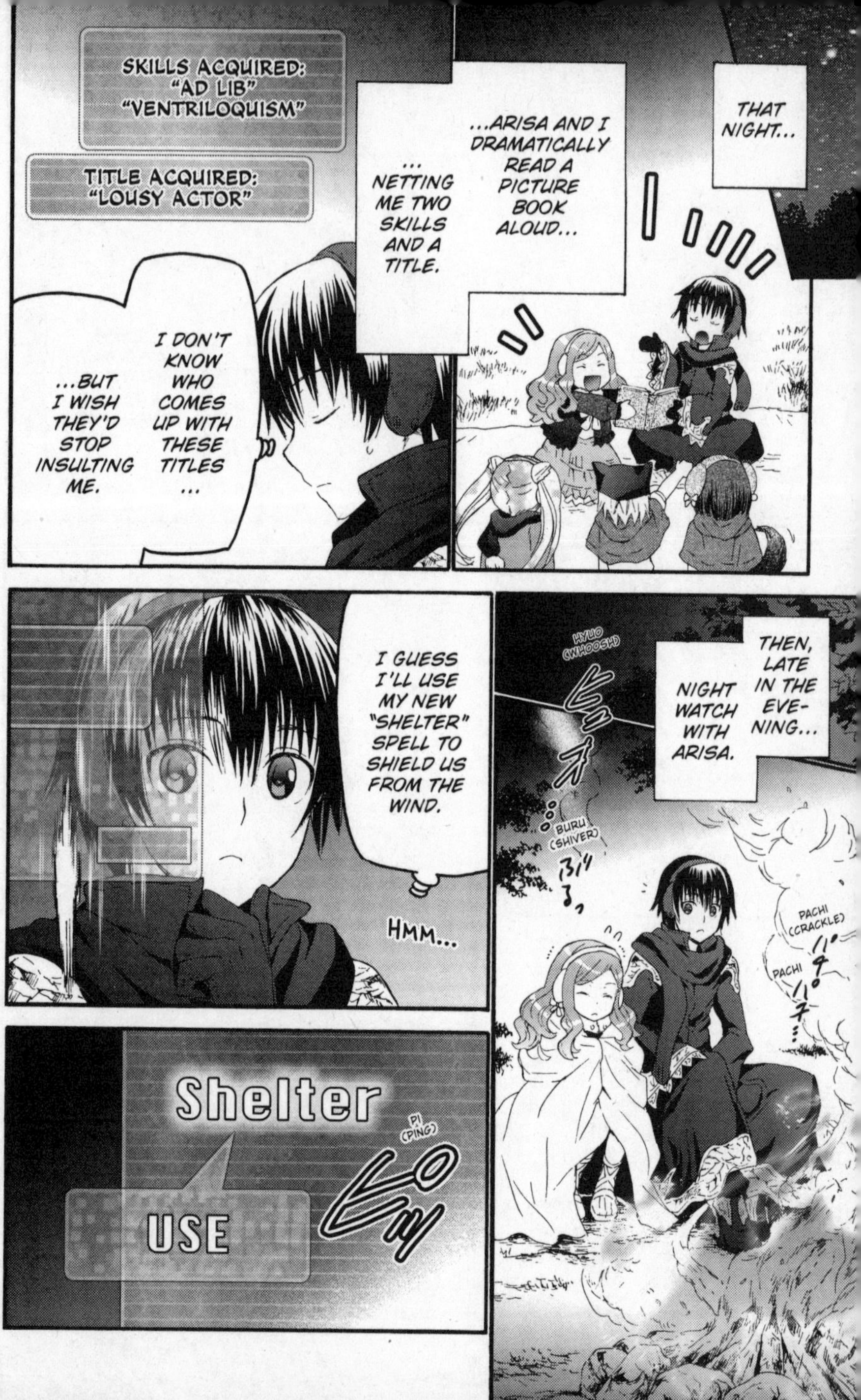
THAT NIGHT...
...ARISA AND I DRAMATICALLY READ A PICTURE BOOK ALOUD...
...NETTING ME TWO SKILLS AND A TITLE.
SKILLS ACQUIRED: "AD LIB" "VENTRILOQUISM"
TITLE ACQUIRED: "LOUSY ACTOR"
I DON'T KNOW WHO COMES UP WITH THESE TITLES...
...BUT I WISH THEY'D STOP INSULTING ME.
THEN, LATE IN THE EVENING...
NIGHT WATCH WITH ARISA.
HYUO (WHOOSH)
BURU (SHIVER)
PACHI (CRACKLE)
PACHI
I GUESS I'LL USE MY NEW "SHELTER" SPELL TO SHIELD US FROM THE WIND.
HMM...
Shelter
USE
PI (PING)

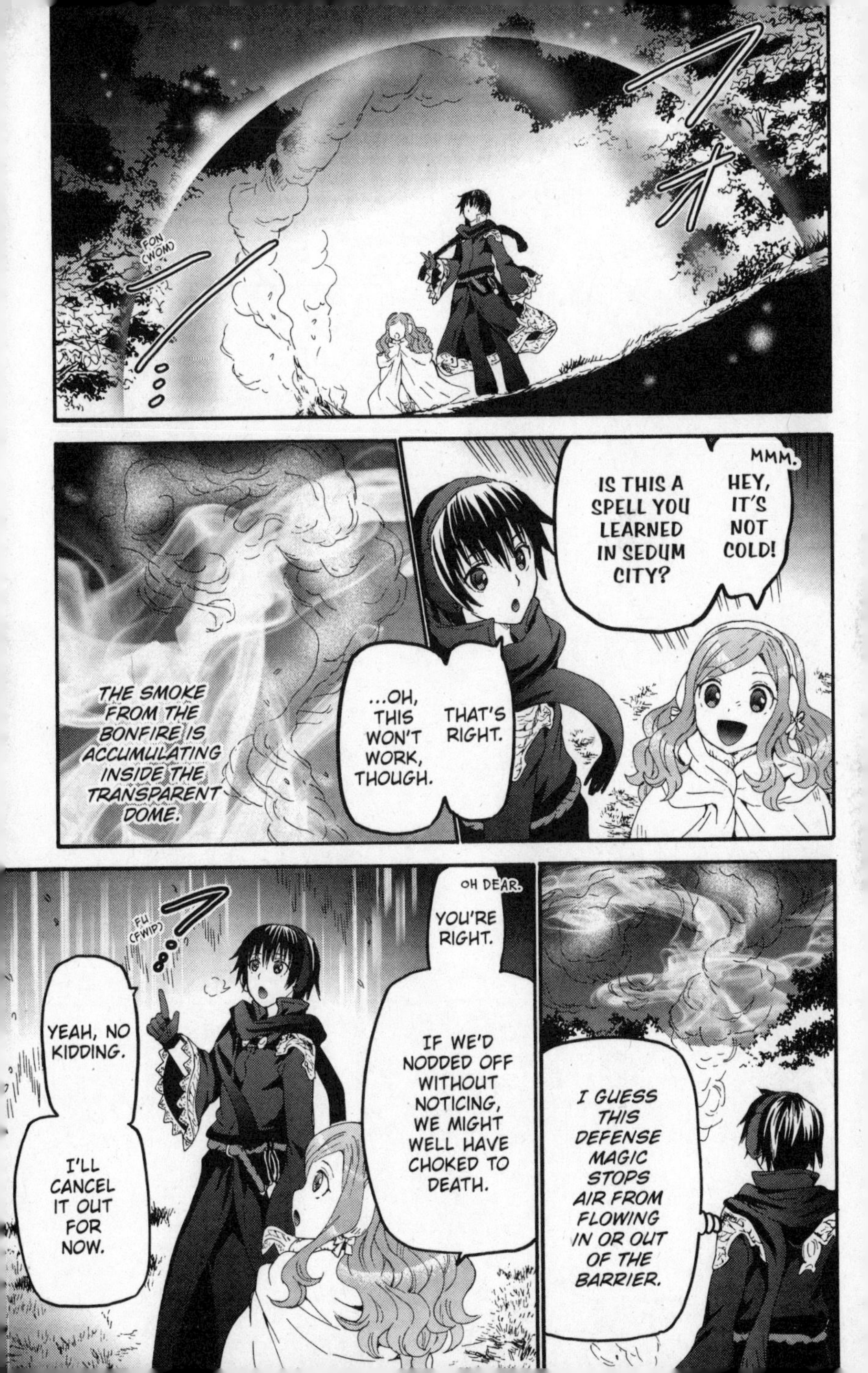
FON (WOM)
MMM.
HEY, IT'S NOT COLD!
IS THIS A SPELL YOU LEARNED IN SEDUM CITY?
THAT'S RIGHT.
...OH, THIS WON'T WORK, THOUGH.
THE SMOKE FROM THE BONFIRE IS ACCUMULATING INSIDE THE TRANSPARENT DOME.
I GUESS THIS DEFENSE MAGIC STOPS AIR FROM FLOWING IN OR OUT OF THE BARRIER.
OH DEAR.
YOU'RE RIGHT.
IF WE'D NODDED OFF WITHOUT NOTICING, WE MIGHT WELL HAVE CHOKED TO DEATH.
FU (FWIP)
YEAH, NO KIDDING.
I'LL CANCEL IT OUT FOR NOW.

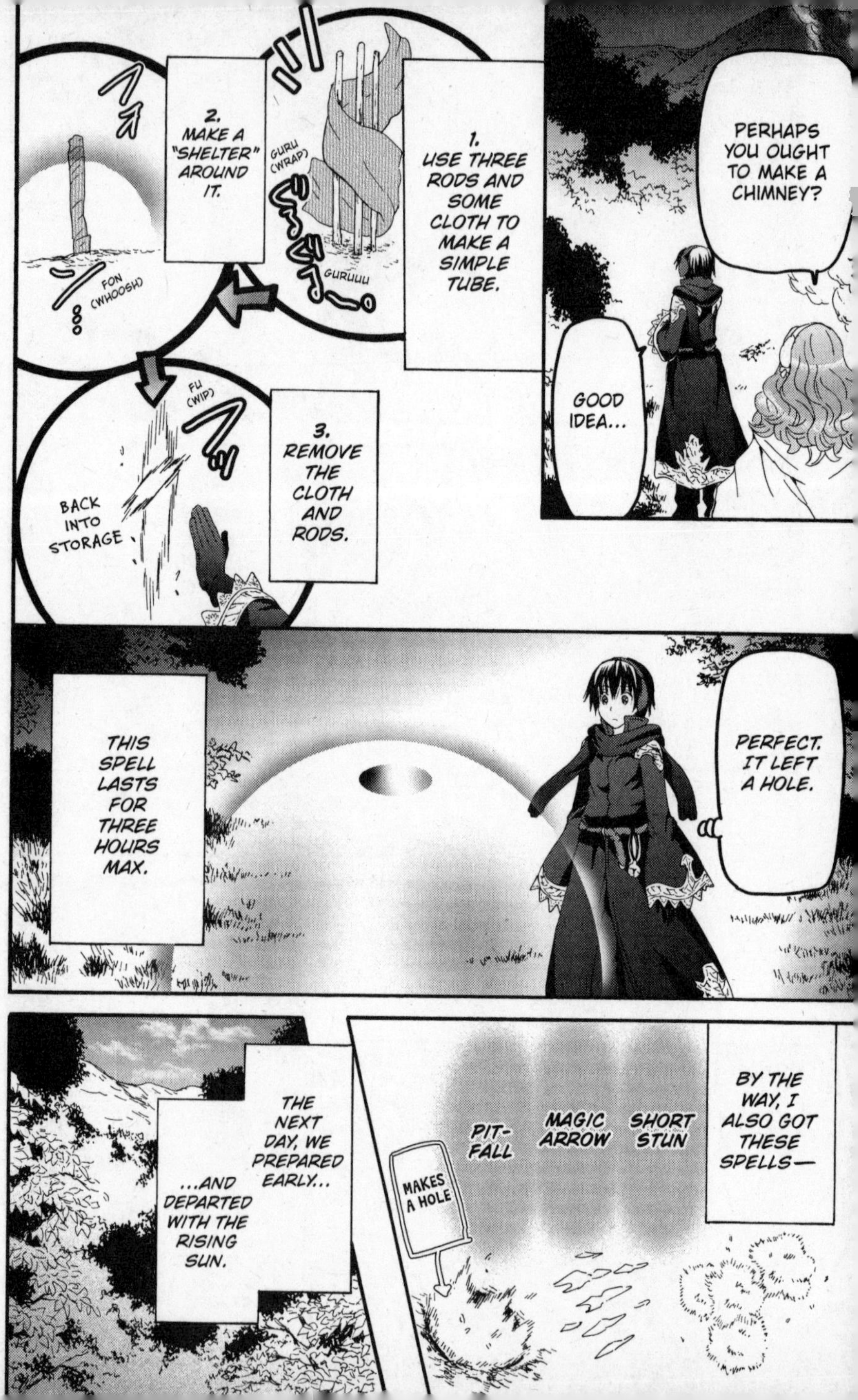
PERHAPS YOU OUGHT TO MAKE A CHIMNEY?
GOOD IDEA...
1. USE THREE RODS AND SOME CLOTH TO MAKE A SIMPLE TUBE.
GURU (WRAP)
GURUUU
2. MAKE A "SHELTER" AROUND IT.
FON (WHOOSH)
3. REMOVE THE CLOTH AND RODS.
FU (WIP)
BACK INTO STORAGE
PERFECT. IT LEFT A HOLE.
THIS SPELL LASTS FOR THREE HOURS MAX.
BY THE WAY, I ALSO GOT THESE SPELLS—
SHORT STUN
MAGIC ARROW
PIT-FALL
MAKES A HOLE
THE NEXT DAY, WE PREPARED EARLY...
...AND DEPARTED WITH THE RISING SUN.

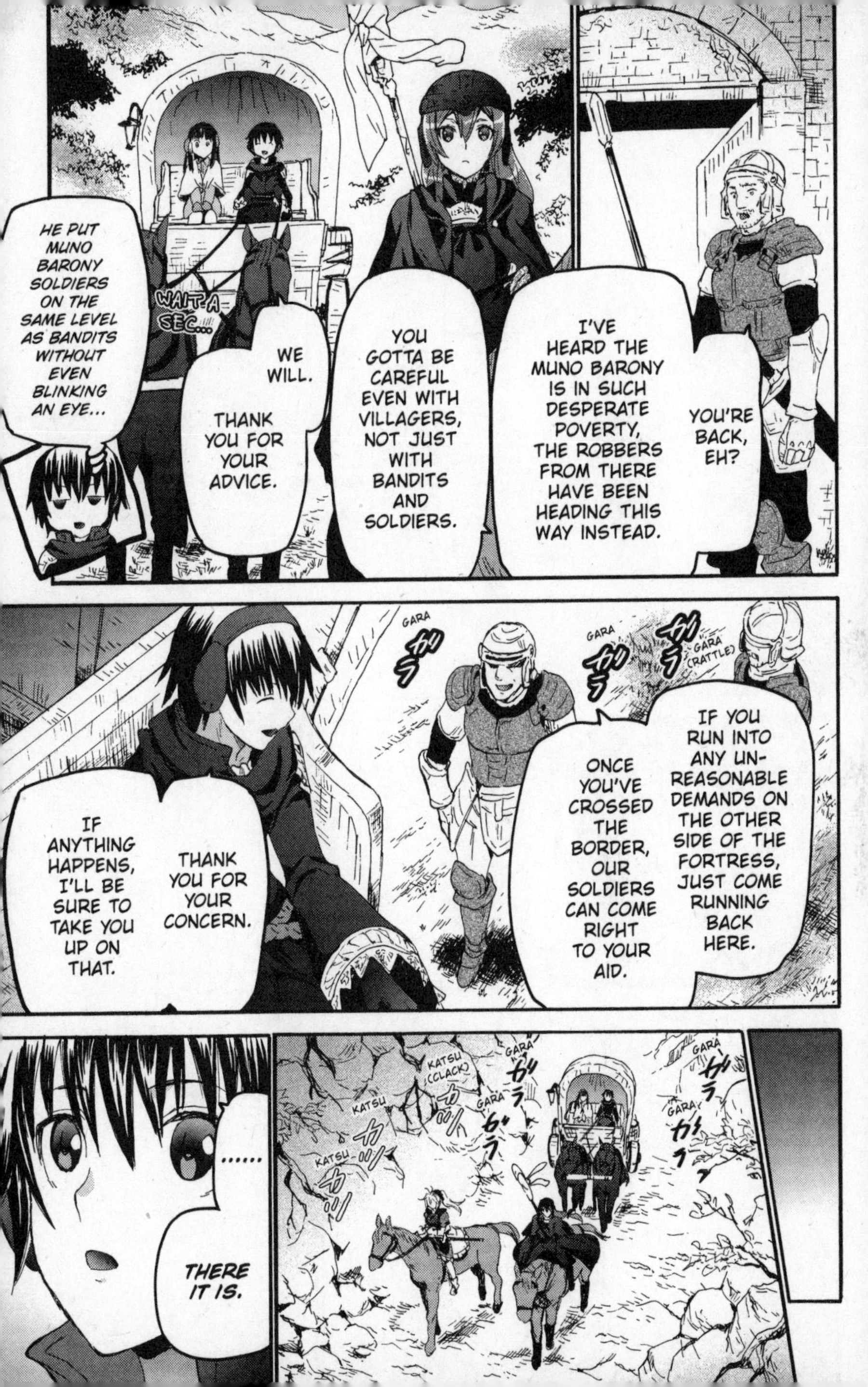

YOU'RE BACK, EH?
I'VE HEARD THE MUNO BARONY IS IN SUCH DESPERATE POVERTY, THE ROBBERS FROM THERE HAVE BEEN HEADING THIS WAY INSTEAD.
YOU GOTTA BE CAREFUL EVEN WITH VILLAGERS, NOT JUST WITH BANDITS AND SOLDIERS.
WE WILL.
THANK YOU FOR YOUR ADVICE.
WAIT A SEC...
HE PUT MUNO BARONY SOLDIERS ON THE SAME LEVEL AS BANDITS WITHOUT EVEN BLINKING AN EYE...
GARA (RATTLE)
GARA
GARA
IF YOU RUN INTO ANY UN-REASONABLE DEMANDS ON THE OTHER SIDE OF THE FORTRESS, JUST COME RUNNING BACK HERE.
ONCE YOU'VE CROSSED THE BORDER, OUR SOLDIERS CAN COME RIGHT TO YOUR AID.
THANK YOU FOR YOUR CONCERN.
IF ANYTHING HAPPENS, I'LL BE SURE TO TAKE YOU UP ON THAT.
GARA
GARA
GARA
GARA
KATSU (CLACK)
KATSU
KATSU
......
THERE IT IS.

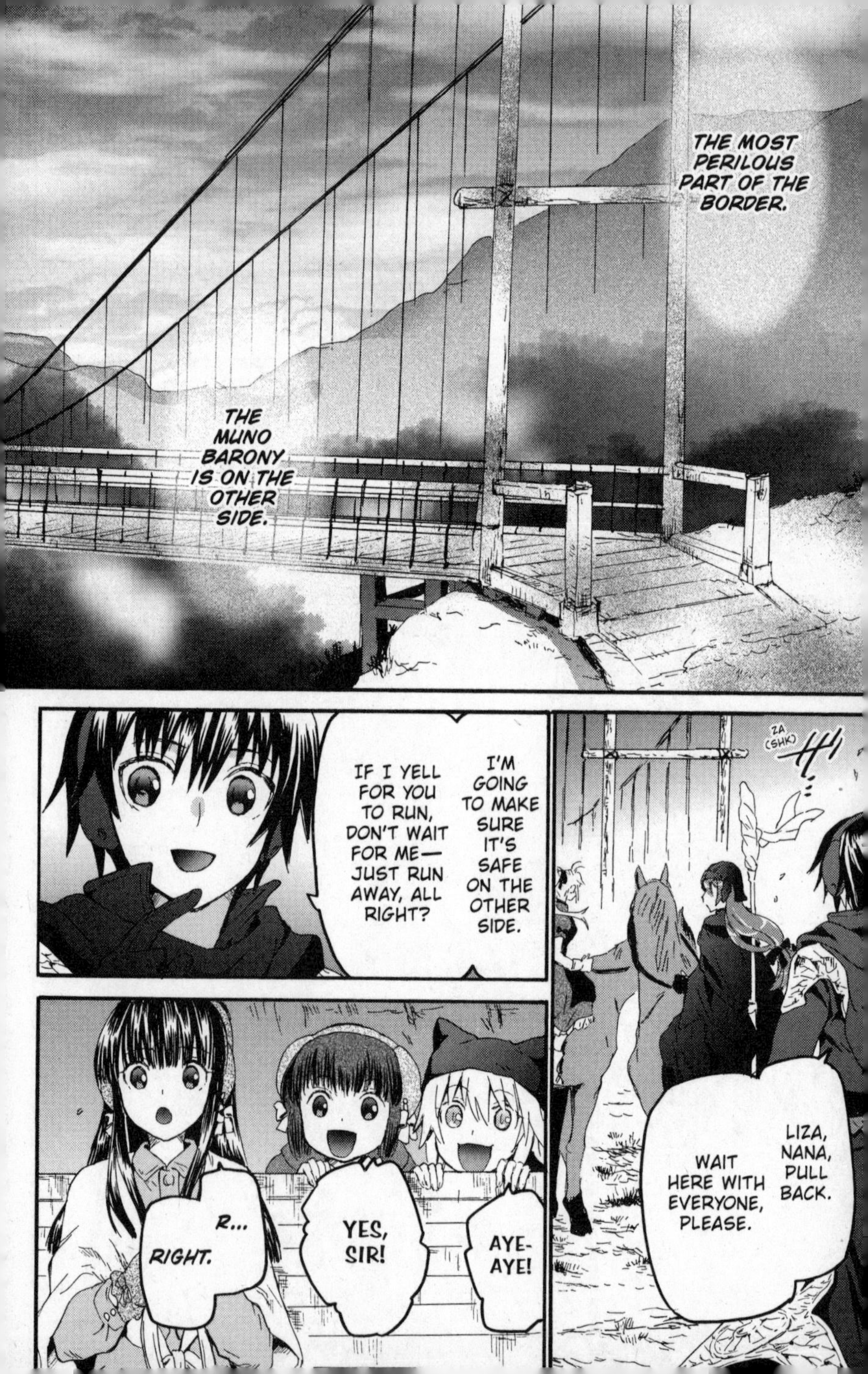
THE MOST PERILOUS PART OF THE BORDER.
THE MUNO BARONY IS ON THE OTHER SIDE.
ZA (SHK)
LIZA, NANA, PULL BACK.
WAIT HERE WITH EVERYONE, PLEASE.
I'M GOING TO MAKE SURE IT'S SAFE ON THE OTHER SIDE.
IF I YELL FOR YOU TO RUN, DON'T WAIT FOR ME—JUST RUN AWAY, ALL RIGHT?
AYE-AYE!
YES, SIR!
R... RIGHT.

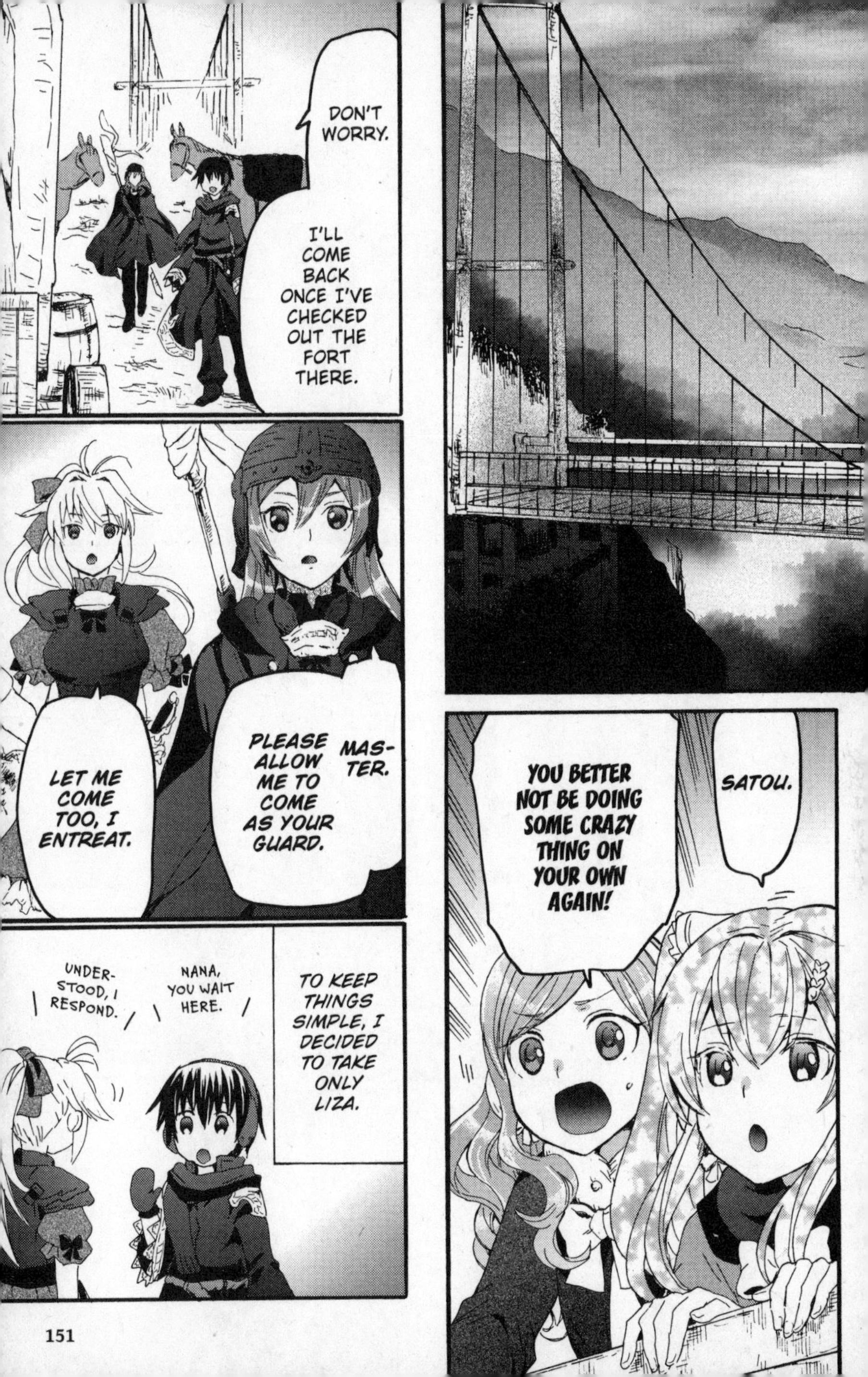
SATOU.
YOU BETTER NOT BE DOING SOME CRAZY THING ON YOUR OWN AGAIN!
DON'T WORRY.
I'LL COME BACK ONCE I'VE CHECKED OUT THE FORT THERE.
MAS-TER.
PLEASE ALLOW ME TO COME AS YOUR GUARD.
LET ME COME TOO, I ENTREAT.
TO KEEP THINGS SIMPLE, I DECIDED TO TAKE ONLY LIZA.
NANA, YOU WAIT HERE.
UNDER-STOOD, I RESPOND.

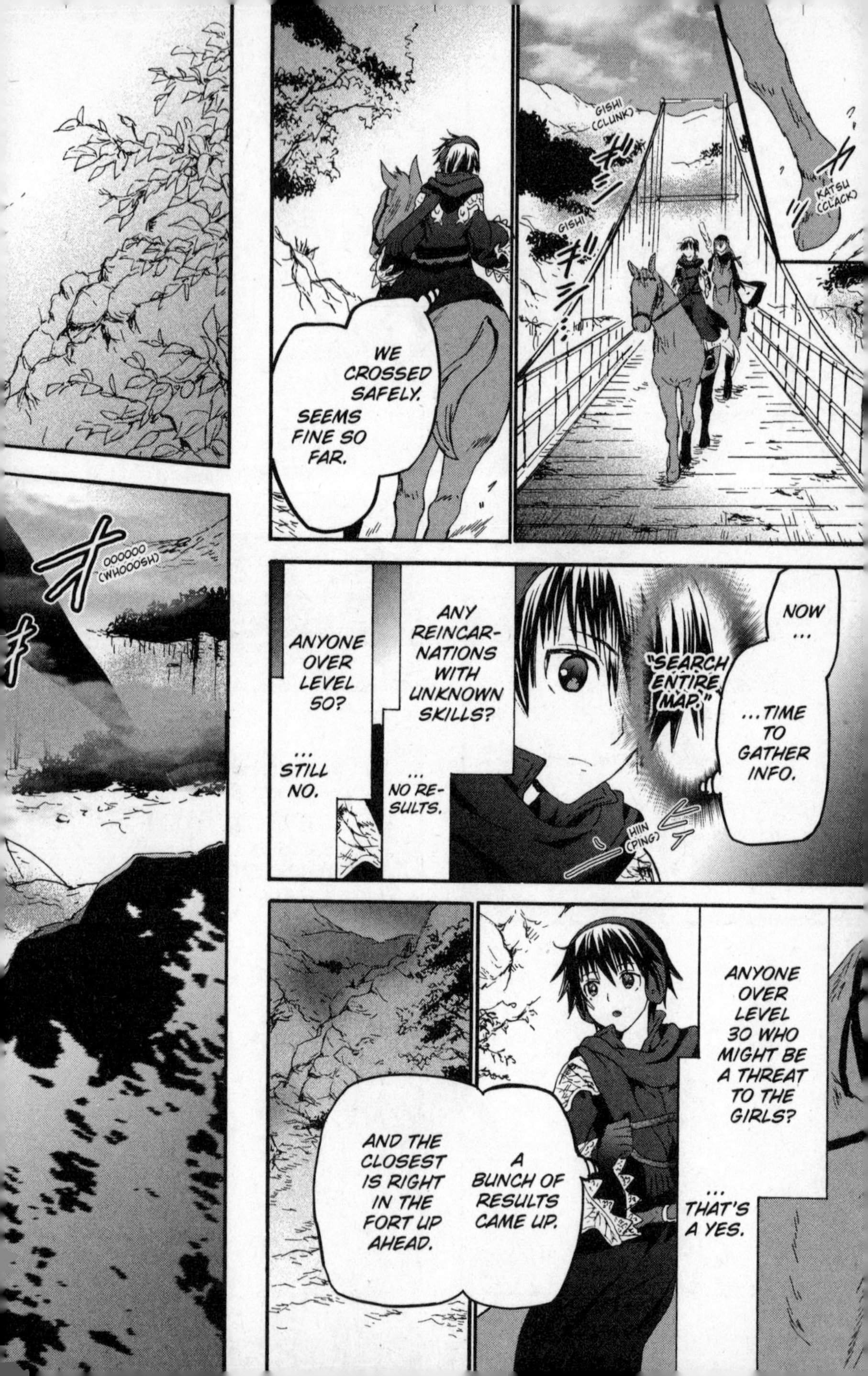
KATSU (CLACK)
GISHI (CLUNK)
GISHI
WE CROSSED SAFELY.
SEEMS FINE SO FAR.
NOW ...
"SEARCH ENTIRE MAP."
...TIME TO GATHER INFO.
HIIN (PING)
ANY REINCARNATIONS WITH UNKNOWN SKILLS?
... NO RESULTS.
ANYONE OVER LEVEL 50?
... STILL NO.
ANYONE OVER LEVEL 30 WHO MIGHT BE A THREAT TO THE GIRLS?
... THAT'S A YES.
A BUNCH OF RESULTS CAME UP.
AND THE CLOSEST IS RIGHT IN THE FORT UP AHEAD.
OOOOOO (WHOOOOSH)

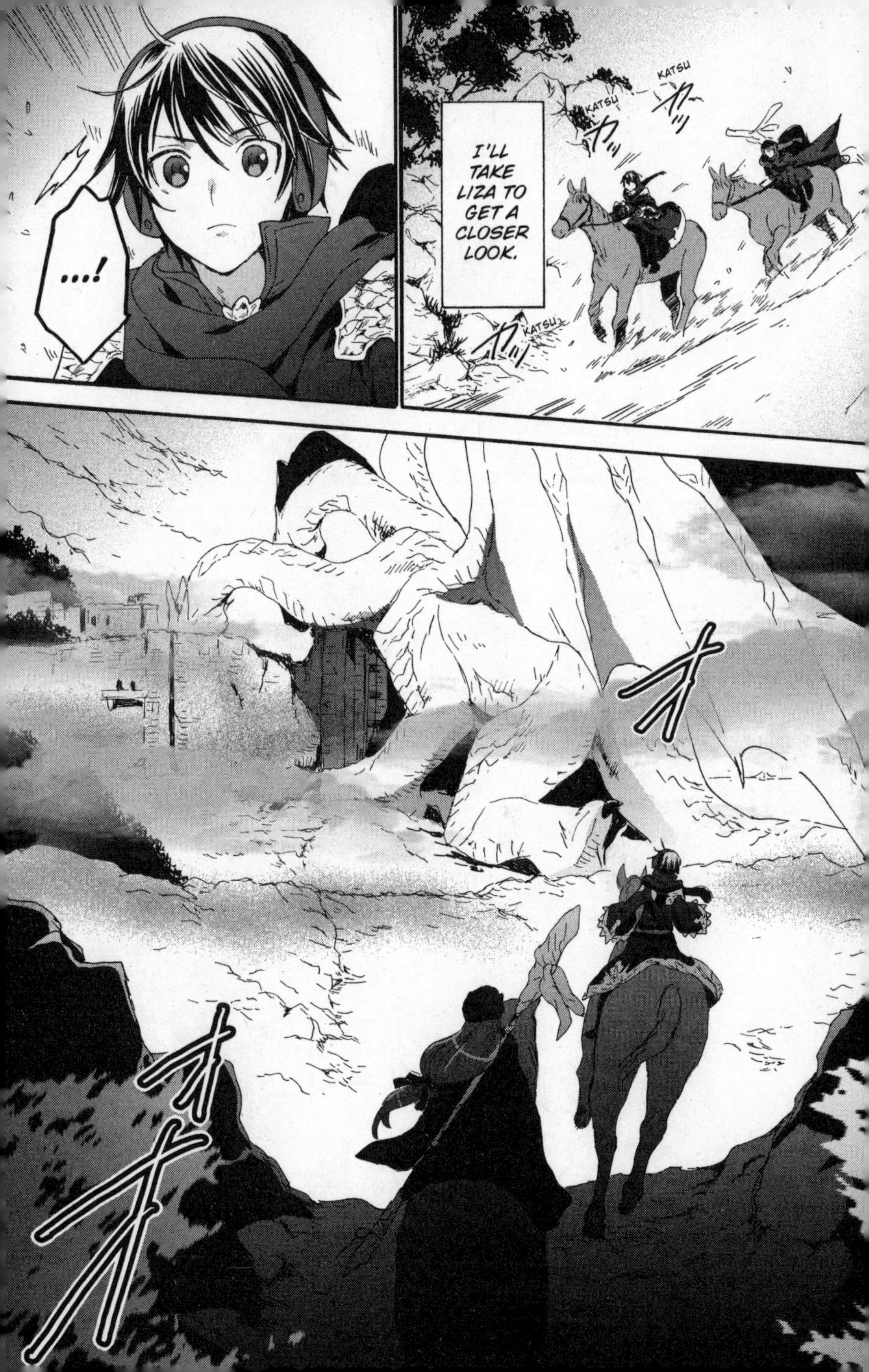

KATSU
KATSU
I'LL TAKE LIZA TO GET A CLOSER LOOK.
KATSU
...!

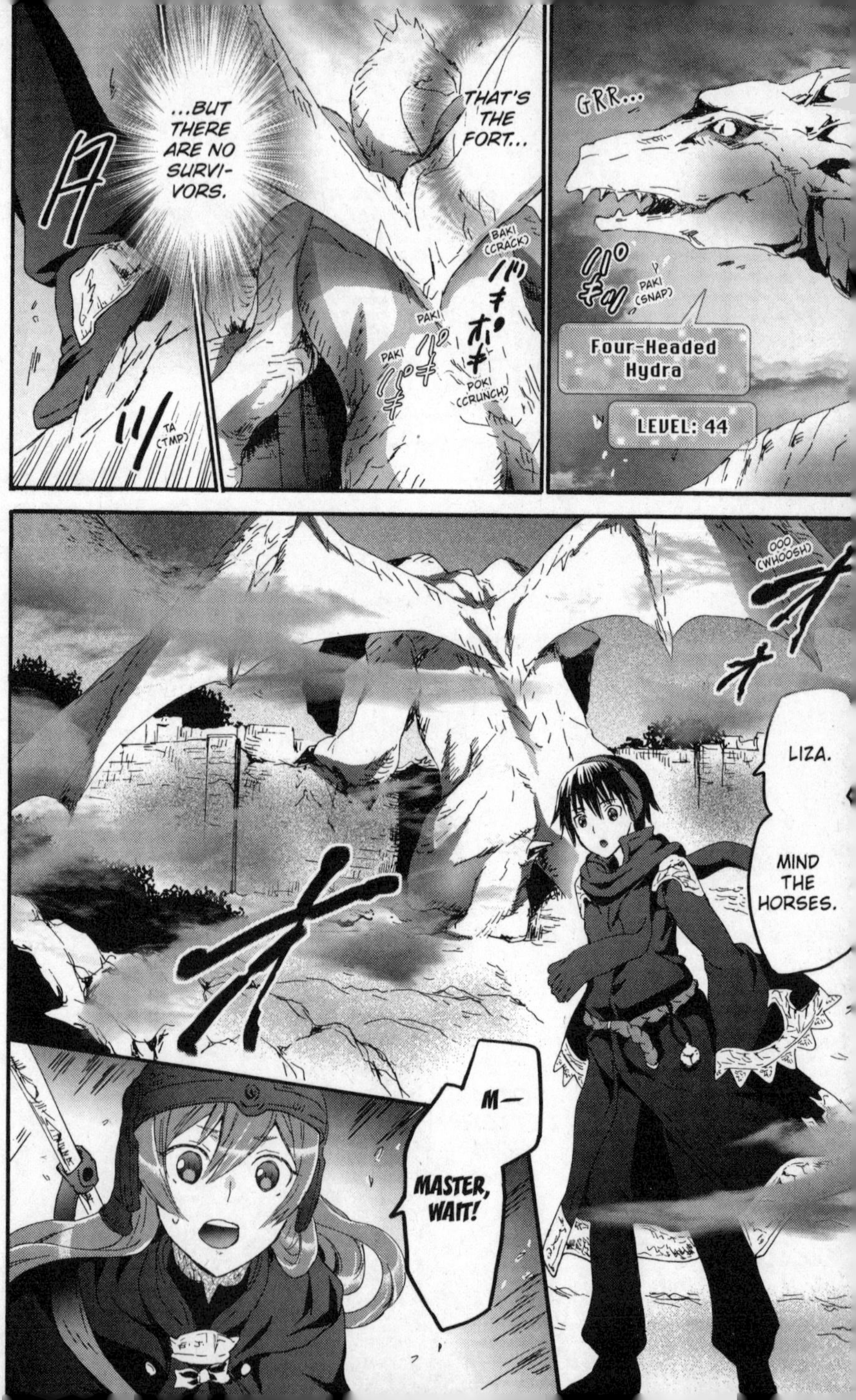
GRR...
PAKI (SNAP)
Four-Headed Hydra
LEVEL: 44
THAT'S THE FORT...
BAKI (CRACK)
PAKI
PAKI
POKI (CRUNCH)
...BUT THERE ARE NO SURVIVORS.
TA (TMP)
OOO (WHOOSH)
LIZA.
MIND THE HORSES.
M—
MASTER, WAIT!

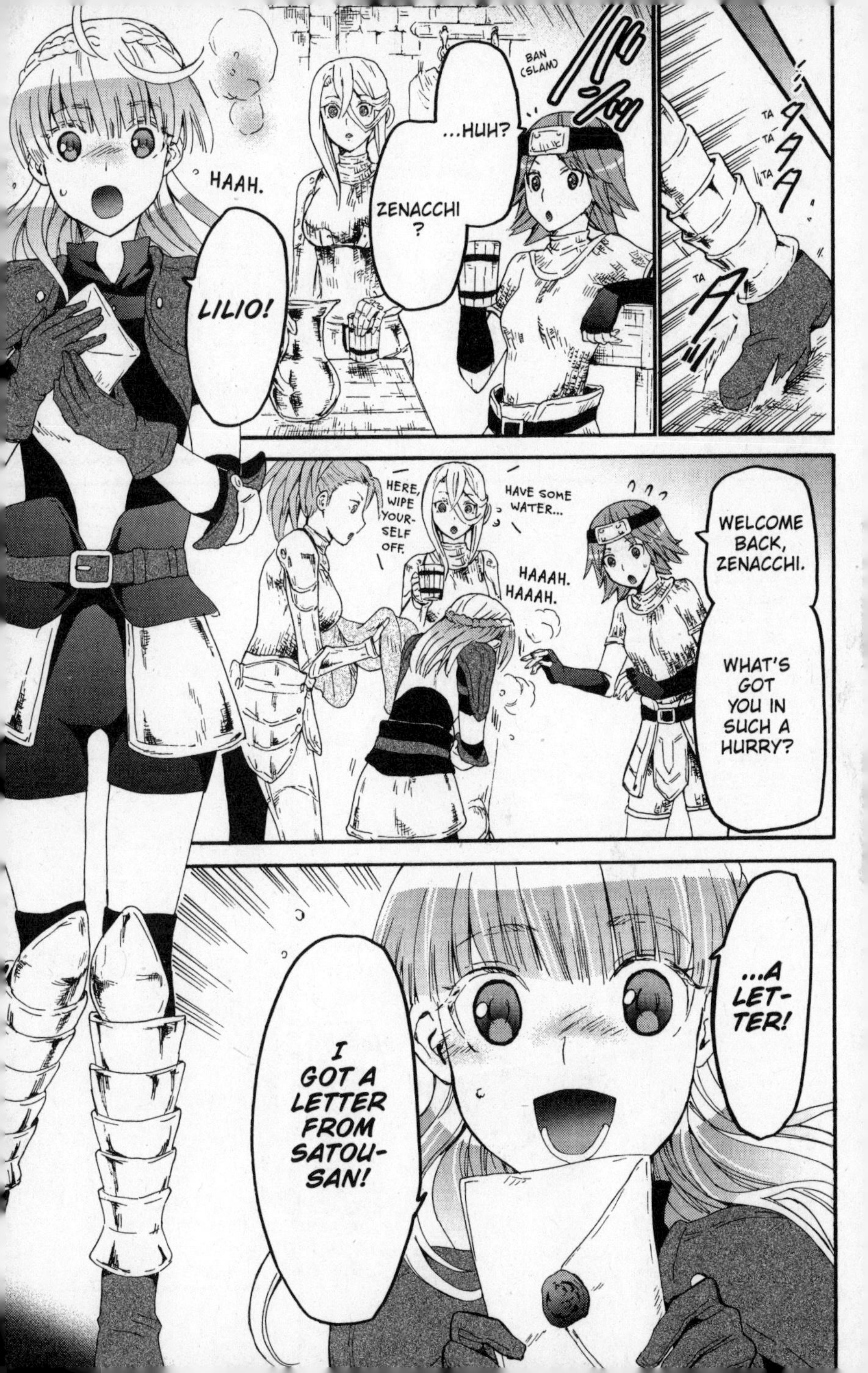
TA TA TA TA
BAN (SLAM)
...HUH?
ZENACCHI?
HAAH.
LILIO!
WELCOME BACK, ZENACCHI.
WHAT'S GOT YOU IN SUCH A HURRY?
HAVE SOME WATER...
HERE, WIPE YOURSELF OFF.
HAAAH. HAAAH.
...A LETTER!
I GOT A LETTER FROM SATOU-SAN!

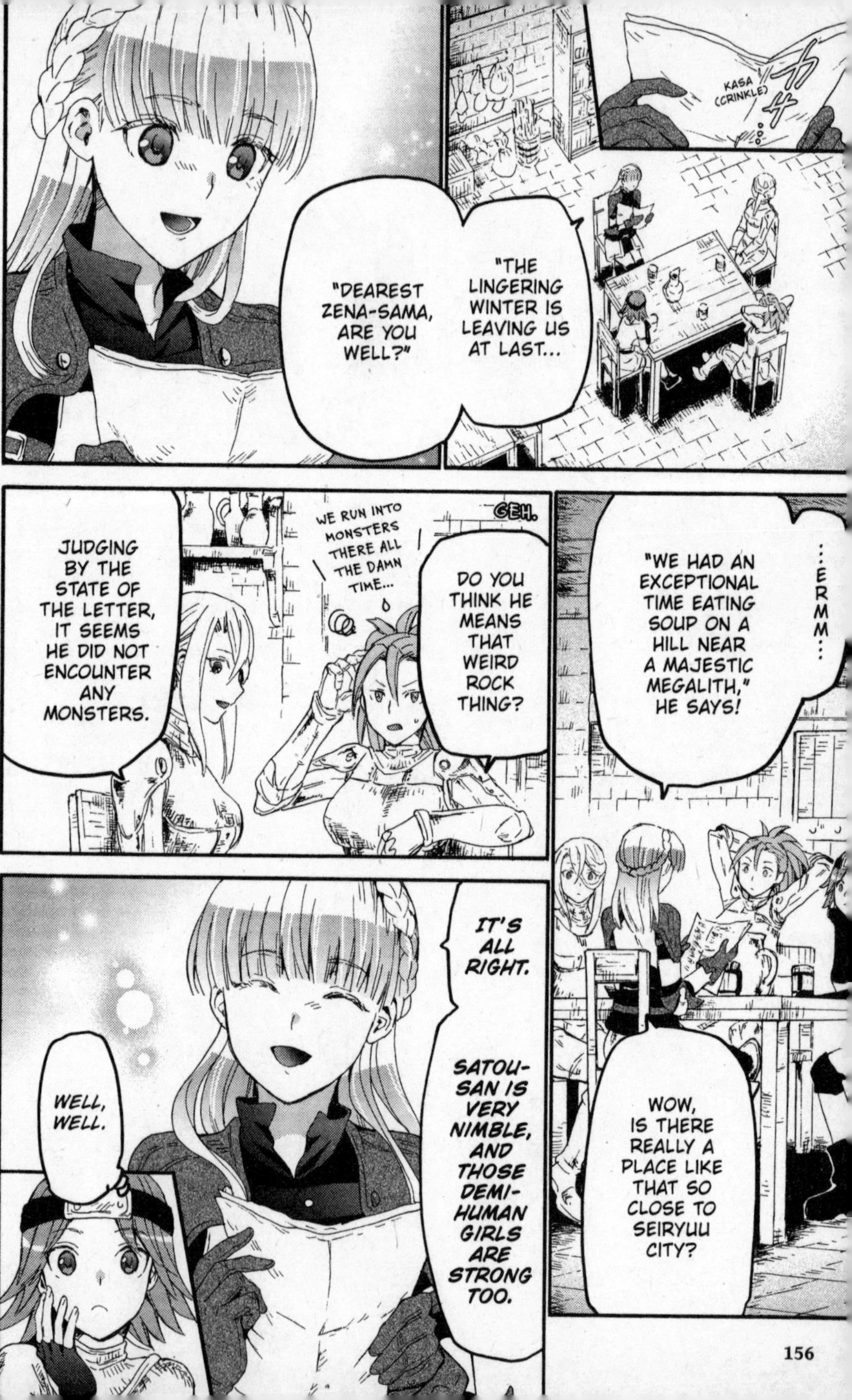
KASA (CRINKLE)
"DEAREST ZENA-SAMA, ARE YOU WELL?"
"THE LINGERING WINTER IS LEAVING US AT LAST...
...ERMM...
"WE HAD AN EXCEPTIONAL TIME EATING SOUP ON A HILL NEAR A MAJESTIC MEGALITH," HE SAYS!
WOW, IS THERE REALLY A PLACE LIKE THAT SO CLOSE TO SEIRYUU CITY?
GEH.
DO YOU THINK HE MEANS THAT WEIRD ROCK THING?
WE RUN INTO MONSTERS THERE ALL THE DAMN TIME...
JUDGING BY THE STATE OF THE LETTER, IT SEEMS HE DID NOT ENCOUNTER ANY MONSTERS.
IT'S ALL RIGHT.
SATOU-SAN IS VERY NIMBLE, AND THOSE DEMI-HUMAN GIRLS ARE STRONG TOO.
WELL, WELL.

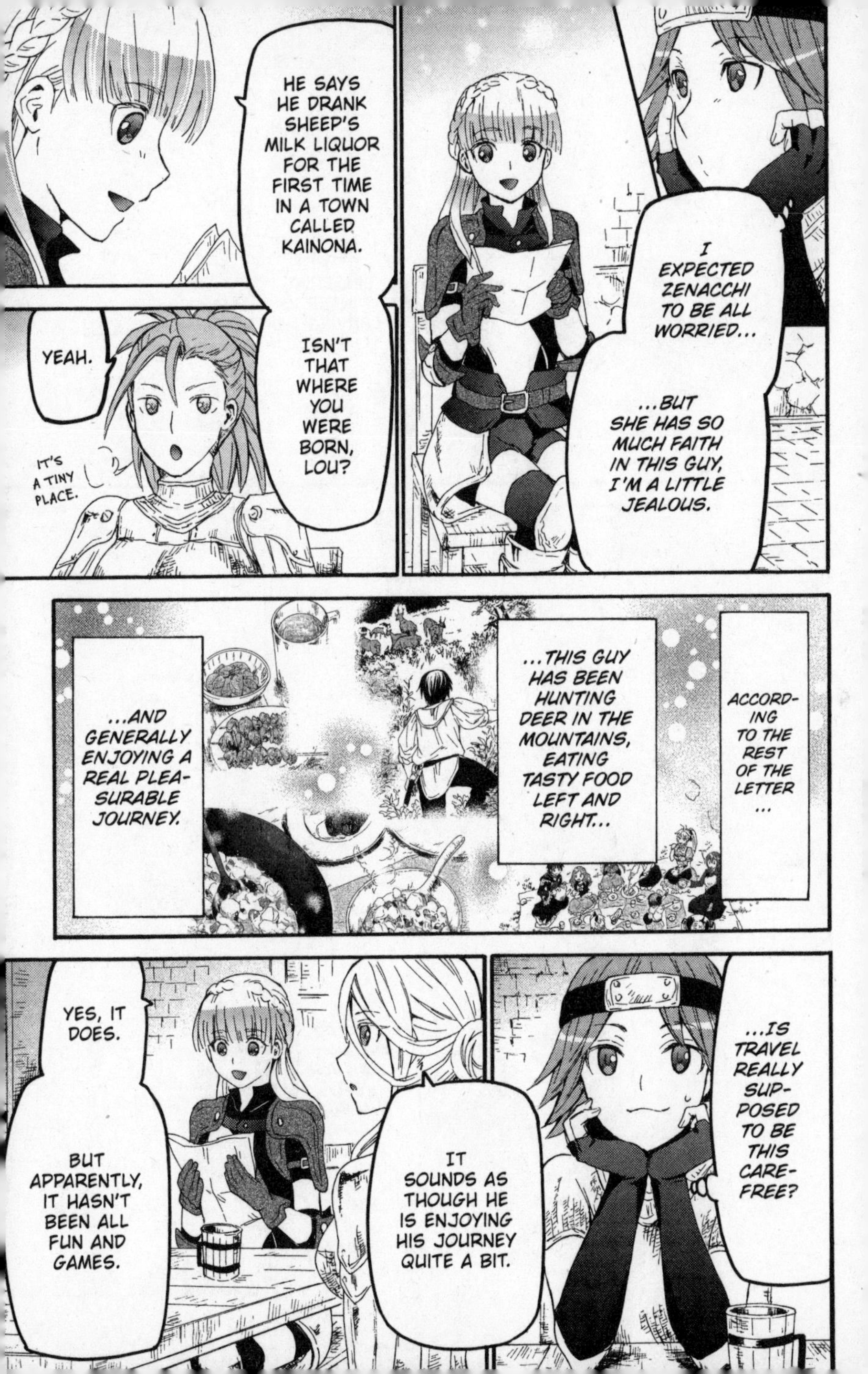
I EXPECTED ZENACCHI TO BE ALL WORRIED...
...BUT SHE HAS SO MUCH FAITH IN THIS GUY, I'M A LITTLE JEALOUS.
HE SAYS HE DRANK SHEEP'S MILK LIQUOR FOR THE FIRST TIME IN A TOWN CALLED KAINONA.
ISN'T THAT WHERE YOU WERE BORN, LOU?
YEAH.
IT'S A TINY PLACE.
ACCORD-ING TO THE REST OF THE LETTER...
...THIS GUY HAS BEEN HUNTING DEER IN THE MOUNTAINS, EATING TASTY FOOD LEFT AND RIGHT...
...AND GENERALLY ENJOYING A REAL PLEA-SURABLE JOURNEY.
...IS TRAVEL REALLY SUP-POSED TO BE THIS CARE-FREE?
IT SOUNDS AS THOUGH HE IS ENJOYING HIS JOURNEY QUITE A BIT.
YES, IT DOES.
BUT APPARENTLY, IT HASN'T BEEN ALL FUN AND GAMES.

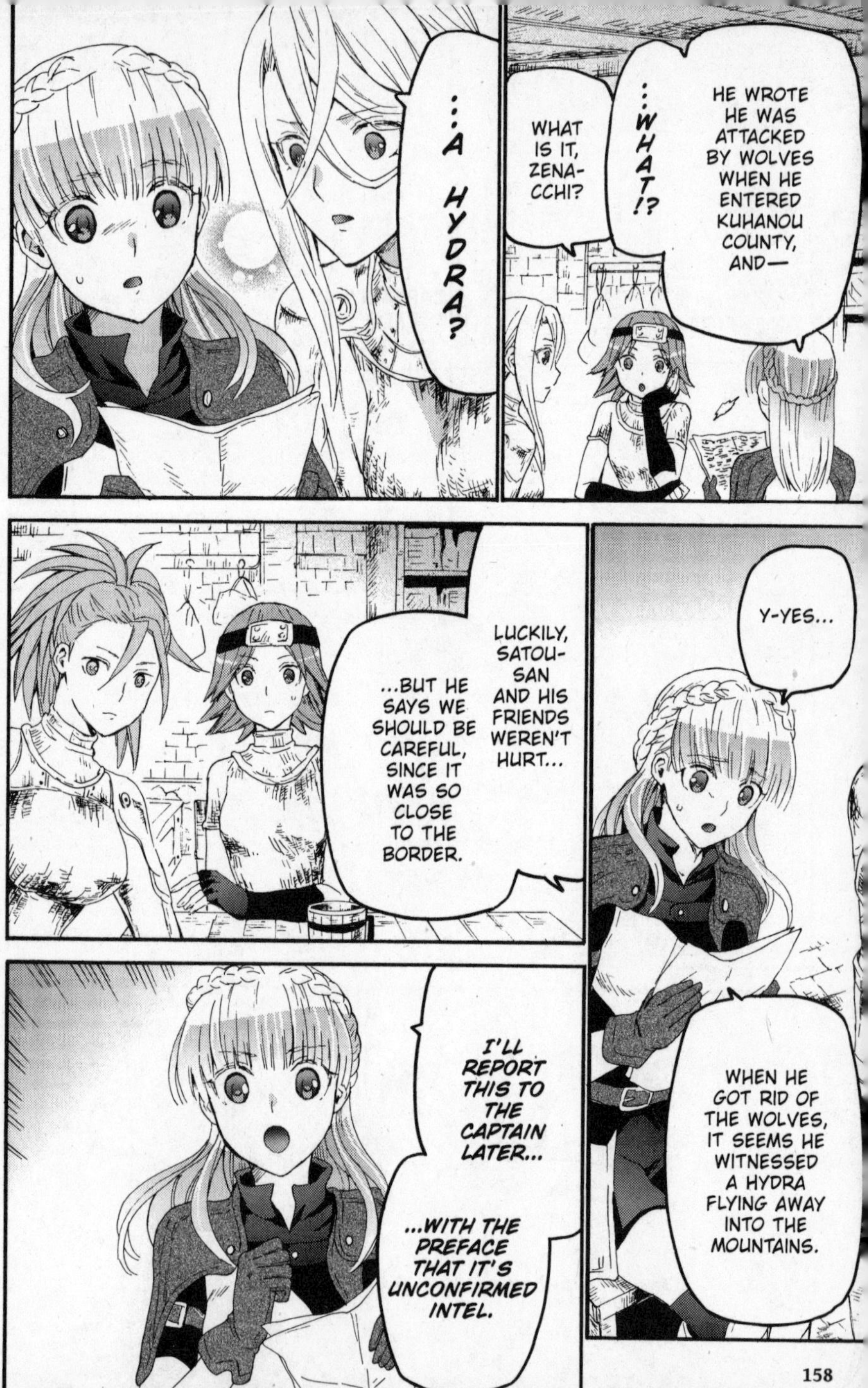
HE WROTE HE WAS ATTACKED BY WOLVES WHEN HE ENTERED KUHANOU COUNTY, AND—
...WHAT!?
WHAT IS IT, ZENA-CCHI?
...A HYDRA?
Y-YES...
WHEN HE GOT RID OF THE WOLVES, IT SEEMS HE WITNESSED A HYDRA FLYING AWAY INTO THE MOUNTAINS.
LUCKILY, SATOU-SAN AND HIS FRIENDS WEREN'T HURT...
...BUT HE SAYS WE SHOULD BE CAREFUL, SINCE IT WAS SO CLOSE TO THE BORDER.
I'LL REPORT THIS TO THE CAPTAIN LATER...
...WITH THE PREFACE THAT IT'S UNCONFIRMED INTEL.

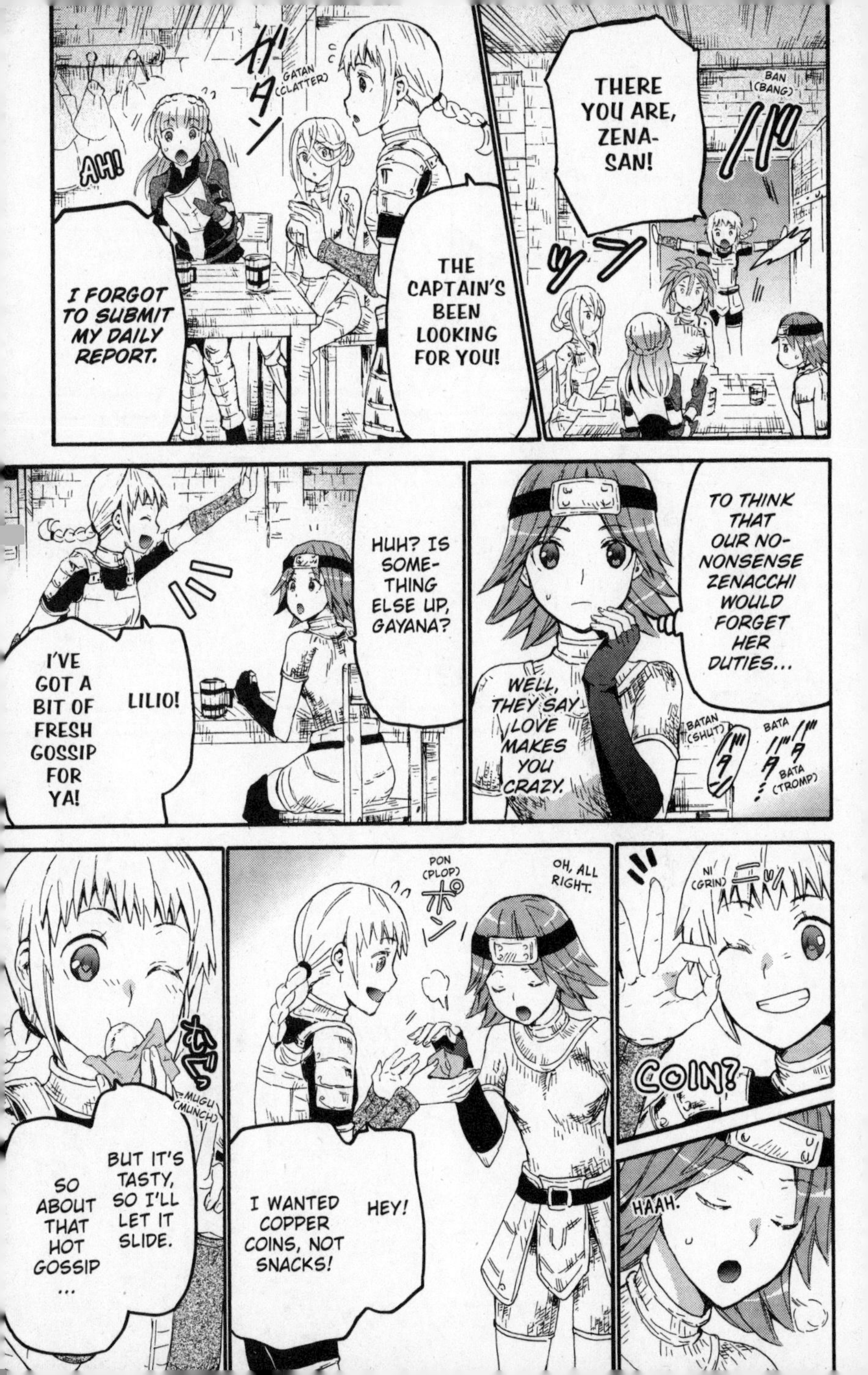
THERE YOU ARE, ZENA-SAN!
BAN (BANG)
GATAN (CLATTER)
THE CAPTAIN'S BEEN LOOKING FOR YOU!
AH!
I FORGOT TO SUBMIT MY DAILY REPORT.
TO THINK THAT OUR NO-NONSENSE ZENACCHI WOULD FORGET HER DUTIES...
WELL, THEY SAY LOVE MAKES YOU CRAZY.
BATA BATA (TROMP)
BATAN (SHUT)
HUH? IS SOME-THING ELSE UP, GAYANA?
LILIO!
I'VE GOT A BIT OF FRESH GOSSIP FOR YA!
NI (GRIN)
COIN?
HAAH.
OH, ALL RIGHT.
PON (PLOP)
HEY!
I WANTED COPPER COINS, NOT SNACKS!
MUGU (MUNCH)
BUT IT'S TASTY, SO I'LL LET IT SLIDE.
SO ABOUT THAT HOT GOSSIP...

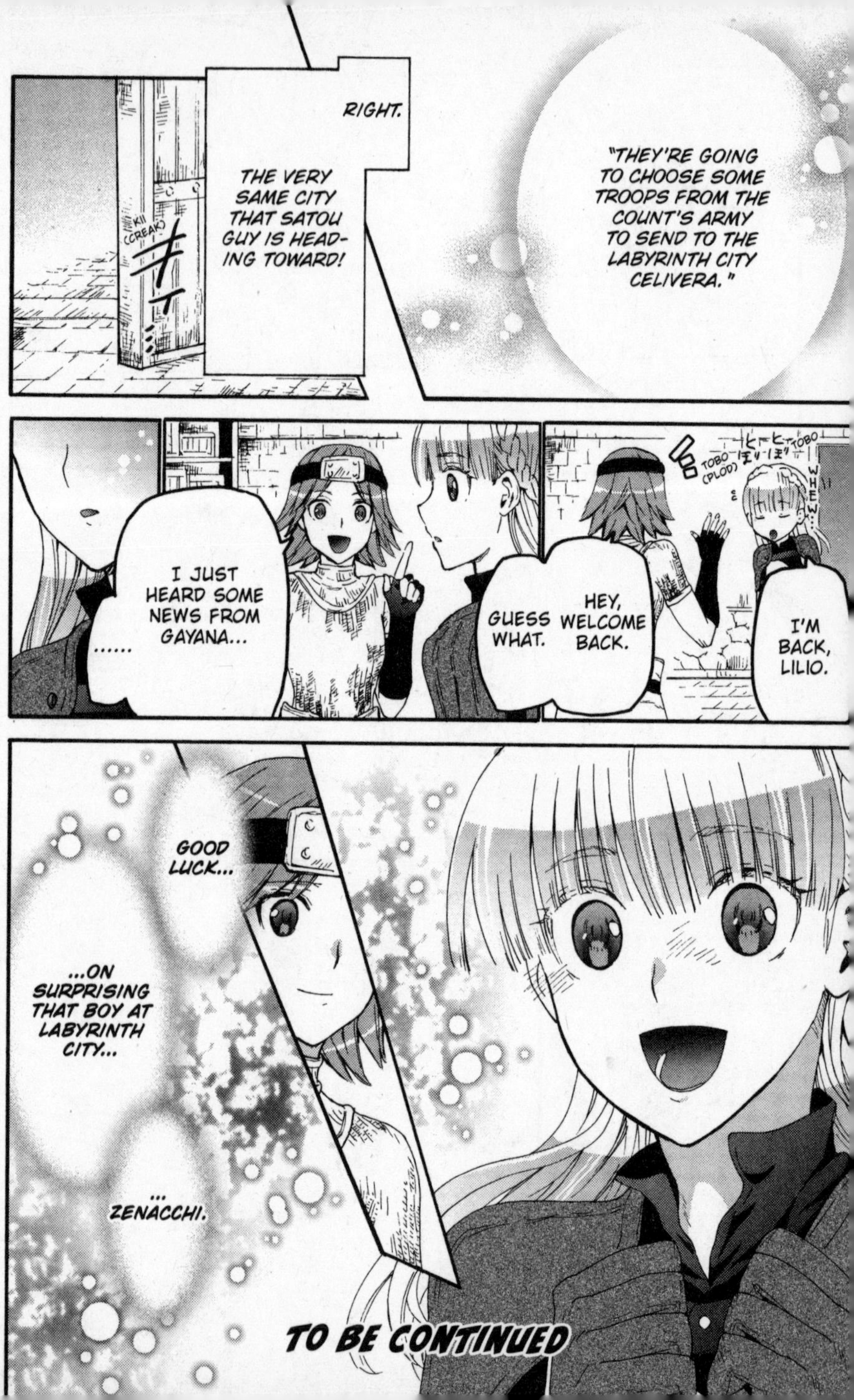
"THEY'RE GOING TO CHOOSE SOME TROOPS FROM THE COUNT'S ARMY TO SEND TO THE LABYRINTH CITY CELIVERA."
RIGHT.
THE VERY SAME CITY THAT SATOU GUY IS HEADING TOWARD!
KII (CREAK)
TOBO TOBO (PLOD)
WHEW...
I'M BACK, LILIO.
HEY, WELCOME BACK.
GUESS WHAT.
I JUST HEARD SOME NEWS FROM GAYANA...
......
GOOD LUCK...
...ON SURPRISING THAT BOY AT LABYRINTH CITY...
... ZENACCHI.
TO BE CONTINUED

THANK-YOU LANTERN

An illumination magic tool that uses "Light Drops."

A lantern that uses magic instead of oil to produce an LED-like light.

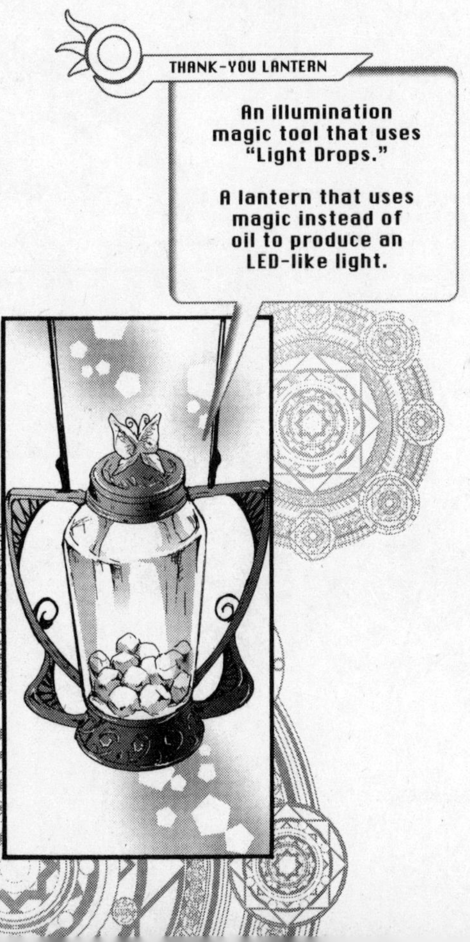

This is Volume 7.

I didn't know anything about clay or pottery, so I took a ceramics class.

The course covered shaping, glazing, and even adding simple pictures.

The teacher did most of the shaping for us. I was there for research purposes, not to make things, so that was fine with me. Guess I'm a bit lazy.

After the vessels dried, it was time to glaze them. There were a lot of varieties of glaze, with many different colors, which was a lot of fun. I was very interested in making the outside and inside different colors, so I gave it a try, without hesitation.

It left my fingers really cramped, though...

I made three vessels total, all of which came out pretty stylish. My sincere thanks to the teacher who helped me so much.

That experience really helped me draw the real thing...at least, I hope so.

Now Satou and company have finally reached the Muno Barony.

I'll be looking forward to what happens next with the rest of you as I continue to work hard on the manga.

I hope we can meet again in the next volume. Thank you for your support.

–Ayamegumu

...Special Thanks

● Manuscript production collaborators
Kaname Yukishiro-sama
Satoru Ezaki-sama
Yuna Kobayashi-sama
Hacchan-sama

● Editors
Toyohara-sama
Hagiwara-sama
Kuwazuru-sama
Arakawa-sama
Ishiguro-sama

● Binding
coil-sama

● Supervision
Hiro Ainana-sama
shri-sama

● Everyone who helped with the production and publication of this book

And you!

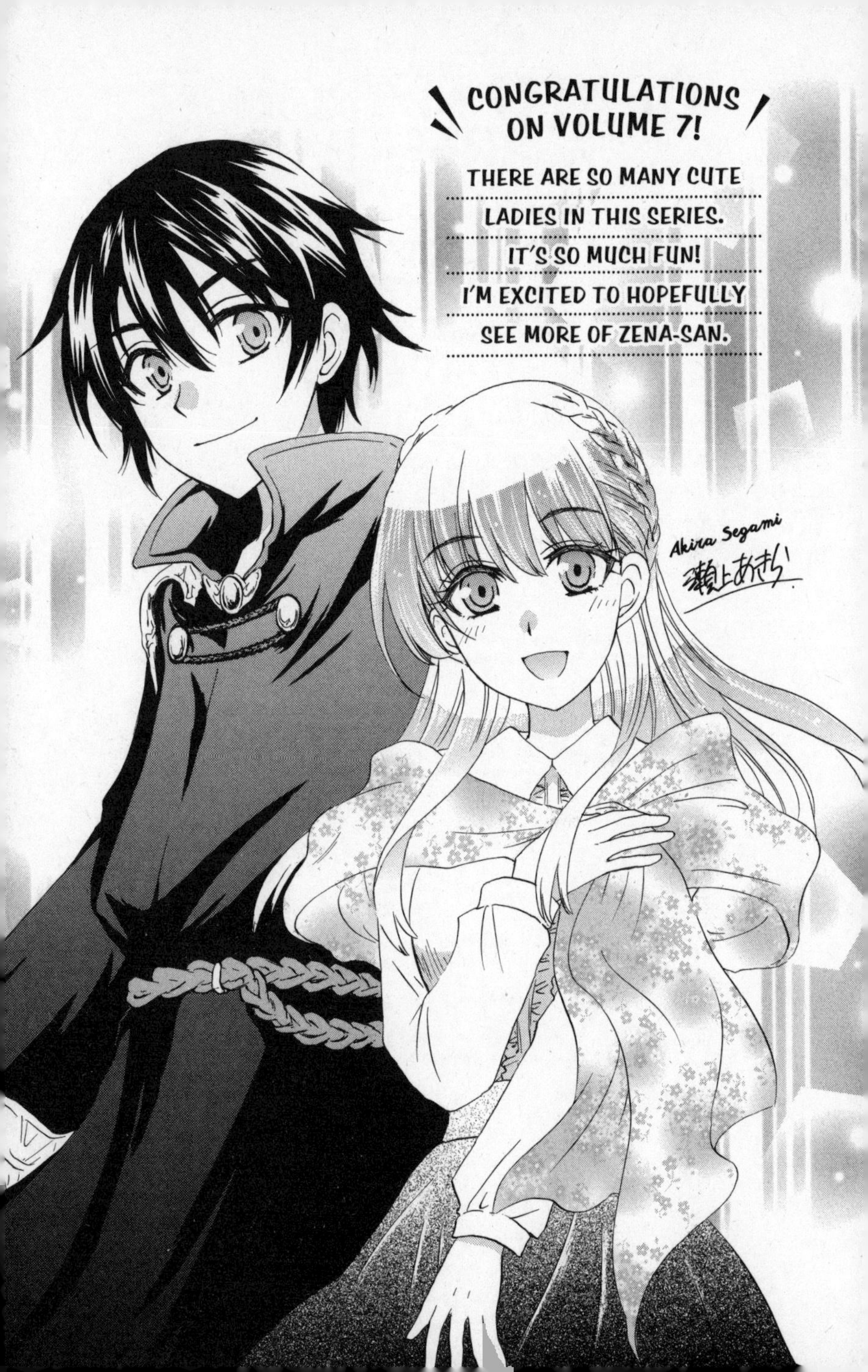
CONGRATULATIONS ON VOLUME 7!
THERE ARE SO MANY CUTE LADIES IN THIS SERIES. IT'S SO MUCH FUN! I'M EXCITED TO HOPEFULLY SEE MORE OF ZENA-SAN.
Akira Segami
瀬上あきら

DEATH MARCH ⑦
TO THE
PARALLEL WORLD RHAPSODY

Original Story: Hiro Ainana
Art: AYAMEGUMU
Character Design: shri

Translation: Jenny McKeon ◆ Lettering: Rochelle Gancio

DEATH MARCHING TO THE PARALLEL WORLD RHAPSODY Vol. 7

©AYAMEGUMU 2018
©HIRO AINANA, shri 2018
First published in Japan in 2018 by KADOKAWA CORPORATION, Tokyo. English translation rights arranged with KADOKAWA CORPORATION, Tokyo through TUTTLE-MORI AGENCY, INC., Tokyo.

English translation © 2019 by Yen Press, LLC

Yen Press
1290 Avenue of the Americas
New York, NY 10104

Visit us at yenpress.com
facebook.com/yenpress
twitter.com/yenpress
yenpress.tumblr.com
instagram.com/yenpress

First Yen Press Edition: April 2019

Yen Press is an imprint of Yen Press, LLC.
The Yen Press name and logo are trademarks of Yen Press, LLC.

The publisher is not responsible for websites (or their content) that are not owned by the publisher.

Library of Congress Control Number: 2016946043

ISBNs: 978-1-9753-0412-6 (paperback)
978-1-9753-5798-6 (ebook)

10 9 8 7 6 5 4 3 2 1

WOR

Printed in the United States of America